HIMSELF

Mark Twain

HIMSELF

Produced by

MILTON MELTZER

WINGS BOOKS

NEW YORK • AVENEL, NEW JERSEY

This 1993 edition is published by Wings Books,
distributed by Outlet Book Company, Inc., a Random House Company,
40 Engelhard Avenue, Avenel, New Jersey 07001,
by arrangement with Thomas Y. Crowell Company.

Random House
New York • Toronto • London • Sydney • Auckland

Printed and bound in the United States of America

Library of Congress Cataloging-in-Publication Data

Meltzer, Milton, 1915-
Mark Twain himself / produced by Milton Meltzer.
p.   cm.
Originally published: New York : Bonanza Books, 1960.
Includes bibliographical references and index.
ISBN 0-517-01248-0
1. Twain, Mark, 1835-1910—Biography.   2. Authors, American—
19th century—Biography.   I. Title.
PS1331.M38—dc20
[B]
92-42530
CIP

8   7   6   5   4   3   2   1

ACKNOWLEDGMENTS

I wish to express my appreciation to Harper & Brothers for permission to quote from the following published works by Mark Twain:

The uniform edition of Mark Twain's works, which comprises twenty-five volumes (1899-1910). Also *Mark Twain's Autobiography*, copyright 1924, renewed 1952 by Clara Clemens Samossoud; *Mark Twain in Eruption*, edited by Bernard De Voto, copyright 1940 by The Mark Twain Co.; *The Autobiography of Mark Twain*, edited by Charles Neider, copyright 1958, 1959 by The Mark Twain Co.; *Mark Twain's Letters*, edited by Albert Bigelow Paine, copyright 1917 by The Mark Twain Co., renewed 1945 by Clara Clemens Samossoud; *Mark Twain's Notebook*, edited by Albert Bigelow Paine, copyright 1935 by The Mark Twain Co.; *Mark Twain's Speeches*, edited by Albert Bige-low Paine, copyright 1923, renewed 1951 by The Mark Twain Co.; *Mark Twain: A Biography*, by Albert Bigelow Paine, copyright 1912 by Harper & Brothers, renewed 1940 by Dora L. Paine; *The Love Letters of Mark Twain*, edited by Dixon Wecter, copyright 1947, 1949 by The Mark Twain Co.

Grateful acknowledgement is made also to the authors and publishers for permission to quote from the following copyrighted publications:

Mark Twain's Travels with Mr. Brown, copyright 1940 by Alfred A. Knopf, Inc.

Mark Twain of the Enterprise, edited by Henry Nash Smith, University of California Press, © 1957 by The Mark Twain Co.

For Hildy, Jane, and Amy

Preface

For *Mark Twain Himself* I have gone not only to his autobiography but to his letters, notebooks, speeches, sketches, to newspaper and magazine pieces, travel books, and fiction. These sources are as personal as the autobiography; many are far closer in time to the events they relate; and they are at least as reliable—which is to say, trivial facts are never permitted to stand in the way of the artist.

Of course this book cannot pretend to include everything. Mark Twain is a big territory to roam around in. He was a printer, river pilot, soldier, miner, reporter, editor, lecturer, inventor, investor, businessman, traveler, publisher—and writer. He lived in many places: Florida (Missouri), Hannibal, St. Louis, Philadelphia, Muscatine, Keokuk, Cincinnati, Carson City, Virginia City, San Francisco, Washington, Buffalo, Elmira, New York, Redding, and several in Europe. His seventy-four years spanned the enormous changes between Andrew Jackson and William Howard Taft. Perhaps no writer has ever known American life so intimately. None has been so widely read or deeply loved. Few have been as complex and contradictory.

In general, the movement of the book is chronological, but now and then gaps in time are leaped to bring together the picture of Twain as lecturer, family man, inventor. It is the convention of this book to use "Mark Twain" throughout, although Samuel Clemens did not adopt the pen name until he was twenty-seven. Finally, the reader is warned that extracts from Mark Twain's work are sometimes telescoped for the sake of pulling together things he may have said at different times or places.

The pictures include daguerrreotypes, tintypes, stereographs, photographs, prints, drawings (including his own), paintings, broadsides, posters, cartoons, caricatures, illustrations from first editions, maps, news clippings, holographs, even his handprint.

In combing the country for Twain pictures I have been helped by a great many people. They not only have allowed me to use material from their collections, private and public, but have made valuable suggestions and offered warm encouragement. The pleasure of attempting a task such as this is multiplied by the friends made in carrying it out. To all these friends I am most grateful.

I owe special thanks to Mrs. Clara Clemens Samossoud; Thomas G. Chamberlain; Mr. and Mrs. Samuel C. Webster; James B. Pond; Anne Coldewey; Harold L. Mueller; Virginia Daiker and Milton Kaplan of the Library of Congress; Romana Javetz of the New York Library; Henry Nash Smith, literary executor of the Mark Twain Estate, and his assistant, Frederick Anderson; Donald Gallup of the Yale University Library; John Winkler, chairman of the Mark Twain Municipal Board, Hannibal, Missouri; Mrs. Mary L. Peck of the Mark Twain Library and Memorial Commission, Hartford, Connecticut; and Daniel Jones and Rhoda Grady of the National Broadcasting Company's Special Projects group.

Contents

Mark Twain Himself

Real estate boosters promised much for Florida in this ad in the Columbia *Missouri Intelligencer*, April 16, 1831.

A rented two-room frame house was the birthplace of Mark Twain.

Two one-room cabins joined together was the third Clemens home in Florida, built by Mark's father.

Missouri Boyhood

I DID IT FOR FLORIDA

West of little Florida's two muddy streets lay Indian territory—just two hundred miles off. Two stores served the village. It was the owner of one, John A. Quarles, brother-in-law to Jane Clemens, who had invited the Clemenses to make their fortune in Florida. Two months ahead of schedule, as Halley's Comet blazed through the skies, Jane Clemens bore her fifth child, christened Samuel Langhorne Clemens.

"I was born," Mark Twain wrote, "the 30th of November, 1835, in the almost invisible village of Florida, Monroe County, Missouri. My parents removed to Missouri in the early 'thirties; I do not remember just when, for I was not born then and cared nothing for such things. It was a long journey in those days and must have been a rough and tiresome one. The village contained a hundred people and I increased the population by 1 per cent. It is more than many of the best men in history could have done for a town. It may not be modest in me to refer to this but it is true. There is no record of a person doing as much—not even Shakespeare. But I did it for Florida and it shows that I could have done it for any place—even London, I suppose.

"Recently some one in Missouri has sent me a picture of the house I was born in. Heretofore I have always stated that it was a palace but I shall be more guarded now.

"The village had two streets, each a couple of hun-

dred yards long; the rest of the avenues mere lanes, with railfences and cornfields on either side. Both the streets and the lanes were paved with the same material —tough black mud in wet times, deep dust in dry.

"Most of the houses were of logs—all of them, indeed, except three or four; these latter were frame ones. There were none of brick and none of stone."

John Clemens dreamed that the Salt River could be made navigable for boats to come up its 85 miles from the Mississippi to the village of Florida. But neither Florida nor Mark's father would ever strike it rich.

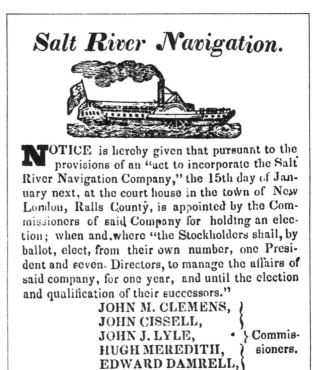

Salt River Navigation.

NOTICE is hereby given that pursuant to the provisions of an "act to incorporate the Salt River Navigation Company," the 15th day of January next, at the court house in the town of New London, Ralls County, is appointed by the Commissioners of said Company for holding an election; when and where "the Stockholders shall, by ballot, elect, from their own number, one President and seven Directors, to manage the affairs of said company, for one year, and until the election and qualification of their successors."

JOHN M. CLEMENS,
JOHN CISSELL,
JOHN J. LYLE, } Commis-
HUGH MEREDITH, } sioners.
EDWARD DAMRELL,

November 11, 1837.

☞ Shareholders may "vote by proxy duly made in writing."

Hannibal, Missouri, as seen by artist Henry Lewis, boating up the Mississippi in the summers of 1846–48.

BOYHOOD IN HANNIBAL

Neither farming, storekeeping, nor law practice would bring John Clemens' growing family prosperity. Of mixed English middle-class and Irish stock, both of Twain's parents took pride in their pre-Revolutionary War heritage. Both came from small and unprosperous slaveholder families. John Clemens, genteel, educated, enterprising, civic-minded, spent his brief life making fresh starts. After failure in Florida came the promise of Hannibal, thirty miles away. In November, 1839, the Clemenses arrived, and young Mark's father opened another general store, on Main Street. The village was a few new brick houses scattered among old log cabins, frame dwellings, and vacant lots, with the river running past one side and forest and prairie surrounding all the rest. No one could make a fortune in the farmers' markets and small shops of the sleepy river town. But out of the fourteen youthful years he spent in that "half-forgotten Paradise," Mark Twain was to draw the memories from which he made *Tom Sawyer* and *Huckleberry Finn* and *Life on the Mississippi*.

The river's vast variety, the woods and birds on its sandbars and islands, the villages along the shore, the keelboats and barges and broadhorns and flatboats and steamboats that moved up and down the muddy waters and the human democracy they carried—all went into the making of an artist. Many years later, roaming the world, Mark Twain found no one, he said, whom he had not met before on the river.

The St. Louis riverfront in 1853.

MY SCHOOL DAYS

"My school days began when I was four years and a half old," wrote Mark Twain in his *Autobiography*. "There were no public schools in Missouri in those early days, but there were two private schools—terms twenty-five cents per week per pupil and collect it if you can. Mrs. Horr taught the children in a small log house at the southern end of Main Street. . . . I was sent to Mrs. Horr's school.

"Mrs. Horr was a New England lady of middle age with New England ways and principles, and she always opened school with prayer and a chapter from the New Testament; also she explained the chapter with a brief talk. In one of these talks she dwelt upon the text, 'Ask and ye shall receive,' and said that whosoever prayed for a thing with earnestness and strong desire need not doubt that his prayer would be answered.

"I was so forcibly struck by this information and so gratified by the opportunities which it offered that this was probably the first time I had heard of it. I thought I would give it a trial. I believed in Mrs. Horr thoroughly and I had no doubts as to the result. I prayed for gingerbread. Margaret Kooneman, who was the baker's daughter, brought a slab of gingerbread to school every morning; she had always kept it out of sight before but when I finished my prayer and glanced up, there it was in easy reach and she was looking the other way. In all my life I believe I never enjoyed an answer to prayer more than I enjoyed that one; and I was a convert, too. I had no end of wants and they had always remained unsatisfied up to that time, but I meant to supply them and extend them now that I had found out how to do it."

Mrs. Horr was assisted by her daughter and two other ladies. Good manners, spelling, and reading were the staples of the dame school, and piety taught on weekdays was declaimed on Sundays, too. A few years later William Cross's common school inspired Mark to the anonymous verse:

> "Cross by name and cross by nature—
> Cross jumped over an Irish potato."

Finally, there were J. D. Dawson's classes for children "of good morals," immortalized as Dobbins' school in *Tom Sawyer*. For those who wanted more, Hannibal offered a library, a few bookstores, magazines published back East, local newspapers, itinerant lecturers, and homemade political oratory. Mark was not an eager pupil: if he won any prizes for learning, they haven't been found. The most important things he learned were not picked up at school.

One of the Hannibal schools Mark Twain attended.

Elizabeth Horr, Mark's first teacher, and her husband Benjamin, the village cooper.

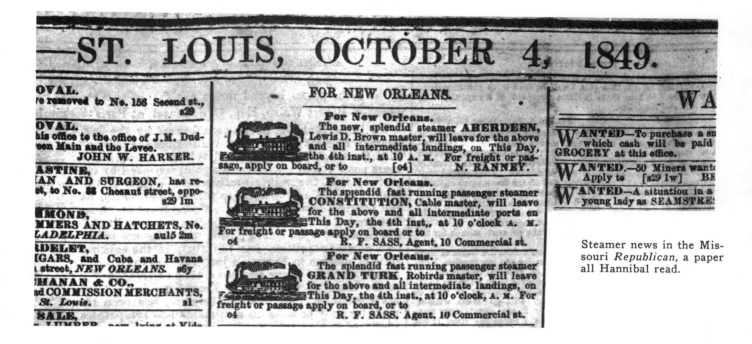

Steamer news in the Missouri *Republican*, a paper all Hannibal read.

S-T-E-A-M-B-O-A-T A-COMIN'!

"When I was a boy," Mark Twain recalled in *Life on the Mississippi*, "there was but one permanent ambition among my comrades in our village on the west bank of the Mississippi River. We had transient ambitions of other sorts, but they were only transient. When a circus came and went, it left us all burning to become clowns; the first Negro minstrel show that ever came to our section left us all suffering to try that kind of life; now and then we had a hope that, if we lived and were good, God would permit us to be pirates. These ambitions faded out, each in its turn; but the ambition to be a steamboatman always remained.

"Once a day a cheap, gaudy packet arrived upward from St. Louis, and another down from Keokuk. Before these events, the day was glorious with expectancy; after them, the day was a dead and empty thing. Not only the boys, but the whole village, felt this. After all these years I can picture that old time to myself now, just as it was then: the white town drowsing in the sunshine of a summer's morning; the streets empty, or pretty nearly so; one or two clerks sitting in front of the Water Street stores, with their splint-bottomed chairs tilted back against the walls, chins on breasts, hats slouched over their faces, asleep —with shingle-shavings enough around to show what broke them down; a sow and a litter of pigs loafing along the sidewalk, doing a good business in watermelon rinds and seeds; two or three lonely little freight piles scattered about the 'levee'; a pile of 'skids' on the slope of the stone-paved wharf, and the fragrant town drunkard asleep in the shadow of them; two or three wood flats at the head of the wharf, but nobody to listen to the peaceful lapping of the wavelets against them; the great Mississippi, the majestic, the magnificent Mississippi, rolling its mile-wide tide along, shining in the sun; the dense forest away on the other side; the 'point' above the town, and the 'point' below, bounding the river-glimpse and turning it into a sort of sea, and withal a very still and brilliant and lonely one. Presently a film of dark smoke appears above one of those remote 'points'; instantly a Negro drayman, famous for his quick eye and prodigious voice, lifts up the cry, 'S-t-e-a-m-boat a-comin'!' and the scene changes! The town drunkard stirs, the clerks wake up, a furious clatter of drays follows, every house and store pours out a human contribution, and all in a twinkling the dead town is alive and moving. Drays, carts, men, boys, all go hurrying from many quarters to a common center, the wharf. Assembled there, the people fasten their eyes upon the coming

The permanent ambition.

boat as upon a wonder they are seeing for the first time. And the boat is rather a handsome sight, too. She is long and sharp and trim and pretty; she has two tall, fancy-topped chimneys, with a gilded device of some kind swung between them; a fanciful pilot-house, all glass and 'gingerbread,' perched on top of the 'texas' deck behind them; the paddle-boxes are gorgeous with a picture or with gilded rays above the boat's name; the boiler deck, the hurricane deck, and the texas deck are fenced and ornamented with clean white railings; there is a flag gallantly flying from the jack-staff; the furnace doors are open and the fires glaring bravely; the upper decks are black with passengers; the captain stands by the big bell, calm, imposing, the envy of all; great volumes of the blackest smoke are rolling and tumbling out of the chimneys—a hus-banded grandeur created with a bit of pitch pine just before arriving at a town; the crew are grouped on the forecastle; the broad stage is run far out over the port bow, and an envied deck-hand stands picturesquely on the end of it with a coil of rope in his hand; the pent steam is screaming through the gauge-cocks; the cap-tain lifts his hand, a bell rings, the wheels stop; then they turn back, churning the water to foam, and the steamer is at rest. Then such a scramble as there is to get aboard, and to get ashore, and to take in freight and to discharge freight, all at once and the same time; and such a yelling and cursing as the mates facilitate it all with! Ten minutes later the steamer is under way again, with no flag on the jack-staff and no black smoke issuing from the chimneys. After ten more minutes the town is dead again, and the town drunkard asleep by the skids once more. . . .

"Boy after boy managed to get on the river. The minister's son became an engineer. The doctor's and the postmaster's sons became 'mud clerks'; the whole-sale liquor dealer's son became a barkeeper on a boat;

Hurrying down to the wharf.

Sam Bowen, river pilot. As boys, he and his brothers, Will and Hart, were playmates of Mark Twain. They all grew up to become pilots.

four sons of the chief merchant, and two sons of the county judge, became pilots. Pilot was the grandest position of all. The pilot, even in those days of trivial wages, had a princely salary—from a hundred and fifty to two hundred and fifty dollars a month, and no board to pay. Two months of his wages would pay a preacher's salary for a year. Now some of us were left disconsolate. We could not get on the river—at least our parents would not let us.

"So, by and by, I ran away. I said I would never come home again till I was a pilot and could come in glory. But somehow I could not manage it. I went meekly aboard a few of the boats that lay packed to-gether like sardines at the long St. Louis wharf, and humbly inquired for the pilots, but got only a cold shoulder and short words from mates and clerks. I had to make the best of this sort of treatment for the time being, but I had comforting day-dreams of a future when I should be a great and honored pilot, with plenty of money, and could kill some of these mates and clerks and pay for them."

The Mark Twain home at 206 Hill Street, Hannibal, built by Judge Clemens in the 1840's. The two-story frame house, quite small, now stands next to a museum packed with Twain mementos.

Tom Blankenship, the barefoot "kindly young heathen" who was the original for Huck Finn, lived in this barnlike house on North Street, close by the Clemens family. The house is long gone.

Laura Hawkins, Tom Sawyer's Becky Thatcher. She lived opposite the Clemenses on Hill Street. She was two years younger than Mark and one of the many "little girl-friends of my early boyhood" with whom he was a favorite because of his gaiety and gallantry. Laura married Dr. James Frazer, and lived to be 91. She remembered Mark as "only a common place boy" with a "drawling, appealing voice," who often played hooky. He used her name in *The Gilded Age,* and her character in *Tom Sawyer.*

John Briggs, the Joe Harper of Tom Sawyer's gang. One of Mark's closest boyhood friends, he was 18 months younger. They met for the last time in 1902, on Mark's final visit to Hannibal. "We were like brothers once," Mark said.

PEOPLE AND PLACES

The "Becky Thatcher house." One of its rooms is now restored to the 1840's period, when young Laura Hawkins lived in it.

A HEAVENLY PLACE FOR A BOY

"I spent some part of every year at the farm until I was twelve or thirteen years old. The life which I led there with my cousins was full of charm, and so is the memory of it yet. I can call back the solemn twilight and mystery of the deep woods, the earthy smells, the faint odors of the wild flowers, the sheen of rain-washed foliage, the rattling clatter of drops when the wind shook the trees, the far-off hammering of woodpeckers and the muffled drumming of wood pheasants in the remoteness of the forest, the snapshot glimpses of disturbed wild creatures scurrying through the grass—I can call it all back and make it as real as it ever was, and as blessed. I can call back the prairie, and its loneliness and peace, and a vast hawk hanging motionless in the sky, with his wings spread wide and the blue of the vault showing through the fringe of their end feathers. I can see the woods in their autumn dress, the oaks purple, the hickories washed with gold, the maples and the sumachs luminous with crimson fires, and I can hear the rustle made by the fallen leaves as we plowed through them. I can see the blue clusters of wild grapes hanging among the foliage of the saplings, and I remember the taste of them and the smell. I know how the wild black-berries looked, and how they tasted, and the same with the paw-paws, the hazelnuts, and the persimmons; and I can feel the thumping rain, upon my head, of hickory nuts and walnuts when we were out in the frosty dawn to scramble for them with the pigs, and the gusts of wind loosened them and sent them down. I know the stain of blackberries, and how pretty it is, and I know the stain of walnut hulls, and how little it minds soap and water, also what grudged experience it had of either of them. I know the taste of maple sap, and when to gather it, and how to arrange the troughs and the delivery tubes, and how to boil down the juice, and how to hook the sugar after it is made, also how much better hooked sugar tastes than any that is honestly come by, let bigots say what they will. I know how a prize watermelon looks when it is sunning its fat rotundity among pumpkin vines and 'simblins'; I know how to tell when it is ripe without 'plugging' it; I know how inviting it looks when it is cooling itself in a tub of water under the bed, waiting; I know how it looks when it lies on the table in the sheltered great floor space between house and kitchen,

and the children gathered for the sacrifice and their mouths watering; I know the crackling sound it makes when the carving knife enters its end, and I can see the split fly along in front of the blade as the knife cleaves its way to the other end; I can see its halves fall apart and display the rich red meat and the black seeds, and the heart standing up, a luxury fit for the elect; I know how a boy looks behind a yard-long slice of that melon, and I know how he feels; for I have been there. I know the taste of the watermelon which has been honestly come by, and I know the taste of the watermelon which has been acquired by art. Both taste good, but the experienced know which tastes best. I know the look of green apples and peaches and pears on the trees, and I know how entertaining they are when they are piled in pyramids under the trees, and how pretty they are and how vivid their colors. I know how a frozen apple looks, in a barrel down cellar in the wintertime, and how hard it is to bite, and how the frost makes the teeth ache, and yet how good it is, notwithstanding. I know the disposition of elderly people to select the speckled apples for the children, and I once knew ways to beat the game. I know the look of an apple that is roasting and sizzling on a hearth on a winter's evening, and I know the comfort that comes of eating it hot, along with some sugar and a drench of cream. I know the delicate art and mystery of so cracking hickory nuts and walnuts on a flatiron with a hammer that the kernels will be delivered whole, and I know how the nuts, taken in conjunction with winter apples, cider, and doughnuts, make old people's old tales and old jokes sound fresh and crisp and enchanting, and juggle an evening away before you know what went with the time. I know the look of Uncle Dan'l's kitchen as it was on the privileged nights, when I was a child, and I can see the white and black children grouped on the hearth, with the firelights playing on their faces and the shadows flickering upon the walls, clear back toward the cavernous gloom of the rear, and I can hear Uncle Dan'l telling the immortal tales which Uncle Remus Harris was to gather into his books and charm the world with, by and by; and I can feel again the creepy joy which quivered through me when the time for the ghost story of the 'Golden Arm' was reached—and the sense of regret, too, which came over me, for it was always the last story of the evening and there was nothing between it and the unwelcome bed.

"I can remember the bare wooden stairway in my uncle's house, and the turn to the left above the landing, and the rafters and the slanting roof over my bed, and the squares of moonlight on the floor, and the white cold world of snow outside, seen through the curtainless window. I can remember the howling of the wind and the quaking of the house on stormy nights, and how shut and cozy one felt, under the blankets, listening; and how the powdery snow used to sift in, around

Uncle John Quarles had a farm near Mark's birthplace, Florida, Missouri. He married the younger sister of Mark's mother. They had eight children and owned 30 slaves. "It was a heavenly place for a boy, that farm of my uncle John's," wrote Mark. He spent six or seven summers there, storing up impressions that would enrich many pages of *Tom Sawyer* and *Huckleberry Finn*. Of Uncle John he wrote, some 50 years later, "I have not come across a better man than he was."

the sashes, and lie in little ridges on the floor and make the place look chilly in the morning and curb the wild desire to get up—in case there was any. I can remember how very dark that room was, in the dark of the moon, and how packed it was with ghostly stillness when one woke up by accident away in the night, and forgotten sins came flocking out of the secret chambers of the memory and wanted a hearing; and how ill chosen the time seemed for this kind of business; and how dismal the hoo-hooing of the owl and the wailing of the wolf, sent mourning by on the night wind.

"I remember the raging of the rain on that roof, summer nights, and how pleasant it was to lie and listen to it, and enjoy the white splendor of the lightning and the majestic booming and crashing of the thunder. It was a very satisfactory room, and there was a lightning rod which was reachable from the window, an adorable and skittish thing to climb up and down, summer nights, when there were duties on hand of a sort to make privacy desirable.

"I remember the 'coon and 'possum hunts, nights, with the Negroes, and the long marches through the black gloom of the woods, and the excitement which fired everybody when the distant bay of an experienced dog announced that the game was treed; then the wild scramblings and stumblings through briers and bushes and over roots to get to the spot; then the lighting of a fire and the felling of the tree, the joyful frenzy of the dogs and the Negroes, and the weird picture it all made in the red glare—I remember it all well, and the delight that everyone got out of it, except the 'coon.

"I remember the pigeon seasons, when the birds would come in millions and cover the trees and by their weight break down the branches. They were clubbed to death with sticks; guns were not necessary and were not used. I remember the squirrel hunts, and prairie-chicken hunts, and wild-turkey hunts, and all that; and how we turned out, mornings, while it was still dark, to go on these expeditions, and how chilly and dismal it was, and how often I regretted that I was well enough to go. A toot on a tin horn brought twice as many dogs as were needed, and in their happiness they raced and scampered about, and knocked small people down, and made no end of unnecessary noise. At the word, they vanished away toward the woods, and we drifted silently after them in the melancholy gloom. But presently the gray dawn stole over the world, the birds piped up, then the sun rose and poured light and comfort all around, everything was fresh and dewy and fragrant, and life was a boon again. After three hours of tramping we arrived back wholesomely tired, overladen with game, very hungry, and just in time for breakfast."

11

THE CADET.

"Never smoke more than one cigar at a time" was Mark's sole rule of abstinence when he grew up. Earlier, at 14, he had a brief spasm of interest in the Hannibal chapter of the Cadets of Temperance. *Right:* The roster shows Sam's name led all the rest, but after it is the notation "with^d." He lasted through two "cold water army" parades, on May Day and the Fourth of July in 1850, strutting the uniform illustrated (*above*) in *Tom Sawyer*.

THE CADETS OF TEMPERANCE

"Hannibal always had a weakness for the Temperance cause. I joined the Cadets myself, although they didn't allow a boy to smoke, or drink or swear, but I thought I never could be truly happy till I wore one of those stunning red scarfs and walked in procession when a distinguished citizen died. I stood it four months, but never an infernal distinguished citizen died during the whole time; and when they finally pronounced old Dr. Norton convalescent (a man I had been depending on for seven or eight weeks), I just drew out. I drew out in disgust, and pretty much all the distinguished citizens in the camp died within the next three weeks."

A little later, Mark modified his explanation: "Nothing pleases a child so much as to be a member of something or other. Your rightly constituted child don't care shucks what it is, either. I joined the Cadets of Temperance, once, when I was a boy. That was an awful take-in; no smoking or anything allowed—not even any bad language; but they had beautiful red scarfs. I stood it three months, and then sidled out. I liked the red scarfs well enough, but I could not stand the morality."

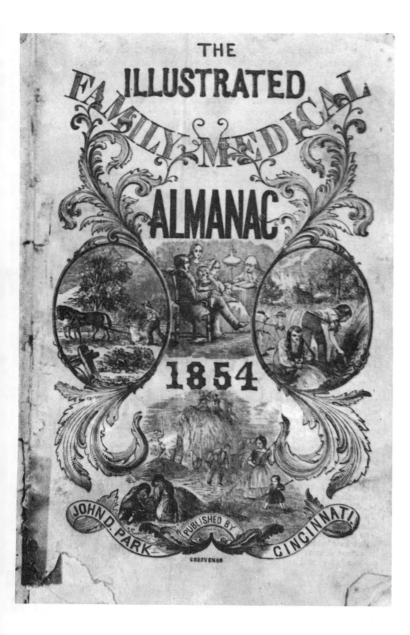

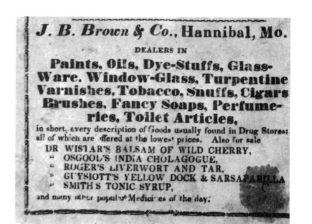

Like Aunt Polly in *Tom Sawyer*, Mark's mother was "infatuated with patent medicines" and found plenty of opportunity to test them on her sickly boy. This *Family Medical Almanac* listed the rich variety of balms, bitters and balsams Jane Clemens could draw on at Brown's drugstore.

AUNT POLLY AND HER PAIN KILLER

"She was one of those people who are infatuated with patent medicines and all new-fangled methods of producing health or mending it. She was an inveterate experimenter in these things. When something fresh in this line came out she was in a fever, right away, to try it; not on herself, for she was never ailing, but on anybody else that came handy. She was a subscriber for all the 'Health' periodicals and phrenological frauds; and the solemn ignorance they were inflated with was breath to her nostrils. All the 'rot' they contained about ventilation, and how to go to bed, and how to get up, and what to eat, and what to drink, and how much exercise to take, and what frame of mind to keep one's self in, and what sort of clothing to wear, was all gospel to her, and she never observed that her health-journals of the current month customarily upset everything they had recommended the month before. She was as simple-hearted and honest as the day was long, and so she was an easy victim. She gathered together her quack periodicals and her quack medicines, and thus armed with death, went about on her pale horse, metaphorically speaking, with 'hell following after.' But she never suspected that she was not an angel of healing and the balm of Gilead in disguise, to the suffering neighbors."

Dan Rice's Hippodrome.

THIS stupendous establishment, organized at an expense of FIFTY THOUSAND DOLLARS numbering over Two Huudred Men and Horses, and being the first effort ever made to introduce the sports of the GENUINE HIPPODROME in this country, Will be opened at HANNIBAL, TUESDAY, AUGUST 31st.

The Afternoon Performance will Commence at 2 o'clock, and the Evening at 7 1-2 o'clock.

Among the truly Magnificent Pageants presented, may be enumerated the grand scena of the

BEDOUINS OF THE DESERT;
THE GAMES OF THE CURRICULUM;
THE TOURNAMENT;
FEATS OF THE GYMNASIUM;
OLYMPIC SPORTS;
ABROBATICS;
TERPSICHOREA;

The performance of the Celebrated CREOLE BALLET TROUPE, numbering over forty members; with all the gems of the Modern Circus, by artists of superior merit in every instance, and in some cases by those who have outstripped all rivalry.

The Spectacle is accompanied and enlivened by strains of choicest music, by a
DOUBLE BRASS BAND;
Led by Almon Mentor, the Wizard Bugler!
The IMMENSE PAVILION will hold comfortably 10,000 PERSONS, and is provided with every convenience of seats, so arranged that fatigue cannot occur while witnessing the performance.

☞ In consequence of the great expense of the ompany, the prices of admission will invariably be 50 cents; children half price.

☞ Tickets may be procured on board of the boat immediately after its landing.

☞ All bills must be presented for payment at the office on board.

☞ For particulars see Pamphlets, Posters, etc.
C. H. CASTLE, Agent.

FOR FALL OF 1852.

Left: Bedouins, ballerinas and brass bands delighted the villagers in Mark's youth. Dan Rice, a favorite with his circus or blackface show, advertised in the Hannibal *Press. Below:* Chang and Eng enthralled Mark. Later he was to use them in *The Siamese Twins,* and again in *Those Extraordinary Twins* which grew into *Pudd'nhead Wilson.*

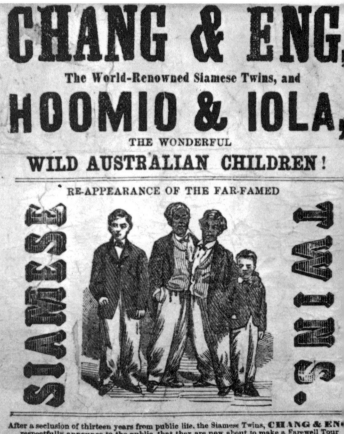

CHANG & ENG,
The World-Renowned Siamese Twins, and
HOOMIO & IOLA,
THE WONDERFUL
WILD AUSTRALIAN CHILDREN!

RE-APPEARANCE OF THE FAR-FAMED

SIAMESE TWINS

After a seclusion of thirteen years from public life, the Siamese Twins, **CHANG & ENG** respectfully announce to the public that they are now about to make a Farewell Tour of the United States, when they trust that the same liberal patronage bestowed on their first traveling tour will be accorded them, on these, their

GRAND FAREWELL ENTERTAINMENTS.

GRIM VISAGED WAR, which for four years swept with relentless fury over our land, destroying the farm owned by the Siamese Twins in North Carolina, and where, for thirteen years, they dwelt in quiet seclusion, surrounded by their families. The fierce onset of contending armies having laid waste their property, and having been repeatedly importuned to appear once more in public, they have concluded to give this series of entertainments, which will be conducted on the same plan as those heretofore given with such marked success before the crowned heads and nobility of France, Germany and England, where their sen created a furore equalled only by the immense crowds who thronged to witness them in the principal cities of the United States.

CHANG AND ENG,
— WILL BE —
Accompanied by their Children
WHO HAVE BEEN BORN SINCE THEIR LAST APPEARANCE IN PUBLIC.

It would be superfluous to dwell upon .... Twins as a rare curiosity, the most eminent physicians and .... unanimous in pronouncing the .... the
GREATEST CURIOSITY IN THE WORLD!

14

News of gold at Sutter's Mill in 1848 infected many Hannibal villagers with the California yellow fever. Bankrupt Ben Horr, husband of Mark's first school-teacher, headed west and so did Mark's playmate, John Robards, whose father captained a local company, reported in this news item. One day, as the gold-hunters streamed westward, Mark found in the streets a page torn from a book about Joan of Arc, telling of her prison days. It led Mark to wide reading in medieval history, opening the path to his own *Joan, The Prince and the Pauper,* and *A Connecticut Yankee.*

A GLAD AND STUNNING SURPRISE

"Where now is Billy Rice? He was a joy to me, and so were the other stars . . . Billy Birch, David Wambold, Backus, and a delightful dozen of their brethren who made life a pleasure to me forty years ago and later.

"I remember the first Negro musical show I ever saw. It must have been in the early forties. It was a new institution. In our village of Hannibal we had not heard of it before, and it burst upon us as a glad and stunning surprise.

"The show remained a week and gave a performance every night. Church members did not attend these performances, but all the worldlings flocked to them and were enchanted.

"The minstrel troupes had good voices and both their solos and their choruses were a delight to me as long as the Negro show continued in existence. In the beginning the songs were rudely comic, such as 'Buffalo Gals,' 'Camptown Races,' 'Old Dan Tucker,' and so on; but a little later sentimental songs were introduced, such as 'The Blue Juniata,' 'Sweet Ellen Bayne,' 'Nelly Bly,' 'A Life on the Ocean Wave,' 'The Larboard Watch,' etc.

"The minstrel show was born in the early forties and it had a prosperous career for about thirty-five years; then it degenerated into a variety show and was nearly all variety show with a Negro act or two thrown in incidentally. The real Negro show has been stone dead for thirty years. To my mind it was a thoroughly delightful thing, and a most competent laughter-compeller and I am sorry it is gone."

The Emigration.

As near as can be ascertained, the number of persons who have emigrated from this City to California is about eighty. We are indebted to the last Journal for a list of the various messes, and the names of those composing them, numbered as follows:

Mess No: 1.—John McKee, Samuel Cross, Wm. M. Ferguson, Henry Mc-Kee.

No. 2.—Tubman Ayres, Philander Anderson.

No. 3.—E. C. McDonald, Robert Sherrard, John Bias.

No. 5.—James Brady, John M. Brady, C. C. Brady.

No. 6.—A Shearer and family, Jacob Lafever, Rev. Mr. Granger and family.

No. 7.—Jos. M. Davis, J. W. Marsh, John Tisdale.

No. 8.—A. S. Robards, E. A. Lockwood, Jas. Wickersham, Jacob D. Atkinson, Peter O. Atkinson, Joshua Richmond, James Munson, Wm. Munson, Wm. Settles, Dr. J. F. Bull, Rev. B. Stevens.

No. 9.—Wm. Nash, Henry Sarver, Wm. Coffman.

No. 10.—Dr H. Meredith, Jno. Jones, Chas. Meredith.

No. 11.—J. F. Hawkins, B. M. Hawkins, G. W. Hawkins.

No. 12.—J. R. Smith, Wm. Bird, Isham Winn, James E. Murnell, Henry Howell, Franklin Bull, R. C. McFarland.

No. 13.—V. P. Draper, Wm. Marr, Wm. Curts, Marion McGinnis.

No. 14.—J. M. Lasley and servant, John Hawkins, T. J. Wilson, C. C. Carter, Clay Price.

No. 15.—Wm. Briggs, Henry Snider, Charles Snider, Wm. Coontz.

No. 16.—Wm. H. Davidson, Solomon Funk, G. W. Harris.

No. 17.—Captain P. H. Hickman, Dr. I. B. Brittingham, A. S. Brittingham.

The following persons have gone but we have not been able to class them in any particular mess:

Wm. E. Holt, Thomas Sunderland, Cook Campbell, Wm. Ewing, Orion Holmes, Joseph Peyton, Archibald Davis, Thomas Fenner, J. T. Williams.

Slave sale advertisements that young Mark saw in the local papers.

AT FIRST MY FATHER OWNED SLAVES . . .

"At first my father owned slaves but by and by he sold them and hired others by the year from the farmers. For a girl of fifteen he paid twelve dollars a year and gave her two linsey-woolsey frocks and a pair of 'stogy' shoes—cost, a modification of nothing; for a Negro woman of twenty-five, as general house servant,

The Clemens children remembered seeing a captured runaway slave brought back to Florida. But thousands of other runaways, like Huck's friend Jim, escaped to freedom with the help of the Underground Railroad.

An ex-slave, once Mark Twain's nurse on his Uncle John Quarles' farm.

300 DOLLARS
REWARD!

RUNAWAY from John S. Doak on the 21st inst., two NEGRO MEN; LOGAN 45 years of age, bald-headed, one or more crooked fingers; DAN 21 years old, six feet high. Both black. I will pay ONE HUNDRED DOLLARS for the apprehension and delivery of LOGAN, or to have him confined so that I can get him. I will also pay TWO HUNDRED DOLLARS for the apprehension of DAN, or to have him confined so that I can get him.
JOHN S. DOAKE,
Springfield, Mo., April 24th, 1857.

he paid twenty-five dollars a year and gave her shoes and the aforementioned linsey-woolsey frocks; for a strong Negro woman of forty, as cook, washer, etc., he paid forty dollars a year and the customary two suits of clothes; and for an able-bodied man he paid from seventy-five to a hundred dollars a year and gave him two suits of jeans and two pairs of 'stogy' shoes—an outfit that cost about three dollars. . . .

"In my schoolboy days I had no aversion to slavery. I was not aware that there was anything wrong about it. No one arraigned it in my hearing; the local papers said nothing against it; the local pulpit taught us that God approved it, that it was a holy thing and that the doubter need only look in the Bible if he wished to settle his mind—and then the texts were read aloud to us to make the matter sure; if the slaves themselves had an aversion to slavery they were wise and said nothing. In Hannibal we seldom saw a slave misused; on the farm never.

". . . there was nothing about the slavery of the Hannibal region to rouse one's dozing humane instincts to activity. It was the mild domestic slavery, not the brutal plantation article. Cruelties were very rare and exceedingly and wholesomely unpopular. To separate and sell the members of a slave family to different masters was a thing not well liked by the people and so it was not often done, except in the settling of estates. I have no recollection of ever seeing a slave auction in that town; but I am suspicious that that is because the thing was a common and commonplace spectacle, not an uncommon and impressive one. I vividly remember seeing a dozen black men and women chained to one another, once, and lying in a group on the pavement, awaiting shipment to the Southern slave market. Those were the saddest faces I have ever seen. Chained slaves could not have been a common sight or this picture would not have made so strong and lasting an impression upon me.

"The 'nigger trader' was loathed by everybody. He was regarded as a sort of human devil who bought and conveyed poor helpless creatures to hell—for to our whites and blacks alike the Southern plantation was simply hell; no milder name could describe it. If the threat to sell an incorrigible slave 'down the river' would not reform him, nothing would—his case was past cure. Yet I remember that once when a white man killed a Negro man for a trifling offence everybody seemed indifferent about it—as regarded the slave—though considerable sympathy was felt for the slave's owner, who had been bereft of valuable property by a worthless person who was not able to pay for it.

"It is commonly believed that an infallible effect of slavery was to make such as lived in its midst hard-hearted. I think it had no such effect—speaking in general terms. I think it stupefied everybody's humanity as regarded the slave, but stopped there. There were no hard-hearted people in our town—I mean there were no more than would be found in any other town of the same size in any other country; and in my experience hard-hearted people are very rare everywhere. . . .

"All of the Negroes were friends of ours, and with those of our own age we were in effect comrades. I say in effect, using the phrase as a modification. We were comrades and yet not comrades; color and condition interposed a subtle line which both parties were conscious of and which rendered complete fusion impossible. We had a faithful and affectionate good

This illustration is from a booklet that tells the story of three abolitionists who were caught helping five Negroes escape from Missouri in 1841. Mark Twain's father, John Clemens, was a member of the jury that sentenced the whites to 12 years in jail for a crime rated more serious than murder in the South. Five years later the Governor pardoned the three men.

friend, ally and adviser in 'Uncle Dan'l,' a middle-aged slave whose head was the best one in the Negro quarter, whose sympathies were wide and warm and whose heart was honest and simple and knew no guile. He has served me well these many, many years. I have not seen him for more than half a century and yet spiritually I have had his welcome company a good part of that time and have staged him in books under his own name and as 'Jim,' and carted him all around—to Hannibal, down the Mississippi on a raft and even across the Desert of Sahara in a balloon—and he has endured it all with the patience and friendliness and loyalty which were his birthright. It was on the farm that I got my strong liking for his race and my appreciation of certain of his fine qualities. This feeling and this estimate have stood the test of sixty years and more and have suffered no impairment. The black face is as welcome to me now as it was then."

VOL. II.   FOR THE AMUSEMENT OF THE READER.   NO. 5.

Written for the Carpet-Bag

The Dandy Frightening the Squatter.

BY S. L. C.

About thirteen years ago, when the now flourishing young city of Hannibal, on the Mississippi River, was but a "wood-yard," surrounded by a few huts, belonging to some hardy "squatters," and such a thing as a steamboat was considered quite a sight, the following incident occurred

A tall, brawny woodsman stood leaning against a tree which stood upon the bank of the river, gazing at some approaching object, which our readers would easily have discovered to be a steamboat.

About half an hour elapsed, and the boat was moored, and the hands busily engaged in taking on wood.

Now among the many passengers on this boat, both male and female, was a spruce young dandy, with a killing moustache, &c., who seemed bent on making an impression upon the hearts of the young ladies on board, and to do this, he thought he must perform some heroic deed. Observing our squatter friend, he imagined this to be a fine opportunity to bring himself into notice; so stepping into the cabin, he said:

"Ladies, if you wish to enjoy a good laugh step out on the guards. I intend to frighten that gentleman into fits who stands on the bank."

The ladies complied with the request, and our dandy drew from his bosom a formidable looking bowie-knife, and thrust it into his belt; then, taking a large horse-pistol in each hand, he seemed satisfied that all was right. Thus equipped, he strode on shore, with an air which seemed to say—"The hopes of a nation depend on me." Marching up to the woodsman, he exclaimed:

"Found you at last, have I! You are the very man I've been looking for these three weeks! Say your prayers!" he continued, presenting his pistols, "you'll make a capital barn door, and I shall drill the key-hole myself!"

The squatter calmly surveyed him a moment, and then, drawing back a step, planted his huge fist directly between the eyes of his astonished antagonist, who, in a moment, was floundering in the turbid waters of the Mississippi.

Every passenger on the boat had by this time collected on the guards, and the shout that now went up from the crowd speedily restored the crest-fallen hero to his senses, and, as he was sneaking off towards the boat, was thus accosted by his conqueror:

"I say, yeou, next time yeou come around drillin' key-holes, don't forget yer old acquaintances!"

The ladies unanimously voted the knife and pistols to the victor.

On May 1, 1852, the Boston comic weekly, *The Carpet-Bag,* published a brief humorous sketch sent in by someone signing himself simply "S.L.C." It was Mark's first appearance in print outside Hannibal.

The second floor of this building housed Joseph Ament's *Missouri Courier* and job-printing office. About the middle of 1848 Mark was apprenticed to Ament for bed and board, two suits per year—and no wages. The bed was a pallet on the shop floor, the first suit was a hand-me-down that fitted like a circus tent, the second suit he never got. Mark's compositor's case stood at the window marked "A." From drudge he soon rose to sub-editor.

Apprentice printer at 15: Mark Twain in the earliest picture of him known. Notice the belt buckle? He began part-time work as a printer's apprentice probably late in 1847. Two years later he was working for his brother Orion, and began to learn to write.

PRINTER'S DEVIL

From the age of thirteen the printer's devil began the cheap boardinghouse life he was not to escape from until his marriage in 1870, some twenty-two years later. The early years were miserable and lonely, except for companionship with apprentices with whom he shared the bleak bed and board. Mark proved to be a fast and capable journeyman, who never lost his feeling for the printshop. For him, too, it was to be "the poor boy's college."

"About 1849 or 1850 Orion severed his connection with the printing-house in St. Louis and came up to Hannibal and bought a weekly paper called the Hannibal Journal, together with its plant and its good-will, for the sum of five hundred dollars cash. He borrowed the cash at ten per cent interest from an old farmer named Johnson who lived five miles out of town. Then he reduced the subscription price of the paper from two dollars to one dollar. He reduced the rates for advertising in about the same proportion and thus he created

one absolute and unassailable certainty—to wit: that the business would never pay him a single cent of profit.

"He took me out to the Courier office and engaged my services in his own at three dollars and a half a week, which was an extravagant wage, but Orion was always generous, always liberal with everybody but himself. It cost him nothing in my case, for he never was able to pay me a single penny as long as I was with him. By the end of the first year he found he must make some economies. The office rent was cheap but it was not cheap enough. He could not afford to pay rent of any kind, so he moved the whole plant into the house we lived in, and it cramped the dwelling-place cruelly. He kept that paper alive during four years but I have at this time no idea how he accomplished it. Toward the end of each year he had to turn out and scrape and scratch for the fifty dollars of interest due Mr. Johnson, and that fifty dollars was about the only cash he ever received or paid out, I suppose, while he was proprietor of that newspaper, except for ink and printing-paper. The paper was a dead failure. It had to be that from the start."

"LOCAL" RESOLVES TO COMMIT SUICIDE.

'Local,' disconsolate from receiving no further notice from 'A Dog-be-Deviled Citizen,' contemplates Suicide. His 'pocket-pistol' (i. e. the *bottle*,) failing in the patriotic work of ridding the country of a nuisance, he resolves to 'extinguish his chunk' by feeding his carcass to the fishes of Bear Creek, while friend and foe are wrapt in sleep. Fearing, however, that he may get out of his depth, he *sounds the stream with his walking-stick.*

The artist has, you will perceive, Mr. Editor, caught the gentleman's countenance as correctly as the thing could have been done with the real *dog*-gerytype apparatus. Ain't he pretty? and don't he step along through the mud with an air? 'Peace to his *re*-manes.'

            'A Dog-be-Deviled Citizen.'

Scott Mass Meeting.

The column in the Hannibal *Journal* for September 16, 1852, in which Mark ("A Dog-be-Deviled Citizen") taunted a jilted rival editor.

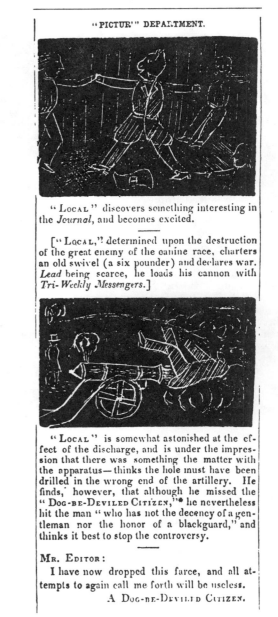

"PICTURE" DEPARTMENT.

" Local" discovers something interesting in the *Journal*, and becomes excited.

["Local," determined upon the destruction of the great enemy of the canine race, charters an old swivel (a six pounder) and declares war. *Lead* being scarce, he loads his cannon with *Tri-Weekly Messengers*.]

"Local" is somewhat astonished at the effect of the discharge, and is under the impression that there was something the matter with the apparatus—thinks the hole must have been drilled in the wrong end of the artillery. He finds, however, that although he missed the " Dog-be-Deviled Citizen,"* he nevertheless hit the man " who has not the decency of a gentleman nor the honor of a blackguard," and thinks it best to stop the controversy.

Mr. Editor:
  I have now dropped this farce, and all attempts to again call me forth will be useless.
           A Dog-be-Deviled Citizen.

Another gibe, with two more "villainous cuts." Years later, it was worked into "My First Literary Venture."

MY FIRST LITERARY VENTURE

"I was a very smart child at the age of thirteen—an unusually smart child, I thought at the time. It was then that I did my first newspaper scribbling, and most unexpectedly to me it stirred up a fine sensation in the community. It did, indeed, and I was very proud of it, too. I was a printer's 'devil,' and a progressive and aspiring one. My uncle had me on his paper (the *Weekly Hannibal Journal*, two dollars a year in advance—five hundred subscribers, and they paid in cordwood, cabbages, and unmarketable turnips), and on a lucky summer's day he left town to be gone a week, and asked me if I thought I could edit one issue of the paper judiciously. Ah! didn't I want to try! Higgins was the editor on the rival paper. He had lately been jilted, and one night a friend found an open note on the poor fellow's bed, in which he stated that he could no longer endure life and had drowned himself in Bear Creek. The friend ran down there and discovered Higgins wading back to shore! He had concluded he wouldn't. The village was full of it for several days, but Higgins did not suspect it. I thought this was a fine opportunity. I wrote an elaborately wretched account of the whole matter, and then illustrated it with villainous cuts engraved on the bottoms of wooden type with a jack-knife—one of them a picture of Higgins wading out into the creek in his shirt, with a lantern, sounding the depth of the water with a walking-stick. I thought it was desperately funny, and was densely unconscious that there was any moral obliquity about such a publication. Being satisfied with this effort I looked around for other worlds to conquer, and it struck me that it would make good, interesting matter to charge the editor of a neighboring country paper with a piece of gratuitous rascality and 'see him squirm.'

"I did it, putting the article into the form of a parody on the 'Burial of Sir John Moore'—and a pretty crude parody it was, too.

"Then I lampooned two prominent citizens outrageously—not because they had done anything to deserve it, but merely because I thought it was my duty to make the paper lively.

"Next I gently touched up the newest stranger—the lion of the day, the gorgeous journeyman tailor from Quincy. He was a simpering coxcomb of the first water, and the 'loudest' dressed man in the State. He was an inveterate woman-killer. Every week he wrote lushy 'poetry' for the *Journal*, about his newest conquest. His rhymes for my week were headed 'To MARY IN H — L,' meaning to Mary in Hannibal, of course. But while setting up the piece I was suddenly riven from head to heel by what I regarded as a perfect thunderbolt of humor, and I compressed it into a snappy footnote at the bottom—thus:—'We will let this thing pass, just this once; but we wish Mr. J. Gordon Runnels to understand distinctly that we have a character to sustain, and from this time forth when he wants to commune with his friends in h—l, he must select some other medium than the columns of this journal!'

"The paper came out, and I never knew any little thing to attract so much attention as those playful trifles of mine.

"For once the *Hannibal Journal* was in demand—a novelty it had not experienced before. The whole town was stirred. Higgins dropped in with a double-barrelled shot-gun early in the forenoon. When he found that it was an infant (as he called me) that had done him the damage, he simply pulled my ears and went away; but he threw up his situation that night and left town for good. The tailor came with his goose and a pair of shears; but he despised me too, and departed for the South that night. The two lampooned citizens came with threats of libel, and went away incensed at my insignificance. The country editor pranced in with a

warwhoop next day, suffering for blood to drink; but he ended by forgiving me cordially and inviting me down to the drug store to wash away all animosity in a friendly bumper of 'Fahnestock's Vermifuge.' It was his little joke. My uncle was very angry when he got back—unreasonably so, I thought, considering what an impetus I had given the paper, and considering also that gratitude for his preservation ought to have been uppermost in his mind, inasmuch as by his delay he had so wonderfully escaped dissection, tomahawking, libel, and getting his head shot off. But he softened when he looked at the accounts and saw that I had actually booked the unparalleled number of thirty-three new subscribers, and had the vegetables to show for it, cordwood, cabbage, beans, and unsalable turnips enough to run the family for two years!"

The front page of the new Hannibal *Daily Journal* for May 6, 1853. Orion Clemens, undaunted by his failing weekly, piled a daily on top of it. This issue, edited by Mark in his brother's absence, contained his famous "To Miss Katie of H——L" love poem.

Four generations photographed in New York on Jane Clemens' seventy-ninth birthday, June 18, 1882. Seated are Mark's mother and her daughter Pamela Clemens Moffett, with her daughter Annie Moffett Webster standing, and her daughter Jean Webster clutching a doll.

MY MOTHER, JANE CLEMENS

"When my mother died in October 1890 she was well along in her eighty-eighth year, a mighty age, a well-contested fight for life for one who at forty was so delicate of body as to be accounted a confirmed invalid and destined to pass soon away. I knew her well during the first twenty-five years of my life; but after that I saw her only at wide intervals, for we lived many days' journey apart.

"Technically speaking, she had no career; but she had a character and it was of a fine and striking and lovable sort.

"She had a slender, small body but a large heart—a heart so large that everybody's grief and everybody's joys found welcome in it and hospitable accommodation. The greatest difference which I find between her and the rest of the people whom I have known is this,

and it is a remarkable one: those others felt a strong interest in a few things, whereas to the very day of her death she felt a strong interest in the whole world and everything and everybody in it. In all her life she never knew such a thing as a half-hearted interest in affairs and people, or an interest which drew a line and left out certain affairs and was indifferent to certain people.

"Her interest in people and other animals was warm, personal, friendly. She always found something to excuse, and as a rule to love, in the toughest of them—even if she had to put it there herself. She was the natural ally and friend of the friendless.

"When her pity or her indignation was stirred by hurt or shame inflicted upon some defenseless person or creature, she was the most eloquent person I have heard speak. It was seldom eloquence of a fiery or violent sort, but gentle, pitying, persuasive, appealing; and so genuine and so nobly and simply worded and so touchingly uttered, that many times I have seen it win the reluctant and splendid applause of tears."

MY BROTHER ORION

Mark's brother, Orion Clemens, and his wife Mollie. Orion died in 1897.

"Orion Clemens was born in Jamestown, Tennessee, in 1825. He was the family's first-born.

"One of his characteristics was eagerness. He woke with an eagerness about some matter or other every morning; it consumed him all day; it perished in the night and he was on fire with a fresh new interest next morning before he could get his clothes on. He exploited in this way three hundred and sixty-five red-hot new eagernesses every year of his life—until he died sitting at a table with a pen in his hand, in the early morning, jotting down the conflagration for that day and preparing to enjoy the fire and smoke of it until night should extinguish it. He was then seventy-two years old. But I am forgetting another characteristic, a very pronounced one. That was his deep glooms, his despondencies, his despairs; these had their place in each and every day along with the eagernesses. Thus his day was divided—no, not divided, mottled—from sunrise to midnight with alternating brilliant sunshine and black cloud. Every day he was the most joyous and hopeful man that ever was, I think, and also every day he was the most miserable man that ever was.

"Innumerable were Orion's projects for acquiring the means to pay off his debt to me. These projects extended straight through the succeeding thirty years, but in every case they failed. During all those thirty years Orion's well-established honesty kept him in offices of trust where other people's money had to be taken care of but where no salary was paid. He was treasurer of all the benevolent institutions; he took care of the money and other property of widows and orphans; he never lost a cent for anybody and never made one for himself. Every time he changed his religion the church of his new faith was glad to get him; made him treasurer at once and at once he stopped the graft and the leaks in that church. He exhibited a facility in changing his political complexion that was a marvel to the whole community.

"He was a most strange creature—but in spite of his eccentricities he was beloved all his life in whatsoever community he lived. And he was also held in high esteem for at bottom he was a sterling man."

When John Clemens' debts forced him out of house and furniture on Hill Street, the family moved over the drugstore in the "House of the Pilasters"—still standing at the corner of Hill and Main. A few months later, on March 24, 1847, Mark's father died here of pneumonia, leaving his family in the same poverty they had known for many years.

Above: This tintype of Mark was made in 1853. *Below:* The same year, "Love Concealed," the poem signed "Rambler," appeared in the Hannibal *Daily Journal* on May 6, and a month later its author was on his way east for the first time. Restless in his brother's newspaper shop, and excited by reports of the Crystal Palace Fair in New York, he left Hannibal for good. He got a compositor's job in New York and went out to see the town.

LOVE CONCEALED.

TO MISS KATIE OF H——L.

Oh, thou wilt never know how fond a love
 This heart could have felt for thee;
Or ever dream how love and friendship strove,
 Through long, long hours for mastery;
How passion often urged, but pride restrained,
 Or how thy coldness grieved, but kindness pained.

How hours have soothed the feelings, then that were
 The torture of my lonely life—
But ever yet will often fall a tear,
 O'er wildest hopes and thoughts then rife;
Where'er recalled by passing word or tone,
 Fond memory mirrors all those visions flown.

For much I fear he has won thy heart,
 And thou art but a friend to me;
I feel that in thy love I have no part,
 I know how much he worships thee;
Yet still often will there rise a gleam of hope,
 Wherewith but only time and pride can cope.
Hannibal, May 4th, 1853.   RAMBLER.

Tramp Printer

A GLORIOUS SIGHT

Soon after arriving in New York, Mark sent his sister Pamela these impressions of the World's Fair in the Crystal Palace:

"From the gallery (second floor) you have a glorious sight—the flags of the different countries represented, the lofty dome, glittering jewelry, gaudy tapestry, etc., with the busy crowd passing to and fro—'tis a perfect fairy palace—beautiful beyond description.

"The machinery department is on the main floor, but I cannot enumerate any of it on account of the lateness of the hour (past 1 o'clock). It would take more than a week to examine everything on exhibition; and I was only in a little over two hours to-night. I only glanced at about one-third of the articles; and, having a poor memory, I have enumerated scarcely any of the principal objects. The visitors to the Palace average 6,000 daily—double the population of Hannibal. The price of admission being 50 cents, they take in about $3,000.

"The Latting Observatory (height about 280 feet) is near the Palace—from it you can obtain a grand view of the city and the country around. The Croton Aqueduct, to supply the city with water, is the greatest wonder yet. Immense sewers are laid across the bed of the Hudson River, and pass through the country to Westchester County, where a whole river is turned from its course and brought to New York. From the reservoir in the city to the Westchester County reservoir the distance is thirty-eight miles and, if necessary, they could easily supply every family in New York with one hundred barrels of water per day!

"You ask where I spent my evenings. Where would you suppose, with a free printer's library containing more than 4,000 volumes within a quarter of a mile of me, and nobody at home to talk to? Write soon."

The Crystal Palace housed America's first world's fair, on Fifth Avenue and 42nd Street, near the spot where the Public Library stands today. The fair was "a perfect fairy palace" to Mark, but an economic failure. Even P. T. Barnum's press agentry failed to keep it open for a full year.

New York in 1853, looking south from 42nd Street. In right foreground is the Crystal Palace, standing beside the city reservoir.

LETTER FROM NEW YORK.

The free and easy impudence of the writer of the following letter will be appreciated by those who recognize him. We should be pleased to have more of his letters:

NEW YORK,
Wednesday, August 24th, 1853.

MY DEAR MOTHER: you will doubtless be a little surprised, and somewhat angry when you receive this, and find me so far from home; but you must bear a little with me, for you know I was always the best boy you had, and perhaps you remember the people used to say to their children—"Now don't do like O. and H. C— but take S. for your guide!"

Well, I was out of work in St. Louis, and did'nt fancy loafing in such a dry place, where there is no pleasure to be seen without paying well for it, and so I thought I might as well go to New York. I packed up my "duds" and left for this village, where I arrived, all right, this morning.

It took a day, by steamboat and cars, to go from St. Louis to Bloomington, Ill; another day by railroad, from there to Chicago, where I laid over all day Sunday; from Chicago to Monroe, in Michigan, by railroad, another day; from Monroe, across Lake Erie, in the fine Lake palace, "Southern Michigan," to Buffalo, another day; from Buffalo to Albany, by railroad, another day; and from Albany to New York, by Hudson river steamboat, another day—an awful trip, taking five days, where it should have been only three. I shall wait a day or so for my insides to get settled, after the jolting they received, when I shall look out for a sit; for they say there is plenty of work to be had for *sober* compositors.

New York evoked Mark's first travel letter, directed to his mother and published by Orion in the Hannibal *Journal* September 8, 1853.

I LIKE THE ABOMINABLE PLACE

In October, 1853, Mark wrote his sister Pamela in St. Louis:

"My Dear Sister—I have not written to any of the family for some time, from the fact, *firstly*, that I didn't know where they were, and *secondly*, because I have been fooling myself with the idea that I was going to leave New York every day for the last two weeks. I have taken a liking to the abominable place, and every time I get ready to leave, I put it off a day or so, from some unaccountable cause. It is as hard on my conscience to leave New York, as it was easy to leave Hannibal. I think I shall get off Tuesday, though.

"Edwin Forrest has been playing, for the last sixteen days, at the Broadway Theatre, but I never went to see him till last night. The play was the 'Gladiator.' I did not like parts of it much, but other portions were really splendid. In the latter part of the last act, where the 'Gladiator' (Forrest) dies at his brother's feet (in all the fierce pleasure of gratified revenge), the man's whole soul seems absorbed in the part he is playing; and it is really startling to see him. I am sorry I did not see him play 'Damon and Pythias'—the former character being his greatest.

"If my letters do not come often, you need not bother yourself about me; for if you have a brother nearly eighteen years of age, who is not able to take care of himself a few miles from home, such a brother is not worth one's thoughts: and if I don't manage to take care of No. 1, be assured you will never know it. I am not afraid, however; I shall ask favors from no one, and endeavor to be (and shall be) as 'independent as a wood-sawyer's clerk.'

"I never saw such a place for military companies as New York. Go on the street when you will, you are sure to meet a company in full uniform, with all the usual appendages of drums, fifes, etc. I saw a large company of soldiers of 1812 the other day, with a '76 veteran scattered here and there in the ranks. And as I passed through one of the parks lately, I came upon a company of *boys* on parade. Their uniforms were neat, and their muskets about half the common size. Some of them were not more than seven or eight years of age; but had evidently been well-drilled.

"Passage to Albany (160 miles) on the finest steamers that ply the Hudson, is now 25 cents—cheap enough, but is generally cheaper than that in the summer."

Mark enjoyed Edwin Forrest as Spartacus at the Broadway Theatre.

Right: East of the Crystal Palace, 42nd Street looked like this. It was a squatters' village, perched on rock.

Left: The notorious Five Points neighborhood in New York, where poverty and sin abounded.

Franklin Square, close by Mark's employers, the printers Gray and Green. He saw the Harper's Building on the way to work, the publishers who were to sign a handsome contract for all his work years later.

PHILADELPHIA CORRESPONDENT

After two months in New York, Mark wandered off to Philadelphia, where he found work in a newspaper's composing room. A letter reported his move to his brother. Orion, meanwhile, had given up Hannibal and bought into the Muscatine, Iowa, *Journal,* where he printed Mark's letters as "Philadelphia Correspondence."

"I am subbing at the Inquirer office. I go to work at 7 o'clock in the evening, and work till 3 o'clock the next morning. I can go to the theatre and stay till 12 o'clock in the evening, and work till 3 o'clock the next morning, when I go to bed, and sleep till 11 o'clock, then get up and loaf the rest of the day.

"Unlike New York, I like this Philadelphia amazingly, and the people in it. There is only one thing that gets my 'dander' up—and that is the hands are always encouraging me: telling me 'it's no use to get discouraged—no use to be downhearted, for there is more work here than you can do!' 'Downhearted,' the devil! I

Mark made a pilgrimage to the tomb in Christ Churchyard of that other poor boy who began life as a printer—Ben Franklin. The Philadelphia printers, Mark wrote Orion, had just raised $1,000 at a ball and supper to help erect a monument to Franklin.

have not had a particle of such a feeling since I left Hannibal, more than four months ago. I fancy they'll have to wait some time till they see me downhearted or afraid of starving while I have strength to work and am in a city of 400,000 inhabitants. When I was in Hannibal, before I had scarcely stepped out of the town limits, nothing could have convinced me that I would starve as soon as I got a little way from home."

WASHINGTON CORRESPONDENT

Mark stayed in Philadelphia through the winter of 1853–54, visiting Washington in February. His letters home do not attempt humor. They are the simple and direct accounts of a diligent tourist with an eye for concrete and vivid detail:

"When I came out on the street this morning to take a view of Washington, the ground was perfectly white, and it was snowing as though the heavens were to be emptied, and that, too, in as short a time as possible. The snow was falling so thickly that I could scarcely see across the street. I started toward the capitol, but there being no sidewalk, I sank ankle deep in mud and snow at every step. When at last I reached the capitol, I found that Congress did not sit till 11 o'clock; so I thought I would stroll around the city for an hour or two.

"The Treasury Building is a pretty edifice, with a long row of columns in front, and stands about a square from the President's house. Passing into the park in front of the White House, I amused myself with a gaze at Clark Mills' great equestrian statue of Jackson. It is a beautiful thing and well worth a long walk on a stormy day to see. The public buildings of Washington are all fine specimens of architecture, and would add greatly to the embellishment of such a city as New York—but here they are sadly out of place; looking like so many palaces in a Hottentot village. The streets, indeed, are fine—wide, straight, and level as a floor. But the buildings, almost invariably, are very poor—two and three story brick houses, and strewed about in clusters; you seldom see a compact square off Pennsylvania Avenue. They look as though they might have been emptied out of a sack by some Brobdignagian gentleman, and when falling, been scattered abroad by the winds. There are scarcely any pavements, and I might almost say *no* gas, off *the* thoroughfare, Pennsylvania Avenue. Then, if you should be seized with a desire to go to the Capitol, or somewhere else, you may stand in a puddle of water, with the snow driving in your face for fifteen minutes or more, before an omnibus rolls lazily by; and when one does come, ten to one there are nineteen passengers inside and fourteen outside, and while the driver casts

Washington was a straggling town when Mark reached it in February, 1854. He didn't bother to describe the Capitol, in the foreground of this contemporary print, but thought the Patent Office Museum magnificent. Later, Twain the inventor would contribute to it.

on you a look of commiseration, you have the inexpressible satisfaction of knowing that you closely resemble a very moist dishrag (and *feel* so, too), at the same time that you are unable to discover what benefit you have derived from the fifteen minutes' soaking; and so, driving your fists into the inmost recesses of your breeches pockets, you stride away in despair, with a step and a grimace that would make the fortune of a tragedy actor, while your 'onery' appearance is greeted with 'screams of laftur' from a pack of vagabond boys over the way. Such is life, and such is Washington!

"The Capitol is a very fine building, but it has been so often described, that I will not attempt another portrait. The statuary with which it is adorned is most beautiful; but as I am no connoisseur in such matters, I will let that pass also. The large hall between the two Congressional Chambers is embellished with numerous large paintings, portraying some of the principal events in American history. One, the 'Embarkation of the Pilgrims in the Mayflower,' struck me as very fine—so fresh and natural. The 'Baptism of Pocahontas' is also a noble picture, and worthy the place it occupies.

"I passed into the Senate Chamber to see the men who give the people the benefit of their wisdom and learning for a little glory and eight dollars a day. The Senate is now composed of a different material from what it once was. Its glory hath departed. Its halls no longer echo the words of Clay, or Webster, or Calhoun.

They have played their parts and retired from the stage; and though they are still occupied by others, the void is felt. The Senators dress very plainly as they should, and all avoid display, and do not speak unless they have something to say—and that cannot be said of the Representatives. Mr. Cass is a fine looking old man; Mr. Douglas, or 'Young America,' looks like a lawyer's clerk, and Mr. Seward is a slim, dark, bony individual, and looks like a respectable wind would blow him out of the country.

"In the House nearly every man seemed to have something weighing on his mind on which the salvation of the Republic depended, and which he appeared very anxious to ease himself of; and so there were generally half a dozen of them on the floor, and 'Mr. Chairman! Mr. Chairman!' was echoed from every part of the house. Mr. Benton sits silent and gloomy in the midst of the din, like a lion imprisoned in a cage of monkeys, who, feeling his superiority, disdains to notice their chattering.

"The Washington Monument is as yet but a plain white marble obelisk 150 feet high. It will no doubt be very beautiful when finished. When completed, an iron staircase will run up within 25 feet of the top. It is to be 550 feet high. If Congress would appropriate $200,000 to the Monument fund, this sum, with the contributions of the people, would build it in four years.

"Mr. Forrest played Othello at the National Theatre last night, to a good audience. This is a very large theatre, and the only consequence in Washington."

A thousand years from now this race may have passed away, and in its stead a people spring up, wearing the skins of animals for raiment, and for food eating the berries that may grow where now stand the proudest buildings of this town. And this people will dig up with their rude instruments some memorial of the forgotten race — a steam boiler, perhaps — and gaze with astonishment upon it, and wonder who made it; what they made it for, whence they came, and whither they are gone.

A page from Mark's first notebook, written at nineteen.

TRAMP PRINTER

In the summer of 1855, Mark joined Orion again, this time in Keokuk, Iowa. With his younger brother Henry he worked in Orion's Ben Franklin Book and Job Printing Office, for five dollars a week and board. They lived in the printshop above the Patterson Shoe Company. Mark stayed on for 18 months.

Advertising another failure, Orion offers the Muscatine paper for sale. Keokuk was next.

Mark went back to typesetting for the St. Louis *Evening News* in the winter of 1854–1855 entertaining himself and the readers of Orion's Muscatine (Iowa) *Journal* with newsletters. He roomed with a young chairmaker, Frank Burrough, who introduced him to Thackeray, Scott and Dickens. The new friend was to write him 22 years later, letting Mark see himself as he had been at 19. "The portrait is correct," Mark replied to Burrough. "You think I have grown some; upon my word there was room for it. You have described a callow fool, a self-sufficient ass, a mere human tumble-bug, stern in air, heaving at his bit of dung, imagining that he is remodeling the world and is entirely capable of doing it right . . . That is what I was at 19–20."

31

I CAN SEE THAT PRINTING OFFICE YET

In an 1886 speech, Mark reminisced about his days as a tramp printer:

"It may be that the printer of to-day is not the printer of thirty-five years ago. I was no stranger to him. I knew him well. We had a hundred town subscribers and three hundred and fifty country ones; the town subscribers paid in groceries and the country ones in cabbages and cordwood—when they paid at all, which was merely sometimes, and then we always stated the fact in the paper, and gave them a puff; and if we forgot it they stopped the paper. Every man on the town list helped edit the thing—that is, he gave orders as to how it was to be edited; dictated its opinions, marked out its course for it, and every time the boss failed to connect he stopped his paper. We were just infested with critics, and we tried to satisfy them all over. We had one subscriber who paid cash, and he was more trouble than all the rest. He bought us once a year, body and soul, for two dollars. He used to modify our politics every which way, and he made us change our religion four times in five years. If we ever tried to reason with him, he would threaten to stop his paper, and, of course, that meant bankruptcy and destruction.

"I can see that printing office of prehistoric times yet, with its horse bills on the walls, its 'd' boxes clogged with tallow, because we always stood the candle in the 'k' box nights, its towel, which was not considered soiled until it could stand alone, and other signs and symbols that marked the establishment of that kind in the Mississippi Valley; and I can see, also, the tramping 'jour,' who flitted by in the summer and tarried a day, with his wallet stuffed with one shirt and a hatful of handbills, for if he couldn't get any type to set he would do a temperance lecture. His way of life was simple, his needs not complex; all he wanted was plate and bed and money enough to get drunk on, and he was satisfied."

Early in August, 1856, Mark wrote from Keokuk to his brother Henry:

". . . determined to start to Brazil, if possible, in *six weeks* from now. Ma knows my determination, but *even she* counsels me to keep it from Orion. She says I can treat him as I did her when I started to St. Louis and went to New York—I can start to New York and go to South America! Although Orion talks grandly about furnishing me with fifty or a hundred dollars in six weeks, I could not depend upon him for ten dollars, so I have 'feelers' out in several directions, and have already asked for a hundred dollars from one source (keep it to yourself). I will lay on my oars for awhile, and see how the wind sets, when I may probably try to get more. I shall take care that Ma and Orion are plentifully supplied with South American books. They have Herndon's Report now. Between you and I, I believe that the secret of Ma's willingness to allow me to go to South America lies in the fact that she is afraid I am going to get married! Success to the hallucination."

Mark moved fast when a lucky wind blew a fifty-dollar bill down Main Street and into his hand. Arranging for a series of travel letters to the Keokuk *Post*—at $5 each—he left, on a roundabout route, for Brazil. The letters began appearing in October, 1856, datelined from St. Louis and Cincinnati. They were in the current genre, relying on illiterate dialect and misspellings for humor, and were signed "Snodgrass." This "Diarrea" added nothing to Mark's reputation, but it brought him his first earnings as a writer.

For the Post.
Snodgrass' Ride on the Railroad.
CINCINNATI Nov. 14, 1856.
MISTER EDITORS:—Well, now, dang my skin if I don't feel rather curus, "so fat from home and all them that's dear to me," as the bordin-school gals say the first time they write to their friends—still, I ain't takin on about it to speak of—all the difference I kin see is, I feel a little more religious, maybe, when I get a little sick, than I used to.

You know arter going down there to St. Louis, and seein so many wonderful things,

Using the pen name of Thomas Jefferson Snodgrass, Mark wrote a few five-dollar travel letters to the Keokuk *Post* to raise cash for his Amazon expedition.

Jane Clemens, in a portrait done in St. Louis in 1858–59 by an itinerant painter named Brady.

Mississippi Pilot

LEARNING THE MISSISSIPPI

With winter in Cincinnati over, Mark again began dreaming about coca hunting in the Amazon. In April 1857 he boarded the *Paul Jones,* bound for New Orleans. As it steamed slowly down the Ohio, the "permanent ambition" of Hannibal boyhood reawakened. The Bowen boys had all become pilots; maybe he could, too. Horace Bixby was at the wheel of the *Paul Jones.* He thought cub pilots were more trouble than they were worth but, as Mark recalled in *Life on the Mississippi,* "I planned a siege against my pilot, and at the end of three hard days he surrendered. He agreed to teach me the Mississippi River from New Orleans to St. Louis for five hundred dollars, payable out of the first wages I should receive after graduating. I entered upon the small enterprise of 'learning' twelve or thirteen hundred miles of the great Mississippi River with the easy confidence of my time of life. If I had really known what I was about to require of my faculties, I should not have had the courage to begin. I supposed that all a pilot had to do was to keep his boat in the river, and I did not consider that that could be much of a trick, since it was so wide."

Horace Bixby, the pilot who taught Mark Twain the river. From New Orleans Captain Bixby took his cub up to St. Louis, where a mile of steamboats flanked the levee. There Mark borrowed from his brother-in-law, Will Moffett, the first $100 due Bixby. Sam stayed with Pamela and Will during his piloting years.

Mark Twain, in a portrait painted about 1859, now in the Keokuk Public Library.

THE RIVER WAS A WONDERFUL BOOK

"My chief was presently hired to go on a big New Orleans boat," Mark wrote, in *Life on the Mississippi*, "and I packed my satchel and went with him. She was a grand affair. When I stood in her pilot-house I was so far above the water that I seemed perched on a mountain; and her decks stretched so far away, fore and aft, below me, that I wondered how I could ever have considered the little *Paul Jones* a large craft. There were other differences, too. The *Paul Jones'* pilot-house was a cheap, dingy, battered rattletrap, cramped for room; but here was a sumptuous glass temple; room enough to have a dance in; showy red and gold window-curtains; an imposing sofa; leather cushions and a back to the high bench where visiting pilots sit, to spin yarns and 'look at the river'; bright, fanciful 'cuspadores,' instead of a broad wooden box filled with sawdust; nice new oilcloth on the floor; a hospitable big stove for winter; a wheel as high as my head, costly with inlaid work; a wire tiller-rope; bright brass knobs

Mark Twain, photographed in his pilot days, about 1859–60.

for the bells; and a tidy, white-aproned, black 'texas-tender,' to bring up tarts and ices and coffee during mid-watch, day and night. Now this was 'something like'; and so I began to take heart once more to believe that piloting was a romantic sort of occupation after all. The moment we were under way I began to prowl about the great steamer and fill myself with joy. She was as clean and as dainty as a drawing-room; when I looked down her long, gilded saloon, it was like gazing through a splendid tunnel; she had an oil-picture, by some gifted sign-painter, on every state-room door; she glittered with no end of prism-fringed chandeliers; the clerk's office was elegant, the bar was marvelous, and the barkeeper had been barbered and upholstered at incredible cost. The boiler-deck (i.e., the second story of the boat, so to speak), was as spacious as a church, it seemed to me; so with the forecastle; and there was no pitiful handful of deck-hands, firemen, and rousta-bouts down there, but a whole battalion of men. The fires were fiercely glaring from a long row of furnaces, and over them were eight huge boilers! This was unutterable pomp. The mighty engines—but enough of this. I had never felt so fine before. And when I found that the regiment of natty servants respectfully 'sir'd' me, my satisfaction was complete.

"The face of the water, in time, became a wonderful book—a book that was a dead language to the uneducated passenger, but which told its mind to me without reserve, delivering its most cherished secrets as clearly as if it uttered them with a voice. And it was not a book to be read once and thrown aside, for it had a new story to tell every day. Throughout the long twelve hundred miles there was never a page that was void of interest, never one that you could leave unread without loss, never one that you would want to skip, thinking you could find higher enjoyment in some other thing. There never was so wonderful a book written by man; never one whose interest was so absorbing, so unflagging, so sparklingly renewed with every re-perusal. The passenger who could not read it was charmed with a peculiar sort of faint dimple on its surface (on the rare occasions when he did not overlook it altogether); but to the pilot that was an italicized passage; indeed, it was more than that, it was a legend of the largest capitals, with a string of shouting exclamation points at the end of it, for it meant that a wreck or a rock was buried there that could tear the life out of the strongest vessel that ever floated. It is the faintest and simplest expression the water ever makes, and the most hideous to a pilot's eye. In truth, the passenger who could not read this book saw nothing but all the manner of pretty pictures in it, painted by the sun and shaded by the clouds, whereas to the trained eye these were not pictures at all, but the grimmest and most dead-earnest of reading matter.

"Now when I had mastered the language of this water, and had come to know every trifling feature that bordered the great river as familiarly as I knew the letters of the alphabet, I had made a valuable acquisition. But I had lost something, too. I had lost something which could never be restored to me while I lived. All the grace, the beauty, the poetry, had gone out of the majestic river! I still kept in mind a certain wonderful sunset which I witnessed when steamboating was new to me. A broad expanse of the river was turned to blood; in the middle distance the red hue brightened into gold, through which a solitary log came floating, black and conspicuous; in one place a long, slanting mark lay sparkling upon the water; in another the surface was broken by boiling, tumbling rings, that were as many-tinted as an opal; where the ruddy flush was faintest, was a smooth spot that was covered with graceful circles and radiating lines, ever so delicately traced; the shore on our left was densely wooded, and the somber shadow that fell from this forest was broken in one place by a long, ruffled trail that shone like silver; and high above the forest wall a clean-stemmed dead tree waved a single leafy bough that glowed like a flame in the unobstructed splendor that was flowing from the sun. There were graceful curves, reflected images, woody heights, soft distances; and over the whole scene, far and near, the dissolving lights drifted steadily enriching it every passing moment with new marvels of coloring.

"I stood like one bewitched. I drank it in, in a speechless rapture. The world was new to me, and I had never seen anything like this at home. But as I have said, a day came when I began to cease from noting the glories and the charms which the moon and the sun and the twilight wrought upon the river's face; another day came when I ceased altogether to note them. Then, if that sunset scene had been repeated, I should have looked upon it without rapture, and should have commented upon it, inwardly, after this fashion: 'The sun means that we are going to have wind to-morrow; that floating log means that the river is rising, small thanks to it; that slanting mark on the water refers to a bluff reef which is going to kill somebody's steamboat one of these nights, if it keeps on stretching out like that; those tumbling "boils" show a dissolving bar and a changing channel there; the lines and circles in the slick water over yonder are a warning that that troublesome place is shoaling up dangerously; that silver streak in the shadow of the forest is the "break" from a new snag, and he has located himself in the very best place he could have found to fish for steamboats; that tall dead tree, with a single living branch, is not going to last long, and then how is a body ever going to get through this blind place at night without the friendly old landmark?'

"No, the romance and the beauty were all gone from

The Pilot's Certificate given Samuel L. Clemens by the District of St. Louis inspectors on April 9, 1859.

the river. All the value any feature of it had for me now was the amount of usefulness it could furnish toward compassing the safe piloting of a steamboat. Since those days, I have pitied doctors from my heart. What does the lovely flush in a beauty's cheek mean to a doctor but a 'break' that ripples above some deadly disease? Are not all her visible charms sown thick with what are to him the signs and symbols of hidden decay? Does he ever see her beauty at all, or doesn't he simply view her professionally, and comment upon her unwholesome condition all to himself? And doesn't he sometimes wonder whether he has gained most or lost most by learning his trade?"

35

The *Cora Anderson,* left, and the *John J. Roe,* right, at the St. Louis docks. A freight boat, the *Roe,* Mark said, was "as slow as an island and as comfortable as a farm." Mark continued piloting lessons on the *Roe* while Bixby was busy elsewhere.

A DELIGHTFUL OLD TUG

"There is a great difference in boats, of course. For a long time I was on a boat that was so slow we used to forget what year it was we left port in. But of course this was at rare intervals. Ferry-boats used to lose valuable trips because their passengers grew old and died, waiting for us to get by. This was at still rarer intervals. I had the documents for these occurrences, but through carelessness they have been mislaid. This boat, the *John J. Roe,* was so slow that when she finally sunk in Madrid Bend it was five years before the owners heard of it. That was always a confusing fact to me, but it is according to the record, anyway. She was dismally slow; still, we often had pretty exciting times racing with islands, and rafts, and such things."

Again, in his autobiography, Mark wrote about life "on the *John J. Roe,* a steamboat whose officers I knew very well, as I had served a term as steersman in that boat's pilot-house. She was a freighter. She was not licensed to carry passengers but she always had a dozen on board and they were privileged to be there because they were not registered; they paid no fare; they were guests of the Captain and nobody was responsible for them if anything of a fatal nature happened to them.

"It was a delightful old tug and she had a very spacious boiler-deck—just the place for moonlight dancing and daylight frolics, and such things were always happening. She was a charmingly leisurely boat and the slowest one on the planet. Up-stream she couldn't even beat an island; down-stream she was never able to overtake the current. But she was a love of a steamboat."

The *Philadelphia*, a steamboat just like the *Pennsylvania*, which exploded in June, 1858, killing Mark's brother Henry.

While other young pilots were idle, lucky Mark landed a job on the boat pictured here. *"The City of Memphis,"* he wrote Orion, "is the largest boat in the trade, and the hardest to pilot, and consequently I can get a reputation on her. . . . The young pilots who used to tell me, patronizingly, that I could never learn the river, cannot keep from showing their chagrin at seeing me so far ahead of them. Permit me to 'blow my horn,' for I derive a living pleasure from these things. . . . You will despise this egotism, but I tell you there is 'stern joy' in it."

CAPTAIN SELLERS: PATRIARCH OF PILOTS

"He was a fine man, a high-minded man, and greatly respected both ashore and on the river. He was very tall, well built, and handsome; and in his old age—as I remember him—his hair was as black as an Indian's, and his eye and hand were as strong and steady and his nerve and judgment as firm and clear as anybody's, young or old, among the fraternity of pilots. He was the patriarch of the craft; he had been a keelboat pilot before the day of steamboats; and a steamboat pilot before any other steamboat pilot, still surviving at the time I speak of, had ever turned a wheel. Consequently, his brethren held him in the sort of awe in which illustrious survivors of a bygone age are always held

Captain Isaiah Sellers, a retired pilot, wrote a pontifical column of river notes for the New Orleans *Picayune*. As a young pilot, Mark burlesqued the column in the *Daily Crescent* on May 17, 1859, changing Captain Sellers to "Sergeant Fathom." In *Life on the Mississippi*, 24 years later, Mark launched the myth that he had borrowed his "Mark Twain" pseudonym from Sellers, but Sellers never used that name. In any case, the *Crescent* piece, reproduced in part here, was Mark's first attempt at writing in three years.

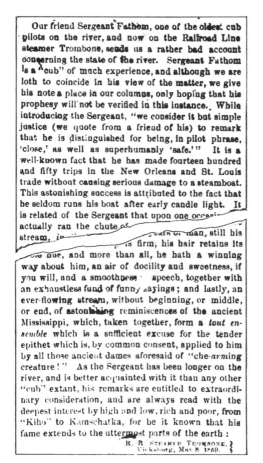

Our friend Sergeant Fathom, one of the oldest cub pilots on the river, and now on the Railroad Line steamer Trombone, sends us a rather bad account concerning the state of the river. Sergeant Fathom is a "cub" of much experience, and although we are loth to coincide in his view of the matter, we give his note a place in our columns, only hoping that his prophesy will not be verified in this instance. While introducing the Sergeant, "we consider it but simple justice (we quote from a friend of his) to remark that he is distinguished for being, in pilot phrase, 'close,' as well as superhumanly 'safe.'" It is a well-known fact that he has made fourteen hundred and fifty trips in the New Orleans and St. Louis trade without causing serious damage to a steamboat. This astonishing success is attributed to the fact that he seldom runs his boat after early candle light. It is related of the Sergeant that upon one occa—
actually ran the chute of...
stream, i—
...is firm; his hair retains its
...hue, and more than all, he hath a winning way about him, an air of docility and sweetness, if you will, and a smoothness speech, together with an exhaustless fund of funny sayings; and lastly, an ever-flowing stream, without beginning, or middle, or end, of astonishing reminiscences of the ancient Mississippi, which, taken together, form a *tout ensemble* which is a sufficient excuse for the tender epithet which is, by common consent, applied to him by all those ancient dames aforesaid of "che-arming creature!" As the Sergeant has been longer on the river, and is better acquainted with it than any other "cub" extant, his remarks are entitled to extraordinary consideration, and are always read with the deepest interest by high and low, rich and poor, from "Kiho" to Kamschatka, for be it known that his fame extends to the uttermost parts of the earth:
R. R. STEAMER TROMBONE,
Vicksburg, May 8, 1859.

by their associates. He knew how he was regarded, and perhaps this fact added some trifle of stiffening to his natural dignity, which had been sufficiently stiff in its original state. . . .

"The old gentleman was not of literary turn or capacity, but he used to jot down brief paragraphs of plain, practical information about the river, and sign them 'MARK TWAIN,' and give them to the New Orleans Picayune. They related to the stage and condition of the river, and were accurate and valuable; and thus far they contained no poison. But in speaking of the stage of the river to-day at a given point, the captain was pretty apt to drop in a little remark about this being the first time he had seen the water so high or so low at that particular point in forty-nine years; and now and then he would mention Island so and so, and follow it, in parentheses, with some such observation as 'disappeared in 1807, if I remember rightly.' In these antique interjections lay poison and bitterness for the other old pilots, and they used to chaff the 'Mark Twain' paragraphs with unsparing mockery.

"It so chanced that one of these paragraphs became the text for my first newspaper article. I burlesqued it broadly, very broadly, stringing my fantastics out to the extent of eight hundred or a thousand words. I was a 'cub' at the time. I showed my performance to some pilots, and they eagerly rushed it into print in the New Orleans True Delta. It was a great pity; for it did nobody any worthy service, and it sent a pang deep into a good man's heart. There was no malice in my rubbish; but it laughed at the captain. It laughed at a man to whom such a thing was new and strange and dreadful. I did not know then, though I do now, that there is no suffering comparable with that which a private person feels when he is for the first time pilloried in print.

"Captain Sellers did me the honor to profoundly detest me from that day forth. When I say he did me the honor, I am not using empty words. It was a very real honor to be in the thoughts of so great a man as Captain Sellers, and I had wit enough to appreciate it and be proud of it. It was distinction to be loved by such a man; but it was a much greater distinction to be hated by him, because he loved scores of people; but he didn't sit up nights to hate anybody but me.

"He never printed another paragraph while he lived, and he never again signed 'Mark Twain' to anything. At the time that the telegraph brought the news of his death, I was on the Pacific coast. I was a fresh, new journalist, and needed a nom de guerre; so I confiscated the ancient mariner's discarded one, and have done my best to make it remain what it was in his hands—a sign and symbol and warrant that whatever is found in its company may be gambled on as being the petrified truth. How I've succeeded, it would not be modest in me to say."

I LOVED THE PROFESSION

How Mark Twain felt about the craft of piloting he told in *Life on the Mississippi:*

"If I have seemed to love my subject, it is no surprising thing, for I loved the profession far better than any I have followed since, and I took a measureless pride in it. The reason is plain: a pilot, in those days, was the only unfettered and entirely independent human being that lived in the earth. Kings are but the hampered servants of parliament and the people; parliaments sit in chains forged by their constituency; the editor of a newspaper cannot be independent, but must work with one hand tied behind him by party and patrons, and be content to utter only half or two-thirds of his mind; no clergyman is a free man and may speak the whole truth, regardless of his parish's opinions; writers of all kinds are manacled servants of the public. We write frankly and fearlessly, but then we 'modify' before we print. In truth, every man and woman and child has a master, and worries and frets in servitude; but, in the day I write of, the Mississippi pilot had none. The captain could stand upon the hurricane-deck, in the pomp of a very brief authority, and give him five or six orders while the vessel backed in the stream, and then that skipper's reign was over. The moment that the boat was under way in the river, she was under

Henry Clemens.

Captain John Klinefelter commanded the packet *Pennsylvania* in May, 1858, when Mark was a cub pilot and his brother Henry mud clerk on her. When Tom Brown, the pilot, struck Henry in a quarrel, Mark beat up Brown. The captain offered Brown's job to Mark, but Mark didn't feel up to the responsibility and left the boat at New Orleans, with Henry staying on. The *Pennsylvania* blew up four days later, killing 150, including Henry Clemens. Mark always blamed himself for his brother's death.

the sole and unquestioned control of the pilot. He could do with her exactly as he pleased, run her when and whither he chose, and tie her up to the bank whenever his judgment said that that course was best. His movements were entirely free; he consulted no one, he received commands from nobody, he promptly resented even the merest suggestions. Indeed, the law of the United States forbade him to listen to commands or suggestions, rightly considering that the pilot necessarily knew better how to handle the boat than anybody could tell him. So here was the novelty of a king without a keeper, an absolute monarch who was absolute in sober truth and not by a fiction of words. I have seen a boy of eighteen taking a great steamer serenely into what seemed almost certain destruction and the aged captain standing mutely by, filled with apprehension but powerless to interfere. His interference, in that particular instance, might have been an excellent thing, but to permit it would have been to establish a most pernicious precedent. It will easily be guessed, considering the pilot's boundless authority, that he was a great personage in the old steamboating days. He was treated with marked courtesy by the captain and with marked deference by all the officers and servants; and this deferential spirit was quickly communicated to the passengers, too. I think pilots were about the only people I ever knew who failed to show, in some degree, embarrassment in the presence of traveling foreign princes. But then, people in one's own grade of life are not usually embarrassing objects.

"By long habit, pilots came to put all their wishes in the form of commands. It 'gravels' me, to this day, to put my will in the weak shape of a request, instead of launching it in the crisp language of an order."

Passengers on the guard rail.

Deck passengers on a
Mississippi steamboat.

In a river-boat cabin.

I HAVE KNOWN HIM BEFORE

"I will remark, in passing, that Mississippi steamboatmen were important in landsmen's eyes (and in their own, too, in a degree) according to the dignity of the boat they were on. For instance, it was a proud thing to be of the crew of such stately craft as the *Aleck Scott* or the *Grand Turk*. Negro firemen, deck-hands, and barbers belonging to those boats were distinguished personages in their grade of life, and they were well aware of that fact, too."

"In that brief, sharp schooling I got personally and familiarly acquainted with all the different types of human nature that are to be found in fiction, biography, or history. When I find a well-drawn character in fiction or biography, I generally take a warm personal interest in him, for the reason that I have known him before—met him on the river."

In the election of 1860, Mark Twain wore a Bell-Everett button, siding with the moderates who wanted peace and the Union preserved. In the first months of 1861 he wrote ten "Snodgrass" letters for the New Orleans *Daily Crescent*, satirizing army life. A few days after the news from Sumter blazed across the country, Mark was on his way up the river. "I supposed—and hoped—" he wrote later, "that I was going to follow the river the rest of my days, and die at the wheel when my mission was ended. But by and by the war came, commerce was suspended, my occupation was gone."

CONFEDERATE SOLDIER

What Mark did in the Civil War he described in "The Private History of a Campaign that Failed." The sketch captures the experience of the vast numbers who found it hard to get their bearings and "leaned first this way, then that, then the other way." This fragment from it omits the narrative, unfortunately, but serves to reveal his frame of mind:

"You have heard from a great many people who did something in the war, is it not fair and right that you listen a little moment to one who started out to do something in it, but didn't? Thousands entered the war, got just a taste of it, and then stepped out again permanently. These, by their very numbers, are respectable and are therefore entitled to a sort of a voice—not a loud one but a modest one, not a boastful one but an apologetic one. They ought not to be allowed much space among better people—people who did something. I grant that, but they ought at least to be allowed to state why they didn't do anything and also to explain the process by which they didn't do anything. Surely this kind of light must have a sort of value.

"Out West there was a good deal of confusion in men's minds during the first months of the great trouble—a good deal of unsettledness, of leaning first this way, then that, then the other way. It was hard for us to get our bearings. I call to mind an instance of this. I was piloting on the Mississippi when the news came that South Carolina had gone out of the Union on the 20th of December, 1860. My pilot mate was a New Yorker. He was strong for the Union; so was I. But he would not listen to me with any patience; my loyalty was smirched, to his eye, because my father had owned slaves. I said in palliation of this dark fact that I had heard my father say, some years before he died, that slavery was a great wrong and that he would free the solitary Negro he then owned if he could think it right to give away the property of the family when he was so straitened in means. My mate retorted that a mere impulse was nothing—anybody could pretend to a good impulse, and went on decrying my Unionism and libeling my ancestry. A month later the secession atmosphere had considerably thickened on the Lower Mississippi and I became a rebel; so did he. We were together in New Orleans the 26th of January, when Louisiana went out of the Union. He did his full share of the rebel shouting but was bitterly opposed to letting me do mine. He said that I came of bad stock—of a father who had been willing to set slaves free. In the following summer he was piloting a Federal gunboat and shouting for the Union again and I was in the Confederate army. I held his note for some borrowed money. He was one of the most upright men I ever knew but he repudiated that note without hesitation because I was a rebel and the son of a man who owned slaves.

"In that summer of 1861 the first wash of the wave of war broke upon the shores of Missouri. Our state was invaded by the Union forces. They took possession of St. Louis, Jefferson Barracks, and some other points. The Governor, Claib Jackson, issued his proclamation calling out fifty thousand militia to repel the invader.

"I was visiting in the small town where my boyhood had been spent, Hannibal, Marion County. Several of us got together in a secret place by night and formed ourselves into a military company. One Tom Lyman, a young fellow of a good deal of spirit but of no military experience, was made captain; I was made second lieutenant. We had no first lieutenant; I do not know why; it was long ago. There were fifteen of us. By the advice of an innocent connected with the organization we called ourselves the Marion Rangers. I do not remember that any one found fault with the name. I did not; I thought it sounded quite well. The young fellow who proposed this title was perhaps a fair sample of the kind of stuff we were made of. He was young, ignorant, good-natured, well-meaning, trivial, full of romance, and given to reading chivalric novels and singing forlorn love-ditties. . . .

"The thoughtful will not throw this war paper of mine lightly aside as being valueless. It has this value: it is a not unfair picture of what went on in many and many a militia camp in the first months of the rebellion, when the green recruits were without discipline, without the steadying and heartening influence of trained leaders, when all their circumstances were new and strange and charged with exaggerated terrors, and before the invaluable experience of actual collision in the field had turned them from rabbits into soldiers. If this side of the picture of that early day has not before been put into history, then history has been to that degree incomplete, for it had and has its rightful place there. There was more Bull Run material scattered through the early camps of this country than exhibited itself at Bull Run. And yet it learned its trade presently and helped to fight the great battles later. I could have become a soldier myself if I had waited. I had got part of it learned, I knew more about retreating than the man that invented retreating."

The allegiance of Mark's Missouri was bitterly fought for by North and South. A slave state, it nevertheless voted to stay in the Union. That didn't end personal and local conflicts (inside the Clemens family, too) over the bloody issue in this border state. Pro-Southern Hannibal, when Mark reached it, was now in the hands of Union Home Guards. Probably scenes like this—neighbors whipping neighbors over political differences—took place in Hannibal too.

General Frémont, commanding Union forces in Missouri, ordered the slaves emancipated on August 31, 1861, but Lincoln reversed him in an effort to hold the border state slave-owners. By this time Mark Twain had "resigned" from the Confederate Army after two weeks' service, explaining that he was "incapacitated by fatigue through persistent retreating."

Mark Twain, at about the time he quit the river.

Orion Clemens, about 1861, the year he was appointed Secretary of the Nevada Territory.

I Lit Out for the Territory

OVERLAND STAGE TO NEVADA

Lincoln's inauguration put Edward Bates in the Cabinet and brought his old friend Orion Clemens the post of Secretary of the new Territory of Nevada. Only a few days out of his Confederate uniform, Mark signed on as Secretary's secretary and on July 25, 1861, the brothers boarded the stagecoach for the twenty-day journey west.

"The first thing we did on that glad evening that landed us at St. Joseph," Mark wrote in *Roughing It*, "was to hunt up the stage-office, and pay a hundred and fifty dollars apiece for tickets per overland coach to Carson City, Nevada.

"Each of us put on a rough, heavy suit of clothing, woolen army shirt and 'stogy' boots included; and into the valise we crowded a few white shirts, some underclothing and such things. My brother, the Secretary, took along about four pounds of United States statutes

and six pounds of Unabridged Dictionary; for we did not know—poor innocents—that such things could be bought in San Francisco on one day and received in

Orion and Sam Clemens headed for Nevada by overland stagecoach. With Orion broke as usual, Sam paid for both $150 fares out of his pilot savings. Here is the receipt, made out to Orion on July 25, 1861.

Received St Joseph July 25. 1861 of Mr Orion Clemens Three Hundred Dollars on account of his and Saml L. Clemens fare to Carson City or any other point on our Route East of Placerville in Coach leaving St Joseph July 25th 1861.
$300.00/100
Paul Coburn Agt COC
Per Nat Stein. NPP & Co

Rec'd St Jo. July 25. 1861, of Mr Orion Clemens His acceptance of this date at 30 Days for One Hundred Dollars, favor of B.M. Hughes, Prest — in full for Balance of above fares.
$100.~
Paul Coburn Agt COC & PP Co
Per Nat Stein)

Transcontinental stages began operating from the Mississippi to the Pacific in 1858. At first they ran semi-weekly on a twenty-five day schedule. One-way fares cost from $100 to $200.

Carson City the next. I was armed to the teeth with a pitiful little Smith & Wesson's seven-shooter, which carried a ball like a homoeopathic pill, and it took the whole seven to make a dose for an adult. But I thought it was grand. It appeared to me to be a dangerous weapon. It only had one fault—you could not hit anything with it. One of our 'conductors' practiced awhile on a cow with it, and as long as she stood still and behaved herself she was safe; but as soon as she went to moving about, and he got to shooting at other things, she came to grief. The Secretary had a small-sized Colt's revolver strapped around him for protection against the Indians, and to guard against accidents he carried it uncapped.

"We took two or three blankets for protection against frosty weather in the mountains. In the matter of luxuries we were modest—we took none along but some pipes and five pounds of smoking tobacco. We had two large canteens to carry water in, between stations on the Plains, and we also took with us a little shot-bag of silver coin for daily expenses in the way of breakfast and dinners.

"By eight o'clock everything was ready, and we were on the other side of the river. We jumped into the stage, the driver cracked his whip, and we bowled away and left 'the states' behind us. It was a superb summer morning, and all the landscape was brilliant with sunshine. There was a freshness and breeziness, too, and an exhilarating sense of emancipation from all sorts of cares and responsibilities, that almost made us feel that the years we had spent in the close, hot city, toiling and slaving, had been wasted and thrown away.

"Our coach was a great swinging and swaying stage, of the most sumptuous description—an imposing cradle on wheels. It was drawn by six handsome horses, and by the side of the driver sat the 'conductor,' the legitimate captain of the craft; for it was his business to take charge and care of the mails, baggage, express matter, and passengers. We three were the only passengers, this trip. We sat on the back seat, inside. About all the rest of the coach was full of mail bags—for we had three days' delayed mails with us. Almost touching our knees, a perpendicular wall of mail matter rose up to the roof. There was a great pile of it strapped on top of the stage, and both the fore and hind boots were full. We had twenty-seven hundred pounds of it aboard, the driver said—'a little for Brigham, and Carson, and 'Frisco, but the heft of it for the Injuns, which is powerful troublesome 'thout they get plenty of truck to read.' But as he just then got up a fearful convulsion of his countenance which was suggestive of a wink being swallowed by an earthquake, we guessed that his remark was intended to be facetious, and to mean that we would unload the most of our mail matter somewhere on the Plains and leave it to the Indians, or whosoever wanted it.

45

"We changed horses every ten miles, all day long, and fairly flew over the hard, level road. . . .

"It was now just dawn; and as we stretched our cramped legs full length on the mail sacks, and gazed out through the windows across the wide wastes of greensward clad in cool, powdery mist, to where there was an expectant look in the eastern horizon, our perfect enjoyment took the form of a tranquil and contented ecstasy. The stage whirled along at a spanking gait, the breeze flapping curtains and suspended coats in a most exhilarating way; the cradle swayed and swung luxuriously, the pattering of the horses' hoofs, the cracking of the driver's whip, and his 'Hy-yi! g'lang!' were music; the spinning ground and the waltzing trees appeared to give us a mute hurrah as we went by, and then slack up and look after us with interest, or envy, or something; and as we lay and smoked the pipe of peace and compared all this luxury with the years of tiresome city life that had gone before it, we felt that there was only one complete and satisfying happiness in the world, and we had found it."

"My delight, the driver." This is Hank Monk, known as the prince of stage drivers. He worked for Wells Fargo. Drivers drew salaries as high as $250 a month —the salary Mark Twain got as river pilot.

STAGECOACH

"Our new conductor (just shipped) had been without sleep for twenty hours. Such a thing was very frequent. From St. Joseph, Missouri, to Sacramento, California, by stage-coach, was nearly nineteen hundred miles, and the trip was often made in fifteen days (the cars do it in four and a half, now), but the time specified in the mail contracts, and required by the schedule, was eighteen or nineteen days, if I remember rightly. This was to make fair allowance for winter storms and snows, and other unavoidable causes of detention. The stage company had everything under strict discipline and good system. Over each two hundred and fifty miles of road they placed an agent or superintendent, and invested him with great authority. His beat or jurisdiction of two hundred and fifty miles was called a 'division.' He purchased horses, mules, harness, and food for men and beasts, and distributed these things among his stage stations, from time to time, according to his judgment of what each station needed. He erected station buildings and dug wells. He attended to the paying of the station-keepers, hostlers, drivers, and blacksmiths, and discharged them whenever he chose. He was a very, very great man in his 'division'—a kind of Grand Mogul, a Sultan of the Indies, in whose presence common men were modest of speech and manner, and in the glare of whose greatness even the dazzling stage-driver dwindled to a penny dip. There were about eight of these kings, all told, on the Overland route.

"Next in rank and importance to the division-agent came the 'conductor.' His beat was the same length as the agent's—two hundred and fifty miles. He sat with the driver, and (when necessary) rode that fearful distance, night and day, without other rest or sleep than what he could get perched thus on top of the flying vehicle. Think of it! He had absolute charge of the mails, express matter, passengers, and stage-coach, until he delivered them to the next conductor, and got his receipt for them. Consequently he had to be a man of intelligence, decision, and considerable executive ability. He was usually a quiet, pleasant man, who attended closely to his duties, and was a good deal of a gentleman. It was not absolutely necessary that the division-agent should be a gentleman, and occasionally he wasn't. But he was always a general in administrative ability, and a bull-dog in courage and determination—otherwise the chieftainship over the lawless underlings of the Overland service would never in any instance have been to him anything but an equivalent for a month of insolence and distress and a bullet and a coffin at the end of it. There were about sixteen or eighteen conductors on the Overland, for there was a daily stage each way, and a conductor on every stage.

"Next in real and official rank and importance, after the conductor, came my delight, the driver—next in real but not in apparent importance—for we have seen that in the eyes of the common herd the driver was to the conductor as an admiral is to the captain of the flag-ship. The driver's beat was pretty long, and his sleeping-time at the stations pretty short, sometimes; and so, but for the grandeur of his position his would have been a sorry life, as well as a hard and a wearing one. We took a new driver every day or every night (for they drove backward and forward over the same piece of road all the time), and therefore we never got as well acquainted with them as we did with the conductors; and besides, they would have been above being familiar with such rubbish as passengers, anyhow, as a general thing. Still, we were always eager to get a sight of each and every new driver as soon as the watch changed, for each and every day we were either anxious to get rid of an unpleasant one, or loath to part with a driver we had learned to like and had come to be sociable and friendly with. And so the first question we asked the conductor whenever we got to where we were to exchange drivers, was always, 'Which is him?' The grammar was faulty, maybe, but we could not know, then, that it would go into a book some day. As long as everything went smoothly, the Overland driver was well enough situated, but if a fellow driver got sick suddenly it made trouble, for the coach must go on, and so the potentate who was about to climb down and take a luxurious rest after his long night's siege in the midst of wind and rain and darkness, had to stay where he was and do the sick man's work. Once in the Rocky Mountains, when I found a driver sound asleep on the box, and the mules going at the usual break-neck pace, the conductor said never mind him, there was no danger, and he was doing double duty—had driven seventy-five miles on one coach, and was now going back over it on this without rest or sleep. A hundred and fifty miles of holding back of six vindictive mules and keeping them from climbing the trees! It sounds incredible, but I remember the statement well enough.

"The station-keepers, hostlers, etc., were low, rough characters, as already described; and from western Nebraska to Nevada a considerable sprinkling of them might be fairly set down as outlaws—fugitives from justice, criminals whose best security was a section of country which was without law and without even the pretense of it. When the 'division-agent' issued an order to one of these parties he did it with the full understanding that he might have to enforce it with a navy six-shooter, and so he always went 'fixed' to make things go along smoothly. Now and then a division-agent was really obliged to shoot a hostler through the head to teach him some simple matter that he could have taught him with a club if his circumstances and surroundings had been different. But they were snappy, able men, those division-agents, and when they tried to teach a subordinate anything, that subordinate generally 'got it through his head.'

"A great portion of this vast machinery—these hundreds of men and coaches, and thousands of mules and horses—was in the hands of Mr. Ben Holladay. All the western half of the business was in his hands."

The Concord stagecoaches, famous internationally, were built at Concord, New Hampshire. They served the Overland Route for 20 years, until the railroads took over. Ben Holladay, whose system Mark describes, was bought out by Wells Fargo for $2,500,000.

In April, 1860, the first horse and rider of the Pony Express sped out of St. Joseph, Missouri, on the hazardous route across the plains to California. The riders ran up the superhuman record of 650,000 miles with only one mail lost. The system came to an abrupt end in October, 1861, when the telegraph killed it.

THE PONY EXPRESS

The brief career of the Pony Express was immortalized in Twain's *Roughing It:*

"In a little while all interest was taken up in stretching our necks and watching for the 'pony-rider'—the fleet messenger who sped across the continent from St. Joe to Sacramento, carrying letters nineteen hundred miles in eight days! Think of that for perishable horse and human flesh and blood to do! The pony-rider was usually a little bit of a man, brimful of spirit and endurance. No matter what time of the day or night his watch came on, and no matter whether it was winter or summer, raining, snowing, hailing, or sleeting, or whether his 'beat' was a level straight road or a crazy trail over mountain crags and precipices, or whether it led through peaceful regions or regions that swarmed with hostile Indians, he must be always ready to leap into the saddle and be off like the wind! There was no idling-time for a pony-rider on duty. He rode fifty miles without stopping, by daylight, moonlight, starlight, or through the blackness of darkness—just as it happened. He rode a splendid horse that was born for a racer and fed and lodged like a gentleman; kept him at his utmost speed for ten miles, and then, as he came crashing up to the station where stood two men holding fast a fresh, impatient steed, the transfer of rider and mail-bag was made in the twinkling of an eye, and away flew the eager pair and were out of sight before the spectator could get hardly the ghost of a look. Both rider and horse went 'flying light.' The rider's dress was thin, and fitted close; he wore a 'roundabout,' and a skull-cap, and tucked his pantaloons into his boot-tops like a race-rider. He carried no arms—he carried nothing that was not absolutely necessary, for even the postage on his literary freight was worth five dollars a letter. He got but little frivolous correspondence to carry—his bag had business letters in it, mostly. His horse was stripped of all unnecessary weight, too. He wore a little wafer of a racing-saddle, and no visible blanket. He wore light shoes, or none at all. The little flat mail-pockets strapped under the rider's thighs would each hold about the bulk of a child's primer. They held many and many an important business chapter and newspaper letter, but these were written on paper as airy and thin as gold-leaf, nearly, and thus bulk and weight were economized. The stage-coach traveled about a hundred to a hundred and twenty-five miles a day (twenty-four hours), the pony-rider about two hundred and fifty. There were about eighty pony-riders in the saddle all the time, night and day, stretching in a long, scattering procession from Missouri to California, forty flying eastward, and forty toward the west, and among them making four hundred gallant horses earn a stirring livelihood and see a deal of scenery every single day in the year."

Carson City was a straggle of wooden houses on the desert in 1861.

CARSON CITY

On August 14, 1861, the dusty Clemens brothers climbed down from the stage in Carson City. Population: 2,000.

"In the middle of the town," Mark wrote, "opposite the stores, was a 'Plaza,' which is native to all towns beyond the Rocky Mountains, a large, unfenced, level vacancy with a Liberty Pole in it, and very useful as a place for public auctions, horse trades, and mass-meetings, and likewise for teamsters to camp in. Two

Gold and silver hunters crowded Carson's streets.

other sides of the Plaza were faced by stores, offices, and stables. The rest of Carson City was pretty scattering."

The Gold Hill mining property, he wrote his mother, "sells at $5,000 per foot, cash down; 'Wild Cat' isn't worth ten cents. The country is fabulously rich in gold, silver, copper, lead, coal, iron, quicksilver, marble, granite, chalk, plaster of Paris (gypsum), thieves, murderers, desperadoes, ladies, children, lawyers, Christians, Indians, Chinamen, Spaniards, gamblers, sharpers, coyotes (pronounced Ki-yo-ties), poets, preachers, and jackass rabbits. I overheard a gentleman say, the other day, that it was 'the d—dest country under the sun,' and that comprehensive conception I fully subscribe to. It never rains here, and the dew never falls. No flowers grow here, and no green thing gladdens the eye. The birds that fly over the land carry their provisions with them. Only the crow and the raven tarry with us. Our city lies in the midst of a desert of the purest, most unadulterated and uncompromising *sand,* in which infernal soil nothing but that fag-end of vegetable creation, 'sage-brush,' ventures to grow."

Discouraging his sister Pamela's interest in coming West, he wrote: "Some people are malicious enough to think that if the devil were set at liberty and told to confine himself to Nevada Territory, he would come here and look sadly around awhile, and then get homesick and go back to hell again. Why, I have had my whiskers and mustaches so full of alkali dust that you'd have thought I worked in a starch factory and boarded in a flour barrel."

Mark Twain spent the first few months exploring his corner of the frontier. But as winter came on he too caught the mining fever. Speculators went mad over the promise of the new Humboldt mines and in December, 1861, Mark joined a party of four out to make their million.

HUMBOLDT! HUMBOLDT!

" 'Humboldt! Humboldt!' was the new cry, and straightway Humboldt, the newest of the new, the richest of the rich, the most marvelous of the marvelous discoveries in silver-land, was occupying two columns of the public prints to 'Esmeralda's' one. I was just on the point of starting to Esmeralda, but turned with the tide and got ready for Humboldt. . . .

"There was a constantly growing excitement about our Humboldt mines. We fell victims to the epidemic

and strained every nerve to acquire more 'feet.' We prospected and took up new claims, put 'notices' on them and gave them grandiloquent names. We traded some of our 'feet' for 'feet' in other people's claims. In a little while we owned largely in the 'Gray Eagle,' the 'Columbiana,' the 'Branch Mint,' the 'Maria Jane,' the 'Universe,' the 'Root-Hog-or-Die,' the 'Samson and Delilah,' the 'Treasure Trove,' the 'Golconda,' the 'Sultana,' the 'Boomerang,' the 'Great Republic,' the 'Grand Mogul,' and fifty other 'mines' that had never been molested by a shovel or scratched with a pick. We had not less than thirty thousand 'feet' apiece in the 'richest mines on earth' as the frenzied cant phrased it—and were in debt to the butcher. We were stark mad with excitement—drunk with happiness—smothered under mountains of prospective wealth—arrogantly compassionate toward the plodding millions who knew not our marvelous canyon—but our credit was not good at the grocer's.

"It was the strangest phase of life one can imagine. It was a beggars' revel. There was nothing doing in the district—no mining—no milling—no productive effort —no income—and not enough money in the entire

The prospectors' wagons carried provisions, mining tools, cards and beer. It took Twain's party 11 days to cover the 200 miles to Humboldt County.

The assay office in Carson City.

willing to make the sacrifice. Then he would fish a piece of rock out of his pocket, and after looking mysteriously around as if he feared he might be waylaid and robbed if caught with such wealth in his possession, he would dab the rock against his tongue, clap an eyeglass to it, and exclaim:

" 'Look at that! Right there in that red dirt! See it? See the specks of gold? And the streak of silver? That's from the "Uncle Abe." There's a hundred thousand tons like that in sight! Right in sight, mind you! And when we get down on it and the ledge comes in solid, it will be the richest thing in the world! Look at the assay! I don't want you to believe me—look at the assay!'

"Then he would get out a greasy sheet of paper which showed that the portion of rock assayed had given evidence of containing silver and gold in the proportion of so many hundreds or thousands of dollars to the ton. I little knew, then, that the custom was to hunt out the richest piece of rock and get it assayed! Very often, that piece, the size of a filbert, was the only fragment in a ton that had a particle of metal in it—and yet the assay made it pretend to represent the average value of the ton of rubbish it came from!

"On such a system of assaying as that, the Humboldt world had gone crazy. On the authority of such assays its newspaper correspondents were frothing about rock worth four and seven thousand dollars a ton!"

camp to buy a corner lot in an eastern village, hardly; and yet a stranger would have supposed he was walking among bloated millionaires. Prospecting parties swarmed out of town with the first flush of dawn, and swarmed in again at nightfall laden with spoil—rocks. Nothing but rocks. Every man's pockets were full of them; the floor of his cabin was littered with them; they were disposed in labeled rows on his shelves.

"I met men at every turn who owned from one thousand to thirty thousand 'feet' in undeveloped silver mines, every single foot of which they believed would shortly be worth from fifty to a thousand dollars—and as often as any other way they were men who had not twenty-five dollars in the world. Every man you met had his new mine to boast of, and his 'specimens' ready; and if the opportunity offered, he would infallibly back you into a corner and offer as a favor to you, not to him, to part with just a few feet in the 'Golden Age,' or the 'Sarah Jane,' or some other unknown stack of croppings, for money enough to get a 'square meal' with, as the phrase went. And you were never to reveal that he had made you the offer at such a ruinous price, for it was only out of friendship for you that he was

The claim-seller tries to make a deal with the outbound prospector.

51

James W. Nye, ex-police commissioner of New York, was appointed Governor of Nevada Territory. Orion Clemens was his Secretary of State. When Nevada entered the Union, Nye became U.S. Senator. He was the model for the Bill Nye of Bret Harte's "The Heathen Chinee."

Nevada's territorial seal. Orion designed it.

BUTTERFIELD H. Indian Agent, res on Rees River
Butts W. B. boarding, Third bet Plaza and Fall
Buzzard Mr. job-wagon, res Robinson near Carson

C

CALIFORNIA HOUSE (Geo. Darling, proprietor), SE cor Carson and Seventh
Campbell Samuel, stone cutter, res Nevada between Sixth and Seventh
Campton L. Mrs. seamstress, SW cor Curry and Proctor
Carle John, laborer, res Nevada near Ann
CARSON CITY BREWERY, cor Minnesota and King
CARSON CITY BREWERY (Gerheiser & Co.) cor Second and Nevada
Carson City Hay Yard, E side Carson near Spear
CARSON CITY MARKET (Boyd & Gardner, proprietors) S side Plaza bet Carson and Plaza
CARSON HOUSE (Mrs. B. Morton, proptr) SW cor Plaza and Fourth
CARSON AND STEAMBOAT STAGE OFFICE (Lytle & Co.) office Stage Saloon
Carlton Davis, teaming, at brick yard
Carlton Gus. saloon next Magnolia Saloon
Carlton Oscar, laborer at brick yard
Carter Charles, waiter at New York Restaurant
CENTRAL HOUSE, S side Fourth near Carson
Chadwick Chas. G. teamster, res Carson City
Chamberlain Mason, laborer at brick yard
Chambers Jacob C. teamster, res Bryant's Ranch
Chandler G. A. teamster, Plaza near Third
Chandler G. W. Pioneer Cigar Store, Ormsby House
Chase Jas. M. carpenter, bds Penrod House
CHEDIC GEORGE, saw mill, Clear Creek, formerly Coyote Mill, res corner Carson and Ann
CHEEK & HOLLAND, furniture, bedding, etc. NW corner Carson and Fourth
Church John, business manager "Silver Age" office
Clagett Wm. H. attorney-at-law, Carson near Proctor
Clapp H. K. Miss, teacher, NW cor Second and Nevada
Clark Daniel, speculator, bds with B. Henney
CLEMENS ORION, Secretary Nevada Territory, office N side Plaza
Clemens Samuel, Assistant Secretary Nevada Territory
Cline Thos. res corner Fall and Fifth
Clow B. bds Penrod House
Coggeshall W. A. clerk with Winne & Amiraux
Collins G. W. ranchman, SW cor Carson and Sixth

This page from the *First Directory of Nevada Territory*, 1862, shows the Clemens brothers and their official titles. Orion rates caps in this period when he took over the Governor's chair in Nye's absence.

The Aurora cabin Mark shared with Higbie and Howland.

Twain's *Roughing It* is dedicated "To Calvin Higbie of California, an honest man, a genial comrade, and a steadfast friend . . . in memory of the curious time when we two were millionaires for ten days." Higbie (left above), an experienced miner, lived with Mark and Robert Howland (right above) in the Aurora mining camp on the Sierra slopes from February to August, 1862. They prospected the Esmeralda Hills in the bleak winter weather, moving restlessly from one promising ledge to another. "Two years' time will make us capitalists," he promised Orion, who was staking their partnership. But food and tools went up as fast as Orion's savings went down, and there never was a lucky strike. In the roulette wheel and the dance hall the miners tried to forget their failure. Cal Higbie has recorded what Mark was like at one of these frontier balls: "In changing partners, whenever he saw a hand raised he would grasp it with great pleasure and sail off into another set, oblivious to his surroundings. Sometimes he would act as though there was no use in trying to go right or to dance like other people, and with his eyes closed he would do a hoe-down or a double-shuffle all alone, talking to himself and saying that he never dreamed there was so much pleasure to be obtained at a ball. It was all as natural as a child's play. By the second set, all the ladies were falling over themselves to get him for a partner, and most of the crowd, too full of mirth to dance, were standing or sitting around, dying with laughter."

CAPITALISTS IN TWO YEARS

In the "Blind Lead" chapter in *Roughing It,* Mark imagined
he and Cal Higbie had made a million—and lost it.

From Aurora, Mark sent humorous letters which the *Territorial Enterprise* in Virginia City published over the pen name "Josh." As July and Mark's resources came to an end, the *Enterprise* offered the miner $25 a week to turn reporter. On a hot August day—it was 1862—the ex-printer, ex-pilot, ex-soldier and ex-miner dropped into the *Enterprise* office and announced: "My name is Clemens, and I've come to write for the paper." He had hiked the 130 miles to Virginia City to make a new beginning that would, this time, see him through to a dazzling end.

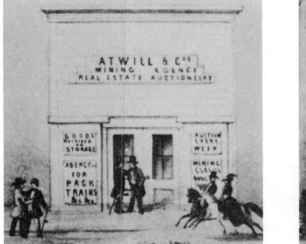

Virginia City (*shown on opposite page in an 1861 lithograph*). Above are sketches of some important places in the town, including the first office of the *Territorial Enterprise,* for which Mark Twain wrote.

DAILY TERRITO

VOL. XIII.

VIRGINIA, NEVADA. TUESD

TERRITORIAL ENTERPRISE

J. T. GOODMAN.................PROPRIETOR

Office, 24 South C St., Virginia.

THE DAILY ENTERPRISE is furnished to subscribers in Virginia, Gold Hill, Silver City, Dayton,
Carson City and San Francisco, at Fifty Cents per week.
Sent by mail, one year, $16; six months, $10; three
months $6.

LETTER FROM WASHINGTON.

[CORRESPONDENCE OF THE ENTERPRISE.]

Equal Suffrage for the District of Columbia—Southern Republican Association
—Its Outspoken Sentiments—Congress
Looking After Presidential Corruption
—The Presidential Mode of Disposing
of Government Property—Department
of Agriculture—The Indians of Kansas
—Colorado and Nebraska to be Admit-
ted as States.

WASHINGTON, D. C., December 13.

To-day marks another advance in national
adjustment. We travel fast towards the
full consummation of the American idea—
equality before the law, perfect liberty in the

distribution of seeds and other duties belonging to the Department, the bill provides
for a Bureau of Mines and Mining, to be under control of the Commissioner. It is not
likely to pass with this clause, as it will
without doubt be deemed more appropriate
to make the Mining Bureau a separate establishment.

The Bureau of Indian Affairs is preparing
for the removal of all the semi-civilized
tribes in Kansas to the Indian Territory
south of that State. When that is accomplished the control of the nomads in Kansas, Nebraska, and in the mountain Terri-
tories, will be turned over to the War Department.

The admission of Colorado as a State is

Among the items of expenditures during the
last year is a sum of $1,906 for the support of
insane patients in our County Hospital, legitim-
ately chargeable to and should be reimbursed by
the State of Nevada. The official reports will
show that the greater number of insane patients
gaining admission into our County Hospital find
their way there from adjoining counties, where
no provision is made for their support. Unlike
our sister States, the State of Nevada is without a
means is without a State institution for the care
and protection of that unfortunate class of our
fellow beings, but the burden of their support
should not fall upon Storey County alone, and it
would seem but an act of justice that the State
should be asked to relieve this county, if not entirely at least in part from such an onerous
charge.

If the foregoing estimates should

Joseph T. Goodman, who bought the *Territorial
Enterprise* and became its editor at 23. The paper's
duty, his editorial manifesto said, "is to keep the
universe thoroughly posted concerning murders and
street fights, and balls and theaters, and packtrains,
and churches, and lectures, and city military affairs,
and highway robberies, and Bible societies, and by-
wagons, and the thousand other things which it is in
the province of local reporters to keep track of and
magnify into undue importance for the instruction of
the readers of a great daily newspaper."

A RUSTY-LOOKING CITY EDITOR

Something over two years before Mark Twain joined
the staff of the *Territorial Enterprise,* as he told it in
Roughing It, "Mr. Goodman and another journeyman
printer had borrowed forty dollars and set out from
San Francisco to try their fortunes in the new city of
Virginia. They found the *Territorial Enterprise,* a
poverty-stricken weekly journal, gasping for breath
and likely to die. They bought it, type, fixtures, good-
will, and all, for a thousand dollars, on long time.
The editorial sanctum, news-room, press-room, publication office, bed-chamber, parlor, and kitchen were all
compressed into one apartment, and it was a small one,
too. The editors and printers slept on the floor, a China-
man did their cooking, and the 'imposing-stone' was the
general dinner table. But now things were changed.
The paper was a great daily, printed by steam; there
were five editors and twenty-three compositors; the
subscription price was sixteen dollars a year; the advertising rates were exorbitant, and the columns crowded.

Sketch of Mark Twain at his newspaper desk, from
Roughing It. He joined the *Enterprise* in September,
1862. Most of the staff were in their twenties. Mark
wrote local news and editorials, filed political reports
from the capital, and concocted occasional hoaxes and
diatribes.

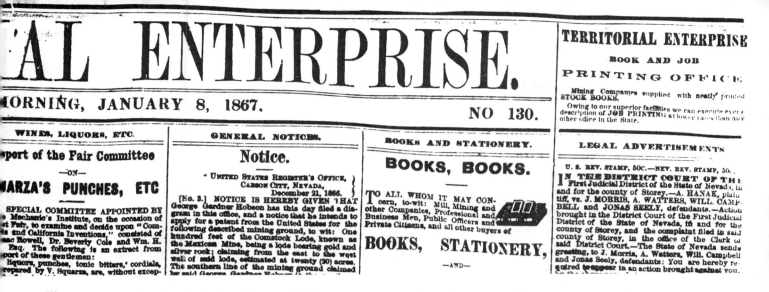
The paper was clearing six to ten thousand dollars a month, and the 'Enterprise Building' was finished and ready for occupation—a stately fireproof brick. Every day from five all the way up to eleven columns of 'live' advertisements were left out or crowded into spasmodic and irregular 'supplements.' . . .

"I was a rusty-looking city editor, I am free to confess—coatless, slouch hat, blue woolen shirt, pantaloons stuffed into boot-tops, whiskered half down to the waist, and the universal navy revolver slung to my belt. But I secured a more Christian costume and discarded the revolver. I had never had occasion to kill anybody, nor ever felt a desire to do so, but had worn the thing in deference to popular sentiment, and in order that I might not, by its absence, be offensively conspicuous, and a subject of remark. But the other editors, and all the printers, carried revolvers. I asked the chief editor and proprietor (Mr. Goodman, I will call him, since it describes him as well as any name could do) for some instructions with regard to my duties, and he told me to go all over town and ask all sorts of people all sorts of questions, make notes of the information gained, and write them out for publication.

"I moralize well, but I did not always practice well when I was a city editor; I let fancy get the upper hand of fact too often when there was a dearth of news. I can never forget my first day's experience as a reporter. I wandered about town questioning everybody, boring everybody, and finding out that nobody knew anything. At the end of five hours my notebook was still barren. I spoke to Mr. Goodman. He said:

"'Dan used to make a good thing out of the hay wagons in a dry time when there were no fires or inquests. Are there no hay wagons in from the Truckee? If there are, you might speak of the renewed activity and all that sort of thing, in the hay business, you know. It isn't sensational or exciting, but it fills up and looks business-like.'

"I canvassed the city again and found one wretched old hay truck dragging in from the country. But I made affluent use of it. I multiplied it by sixteen, brought it into town from sixteen different directions, made six-teen separate items out of it, and got up such another sweat about hay as Virginia City had never seen in the world before.

"This was encouraging."

An ad appearing in the *First Directory of Nevada Territory* in 1862.

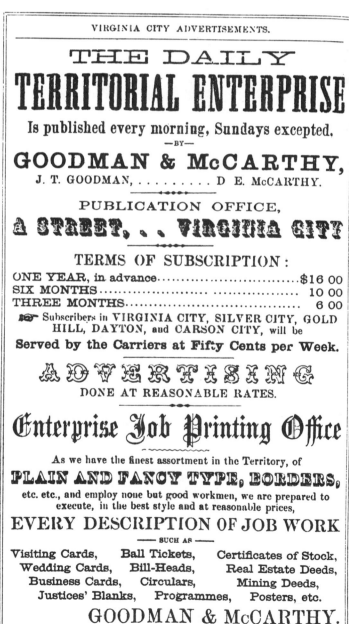

THE PETRIFIED MAN.

Mark's "Petrified Man" hoax appeared in the *Enterprise* in early October, 1862. Why the cub reporter wrote it and how it misfired, he tells below.

HOAXING THE UNSUSPECTING PUBLIC

"Now, to show how really hard it is to foist a moral or a truth upon an unsuspecting public through a burlesque without entirely and absurdly missing one's mark, I will here set down two experiences of my own in this thing. In the fall of 1862, in Nevada and California, the people got to running wild about extraordinary petrifications and other natural marvels. One could scarcely pick up a paper without finding in it one or two glorified discoveries of this kind. The mania was becoming a little ridiculous. I was a brand-new local editor in Virginia City, and I felt called upon to

destroy this growing evil; we all have our benignant fatherly moods at one time or another, I suppose. I chose to kill the petrifaction mania with a delicate, a very delicate satire. But maybe it was altogether too delicate, for nobody ever perceived the satire part of it at all. I put my scheme in the shape of the discovery of a remarkably petrified man. From beginning to end the 'Petrified Man' squib was a string of roaring absurdities, albeit they were told with an unfair pretence of truth that even imposed upon me to some extent, and I was in some danger of believing in my own fraud. But I really have no desire to deceive anybody, and no expectation of doing it. I depended on the way the petrified man was *sitting* to explain to the public that he was a swindle. Yet I purposely mixed that up with other things, hoping to make it obscure—and I did.

"As a *satire* on the petrifaction mania, or anything else, my Petrified Man was a disheartening failure; for everybody received him in innocent good faith, and I was stunned to see the creature I had begotten to pull down the wonder-business with, and bring derision upon it, calmly exalted to the grand chief place in the list of the genuine marvels our Nevada had produced. I was so disappointed at the curious miscarriage of my scheme, that at first I was angry, and did not like to think about it; but by and by, when the exchanges began to come in with the Petrified Man copied and guilelessly glorified, I began to feel a soothing secret satisfaction; and as my gentleman's field of travels broadened, and by the exchanges I saw that he steadily and implacably penetrated territory after territory, State after State, and land after land, till he swept the great globe and culminated in sublime and unimpeached legitimacy in the august London *Lancet,* my cup was full, and I said I was glad I had done it. . . .

"The other burlesque I have referred to was my fine satire upon the financial expedients of 'cooking dividends,' a thing which became shamefully frequent on the Pacific coast for a while. Once more, in my self-complacent simplicity, I felt that the time had arrived for me to rise up and be a reformer. I put this reformatory satire in the shape of a fearful 'Massacre at Empire City.' The San Francisco papers were making a great out-cry about the iniquity of the Daney Silver-Mining Company, whose directors had declared a 'cooked' or false dividend, for the purpose of increasing the value of their stock, so that they could sell out at a comfortable figure, and then scramble from under the tumbling concern. And while abusing the Daney, those papers did not forget to urge the public to get rid of all their silver stocks and invest in sound and safe San Francisco stocks, such as the Spring Valley Water Company, etc. But right at this unfortunate juncture, behold the Spring Valley cooked a dividend too! And so, under the insidious mask of an invented 'bloody massacre,' I

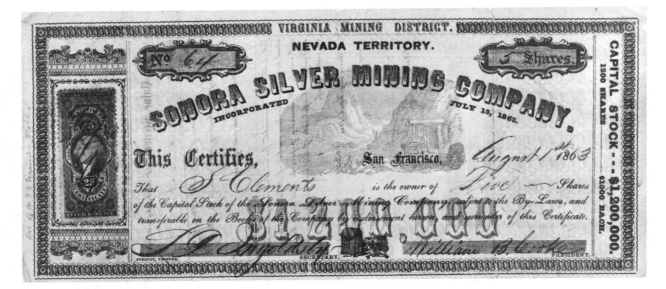

As a distinguished reporter and influential lobbyist, Mark was handed occasional favors, such as these five shares in a silver mine.

stole upon the public unawares with my scathing satire upon the dividend-cooking system. In about half a column of imaginary human carnage I told how a citizen had murdered his wife and nine children, and then committed suicide. And I said slyly, at the bottom, that the sudden madness of which this melancholy massacre was the result, had been brought about by his having allowed himself to be persuaded by the California papers to sell his sound and lucrative Nevada silver stocks, and buy into Spring Valley just in time to get cooked along with that company's fancy dividend, and sink every cent he had in the world.

The "favorite place of resort" in Carson City, advertised in the first Nevada directory, plays a part in another Twain hoax, the "Empire City Massacre."

"Ah, it was a deep, deep satire, and most ingeniously contrived. But I made the horrible details so carefully and conscientiously interesting that the public devoured *them* greedily, and wholly overlooked the following distinctly-stated facts, to wit:—The murderer was perfectly well known to every creature in the land as a *bachelor,* and consequently he could not murder his wife and nine children; he murdered them 'in his splendid dressed-stone mansion just in the edge of the great pine forest between Empire City and Dutch Nick's,' when even the very pickled oysters that came on our tables knew that there was not a 'dressed-stone mansion' in all Nevada Territory; also that, so far from there being a 'great pine forest between Empire City and Dutch Nick's,' there wasn't a solitary tree within fifteen miles of either place; and, finally, it was patent and notorious that Empire City and Dutch Nick's were one and the same place, and contained only six houses anyhow, and consequently there could be no forest *between* them; and on top of all these absurdities I stated that this diabolical murderer, after inflicting a wound upon himself that the reader ought to have seen would kill an elephant in the twinkling of an eye, jumped on his horse and rode *four miles,* waving his wife's reeking scalp in the air, and thus performing entered Carson City with tremendous éclat, and dropped dead in front of the chief saloon, the envy and admiration of all beholders.

"Well, in all my life I never saw anything like the sensation that little satire created. It was the talk of the town, it was the talk of the Territory. Most of the citizens dropped gently into it at breakfast, and they never finished their meal."

This reporters' quintet—three of them on Mark's paper—posed for their portrait on December 10, 1865. From left to right they are William A. Gillespie of the *Enterprise*, Charles E. Parker of the *Gold Hill News*, Dan DeQuille of the *Enterprise*, Robert E. Lowery of the *Union*, and Alf Doten of the *Enterprise*. Apparently they sent this "handsome present" to other Nevada newsmen. When the gift reached Mark Twain in San Francisco he acknowledged it with this item labeled "Convicts."

"By the Mark Twain!"

Left: William Wright (Dan DeQuille) was an Ohioan six years Mark's senior. He joined the *Enterprise* shortly before Mark, and was with it when it suspended in the 1890's. The paper's best mining reporter, he became Mark's closest friend in that period.

POLITICAL CORRESPONDENT

In Carson City Mark covered the legislature and later the Constitutional Convention for the *Enterprise*, a grinding assignment. "Every Saturday I wrote a letter to the paper, in which I made a resume of the week's legislative work, and in order that it might be readable, I put no end of seasoning into it. I signed these letters 'Mark Twain.'" The first record of his use of the pseudonym is a newsletter published February 3, 1863. His straight news copy was still signed Clemens. But the humor and fantasy of the growing literary personality began carrying the Mississippi leadsman's call, "Mark Twain," meaning two fathoms—twelve feet, safe water. The pen name was in the tradition of that noted trio of humorists he was soon to surpass: Charles Farrar Browne (Artemus Ward), David Ross Locke (Petroleum V. Nasby), and Robert H. Newell (Orpheus C. Kerr).

The Nevada legislature paid Mark and the other reporters a bonus on top of their newspaper salaries. A favorite at the Capitol, Mark was invited to deliver the Governor's message to the burlesque Third House on December 11, 1863. Later he sent his sister Pamela the above photo, showing "his excellency Gov. Mark Twain of the Third House, Hon. Wm. H. Claggett of the House of Representatives, and Hon. A. J. Simmons, Speaker of the same." Mark drew a bigger crowd than Artemus Ward, and knew "the gratification of very good judges saying it was the best thing of the kind they had ever listened to." It looked as though a new platform star had been born.

A territorial legislator at work. Mark's close view of the Nevada "sovereigns" seeded a fine contempt for public representatives that blossomed when he covered Congress a few years later.

"That was a fine collection of sovereigns, that first Nevada legislature," Mark said in *Roughing It*. "They levied taxes to the amount of thirty or forty thousand dollars and ordered expenditures to the extent of about a million. Yet they had their little periodical explosions of economy like all other bodies of the kind. A member proposed to save three dollars a day to the nation by dispensing with the Chaplain. And yet that short-sighted man needed the Chaplain more than any other member, perhaps, for he generally sat with his feet on his desk, eating raw turnips, during the morning prayer.

"The legislature sat sixty days, and passed private toll-road franchises all the time. When they adjourned it was estimated that every citizen owned about three franchises, and it was believed that unless Congress gave the Territory another degree of longitude there would not be room enough to accommodate the toll-roads. The ends of them were hanging over the boundary line everywhere like a fringe."

61

THE MENKEN—WRITTEN ESPECIALLY FOR GENTLEMEN

With a friendly rival reporter, C. T. Rice, whom he dubbed the "Unreliable," Mark began enjoying the delights of San Francisco in the summer of 1863. "We fag ourselves out completely every day, and go to sleep without rocking, every night. I am going to the Dickens mighty fast," he wrote his mother. For several weeks the two reporters "lived like a lord to make up for two years of privation" in the "snows and deserts of Washoe." Trips across the bay, yachting excursions, champagne suppers—"we *do* put on the most disgusting airs." Slipped into each of these gay reports home was twenty dollars, but Mark's generosity did not calm Jane Clemens' fears. To her accusations he replied:

"Ma, you have given my vanity a deadly thrust. Behold, I am prone to boast of having the widest

"After the sage-brush and alkali deserts of Washoe," said Mark, "San Francisco was Paradise to me. I lived at the best hotel, exhibited my clothes in the most conspicuous places, infested the opera, and learned to seem enraptured with music. . . . I attended private parties in sumptuous evening dress, simpered and aired my graces like a born beau, and polked and schottisched with a step peculiar to myself —and the kangaroo."

reputation, as a local editor, of any man on the Pacific coast, and you gravely come forward and tell me 'if I work hard and attend closely to my business, I may aspire to a place on a big San Francisco daily, some day.' There's a comment on human vanity for you! Why, blast it, I was under the impression that I could get such a situation as that any time I asked for it. But I don't want it. No paper in the United States can afford to pay me what my place on the 'Enterprise' is worth. If I were not naturally a lazy, idle, good-for-nothing vagabond, I could make it pay me $20,000 a year. But I don't suppose I shall ever be any account. I lead an easy life, though, and I don't care a cent whether school keeps or not. Everybody knows me, and I fare like a prince wherever I go, be it on this side of the mountains or the other. And I am proud to say I am the most conceited ass in the Territory."

A few weeks later, in a letter to the *Enterprise:*

"When I arrived in San Francisco, I found there was no one in town—at least there was nobody in town but 'the Menken'—or rather, that no one was being talked about except that manly young female. I went to see her play 'Mazeppa,' of course. They said she was dressed from head to foot in flesh-colored 'tights,' but I had no opera-glass, and I couldn't see it, to use the language of the inelegant rabble. She appeared to me to have but one garment on—a thin tight white linen one, of unimportant dimensions; I forget the name of the article, but it is indispensable to infants of tender age—I suppose any young mother can tell you what it is, if you have the moral courage to ask the question. With the exception of this superfluous rag, the Menken dresses like the Greek Slave; but some of her postures are not so modest as the suggestive attitude of the latter. She is a finely formed woman down to her knees; if she could be herself that far, and Mrs. H. A. Perry the rest of the way, she would pass for an unexceptionable Venus. Here every tongue sings the praises of her matchless grace, her supple gestures, her charming attitudes. Well, possibly, these tongues are right. In the first act, she rushes on the stage, and goes cavorting around after 'Olinska'; she bends herself back like a bow; she pitches headforemost at the atmosphere like a battering ram; she works her arms, and her legs, and her whole body like a dancing-jack; her every movement is as quick as thought; in a word, without any apparent reason for it, she carries on like a lunatic from the beginning of the act to the end of it. At other times she 'whallops' herself down on the stage, and rolls over as does the sportive pack-mule after his burden is removed. If this be grace then the Menken is eminently graceful. After a while they proceed to strip her, and the high chief Pole calls for the 'fiery untamed steed'; a subordinate Pole brings in the fierce brute, stirring him up occasionally to make him run away, and then hanging to him like death to keep him from doing it;

Adah Menken as the French Spy.

Another publicity photo of the Menken, who fascinated not only Mark Twain, but Whitman, Dumas, Swinburne, and even Longfellow, who inscribed a love poem in her album.

A tantalizing playbill plastered all over town to announce the coming of Menken as Mazeppa in the *Wild Horse of Tartary*.

the monster looks round pensively upon the brilliant audience in the theatre, and seems very willing to stand still—but a lot of those Poles grab him and hold on to him, so as to be prepared for him in case he changes his mind. They are posted as to his fiery untamed nature, you know, and they give him no chance to get loose and eat up the orchestra. They strap Mazeppa on his back, fore and aft, and face uppermost, and the horse goes cantering up-stairs over the painted mountains, through tinted clouds of theatrical mist, in a brisk exciting way, with the wretched victim he bears unconsciously digging her heels into his hams, in the agony of her sufferings, to make him go faster. Then a tempest of applause bursts forth, and the curtain falls. The fierce old circus horse carries his prisoner around through the back part of the theatre, behind the scenery, and although assailed at every step by the savage wolves of the desert, he makes his way at last to his dear old home in Tartary down by the footlights, and beholds once more, O, gods! the familiar faces of the fiddlers in the orchestra. The noble old steed is happy, then, but poor Mazeppa is insensible—'ginned out' by his trip, as it were. Before the act closes, how-ever, he is restored to consciousness and his doting old father, the king of Tartary; and the next day, without taking time to dress—without even borrowing a shirt, or stealing a fresh horse—he starts off on the fiery untamed, at the head of the Tartar nation, to exterminate the Poles, and carry off his own sweet Olinska from the Polish court. He succeeds, and the curtain falls upon a bloody combat, in which the Tartars are victorious. 'Mazeppa' proved a great card for Maguire here; he put it on the boards in first-class style, and crowded houses went crazy over it every night it was played. But Virginians will soon have an opportunity of seeing it themselves, as 'the Menken' will go direct from our town there without stopping on the way. The 'French Spy' was played last night and the night before, and as this spy is a frisky Frenchman, and as dumb as an oyster, Miss Menken's extravagant gesticulations do not seem so over done in it as they do in 'Mazeppa.' She don't talk well, and as she goes on her shape and her acting, the character of a fidgety 'dummy' is peculiarly suited to her line of business. She plays the Spy, without words, with more feeling than she does Mazeppa with them."

others he stretched his visit into a twelve-day period of "continuous celebration." The veteran Ward and the beginner Twain raced on a rising tide of humor that carried them to a walk at dawn over the terraced roofs of the town. A few days later, after Ward had moved on, Mark reported receiving this letter from him:

I arrived here yesterday morning at 2 o'clock. It is a wild, untamable place, but full of lion-hearted boys. I speak tonight. See small bills. . . . I hope, some time, to see you and Kettle-belly Brown in New York. My grandmother—my sweet grandmother—she, thank God, is too far advanced in life to be affected by your hellish wiles. My aunt—she might fall. But didn't Warren fall, at Bunker Hill? [The old woman's safe. And so is the old girl, for that matter.—MARK.] Do not sir, do not, sir, do not flatter yourself that you are the only chastely-humorous writer onto the Pacific slopes. . . . I shall always remember Virginia as a bright spot in my existence, and all others might or rather cannot be, "as it were."

A *Vanity Fair* cartoon, 1862, of Artemus Ward as public lecturer. "The Babes in the Wood" was the kind of totally irrelevant title Ward chose for his talks. Twain got a chance to see an expert when he heard Ward lecture in Virginia City in December, 1863.

Artemus Ward (Charles Farrar Browne) enjoyed an enormous popularity (Lincoln interrupted Cabinet meetings to read Ward's stories aloud) in his brief career as writer and lecturer. He was born in Skowhegan, Maine, in 1834, and by 1867 was dead of consumption. Like Twain he began life as a compositor. His humor, as Twain characterized it later, "was merely an odd trick of speech and of spelling" and its fashion soon faded. Artemus knew a talent when he saw it, and he encouraged the "Wild Humorist of the Pacific Slope" to find a wider market for his work. In February, 1864, the New York *Sunday Mercury* printed two of Mark's contributions. He could now boast of being read from coast to coast.

ARTEMUS WARD AND THE LION-HEARTED BOYS

It was December 18, 1863, when Artemus Ward reached Virginia City on his nationwide lecture tour. The famous newspaper and platform humorist found in the *Enterprise* gang the "lion-hearted boys" he loved. With Twain, Goodman, De Quille and the

A platoon of the Virginia City volunteer fire company poses with its hand-drawn cart. Many of these fire laddies were New Yorkers of the "Bowery B'hoy" tradition, quick to use fist, knife or pistol. Buck Fanshaw in *Roughing It* might have been patterned on big Jack Perry, foreman of a fire company as well as city marshal of Virginia. Demonstrations of equipment provided street holidays for the locals.

In *Sketches, New and Old*, Mark described his first interview with Artemus Ward. It is an early example of the art of double talk, a string of plausibly worded sentences that are meaningless.

John W. Mackay, an Irish immigrant, began his Comstock legend as a mucker in the mines at $4.50 a day and went on to become one of the most powerful bonanza kings. Almost 30 years later, when bankruptcy threatened Mark, he was to seek Mackay's help.

Eds. Golden Era:— Going down to San José last Sunday, to write a letter to the newspaper with which I am connected, I was taken somewhat sick, & the "Unreliable" being along, I ventured to entrust him with my work. I send you the result, for I have no use for it myself. This is the twentieth time I have been deceived by that well-meaning but ~~unstable~~ unstable young man, & it shall be the last. Every time he gets a commission of this kind, he calls himself an editor, & gets drunk — to prove it, perhaps, though I cannot conceive how he hopes to establish such a fact by such an argument.

Yours, sadly,

Mark Twain.

This is perhaps the earliest "Mark Twain" signature in existence. The letter was written to the *Golden Era* literary paper when Mark and C. T. Rice, the "Unreliable," were visiting San Francisco in September, 1863.

THAT SANITARY SACK OF FLOUR

Mark was cock of the walk as 1864 opened. But trouble began in May. It started when the ladies began raising money for the U.S. Sanitary Commission, which provided aid for the wounded Union soldiers. An old Hannibal schoolmate of Mark's, Reuel Gridley, won overnight fame for himself and raised thousands for the fund by roving the Territory with a fifty-pound sack of flour which he auctioned off again and again to hundreds of high-bidding Nevadans.

In the midst of the Sanitary spree Mark got off a paragraph in the *Enterprise* hinting that the funds

The great flour sack procession through Virginia City.

were being diverted to a "Miscegenation Society" back East. The miserable Copperhead joke was disastrous. His weak apology did not dam the tide of scorn channeled through the rival *Union* newspaper. Mark and the *Union* editor swapped insults that culminated in Mark's challenging him to a duel. But it never came off, despite Mark's colorful account of a duel in his autobiography. Instead, he fled west across the mountains, fearing two years in prison for the felony of issuing a challenge.

Duel or no duel, he was about ready to quit the Comstock. "I began to get tired of staying in one place so long," he wrote. "I wanted to see San Francisco. I wanted to go somewhere. I wanted—I did not know what I wanted. I had the 'spring fever.'" On May 29, Mark took the California stage, "bidding a permanent farewell to a city which had afforded me the most vigorous enjoyment of life I had ever experienced."

Reuel Gridley auctioned off the sack all over the country, raising some $150,000 in three months. Prints of this picture were also sold for the Sanitary Fund.

Bret Harte, once miner, schoolteacher, compositor, was now literary mentor of the Golden Gate. After ten years on the Coast he had just begun writing the poems and stories of the West that would soon win him an international reputation.

Mark Twain, photographed not long after his arrival in San Francisco.

Reporter at Large

Orpheus C. Kerr, briefly wed to The Menken, was one of the California figures of this day.

AWFUL SLAVERY FOR A LAZY MAN

Mark Twain "has vamosed, cut stock, absquatulated," noted a Nevada paper the day after his abrupt flight to San Francisco. With him went Steve Gillis, an *Enterprise* compositor and one of his intimates. The two found jobs on the *Morning Call*. But the routine of the *Call* was a disappointment to a veteran of the free and easy *Enterprise*. Police court, street squabbles, fires, a nightly round of the six theaters: "It was fearful drudgery—soulless drudgery—and almost destitute of interest. It was an awful slavery for a lazy man." But the town's literary circle provided relief, and their publications offered new markets for the now professional writer.

San Francisco newspapermen. Number 2 is supposed to be Mark Twain.

Steve Gillis and Mark Twain remained companions until Mark went East in 1866. This picture of Steve was taken long after, in 1907.

Joaquin Miller, the "Byron of the Sierras," had come down from Oregon to join the writers clustered around the *Golden Era*.

69

San Francisco of the 1860's, looking down from Russian Hill. "A truly fascinating city to live in," Mark Twain wrote, "stately and handsome at a fair distance, but close at hand one notes that the architecture is mostly old-fashioned, many streets are made up of decaying, smoke-grimed, wooden houses, and the brown sand-hills towards the outskirts obtrude themselves too prominently."

"Heaven on the half-shell" was Mark's term for life at the Occidental Hotel, on Montgomery Street. He stayed here in 1865.

Know-Nothing prejudice against the foreign-born was common in Twain's boyhood; it was to take many years for him to overcome these feelings. But nevertheless he recognized the rights of minority groups. He would not remain quiet in the face of such outrages as this 1865 riot at the Rope Walk in San Francisco, when several Chinese were murdered.

HEAVEN ON THE HALF SHELL

"I am taking life easy now," Mark wrote his mother and sister, "and I mean to keep it up for a while. I don't work at night any more. I told the *Call* folks to pay me $25 a week and let me work only in daylight. So I get up at ten every morning and quit work at five or six in the afternoon . . . I work as I always did—by fits and starts."

For a while he contributed to the *Golden Era* the kind of sketch he had formerly sent them from Virginia City. Then he quit it for the *Californian*. Although the rates were the same, the *Era* "wasn't high-toned enough." The *Call* was still his daily bread, but when it wouldn't print his attacks on the corruption of local politicians and police, he sent the dispatches to the *Enterprise*. Revolted by the brutal treatment of the Chinese in San Francisco, he damned the mobs that hunted victims in the streets. By the end of 1864, San Francisco was becoming too hot for the crusader.

Mark's first San Francisco job was with the *Call*.

The *Golden Era*'s office was the heart of literary Bohemia. Mark contributed an article a week, at $50 a month.

"The best weekly literary paper in the United States—and I suppose I ought to know," said Mark of the *Californian*. When Harte became its editor Twain joined the staff.

GOLD, WHISKY, FIGHTS, AND FANDANGOES

Life in the California Mother Lode country, as Mark pictured it in *Roughing It:*

"It was in this Sacramento Valley, just referred to, that a deal of the most lucrative of the early gold mining was done, and you may still see, in places, its grassy slopes and levels torn and guttered and disfigured by the avaricious spoilers of fifteen and twenty years ago. You may see such disfigurements far and wide over California—and in some such places, where only meadows and forests are visible—not a living creature, not a house, no stick or stone or remnant of a ruin, and not a sound, not even a whisper to disturb the Sabbath stillness—you will find it hard to believe that there stood at one time a fiercely-flourishing little city, of two thousand or three thousand souls, with its newspaper, fire company, brass band, volunteer militia, bank, hotels, noisy Fourth of July processions and speeches, gambling hells crammed with tobacco smoke, profanity, and rough-bearded men of all nations and colors, with tables heaped with gold dust sufficient for the revenues of a German principality—streets crowded and rife with business—town lots worth four thousand dollars a front foot—labor, laughter, music, dancing, swearing, fighting, shooting, stabbing—a bloody inquest and a man for breakfast every morning—everything that delights and adorns existence—all the appointments and appurtenances of a thriving and prosperous and promising young city,—and now nothing is left of it all but a lifeless, homeless solitude. The men are gone, the houses have vanished, even the name of the place is forgotten. In no other land, in modern times, have towns so absolutely died and disappeared, as in the old mining regions of California.

"It was a driving, vigorous, restless population. It was the only population of the kind that the world has ever seen gathered together, and it is not likely that the world will ever see its like again. For, observe, it was an assemblage of two hundred thousand young men—not simpering, dainty, kid-gloved weaklings, but stalwart, muscular, dauntless young braves, brimful of push and energy, and royally endowed with every attribute that goes to make up a peerless and magnificent manhood—the very pick and choice of the world's glorious ones. No women, no children, no gray and stooping veterans,—none but erect, bright-eyed, quick-moving, strong-handed young giants—the strangest population, the finest population, the most gallant host that ever trooped down the startled solitudes of an unpeopled land. And where are they now? Scattered to the ends of the earth—or prematurely aged and decrepit—or shot or stabbed in street affrays—or dead of disappointed hopes and broken hearts—all gone, or nearly all—victims devoted upon the altar of the golden calf—the noblest holocaust that ever wafted its sacrificial incense heavenward. It is pitiful to think upon.

"It was a splendid population—for all the slow, sleepy, sluggish-brained sloths staid at home—you never find that sort of people among pioneers—you cannot build pioneers out of that sort of material. It was that population that gave to California a name for getting up astounding enterprises and rushing them

This picture of Mark Twain was made in San Francisco around the time he wrote his "Jumping Frog" story. In the dreary winter of 1864–65 Mark tried pocket-mining at Angel's Camp in the Mother Lode country. In the notebook he began to keep in January the most frequent jottings are "rain," "beans," "dishwater." But on one page is the entry: "Coleman with his jumping frog—bet a stranger $50.—stranger had no frog and C. got him one:—In the meantime stranger filled C's frog full of shot and he couldn't jump. The Stranger's frog won." The story—an old one—Mark first heard from Ben Coon, a marathon talker pocketmining at Angel's. Late in February, Mark got back to San Francisco and found a letter from Artemus Ward asking for a sketch for Ward's new book. But Ward's book had gone to press and the story found print in a New York paper instead. It was the beginning of Mark's fiction writing, and a success: papers everywhere copied it.

through with a magnificent dash and daring and a recklessness of cost or consequences, which she bears unto this day—and when she projects a new surprise, the grave world smiles as usual, and says 'Well, that is California all over.'

"But they were rough in those times! They fairly reveled in gold, whisky, fights, and fandangoes, and were unspeakably happy. The honest miner raked from a hundred to a thousand dollars out of his claim a day, and what with the gambling dens and the other entertainments, he hadn't a cent the next morning, if he had any sort of luck. They cooked their own bacon and beans, sewed on their own buttons, washed their own shirts—blue woolen ones; and if a man wanted a fight on his hands without any annoying delay, all he had to do was to appear in public in a white shirt or a stove-pipe hat, and he would be accommodated. For those people hated aristocrats. They had a particular and malignant animosity toward what they called a 'biled shirt.'

"It was a wild, free, disorderly, grotesque society! Men—only swarming hosts of stalwart men—nothing juvenile, nothing feminine, visible anywhere!"

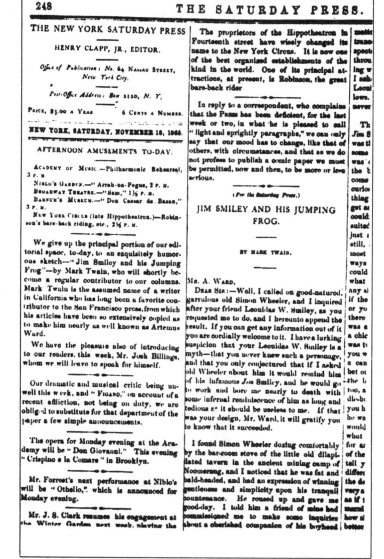

The New York *Saturday Press* for November 18, 1865, with the beginning of Twain's Jumping Frog story. The whole country laughed, but the author complained to Jane and Pamela that people had singled out "a villainous backwoods sketch" to compliment him on.

The three characters of Mark Twain's first piece of fiction: Jim Smiley, Simon Wheeler and the frog Dan'l.

I ENJOYED MY FIRST
EARTHQUAKE

A month after Mark Twain was back in San Francisco, the Civil War ended. But no reflection of the bloody convulsion is found in the potboilers he lived on now. He wrote casual sketches for the West Coast papers, finding fun even in an earthquake. The following account was written seven years later:

"A month afterward I enjoyed my first earthquake. It was one which was long called the 'great' earthquake, and is doubtless so distinguished till this day. It was just after noon, on a bright October day. I was coming down Third street. The only objects in motion anywhere in sight in that thickly-built and populous quarter, were a man in a buggy behind me, and a street car wending slowly up the cross street. Otherwise, all was solitude and a Sabbath stillness. As I turned the corner, around a frame house, there was a great rattle and jar, and it occurred to me that here

This lively lithograph of the San Francisco earthquake Mark Twain "enjoyed" on October 8, 1865, was drawn by Edward Jump. The artist learned his craft designing labels for whisky bottles. Three years after the quake he and Mark roomed in the same boardinghouse in Washington. Later he drew for New York periodicals; he committed suicide in 1883.

was an item!—no doubt a fight in that house. Before I could turn and seek the door, there came a really terrific shock; the ground seemed to roll under me in waves, interrupted by a violent joggling up and down, and there was a heavy grinding noise as of brick houses rubbing together. I fell up against the frame house and hurt my elbow. I knew what it was, now, and from mere reportorial instinct, nothing else, took out my watch and noted the time of day; at that moment a third and still severer shock came, and as I reeled about on the pavement trying to keep my footing, I saw a sight! The entire front of a tall four-story brick building in Third Street sprung outward like a door and fell sprawling across the street, raising a dust like a great volume of smoke! And here came the buggy—overboard went the man, and in less time than I can tell it the vehicle was distributed in small fragments along three hundred yards of street. One could have fancied that somebody had fired a charge of chair-rounds and rags down the thoroughfare. The street car had stopped, the horses were rearing and plunging, the passengers were pouring out at both ends, and one fat man had crashed half way through a glass window on one side of the car, got wedged fast and was squirming and screaming like an impaled madman. Every door of every house, as far as the eye could reach, was vomiting a stream of human beings; and almost before one could execute a wink and begin another, there was a massed multitude of people stretching in endless procession down every street my position commanded. Never was solemn solitude turned into teeming life quicker."

A veteran of domestic newsletters, Mark Twain got his first assignment as foreign correspondent early in 1866. This ship news item reports the steamer *Ajax* left San Francisco on March 7, 1866, and arrived in Honolulu March 18. Aboard was the Sacramento *Union*'s man, Mark Twain. It was the first sea voyage for the ex-river pilot.

THESE ENCHANTED ISLANDS

Out of his original travel letters came some chapters in *Roughing It*. Here is how Mark Twain remembered Hawaii:

"On a certain bright morning the Island hove in sight, lying low on the lonely sea, and everybody climbed to the upper deck to look. After two thousand miles of watery solitude the vision was a welcome one. As we approached, the imposing promontory of Diamond Head rose up out of the ocean, its rugged front softened by the hazy distance, and presently the details of the land began to make themselves manifest: first the line of beach; then the plumed cocoanut trees of the tropics; then cabins of the natives; then the white town of Honolulu, said to contain between twelve and fifteen thousand inhabitants, spread over a dead level; with streets from twenty to thirty feet wide, solid and level as a floor, most of them straight as a line and few as crooked as a corkscrew.

"The further I traveled through the town the better I liked it. Every step revealed a new contrast—disclosed something I was unaccustomed to. In place of the grand mud-colored brown fronts of San Francisco, I saw dwellings built of straw, adobes, and cream-colored pebble-and-shell-conglomerated coral, cut into oblong blocks and laid in cement; also a great number of neat white cottages, with green window-shutters; in place of front yards like billiard-tables with iron fences around them, I saw these homes surrounded by ample yards, thickly clad with green grass, and shaded by tall trees, through whose dense foliage the sun could scarcely penetrate; in place of the customary geranium, calla lily, etc., languishing in dust and general debility, I saw luxurious banks and thickets of flowers, fresh as a meadow after a rain, and glowing with the richest dyes; in place of the dingy horrors of San Francisco's pleasure grove, the 'Willows,' I saw huge-bodied, wide-spreading forest trees, with strange names and stranger appearance—trees that cast a shadow like a thunder-cloud, and were able to stand alone without being tied to green poles; in place of gold fish, wriggling around in glass globes, assuming countless shades and degrees of distortion through the magnifying and diminishing qualities of their transparent prison-house, I saw cats—Tom cats, Mary Ann cats, long-tailed cats, bob-tailed cats, blind cats, one-eyed cats, white cats, yellow cats, striped cats, individual cats, groups of cats, platoons of cats, companies of cats, regiments of cats, armies of cats, multitudes of cats, millions of cats, and all of them sleek, fat, lazy and sound asleep.

"I looked on a multitude of people, some white in white coats, vests, pantaloons, even white cloth shoes, made snowy with chalk duly laid on every morning; but the majority of the people were almost as dark as Negroes—women with comely features, fine black eyes, rounded forms, inclining to the voluptuous, clad

The Honolulu steamer *Ajax* at a San Francisco wharf. With his fame now carried nationwide by the jumping frog, Mark had been invited to visit Hawaii (the Sandwich Islands in those days) on the ship's maiden voyage. He turned down the press party but was commissioned by the Sacramento *Union* to "ransack the islands" for a month. The month stretched out to five.

in a single bright red or white garment that fell free and unconfined from shoulder to heel, long black hair falling loose, gypsy hats, encircled with wreaths of natural flowers of a brilliant carmine tint; plenty of dark men in various costumes, and some with nothing on but a battered stove-pipe hat tilted on the nose, and a very scant breech-clout; certain smoke-dried children were clothed in nothing but sunshine—a very neat fitting and picturesque apparel indeed.

"In place of roughs and rowdies staring and black-guarding on the corners, I saw long-haired, saddle-colored Sandwich Island maidens sitting on the ground in the shade of corner houses, gazing indolently at whatever or whoever happened along; instead of wretched cobble-stone pavements, I walked on a firm foundation of coral, built up from the bottom of the sea by the absurd but persevering insect of that name, with a light layer of lava and cinders overlying the coral, belched up out of fathomless perdition long ago through the seared and blackened crater that stands dead and harmless in the distance now; instead of cramped and crowded street-cars, I met dusky native women sweeping by, free as the wind, on fleet horses and astride, with gaudy riding-sashes, streaming like banners behind them; instead of the combined stenches of Chinadom and Brannan street slaughter-houses, I breathed the balmy fragrance of jessamine, oleander, and the Pride of India; in place of the hurry and bustle and noisy confusion of San Francisco, I moved in the midst of a summer calm as tranquil as dawn in the Garden of Eden; in place of the Golden City's skirting sand-hills and the placid bay, I saw on the one side a frame-work of tall, precipitous mountains close at hand, clad in refreshing green, and cleft by deep cool, chasm-like valleys—and in front the grand sweep of the ocean: a brilliant, transparent green near the shore, bound and bordered by a long white line of foamy spray dashing against the reef, and further out the dead blue water of the deep sea, flecked with 'white caps,' and in the far horizon a single, lonely sail—a mere accent-mark to emphasize a slumberous calm and a solitude that were without sound or limit. When the sun sunk down—the one intruder from other realms and persistent in sugges-tions of them—it was tranced luxury to sit in the per-fumed air and forget that there was any world but these enchanted islands."

The travel letters began in the *Union* in April, 1866, and were promptly popular. Sometimes they even made Page One. Mark was absorbed in new people and places and his fresh responses come through in his travel pieces. "No careworn or eager, anxious faces in this land of happy contentment," he wrote in his notebook. "God, what a contrast with California and Washoe!"

SCENES IN HONOLULU—NO. 12.

[CORRESPONDENCE OF THE UNION.]

Honolulu, May 23, 1866.

Hawaiian Legislature.

I have been reporting the Hawaiian Legisla-ture all day. This is my first visit to the Capi-tol. I expected to be present on the 25th of April and see the King open his Parliament in state and hear his speech, but I was in Maui then and Legislatures had no charms for me.

The Government of the Hawaiian Kingdom is composed of three estates, viz: The King, the Nobles and the Commons or Representa-tives. The Nobles are members of the Legisla-ture by right of their nobility—by blood, if you please—and hold the position for life. They hold the right to sit, at any rate, though that right is not complete until they are formally commissioned as Legislators by the King. Prince William, who is thirty-one years of ... was only so commissioned two years ... is now occupying ... the first time ... ... al was to ... o'clock to-morrow ... and I had nothing to do. I would attend it.]

Explanatory.

It has been six weeks since I touched a pen. In explanation and excuse I offer the fact that I spent that time (with the exception of one week) on the island of Maui. I only got back yesterday. I never spent so pleasant a month before, or bade any place good-bye so regret-fully. I doubt if there is a mean person there, from the homeliest man on the island (Lewers) down to the oldest (Tallant). I went to Maui to stay a week and remained five. I had a jolly time. I would not have fooled away any of it writing letters under any consideration what-ever. It will be five or six weeks before I write again. I sail for the island of Hawaii to-mor-row, and my Maui notes will not be written up until I come back. MARK TWAIN.

FROM THE SANDWICH ISLANDS.

[CORRESPONDENCE OF THE UNION.]

Kealakekua Bay, July, 1866.

A Funny Scrap of History.

In my last I spoke of the old cocoanut stump, all covered with copper plates bearing inscriptions com-memorating the visits of various British naval com-manders to Captain Cook's death-place at Kealakekua Bay. The most magniloquent of these is that left by "the Right Hon. Lord George Paulet, to whom, as the representative of Her Britannic Majesty Queen Vic-toria, the Sandwich Islands were ceded, February 25, 1843."

Lord George, if he is alive yet, would like to tear off that plate and destroy it, no doubt. He was fearfully snubbed by his Government, shortly afterward, for his acts as Her Majesty's representative upon the occasion to which he refers with such manifest satisfact—

A pestilent fellow h— Grea— ... ay so; but I don't see no use of ... spread as you're making. I don't see nothing ... very high-toned about this old rotten chunk. It's about the orneryest thing for a monument I've ever struck yet. If it suits Cook, though, all right; I wish him joy; but if I was planted under it I'd blight it, if it was the last act of my life. Monument! it ain't fit for a dog—I can buy dead loads of just such for six bits. She puts this over Cook—but she put one over that foreigner—what was his name?—Prince Albert—that cost a million dol-lars—and what did he do? Why, he never done any-thing—never done anything but lead a gallus, com-fortable life, at home and out of danger, and raise a large family for Government to board at £300,000 a year apiece. But with this fellow, you know, it was different. However, if you say the old stump's got to go down again, down she goes. As I said before, if its your wishes, I've got nothing to say. Nothing only this—I've fetched her a mild or a mild and a half, and she weighs a hundred and fifty I should judge, and if I would suit Cook just as well to have her planted up here instead of down there, it would be considerable of a favor to me."

I made him shoulder the monument and carry it back, nevertheless. His criticisms on the monument and its patron struck me, though, in spite of myself. The creature has got no sense, but his vaporings sound strangely plausible sometimes.

In due time we arrived at the port of entry once more. MARK TWAIN.

77

Honolulu, seen from the harbor not long after Twain's trip. Hawaii "has been a perfect jubilee to me in the way of pleasure," he wrote Mollie Clemens. He sent the *Union* about 25 letters describing the great volcanoes, cataracts, and mountains, the Kanaka royalty, the broad plantations, and the few friends from Washoe who had strayed this far west. Seasoning the bouillabaisse are the anecdote, satire, and burlesque that characterize all his travel writing.

THOSE ISLES OF THE BLEST

When a baseball team returned from a world tour by way of Hawaii in 1889, Mark Twain delivered the welcome-home speech. His remarks show how captivating he had found the islands:

"Though not a native, as intimated by the chairman, I visited, a great many years ago, the Sandwich Islands—that peaceful land, that beautiful land, that far-off home of profound repose, and soft indolence, and dreamy solitude, where life is one long slumberous Sabbath, the climate one long delicious summer day, and the good that die experience no change, for they but fall asleep in one heaven and wake up in another.

"The native language is soft and liquid and flexible, and in every way efficient and satisfactory—till you get mad; then there you are; there isn't anything in it to swear with. Good judges all say it is the best Sunday language there is; but then all the other six days in the week it just hangs idle on your hands; it isn't any good for business and you can't work a telephone with it. Many a time the attention of the missionaries has been called to this defect, and they are always promising they are going to fix it; but, no, they go fooling along and fooling along and nothing is done. Speaking of education, everybody there is educated, from the highest to the lowest; in fact, it is the only country in the world where education is actually universal. And yet every now and then you run across instances of ignorance that are simply revolting—simply degrading to the human race. Think of it—

there, the ten takes the ace! But let us not dwell on such things; they make a person ashamed. Well, the missionaries are always going to fix that, but they put it off, and put it off, and put it off, and so that nation is going to keep on going down and down and down, till some day you will see a pair of jacks beat a straight flush.

"No alien land in all the world has any deep, strong charm for me but that one, no other land could so longingly and so beseechingly haunt me, sleeping and waking, through half a lifetime, as that one has done. Other things leave me, but it abides; other things

Anson Burlingame, U.S. Minister to China. On his way to his post in 1866, he hunted Twain up in Honolulu and invited him to visit China, a trip that never came off. Twain was deeply impressed by the brilliant diplomat, whom he described as "a man who could be esteemed, respected, and popular anywhere, no matter whether he was among Christians or cannibals."

A rare painting of the clipper ship *Hornet*.

During the 1860's, clipper ships advertised their merits and announced their sailing dates in cards like this. The *Hornet,* built in New York in 1851, beat the famous *Flying Cloud* in the closest sailing match in clipper history. They raced from New York to San Francisco by way of Cape Horn, arriving in 105 days, with the *Hornet* only 40 minutes ahead of her rival.

change, but it remains the same. For me its balmy airs are always blowing, its summer seas flashing in the sun, the pulsing of its surf-beat is in my ear; I can see its garlanded crags, its leaping cascades, its plumy palms drowsing by the shore, its remote summits floating like islands above the cloud rack; I can feel the spirit of its woodland solitudes, I can hear the splash of its brooks; in my nostrils still lives the breath of flowers that perished twenty years ago."

MARK TWAIN'S NEWSPAPER SCOOP

On June 21, 1866, an open boat with fifteen starving seamen washed up on a Hawaiian beach. For forty-three days, with only ten days' provisions, the men had been smashed about on a stormy sea. Their clipper ship, the *Hornet,* had taken fire with a cargo of kerosene aboard and burned to the line. Mark Twain, just back from his island tour, was bedded with boils, but he saw his chance for a great story if he could interview the castaways and get a dispatch aboard a ship sailing for San Francisco the next morning. With Anson Burlingame's help, Twain was carried on a cot to the Honolulu hospital. While the American minister to China questioned the survivors, Mark took notes. Then he stayed awake through the night to write the story of the struggle to survive six weeks of drifting across 4,000 miles of open sea. In the morning, just as the ship cast off for California, Mark's story was flung aboard. He had produced a sensational newspaper scoop, one of the biggest in history.

Mark Twain's account of the *Hornet* disaster was carried safely to the States and on July 19, 1866, the Sacramento *Union* spread it across four columns of the front page. The suffering of the *Hornet*'s crew, and their heroism, created a sensation and added to Twain's fame. On the day the story was published Mark sailed from Hawaii—never to return—and 25 days later he was back in San Francisco. Awaiting him was a $300 bonus for the scoop.

EASTWARD BOUND.—The steamship *America*, for San Juan del Sur this morning, carries the following Eastward bound passengers:

Mark Twain, [Correspondent of the ALTA,]
P. W. Hermans,
J. A. Cornington,
H. Sutherland,
J. Delano and wife,
C. Dowe and wife,
C. C. Reynolds,
N. B. Bartlet and wife,
F. Sylvester,
J. Alexander,
Brown Bryant,
Mrs. Walter,
J. W. Gunn,
W. Holbrook,
L. L. Warner,
G. L. Sammins,
C. J. Thorp,
G. W. Thompson,
A. Dreyfouss,
R. Gillmore and wife,
Edward Stanton,
H. Freedman,
P. P. Street,
Mrs. J. C. Whipple and child,
D. K. Lewis,
H. M. Ross and wife,
R. H. Thayer,
Col. E. L. Kinney,
P. P. Smith,
Dr. C. Luther, wf and 4 ch,
W. Siebert,
W. A. Foss,
E. C. Moore,
W. L. Wilson,
G. W. Goff,
H. J. Kingman,
J. Prince,
Mrs. F. F. Butler and child,
Miss F. Butler,
J. M. Standifer,
Jas. Dunlap, wf. and ch.,
E. D. Fisher,
J. H. River,
A. B. Walker, wife and child,
N. Yost,
W. Whittey,
J. P. Mourand,
E. Wilder,
C. B. Fleming,
E. A. Irving,
C. J. Cobb,
A. A. Warner,
A. E. Scott and wife,
J. Bodine,
G. L. Miller,
A. H. Nolan,
C. C. Parker,
J. A. Carpenter,
B. Bryant,
C. L. Curtis,
Mrs. M. Witty,
Mrs. E. Farley,
R. G. Lewis,
Miss Madeline Perry,
E. F. Cooper and wife,
Capt. Thomas Snow,
Mrs. F. Straight,
J. Brock,
Col. A. M. Woolkfolk,
P. H. Rea,
J. Gibbons,
Jas. Thomas and wife,
Edward Lewin,
R. H. Prince.

The San Francisco shipping news on December 15, 1866, carried this passenger list of the steamer *America*. Mark Twain's name leads all the rest. "My room is the choicest in the ship," he wrote his mother. "I know all the officers."

Captain Ned Wakeman was skipper of the *America*, and one of the most colorful seafarers of Mark Twain's day. He is reincarnated in several of Twain's characters: Captain Ned Blakely, Captain Stormfield, and Captain Hurricane Jones. Wakeman died in 1875.

EASTWARD BOUND: SO LONG, BRIGANDS!

"Sailed from San Francisco in Opposition [Line] steamer *America*, Capt. Wakeman, at noon, 15th December, 1866. Pleasant sunny day, hills brightly clad with green grass and shrubbery." So ran the entry in Mark's notebook that day. On his calendar was a trip around the world, commissioned this time by the *Alta California*. But first he would go home. Over five years ago he had left home, an obscure secretary to his brother Orion, a former printer and pilot. Now, at thirty-one, he had added miner, reporter and lecturer to his professions, and was no longer plain Sam Clemens of Hannibal, but famous Mark Twain—"The Wild Humorist of the Pacific Slope" and "The Moralist of the Main."

The first seven letters Mark sent the *Alta* described the *America*'s adventurous voyage south from San Francisco, through hurricane seas to San Juan del Sur in Nicaragua. The trip was enlivened by Captain Wakeman's stunning forecastle yarns, told with a defiance of grammar and flights of fancy swearing that filled Mark with admiration. The passengers left the ship and crossed the Isthmus to catch the steamer *San Francisco* on the Atlantic side. Only a day out at sea cholera appeared and the passage north became a horror. The sheeted corpses were buried at sea, day after day; when the cholera-stricken ship stopped at Key West, many terrified passengers deserted. Finally, at eight in the morning on January 12, 1867, the *San Francisco* sailed past snow-covered Staten Island and Mark beheld again vast New York spread out beyond, "encircled with its palisades of masts, and adorned with its hundred steeples."

San Juan del Sur, the Pacific terminus of the route across Nicaragua. Mark's letters to the *Alta* described his visit to the town on his way across the Isthmus and then up to New York in 1867.

CAPTAIN NED WAKEMAN

Captain Edgar ("Ned") Wakeman was one of the "most winning and delightful" people Mark ever met. "I'd rather travel with that old portly, hearty, jolly, boisterous, good-natured sailor . . . than with any other man I've ever come across," runs one jotting in

This letter to the *Alta California* was Mark's parting shot at Steve Gillis and the *Enterprise* cronies who had staged a fake robbery in November, taking a carpetbag of silver from him at the point of a gun as he was on his way back from a lecture. This was one joke he didn't see, but he finally forgave the "brigands."

SO-LONG.

Editors Alta: I leave for the States in the Opposition steamer to-morrow, and I ask, as a special favor, that you will allow me to say good-bye to my highway-robber friends of the Gold Hill and Virginia Divide, and convince them that I have got ahead of them. They had their joke in robbing me and returning the money, and I had mine in the satisfaction of knowing that they came near freezing to death while they were waiting two hours for me to come along the night of the robbery. And at this day, so far from bearing them any ill will, I want to thank them kindly for their rascality. I am pecuniarily ahead on the transaction. I got a telegram from New York, last night, which reads as follows:

"New York, December 12th.

" *Mark Twain:* Go to Nudd, Lord & Co., Front street, collect amount of money equal to what highwaymen took from you. (Signed.) A. D. N."

I took that telegram and went to that store and called for a thousand dollars, with my customary modesty; but when I found they were going to pay it, my conscience smote me and I reduced the demand to a hundred. It was promptly paid, in coin, and now if the robbers think they have got the best end of that joke, they are welcome—they have my free consent to go on thinking so. (It is barely possible that the best of the joke is on A. D. N., now.)

Good-bye, felons—good-bye. I bear you no malice. And I sincerely pray that when your cheerful career is closing, and you appear finally before a delighted and appreciative audience to be hanged, that you will be prepared to go, and that it will be as a ray of sunshine amid the gathering blackness of your damning recollections, to call to mind that you never got a cent out of me. So-long, brigands.

MARK TWAIN.

the Twain notebook. This by no means exhausted Mark's store of adjectives, as the following tribute from his memoirs indicates:

"I first knew Capt. Wakeman thirty-nine years ago. I made two voyages with him and we became fast friends. He was a great burly, handsome, weatherbeaten, symmetrically built and powerful creature, with coal-black hair and whiskers and the kind of eye which men obey without talking back. He was full of human nature, and the best kind of human and loving a soul as I have found anywhere and when his temper was up he performed all the functions of an earthquake, without the noise.

"He was all sailor from head to heel; and this was proper enough, for he was born at sea and in the course of his sixty-five years he had visited the edges of all the continents and archipelagoes, but had never been on land except incidentally and spasmodically, as you may say. He had never had a day's schooling in his life but had picked up worlds and worlds of knowledge at secondhand, and none of it correct. He was a liberal talker and inexhaustibly interesting. In the matter of a wide and catholic profanity he had not his peer on the planet while he lived. It was a deep pleasure to me to hear him do his stunts in this line. He knew the Bible by heart and was profoundly and sincerely religious. He was always studying the Bible when it was his watch below and always finding new things, fresh things, and unexpected delights and surprises in it—and he loved to talk about his discoveries and expound them to the ignorant. He believed that he was the only man on the globe that really knew the secret of the Biblical miracles. He had what he believed was a sane and rational explanation of every one of them, and he loved to teach his learning to the less fortunate."

81

key is bound to make a temperance man of a toper in a year or kill him.) If you order a glass of champagne, you must pay for the whole bottle. Peanuts, hickory nuts and roast chestnuts are twenty cents a pint—say $25 a bushel—used to be worth two or three dollars. A choice seat in the theatre costs $1.50, and I suppose they would tax you to let you blow your nose any-

NEW YORK: A SPLENDID DESERT

Safe ashore at last, the *Alta*'s correspondent took rooms on East 16th Street and began to explore the city he had not seen since 1853:

"The town is all changed since I was here, thirteen years ago, when I was a pure and sinless sprout. The streets wind in and out, and this way and that way, in the most bewildering fashion, and two of them will suddenly come together and clamp the last house between them so close, and whittle the end of it down so sharp, that it looms up like the bow of a steamship, and you have to shut one eye to see it. The streets are so crooked in the lower end of town that if you take one and follow it faithfully you will eventually fetch up right where you started from. . . .

"They have increased the population of New York and its suburbs a quarter of a million souls. They have built up her waste places with acres upon acres of costly buildings. They have made five thousand men wealthy, and for a good round million of her citizens they have made it a matter of the closest kind of scratching to get along in the several spheres of life to which they belong. The brown-stone fronter and the rag-picker of the Five Points have about an even thing of it; the times are as hard for one as for the other; both struggle desperately to hold their places, and both grumble and grieve to much the same tune. What advantage there is, though, is all in favor of the rag-picker—he can only starve or freeze, but the other can lose caste, which is worse. . . .

"Everything is high. You pay $20 to $25 and $30 a week for the same sort of private board and lodging you got for $8 and $10 when I was here thirteen years ago. You can board and lodge at the best hotels in the city for the same money—$4.50 a day. Still, both the hotels and the boarding houses are all full. Crossing-sweeps demand toll going and coming, both. An old woman had a pea-nut shelf in a contracted corner—rent, $25 a month; they raised her to $50; she stood the raise and continued business; then they raised her to $75, and this time they raised her out. . . . Simple, 'straight' whiskey, gin, and such things, are fifteen cents; brandy and mixed beverages, twenty-five, (and they don't know how to mix them—besides their whis-

Mark Twain, from an engraving of 1868.

where within the city limits. Hackmen charge you $2.50 to take you around the block, or $10 to $12 a day. Late at night they charge you what they please. Pew rent is just about as high as house rent. Therefore, few men can afford to indulge in matrimony and religion both. In a word, I find that with due moderation, a single man can get along after a fashion for forty to fifty dollars a week. God help the married ones. . . .

"New Yorkers are singular people, somehow, or other. Here, in their own home, they have the name among strangers of being excessively unsociable; but take them in any part of the world, outside their State limits, and they are the most liberal, pleasant and companionable people you can find. . . .

"I have at last, after several months' experience, made up my mind that it is a splendid desert—a domed and steepled solitude, where the stranger is lonely in the midst of a million of his race. A man walks his tedious miles through the same interminable street every day, elbowing his way through a buzzing multitude of men, yet never seeing a familiar face, and never seeing a strange one the second time. He visits a friend once—it is a day's journey—and then stays away from that time forward till that friend cools to a mere acquaintance, and finally a stranger. So there is little sociability, and, consequently, there is little cordiality. Every man seems to feel that he has got the duties of two lifetimes to accomplish in one, and so he rushes, rushes, rushes, and never has time to be companionable—never has any time at his disposal to fool away on matters which do not involve dollars and duty and business.

"All this has a tendency to make the city-bred man impatient of interruption, suspicious of strangers and fearful of being bored, and his business interfered with. The natural result is, that the striking want of heartiness observable here sometimes even among old friends, degenerates into something which is hardly even chilly politeness towards strangers. There is something about this ceaseless buzz, and hurry, and bustle, that keeps a stranger in a state of unwholesome excitement all the time, and makes him restless and uneasy, and saps from him all capacity to enjoy anything or take a strong interest in any matter whatever —something which impels him to try to do everything, and yet permits him to do nothing. He is a boy in a candy-shop—could choose quickly if there were but one kind of candy, but is hopelessly undetermined in the midst of a hundred kinds. A stranger feels unsatisfied, here, a good part of the time. He starts to a library; changes, and moves toward a theatre; changes again and thinks he will visit a friend; goes within a biscuit-toss of a picture-gallery, a billiard-room, a beercellar and a circus, in succession, and finally drifts home and to bed, without having really done anything or gone anywhere. He don't go anywhere because he can't go everywhere, I suppose. This fidgetty, feverish restlessness will drive a man crazy, after a while, or kill him. It kills a good many dozens now—by suicide. I have got to get out of it."

On March 2, 1867, Mark left New York for a visit to Missouri. In St. Louis he found the women petitioning the legislature for the right to vote. With 39 lawmakers already won to the feminists' cause, Mark wrote the *Alta*, "It is time for all good men to tremble for their country." He dashed off three articles for the St. Louis *Democrat*, ridiculing the women's rights movement. One of the pieces, reprinted in the *Alta*, is shown here. Attacking "the monster" in the public prints, Mark wrote, "raised a small female storm, but it occurred to me that it might get uncommon warm for one poor devil against all the crinoline in the camp, and so I anted up and passed out, as the Sabbath School children say."

"MARK TWAIN" ON FEMALE SUFFRAGE.

"The Iniquitous Crusade Against Man's Regal Birthright must be Crushed."

DEAR COUSIN JENNIE: I did not know I had a cousin named Jennie, but I am proud to claim such a relationship with you. I have no idea who you are, but you talk well—you talk exceedingly well. You seem inclined to treat the question of female suffrage seriously, and for once I will drop foolishness, and speak with the gravity the occasion demands. You fully understand the difference between justice and expediency? I am satisfied you do. You know very well that it would have been a righteous act if we had rescued struggling Poland four or five years ago; but you know also that it would not have been good policy to do it. No one will say that it is not just and right that women should vote; no one will say that an educated American woman would not vote with fifty times the judgment and independence exercised by stupid, illiterate newcomers from foreign lands; I will even go so far myself as to say that in my experience only third-rate intelligence is sent to Legislatures to make laws, because the first-rate article will not leave important private interests go unwatched to go and serve the public for a beggarly four or five dollars a day, and a miserably trivial distinction, while it is possible that a talented matron, unincumbered with children, might go with no great detriment to the affairs of her household. We know also that between constable and United States Senator, the one thousand offices of mere honor (though burdened with high responsibilities), are held by third-rate ability because first-rate ability can only afford to hold offices of great emolument—and we know that first-rate female talent *could* afford to hold those offices of mere honor without making business sacrifices. You see I have made a very strong argument for your side; and I repeat that no one will deny the truth of any of the above propositions; but behold that matter of expediency comes in here—policy!

Now, you think I am going to string out a long argument on my own side, but I am not. I only say this: The ignorant foreign women would vote with the ignorant foreign men; the bad women would vote with the bad men; the good women would vote with the good men. The same candidate who would be elected now would be elected then, the only difference being that there might be twice as many votes polled then as now. Then in what respect is the condition of things improved? I cannot see.

So, I conceive that if nothing is to be gained by it, it is inexpedient to extend the suffrage to women. That must be a benefit beyond the power of figures to estimate which can make us consent to take the High Priestess we reverence at the sacred fireside and send her forth to electioneer for votes among a mangy mob who are unworthy to touch the hem of her garment. A lady of my acquaintance came very near putting my feeling in this matter into words the other day, Jennie, when she said she was opposed to female suffrage, because she was not willing to see her sex reduced to a level with negroes and men!

Female suffrage would do harm, my dear—it would actually do harm. A very large proportion of our best and wisest women would still cling to the holy ground of the home circle, and refuse to either vote or hold office—but every grand rascal among your sex would work, bribe and vote with all her might; and, behold, mediocrity and dishonesty would be appointed to conduct the affairs of Government more surely than ever before. You see the policy of the thing is bad, very bad. It would augment the strength of the bad vote. I consider it a very strong point on our side of the question.

I think I could write a pretty strong argument in favor of female suffrage, but I do not want to do it. I never want to see women voting, and gabbling about politics, and electioneering. There is something revolting in the thought. It would shock me inexpressibly for an angel to come down from above and ask me to take a drink with him (though I should doubtless consent); but it would shock me still more to see one of our blessed earthly angels peddling election tickets among a mob of shabby scoundrels she never saw before.

There is one insuperable obstacle in the way of female suffrage, Jennie; I approach the subject with fear and trembling, but it must out: A woman would never vote, because she would have to tell her age at the polls. And even if she did dare to vote once or twice when she was just of age, you know what dire results would flow from "putting this and that together" in after times. For instance, in an unguarded moment, Miss A. says she voted for Mr. Smith. Her auditor, who knows that it has been seven years since Smith ran for anything, easily ciphers out that she is at least seven years over age, instead of the tender young pullet she has been making herself out to be. No, Jennie, this new fashion of registering the name, age, residence and occupation of every voter, is a fatal bar to female suffrage.

Women will never be permitted to vote or hold office, Jennie, and it is a lucky thing for me, and for many other men, that such is the decree of fate. Because, you see, there are some few measures they would all unite on—there are one or two measures that would bring out their entire voting strength, in spite of their antipathy to making themselves

A playbill for an 1867 performance of *The Black Crook!* The New York *Times* called it "a story of sorcery, demonism and wickedness generally." The alluring spectacle was to run 40 years in various forms. On opening night, September 17, 1866, the show ran from 7:45 to 1:15, and everyone stayed "until the gorgeous end."

LAYING SIEGE TO PUBLIC MORALS

Mark wasted little time in getting up to Niblo's Garden where the most elaborate and sensational musical in the town's history was in its sixth month. His vivid report to the *Alta* readers must have set many Californians packing for a trip east:

"I warn you that when they put beautiful clipper-built girls on the stage in this new fashion, with only just barely clothes enough on to be tantalizing, it is a shrewd invention of the devil. It lays a heavier siege to public morals than all the legitimate model artist shows you can bring into action.

"The name of this new exhibition that so touches my missionary sensibilities, is the 'Black Crook.' The scenic effects—the waterfalls, cascades, fountains, oceans, fairies, devils, hells, heavens, angels—are gorgeous beyond anything ever witnessed in America, perhaps, and these things attract the women and the girls. Then the endless ballets and splendid tableaux, with seventy beauties arrayed in dazzling half-costumes, and displaying all possible compromises between nakedness and decency, capture the men and boys —and so Niblo's has taken in twenty-four hundred dollars a night, (seven nights and a matinee a week,) for five months, and sometimes twenty-seven hundred dollars.

". . . The scenery and the legs are everything; the actors who do the talking are the wretchedest sticks on the boards. But the fairy scenes—they fascinate the boys! Beautiful bare-legged girls hanging in flower baskets; others stretched in groups on great sea shells; others clustered around fluted columns; others in all possible attitudes; girls—nothing but a wilderness of girls—stacked up, pile on pile, away aloft to the dome of the theatre, diminishing the size and clothing, till the last row, mere children, dangle high up from invisible ropes, arrayed only in camisa. The whole tableau resplendent with columns, scrolls, and a vast ornamental work, wrought in gold, silver and brilliant colors—all lit up with gorgeous theatrical fires, and witnessed through a great gauzy curtain that counterfeits a soft silver mist! It is the wonders of the Arabian Nights realized.

"Those girls dance in ballet, dressed with a meagreness that would make a parasol blush. And they prance around and expose themselves in a way that is scandalous to me. Moreover, they come trooping on the stage in platoons and battalions, in most princely attire I grant you, but always with more tights in view than anything else. They change their clothes every fifteen

Josephine Invernezzi was one of the "bewitchingly beautiful" ballerinas of *The Black Crook!* which dazzled Mark Twain and millions of others. As the *Tribune* put it, "Children cry for it. Countrymen coming to town clamor for it, and will not be comforted unless they see it. The rural visitor, in fact, divides his time between Niblo's Garden and Trinity Church, and certainly sees a good deal at both places." This photo publicized the dancer in *The White Fawn,* which the producers rushed to the stage in imitation of their first smash hit.

minutes for four hours, and their dresses become more beautiful and more rascally all the time.

"Edwin Booth and the legitimate drama still draw immense houses, but the signs of the times convince me that he will have to make a little change by-and-by and peel some women. Nothing else can chain the popular taste, the way things are going now."

A month later, it was P. T. Barnum's turn:

"Now that Barnum is running for Congress, anything connected with him is imbued with a new interest. Therefore I went to his Museum yesterday, along with the other children. There is little or nothing in the place worth seeing, and yet how it draws! It was crammed with both sexes and all ages. One could keep on going up stairs from floor to floor, and still find scarcely room to turn. There are numerous trifling attractions there, but if there was one grand, absorbing feature, I failed to find it.

"Barnum's Museum is one vast peanut stand, now, with a few cases of dried frogs and other wonders scattered here and there, to give variety to the thing.

"There are some cages of ferocious lions, and other wild beasts, but they sleep all the time. And also an automatic card writer; but something about it is broken, and it don't go now. Also, a good many bugs, with pins stuck through them; but the people do not seem to enjoy bugs any more. In some large glass cases are some atrocious waxen images, done in the very worst style of the art. Queen Victoria is dressed in faded red velvet and glass jewelry, and has a bloated countenance and a drunken leer in her eye, that remind one of convivial Mary Holt, when she used to come in from a spree to get her ticket for the County Jail. And that accursed eye-sore to me, Tom Thumb's wedding party, which airs its smirking imbecility in every photograph album in America, is not only set forth here in ghastly wax, but repeated! Why does not some philanthropist burn the Museum again?"

Barnum's New Museum, at 539 Broadway, was "one vast peanut stand" to Mark. In the Congressional race Mark refers to on this page, Barnum, a Republican candidate in Connecticut, was beaten by a Democrat, also named Barnum.

Charles Henry Webb. In his two years as a journalist in San Francisco he met Mark Twain. Returning to New York, Webb put 27 of Mark's California pieces into a book, with the "Frog" as lead-off sketch. By a nice coincidence the printer was Gray and Green, the same shop Mark had set type for 13 years earlier.

THE GORGEOUS GOLD JUMPING FROG

The publication of Mark Twain's first book on May 1, 1867 (not April 25), was a big event to the author, of course. He didn't mind using his *Alta* letters for personal publicity. He got in everything but an order form:

"Webb ('Inigo') has fixed up a volume of my sketches and he and the American News Company will publish it on Thursday, the 25th of the present month. He has gotten it up in elegant style, and has done everything to suit his own taste, which is excellent. I have made no suggestions. He calls it 'The Celebrated Jumping Frog, and Other Sketches, by "Mark Twain." Edited by C. H. Webb.' Its price is $1.50 a copy. It will have a truly gorgeous gold frog on the back of it, and that frog alone will be worth the money. I don't know but what it would be well to publish the frog and leave the book out. Mail your orders either to C. H. Webb or the American News Company, New York."

Here's the *Frog* again—eleven days later:

"Webb has gotten up my 'Jumping Frog' book in excellent style, and it is selling rapidly. A lot of copies will go to San Francisco per this steamer. I hope my friends will all buy a few copies each, and more especially am I anxious to see the book in the Sunday

School Libraries in the land. I don't know that it would instruct youth much, but it would make them laugh anyway, and therefore no Sunday School Library can be complete without the 'Jumping Frog.' But candidly, now, joking aside, it is really a very handsome book, and you know yourself that it is a very readable one. I have sent a copy to Honolulu for my old friend, Father Damon."

To Bret Harte, the new author wrote:

"The book . . . is full of damnable errors of grammar and deadly inconsistencies of spelling in the Frog sketch, because I was away and did not read proofs; but be a friend and say nothing about these things. When my hurry is over, I will send you a copy to pisen the children with."

A NIGHT IN JAIL

As Mark told the readers of the *Alta,* he once spent a night in jail. Coming home with a friend around midnight, he saw two men fighting in the street and tried to separate them. The police came up and hauled all four off to the Station House. Describing the experience, Mark wrote:

"I have been in the Station House. I staid there all night. I don't mind mentioning it, because anybody can get into the Station House here without commit-

Title page of *Sut Lovingood,* in the edition Mark reviewed.

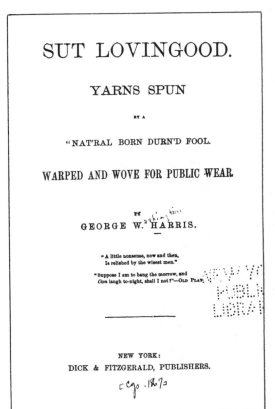

The Black Maria depositing prisoners at the foot of 26th street, where they embarked for Blackwell's Island. These were "the rascals and unfortunates" Mark spent a night in jail with in 1867.

ting an offence of any kind. And so he can anywhere that policemen are allowed to cumber the earth. I complimented this police force in a letter some time ago, and felt like a guilty, degraded wretch when I was doing it, and now I am glad I got into the Station House, because it will teach me never to so far forget all moral principle as to compliment a police force again.

"They put us in separate cells, and I enjoyed the thing considerably for an hour or so, looking through the bars at the dilapidated old hags, and battered and ragged bummers, sorrowing and swearing in the stone-paved halls, but it got rather tiresome after a while. I fell asleep on my stone bench at 3 o'clock, and was called at dawn and marched to the Police Court with a vile policeman at each elbow, just as if I had been robbing a church, or saying a complimentary word about the police, or doing some other supernaturally mean thing.

"At 9 o'clock we went out, one by one, under guard, and stood up before the Judge. I consulted with him about the practicability of contesting my case on the ground of unjust imprisonment, but he said it would be troublesome, and not worth the bother, inasmuch as nobody would ever know I had been in the Station House unless I told it myself, and then he let me go. I staid by and watched them dispense justice a while—

observed that in all small offenses the policeman's charge on the books was received as entirely sufficient, and sentence passed without a question being asked of either accused or witnesses—and then departed, glad I had been in the Station House, because I knew all about it now from personal experience, but not anxious to pursue my investigations any further in that line."

SUT LOVINGOOD

"It was reported, years ago, that this writer was dead—accidentally shot in a Tennessee doggery before the war; but he has turned up again, and is a conductor on a railway train that travels somewhere between Charleston, S.C., and Memphis. His real name is George Harris. I have before me his book, just forwarded by Dick & Fitzgerald, the publishers, New York. It contains all his early sketches, that used to be so popular in the West, such as his story of his father 'actin' hoss,' the lizards in the camp-meeting, etc., together with many new ones. The book abounds in humor, and is said to represent the Tennessee dialect correctly. It will sell well in the West, but the Eastern people will call it coarse and possibly taboo it."

87

SUNDAY AMUSEMENT:
HENRY WARD BEECHER

Mark ran into the local blue laws when he looked about for fun on a Sunday: "You cannot get a taste of the villainous wines and liquors of New York on the Sabbath, for love or money. And all possible places of amusement and public resort are closed up also. The town looks dead and deserted. I could not even find a bootblack yesterday, or a newsboy, or a place where I could buy a newspaper. What was left for me to do? Simply to follow the fashionable mania, and go to church. You cannot imagine what an infatuation church-going has become in New York. Youths and young misses, young gentlemen and ladies, the middle-aged and the old, all swarm to church, morning, noon and night every Sunday. They brave miles of stormy weather to worship and sing praises at the altar, and criticise each other's costumes."

One Sunday, "in a pious frenzy" himself, Mark went over to Brooklyn to see the Reverend Henry Ward Beecher preach:

"Mr. Beecher's altar is an elevated, carpeted, un-railed platform—a sort of stage—with a little pedestal at its front edge for a pulpit. Mr. B. sat in a chair against the wall, his head and body inclining back-ward, with the comfortable air of a manager who has got a good house and expected it. The choir over his head sang charmingly, and then he got up and preached one of the liveliest and most sensible ser-mons I ever listened to. He has a rich, resonant voice, and a distinct enunciation, and makes himself heard all over the church without very apparent effort. His discourse sparkled with felicitous similes and meta-phors (it is his strong suit to use the language of the worldly,) and might be called a striking mosaic work, wherein poetry, pathos, humor, satire and eloquent declamation were happily blended upon a ground work of earnest exposition of the great truths involved in his text.

"Whenever he forsook his notes and went marching up and down his stage, sawing his arms in the air, hurling sarcasms this way and that, discharging rock-ets of poetry, and exploding mines of eloquence, halt-

Henry Ward Beecher in the pulpit, drawn by Thomas Nast. Beecher was pastor of Plymouth Church of Brooklyn from 1847 to his death in 1887. Mark was to cross paths with many of the Beecher clan from this time forward.

ing now and then to stamp his foot three times in suc-cession to emphasize a point, I could have started the audience with a single clap of the hands and brought down the house. I had a suffocating desire to do it.

"Mr. Beecher is a remarkably handsome man when he is in the full tide of sermonizing, and his face is lit up with animation, but he is as homely as a singed cat when he isn't doing anything."

ENOUGH OF SIGHTS AND SHOWS—
I AM READY TO GO!

In his last New York letter, Mark said he had done the big city from end to end, and had had enough. In a farewell paragraph he summarized post-Civil War New York:

"I have a large share of curiosity, but I believe it

is satisfied for the present. I have seen the horse 'Dexter' trot a race—but then I know but little about horses, and I did not appreciate the exhibition; I was present at the great annual meeting of the Quakers a week ago, but between you and I it was excessively dull; I went to a billiard tournament where Phelan and McDevitt played, but I knew beforehand what to expect, and so there was no chance to get up a revivifying astonishment; I have been to three Sunday Schools and have heard all the great guns of the New York pulpit preach, and so that department is exhausted; I have been through the dens of poverty, crime and degradation that hide from the light of day in the Five Points and infinitely worse localities—but I, even I, can blush, and must decline to describe them; I have been in the Bible House, and also in the Station House—pleasant experiences of a day, but nothing worth for a second visit; I have gone the rounds of the newspaper offices and the theatres, and have contrasted the feverish turmoil of Broadway with the still repose of Greenwood Cemetery; I have seen Barnum's Museum, and time and again have looked upon the summer loveliness of Central Park and stood upon its high grounds and wondered how any landscape could be so beautiful as that which stretches abroad right and left over Jersey and far up the river, and yet have no sign of a mountain about it; I have seen Brooklyn, and the ferry-boats, and the *Dunderberg,* and the bootblacks, and Staten Island, and Peter Cooper, and the Fifth Avenue, and the Academy of Design, and Rosa Bonheur's Horse Fair; and have compared the noble architecture of Old Trinity church with the cluster of painted shower baths, they call young Dr. Tyng's church (they don't dare to call it the church of God, notwithstanding it has got a safety-iron fence on its roof, and sixty-two lightning rods,) and behold I have tried the Russian bath, and skated while the winter was here, and did contract to go up in a balloon, but the balloon didn't go. I have seen all there was to see—even the 'Black Crook'—and yet, I say it, that shouldn't say it—all is vanity! There has been a sense of something lacking, something wanting, every time—and I guess that something was the provincial quietness I am used to. I have had enough of sights and shows, and noise and bustle, and confusion, and now I want to disperse. I am ready to go."

Harry Hill's dance hall, or "Concert Saloon." It was at 26 East Houston Street, and featured liquor, music, dancing, girls, and prize fights. Mark Twain's last letter in the *Alta* series described a night at Harry's, "one of the worst dens in all New York."

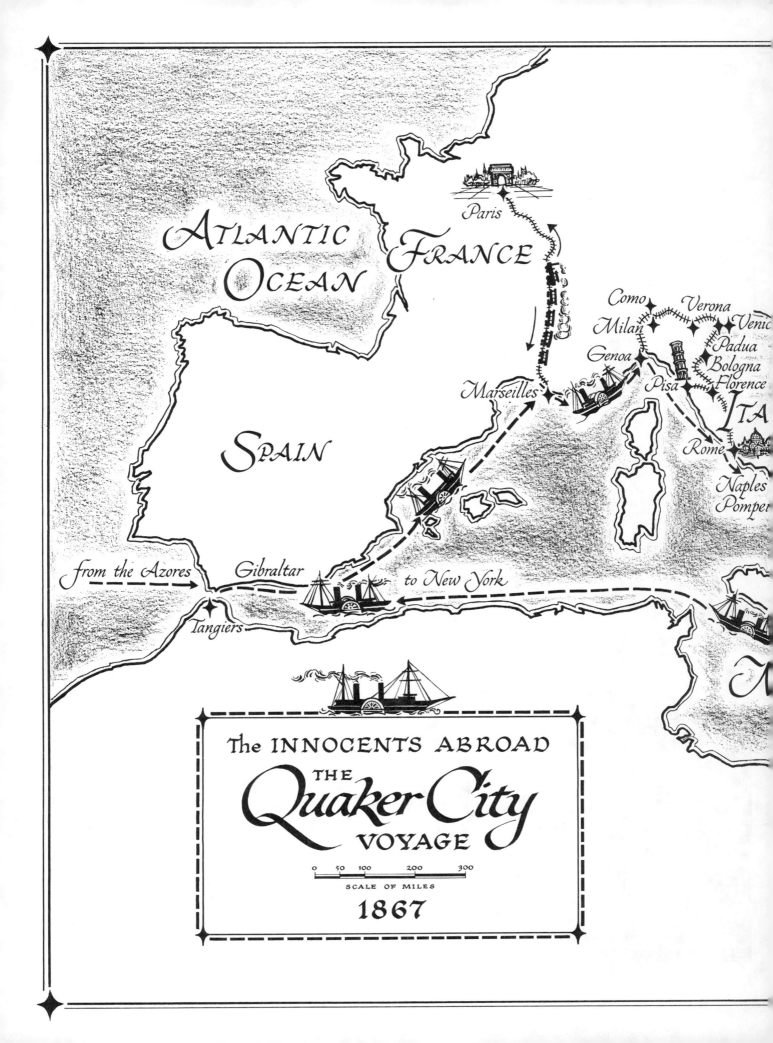

THE HOLY LAND EXCURSION.

LETTER FROM "MARK TWAIN."

[SPECIAL TRAVELLING CORRESPONDENT OF THE ALTA.]

[Number Two.]

The Flag in a Foreign Land---The Gate of the Mediterranean---Impregnable Gibraltar---Sight Seeing---Geologic and Historic---Portrait of an Old Acquaintance---Other Portraits---Brown Redivivus.

GIBRALTAR, June 30th.
Land Ho!

EDITORS ALTA: All hands were called on deck at ten o'clock this morning by the news that land was in sight. Within the hour we were fairly within the Strait of Gibraltar, with the tall yellow-splotched hills of Africa on our right, with their bases vailed in a blue haze and their summits swathed in clouds —the same being according to Scripture, which says that "clouds and darkness are over the land." The words were spoken of this particular portion of Africa, I believe. On our left were the granite-ribbed domes of old Spain. The Strait is only thirteen miles wide in its narrowest part.

At short intervals, along the Spanish shore, were quaint looking old stone towers—Moorish, we thought, but learned better afterwards. In former times the Morocco rascals used to coast along the Spanish Main in their boats till a safe opportunity seemed to present itself, and then dart in and capture a Spanish village, and carry off all the pretty women they could find. It was a pleasant business, and was very popular. The Spaniards built these watch-towers on the hills to enable them to keep a sharper lookout on the Moroccan speculators.

It was a bright, breezy morning, and the picture on either hand was very beautiful to eyes weary of the changeless sea. The ship's company were uncommonly cheerful. But while we stood admiring the cloud-capped peaks and the lowlands robed in misty gloom, a finer picture burst upon us and chained every eye like a magnet—a stately ship, with canvas piled on canvas till she was one towering mass of bellying sail! She came speeding over the sea like a great bird. Africa and Spain were forgotten. All homage was for the beautiful stranger. While everybody gazed, she swept grandly by and flung the Stars and Stripes to the breeze! Quicker than thought, hats and handkerchiefs flashed in the air, and a cheer went up! She was beautiful before—she was radiant now. Many a one on our decks knew then for the first time

THE INNOCENTS ABROAD OR THE NEW PILGRIM'S PROGRESS

The idea for the first pleasure cruise from America to the old country sprang up in Henry Ward Beecher's church. Mark heard of it when the excursion was advertised on February 1, 1867. He got the *Alta*'s editors to send him as correspondent. The paper paid the $1,250 passage and promised twenty dollars apiece for his letters. There were a dozen other reporters aboard the side-wheeler when she steamed out of New York on June 8. A good many of the sixty-seven passengers turned out to be clergy, and most of them considerably older than Mark. But he found a batch of carefree younger spirits who helped make the junket both frolic and adventure. What Mark saw and did in those five months abroad was transmuted into almost a quarter of a million words. He sent fifty-three letters to the *Alta*, six to the New York *Tribune* and three to the New York *Herald*. No traveler was ever busier.

Almost twenty months after the celebrated voyage of

The second letter from "Mark Twain—Special Travelling Correspondent of the Alta"—was printed with these headlines.

This steel engraving of the *Quaker City* in a storm was the frontispiece in the first edition of *The Innocents Abroad*.

the *Quaker City,* Mark Twain's *The Innocents Abroad* was published. In the opening pages he conveyed the exciting promise of the grand European pleasure trip:

"For months the great Pleasure Excursion to Europe and the Holy Land was chatted about in the newspapers every where in America, and discussed at countless firesides. It was a novelty in the way of Excursions—its like had not been thought of before, and it compelled that interest which attractive novelties always command. It was to be a picnic on a gigantic scale. The participants in it, instead of freighting an ungainly steam ferry-boat with youth and beauty and pies and doughnuts, and paddling up some obscure creek to disembark upon a grassy lawn and wear themselves out with a long summer day's laborious frolicking under the impression that it was fun, were to sail away in a great steamship with flags flying and cannon pealing, and take a royal holiday beyond the broad ocean, in many a strange clime and in many a land renowned in history! They were to sail for months over the breezy Atlantic and the sunny Mediterranean; they were to scamper about the decks by day, filling the ship with shouts and laughter—or read novels and poetry in the shade of the smoke-stacks, or watch for the jelly-fish and the nautilus, over the side, and the shark, the whale, and other strange monsters of the deep; and at night they were to dance in the open air, on the upper deck, in the midst of a ball-room that stretched from horizon to horizon, and was domed by the bending heavens and lighted by no meaner lamps than the stars and the magnificent moon—dance, and promenade, and smoke, and sing, and make love, and search the skies for constellations that never associate with the 'Big Dipper' they were so tired of; and they were to see the ships of twenty navies—the customs and costumes of twenty curious peoples—the great cities of half a world—they were to hob-nob with nobility and hold friendly converse with kings and princes, Grand Moguls, and the anointed lords of mighty empires!

"It was a brave conception; it was the offspring of a most ingenious brain. It was well advertised, but it hardly needed it: the bold originality, the extraordinary character, the seductive nature, and the vastness of the enterprise provoked comment every where and advertised it in every household in the land. Who could read the programme of the excursion without longing to make one of the party?"

Captain Charles C. Duncan commanded the *Quaker City*. Ten years after the cruise, Mark Twain would engage in a brief newspaper vendetta with the Captain.

Moses S. Beach, owner of the New York *Sun*. He and his young daughter Emma were favorites of Mark's on the trip.

Mrs. Mary Mason Fairbanks, correspondent on the *Quaker City* for her husband's newspaper, the Cleveland *Herald*. She made herself Mark's editor while on the trip and they became lasting friends. "She was the most refined, intelligent, and cultivated lady in the ship, and altogether the kindest and best. She sewed my buttons on, kept my clothes in presentable trim, fed me on Egyptian jam (when I behaved), lectured me awfully on the quarter-deck on moonlit promenading evenings, and cured me of several bad habits. I am under lasting obligations to her. She looks young, because she is so good. . . ." Although she was Mark's senior by only seven years, he called her "Mother Fairbanks" and for many years after continued to enjoy her attempts to dictate taste, manners, and morals.

Dan Slote was Mark's "splendid, immoral, tobacco-smoking, wine-drinking, godless roommate" on the ship. "As good and true and right-minded a man as ever lived," Mark said of him then; later he wouldn't be able to find strong enough words to damn the man.

Left: Frederick Greer, the "horse-laughing young fellow" Mark detested.

John Van Nostrand, a New Jerseyan who became the renowned "Jack" of the *Innocents*.

Above: Dr. E. Andrews was the know-it-all whom Mark pilloried in this illustration for the *Innocents*.

PARIS AND THE CAN-CAN

In Paris, the modest Mark got his first view of the can-can. . . . "The dance had begun, and we adjourned to the temple. Within it was a drinking-saloon; and all around it was a broad circular platform for the dancers. I backed up against the wall of the temple, and waited. Twenty sets formed, the music struck up, and then—I placed my hands before my face for very shame. But I looked through my fingers. They were dancing the renowned 'can-can.' A handsome girl in the set before me tripped forward lightly to meet the opposite gentleman—tripped back again, grasped her dresses vigorously on both sides with her hands, raised them pretty high, danced an extraordinary jig that had more activity and exposure about it than any jig I ever saw before, and then, drawing her clothes still higher, she advanced gaily to the center and launched a vicious kick full at her vis-a-vis that must infallibly have removed his nose if he had been seven feet high. It was a mercy he was only six.

"That is the can-can. The idea of it is to dance as wildly, as noisily, as furiously as you can; expose yourself as much as possible if you are a woman; and kick as high as you can, no matter which sex you belong to. There is no word of exaggeration in this. Any of the staid, respectable, aged people who were there that night can testify to the truth of that statement. There were a good many such people present. I suppose French morality is not of that strait-laced description which is shocked at trifles.

"I moved aside and took a general view of the can-can. Shouts, laughter, furious music, a bewildering chaos of darting and intermingling forms, stormy jerking and snatching of gay dresses, bobbing heads, flying arms, lightning flashes of white-stockinged calves and dainty slippers in the air, and then a grand final rush,

riot, a terrific hubbub, and a wild stampede! Heavens! Nothing like it has been seen on earth since trembling Tam O'Shanter saw the devil and the witches at their orgies that stormy night in 'Alloway's auld haunted kirk.' "

Last page of a letter Mark wrote home from Marseilles on July 12, 1867, reporting on a "gorgeous time" in Paris and so much excitement he couldn't sleep for 24 hours.

MONKS, MARTYRS, AND OLD MASTERS

Italy was "one vast museum of magnificence and misery" to Mark Twain. The traveler saw endless acres of art. He knew what he liked and did not hesitate to tell his readers about it:

"I ought not to confess it, but still, since one has no opportunity in America to acquire a critical judgment in art, and since I could not hope to become educated in it in Europe in a few short weeks, I may therefore as well acknowledge with such apologies as may be due, that to me it seemed that when I had seen one of these martyrs I had seen them all. They all have a marked family resemblance to each other, they dress alike, in coarse monkish robes and sandals, they are all bald-headed, they all stand in about the same attitude, and without exception they are gazing heavenward with countenances which the Ainsworths, the Mortons, and the Williamses, et fils, inform me are full of 'expression.' To me there is nothing tangible about these imaginary portraits, nothing that I can grasp and take a living interest in. If great Titian had only been gifted with prophecy, and had skipped a martyr, and gone over to England and painted a portrait of Shakespeare, even as a youth, which we could all have confidence in now, the world down to the latest generations would have forgiven him the lost martyr in the rescued seer. I think posterity could have spared one more martyr for the sake of a great historical picture of Titian's time and painted by his brush—such as Columbus returning in chains from the discovery of a world, for instance. The old masters did paint some Venetian historical pictures, and these we did not tire of looking at, notwithstanding representations of the formal introduction of defunct Doges to the Virgin Mary in regions beyond the clouds clashed rather harshly with the proprieties, it seemed to us.

"But, humble as we are, and unpretending, in the matter of art, our researches among the painted monks and martyrs have not been wholly in vain. We have striven hard to learn. We have had some success. We have mastered some things, possibly of trifling import in the eyes of the learned, but to us they give pleasure, and we take as much pride in our little acquirements as do others who have learned far more, and we love to display them full as well. When we see a monk going about with a lion and looking tranquilly up to heaven, we know that that is St. Mark. When

St. Mark, by the Old Masters.

St. Matthew, by the Old Masters.

St. Jerome, by the Old Masters.

St. Sebastian, by the Old Masters.

Art and captions from *The Innocents Abroad.*

St. Unknown, by the Old Masters.

we see a monk with a book and a pen, looking tranquilly up to heaven, trying to think of a word, we know that that is St. Matthew. When we see a monk sitting on a rock, looking tranquilly up to heaven, with a human skull beside him and without other baggage, we know that that is St. Jerome. Because we know that he always went flying light in the matter of baggage. When we see a party looking tranquilly up to heaven, unconscious that his body is shot through and through with arrows, we know that that is St. Sebastian. When we see other monks looking tranquilly up to heaven, but having no trademark, we always ask who those parties are. We do this because we humbly wish to learn. We have seen thirteen thousand St. Jeromes, and twenty-two thousand St. Marks, and sixteen thousand St. Matthews, and sixty thousand St. Sebastians, and four millions of assorted monks, undesignated, and we feel encouraged to believe that when we have seen some more of these various pictures, and had a larger experience, we shall begin to take an absorbing interest in them like our cultivated countrymen from Amerique.

"Now it does give me real pain to speak in this almost unappreciative way of the old masters and their martyrs, because good friends of mine in the ship—friends who do thoroughly and conscientiously appreciate them and are in every way competent to discriminate between good pictures and inferior ones—have urged me for my own sake not to make public the fact that I lack this appreciation and this critical discrimination myself. I believe that what I have written and may still write about pictures will give them pain, and I am honestly sorry for it. I even promised that I would hide my uncouth sentiments in my own breast. But alas! I never could keep a promise. I do not blame myself for this weakness, because the fault must lie in my physical organization.

It is likely that such a very liberal amount of space was given to the organ which enables me to make promises, that the organ which should enable me to keep them was crowded out. But I grieve not. I like no half-way things. I had rather have one faculty nobly developed than two faculties of mere ordinary capacity. I certainly meant to keep that promise, but I find I cannot do it. It is impossible to travel through Italy without speaking of pictures, and can I see them through others' eyes?

"If I did not so delight in the grand pictures that are spread before me every day of my life by that monarch of all the old masters, Nature, I should come to believe, sometimes, that I had in me no appreciation of the beautiful whatsoever."

INQUISITORS NEW AND OLD

"We look out upon many objects of interest from the dome of St. Peter's; and last of all, almost at our feet, our eyes rest upon the building which was once the Inquisition. How times changed, between the older ages and the new! Some seventeen or eighteen centuries ago, the ignorant men of Rome were wont to put Christians in the arena of the Coliseum yonder, and turn the wild beasts in upon them for a show. It was for a lesson as well. It was to teach the people to abhor and fear the new doctrine the followers of Christ were teaching. The beasts tore the victims limb from limb and made poor mangled corpses of them in the twinkling of an eye. But when the Christians came into power, when the holy Mother Church became mistress of the barbarians, she taught them the error of their ways by no such means. No, she put them in this pleasant Inquisition and pointed to the Blessed Redeemer, who was so gentle and so merciful toward all men, and they urged the barbarians to love him; and they did all they could to persuade them to love and honor him—first by twisting their thumbs out of joint with a screw; then by nipping their flesh with pincers—red-hot ones, because they are the most comfortable in cold weather; then by skinning them alive a little, and finally by roasting them in public. They always convinced those barbarians. The true religion, properly administered, as the good Mother Church used to administer it, is very, very soothing. It is wonderfully persuasive, also. There is a great difference between feeding parties to wild beasts and stirring up their finer feelings in an Inquisition. One is the system of degraded barbarians, the other of enlightened, civilized people. It is a great pity the playful Inquisition is no more."

TWAIN MEETS CZAR

When the *Quaker City* steamed into the Black Sea, Czar Alexander II welcomed the tourists to the imperial palace at Yalta. On August 26, 1867, Mark Twain met his first royalty:

"The Emperor wore a cap, frock-coat, and pantaloons, all of some kind of plain white drilling—cotton or linen—and sported no jewelry or any insignia whatever of rank. No costume could be less ostentatious. He is very tall and spare, and a determined-looking man, though a very pleasant-looking one, nevertheless. It is easy to see that he is kind and affectionate. There is something very noble in his expression when his cap is off. There is none of that cunning in his eye that all of us noticed in Louis Napoleon's.

"It seemed strange—stranger than I can tell—to think that the central figure in the cluster of men and women, chatting here under the trees like the most ordinary individual in the land, was a man who could open his lips and ships would fly through the waves, locomotives would speed over the plains, couriers would hurry from village to village, a hundred telegraphs would flash the word to the four corners of an empire that stretches its vast proportions over a seventh part of the habitable globe, and a countless multitude of men would spring to do his bidding. I had a sort of vague desire to examine his hands and see if they were of flesh and blood, like other men's. Here was a man who could do this wonderful thing, and yet if I chose I could knock him down. The case was plain, but it seemed preposterous, nevertheless —as preposterous as trying to knock down a mountain or wipe out a continent. If this man sprained his ankle, a million miles of telegraph would carry the news over mountains—valleys—uninhabited deserts —under the trackless sea—and ten thousand newspapers would prate of it; if he were grievously ill, all the nations would know it before the sun rose again; if he dropped lifeless where he stood, his fall might shake the thrones of half a world! If I could have stolen his coat, I would have done it. When I meet a man like that, I want something to remember him by."

IF WE COULD RENEW OUR EDGES . . .

When Mark Twain compared Europe with America on this first trip, Europe did not always come out second-best:

"Afterward we walked up and down one of the most popular streets for some time, enjoying other people's comfort and wishing we could export some of it to our restless, driving, vitality-consuming marts at home. Just in this one matter lies the main charm of life in Europe—comfort. In America, we hurry— which is well; but when the day's work is done, we go on thinking of losses and gains, we plan for the morrow, we even carry our business cares to bed with us, and toss and worry over them when we ought to be restoring our racked bodies and brains with sleep.

The Address to Alexander II of Russia, presented by the *Quaker City* passengers and drafted by Mark Twain. "Writing addresses to Emperors is not my strong suit," Mark complained in his notebook. The appeal for Russian-American friendship has a twentieth-century ring.

Czar Alexander II.

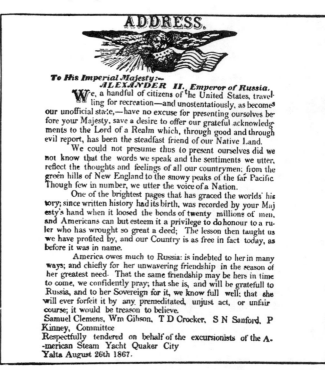

ADDRESS.

To His Imperial Majesty:—
ALEXANDER II, Emperor of Russia.

We, a handful of citizens of the United States, travelling for recreation—and unostentatiously, as becomes our unofficial state,—have no excuse for presenting ourselves before your Majesty, save a desire to offer our grateful acknowledgments to the Lord of a Realm which, through good and through evil report, has been the steadfast friend of our Native Land.

We could not presume thus to present ourselves did we not know that the words we speak and the sentiments we utter, reflect the thoughts and feelings of all our countrymen; from the green hills of New England to the snowy peaks of the far Pacific Though few in number, we utter the voice of a Nation.

One of the brightest pages that has graced the worlds' history; since written history had its birth, was recorded by your Majesty's hand when it loosed the bonds of twenty millions of men, and Americans can but esteem it a privilege to do honour to a ruler who has wrought so great a deed; The lesson then taught us we have profited by, and our Country is as free in fact today, as before it was in name.

America owes much to Russia: is indebted to her in many ways; and chiefly for her unwavering friendship in the season of her greatest need. That the same friendship may be hers in time to come, we confidently pray; that she is, and will be gratefull to Russia, and to her Sovereign for it, we know full well; that she will ever forfeit it by any premeditated, unjust act, or unfair course; it would be treason to believe.

Samuel Clemens, Wm Gibson, T D Crocker, S N Sanford, P Kinney, Committee

Respectfully tendered on behalf of the excursionists of the A-merican Steam Yacht Quaker City

Yalta August 26th 1867.

On October 6, 1867, Mark Twain dropped into Abdullah Frères in Constantinople to have this picture taken.

Charles J. Langdon (*below*) was a gay 18-year-old whose wealthy father, Jervis Langdon, thought the *Quaker City* company would be good for him. Charlie and Mark became friends. One September day, in the Bay of Smyrna, Charlie invited Mark into his cabin and showed him a miniature portrait of sister Olivia Langdon (*above*). "From that day to this," Mark was to write 40 years later, "she has never been out of my mind." His long bachelorhood was soon to end.

We burn up our energies with these excitements, and either die early or drop into a lean and mean old age at a time of life which they call a man's prime in Europe. When an acre of ground has produced long and well, we let it lie fallow and rest for a season; we take no man clear across the continent in the same coach he started in—the coach is stabled somewhere on the plains and its heated machinery allowed to cool for a few days; when a razor has seen long service and refuses to hold an edge, the barber lays it away for a few weeks, and the edge comes back of its own accord. We bestow thoughtful care upon inanimate objects, but none upon ourselves. What a robust people, what a nation of thinkers we might be if we would only lay ourselves on the shelf occasionally and renew our edges!

"I do envy these Europeans the comfort they take. When the work of the day is done, they forget it. Some of them go, with wife and children, to a beer hall, and sit quietly and genteelly drinking a mug or two of ale and listening to music; others walk the streets, others drive in the avenues; others assemble in the great ornamental squares in the early evening to enjoy the sight and the fragrance of flowers and to hear the military bands play—no European city being without its fine military music at eventide; and yet others of the populace sit in the open air in front of the refreshment houses and eat ices and drink mild beverages that could not harm a child. They go to bed moderately early, and sleep well. They are always quiet, always orderly, always cheerful, comfortable, and appreciative of life and its manifold blessings. One never sees a drunken man among them. The change that has come over our little party is surprising. Day by day we lose some of our restlessness and absorb some of the spirit of quietude and ease that is in the tranquil atmosphere about us and in the demeanor of the people. We grow wise apace. We begin to comprehend what life is for."

OBITUARY ON AN EXTRAORDINARY VOYAGE

The *Quaker City* arrived in New York on November 19, 1867. Bumming around the newspaper offices the same day, Mark got a request from the *Herald* for a valedictory on the performances of the pilgrims in foreign lands. He sat down to it at once. The next morning he found "the Quakers all howling on account of the article." He pretended not to understand why his fellow passengers didn't care for the obituary. He liked it—enough to reprint it in his book.

"Wherever we went, in Europe, Asia, or Africa, we made a sensation, and, I suppose I may add, created a famine. None of us had ever been any where before; we all hailed from the interior; travel was a wild novelty to us, and we conducted ourselves in accordance with the natural instincts that were in us, and trammeled ourselves with no ceremonies, no conventionalities. We always took care to make it understood that we were Americans—Americans! When we found that a good many foreigners had hardly ever heard of America, and that a good many more knew it only as a barbarous province away off somewhere, that had lately been at war with somebody, we pitied the ignorance of the Old World, but abated no jot of our importance. Many and many a simple community in the Eastern hemisphere will remember for years the incursion of the strange horde in the year of our Lord 1867, that called themselves Americans, and seemed to imagine in some unaccountable way that they had a right to be proud of it. We generally created a famine, partly because the coffee on the *Quaker City* was unendurable, and sometimes the more substantial fare was not strictly first-class; and partly because one naturally tires of sitting long at the same board and eating from the same dishes.

"The people of those foreign countries are very, very ignorant. They looked curiously at the costumes we had brought from the wilds of America. They observed that we talked loudly at table sometimes. They noticed that we looked out for expenses, and got what we conveniently could out of a franc, and wondered where in the mischief we came from. In Paris they just simply opened their eyes and stared when we spoke to them in French! We never did succeed in making those idiots understand their own language.

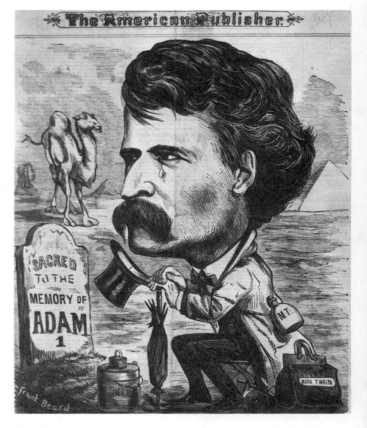

In Jerusalem the Pilgrims visited several Biblical sites, including the reputed tomb of Adam. A cartoonist pictured Mark's tribute to his blood relation.

"The people stared at us everywhere, and we stared at them. We generally made them feel rather small, too, before we got done with them, because we bore down on them with America's greatness until we crushed them. And yet we took kindly to the manners and customs, and especially to the fashions of the various people we visited.

"Well, we were at home in Palestine. It was easy to see that that was the grand feature of the expedition. We had cared nothing much about Europe. We galloped through the Louvre, the Pitti, the Uffizi, the Vatican—all the galleries—and through the pictured and frescoed churches of Venice, Naples, and the cathedrals of Spain; some of us said that certain of the great works of the old masters were glorious creations of genius (we found it out in the guidebook, though we got hold of the wrong picture sometimes), and the others said they were disgraceful old daubs. We examined modern and ancient statuary with a critical eye in Florence, Rome, or anywhere we found it, and praised it if we saw fit, and if we didn't we said we preferred the wooden Indians in front of the cigar stores of America. But the Holy Land brought out all our enthusiasm. We fell into raptures by the barren shores of Galilee; we pondered at Tabor and at Nazareth; we exploded into poetry over the questionable loveliness of Esdraelon; we meditated at Jezreel and Samaria over the missionary zeal of Jehu; we rioted—fairly rioted among the holy places of Jerusalem; we bathed in Jordan and the Dead Sea, reckless whether our accident-insurance policies were extra-hazardous or not, and brought away so many jugs of precious water from both places that all the country from Jericho to the mountains of Moab will suffer from drouth this year, I think. Yet, the pilgrimage part of the excursion was its pet feature—there is no question about that. After dismal, smileless Palestine, beautiful Egypt had few charms for us. We merely glanced at it and were ready for home.

"They wouldn't let us land at Malta—quarantine; they would not let us land in Sardinia; nor at Algiers, Africa; nor at Malaga, Spain, nor Cadiz, nor at the Madeira Islands. So we got offended at all foreigners and turned our backs upon them and came home. I suppose we only stopped at the Bermudas because they were in the programme. We did not care anything about any place at all. We wanted to go home. Homesickness was abroad in the ship—it was epidemic. If the authorities of New York had known how badly we had it, they would have quarantined us here.

"The grand pilgrimage is over. Good-bye to it, and a pleasant memory to it, I am able to say in all kindness. I bear no malice, no ill-will toward any individual that was connected with it, either as passenger or officer. Things I did not like at all yesterday I like very well to-day, now that I am at home, and always hereafter I shall be able to poke fun at the whole gang if the spirit so moves me to do, without

ever saying a malicious word. The expedition accomplished all that its programme promised that it should accomplish, and we ought all to be satisfied with the management of the matter, certainly. Bye-bye!"

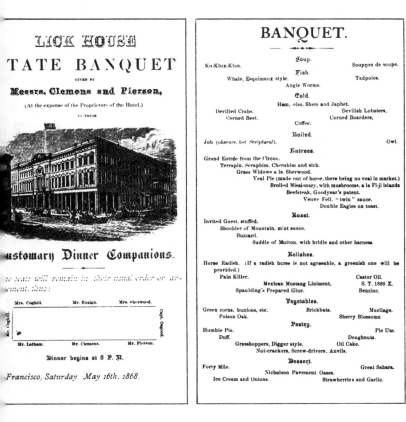

To negotiate with the *Alta* for book use of his travel letters, Mark went to San Francisco in March, 1868. He made money on the side by swinging around the Western lecture circuit. To promote his farewell lecture in San Francisco he concocted this advertisement.

Reworking his *Quaker City* travel letters for a book and lecturing on "The Holy Land" still left Mark time for an occasional frolic with his old Western friends.

THE

INNOCENTS ABROAD,

OR

THE NEW PILGRIMS' PROGRESS;

BEING SOME ACCOUNT OF THE STEAMSHIP QUAKER CITY'S PLEASURE
EXCURSION TO EUROPE AND THE HOLY LAND; WITH
DESCRIPTIONS OF COUNTRIES, NATIONS,
INCIDENTS AND ADVENTURES,
AS THEY APPEARED
TO THE
AUTHOR.

WITH TWO HUNDRED AND THIRTY-FOUR ILLUSTRATIONS.

BY

MARK TWAIN,

(SAMUEL L. CLEMENS.)

(ISSUED BY SUBSCRIPTION ONLY, AND NOT FOR SALE IN THE BOOK-STORES. RESIDENTS OF ANY STATE DESIRING
A COPY SHOULD ADDRESS THE PUBLISHERS, AND AN AGENT WILL CALL UPON THEM.)

HARTFORD, CONN.:

AMERICAN PUBLISHING COMPANY.

BLISS & CO., NEWARK, N. J.; R. W. BLISS & CO., TOLEDO, OHIO.
F. G. GILMAN & CO., CHICAGO, ILL.; NETTLETON & CO., CINCINNATI, OHIO.
F. A. HUTCHINSON & CO., ST. LOUIS, MO.
H. H. BANCROFT AND COMPANY, SAN FRANCISCO, CAL.
1869.

Two days after the *Quaker City* docked, the American Publishing Company invited Mark Twain to work up the travel letters into a book. Refusing an offer of $10,000 cash for his copyright, Mark signed for a five per cent royalty. The book appeared on July 20, 1869, and was a best seller at once.

Mark's publisher advertised in the Hartford press for book agents to sell the 20,000 copies of the first printing.

The author at work on *The Innocents Abroad*.

A LECTURE WITH A MORAL

During the winter of 1868–69 Mark lectured in the East on "The Vandal Abroad," earning $100 a night and promoting his coming book at the same time. The lecture concluded with a moral:

"If there is a moral to this lecture it is an injunction to all Vandals to *travel*. I am glad the American Vandal *goes* abroad. It does him good. It makes a better man of him. It rubs out a multitude of his old unworthy biases and prejudices. It aids his religion, for it enlarges his charity and his benevolence, it broadens his views of men and things; it deepens his generosity and his compassion for the failings and shortcomings of his fellow creatures. Contact with men of various nations and many creeds teaches him that there are *other* people in the world besides his own little clique, and other opinions as worthy of attention and respect as his own. He finds that he and *his* are not the most momentous matters in the universe. Cast into trouble and misfortune in strange lands and being mercifully cared for by those he never saw before, he begins to learn that best lesson of all—that one which culminates in the conviction that God puts *something* good and something lovable in every man his hands create—that the world is *not* a cold, harsh, cruel, prisonhouse, stocked with all manner of selfishness and hate and wickedness. It *liberalizes* the Vandal to travel. You never saw a bigoted, opinionated, stubborn, narrow-minded, self-conceited, *almighty mean man* in your life but he had stuck in one place ever since he was born and thought God made the world and dyspepsia and bile for *his* especial comfort and satisfaction. So I say, *by all means* let the American Vandal go on traveling, and let no man discourage him."

In his first few months in Washington, Mark Twain moved five times, from boardinghouse to boardinghouse. "Shabby furniture and shabby food —*that* is Wash.," he wrote his folks. Here is how Pennsylvania Avenue looked to him in 1868.

WASHINGTON CORRESPONDENT

A day after the satiric *Herald* letter was published, Mark was safely in Washington, as private secretary to Senator William M. Stewart, an old Nevada friend. This observation post on capital life was soon wiped out when differences developed with the pompous politician. Nor did Mark's maneuvers materialize in a hoped-for clerkship for brother Orion. But "hobnobbing with these old Generals and Senators and other humbugs" provided good copy for the newsletters Mark began contributing to the *Tribune* and *Herald* in New York and his old papers out West.

Senator William M. Stewart of Nevada. Mark Twain was his private secretary briefly in 1867. When Stewart wrote his memoirs, he did not remember Mark fondly.

Mark Twain in 1868, the year Washington was being etched in acid on his mind: "It could probably be shown by facts and figures that there is no distinctly native American criminal class except Congress."

104

Newspaper Row in Washington. The offices of several newspapers Mark wrote for can be seen.

For the now famous writer of the *Quaker City* letters, every door was open. "Don't have any more trouble making friends than I did in California. All serene," he wrote home. Running up to New York he got advice from Henry Ward Beecher on how to force the best bargain out of his publisher. "I had my mind made up to *one* thing," he wrote his mother. "I wasn't going to touch a book unless there was *money* in it, and a good deal of it." For a while he toyed with an offer to become postmaster of San Francisco, but the book contract interfered. Influential Washington friends suggested an easy post abroad that would permit him to write more. "I didn't want any of the pie," Mark said, "God knows I am mean enough and lazy enough right now, without being a foreign consul."

SUPPORTING THAT JUG

When the *Innocents* contract with the Hartford publisher was signed late in January, 1868, Mark was broke. He had to eat while writing the book; in his autobiography he describes the birth of his newspaper syndicate:

"I went down to Washington to see if I could earn enough there to keep me in bread and butter while I should write the book. I came across William Swinton, brother of the historian, and together we invented a scheme for our mutual sustenance; we became the fathers and originators of what is a common feature in the newspaper world now, the syndicate. We became the old original first Newspaper Syndicate on the planet; it was on a small scale but that is usual with untried new enterprises. We had twelve journals on our list; they were all weeklies, all obscure and poor and all scattered far away among the back settlements. It was a proud thing for those little newspapers to have a Washington correspondence, and a fortunate thing for us that they felt in that way about it. Each of the twelve took two letters a week from us, at a dollar per letter; each of us wrote one letter per week and sent off six duplicates of it to these benefactors, thus acquiring twenty-four dollars a week to live on, which was all we needed in our cheap and humble quarters.

"Swinton was one of the dearest and loveliest human beings I have ever known, and we led a charmed existence together, in a contentment which knew no bounds. He hadn't a vice, unless a large and grateful sympathy with Scotch whisky may be called by that name. I didn't regard it as a vice, because he was a Scotchman, and Scotch whisky to a Scotchman is as innocent as milk is to the rest of the human race. In Swinton's case it was a virtue and not an economical one. Twenty-four dollars a week would really have been riches to us if we hadn't had to support that jug; because of the jug we were always sailing pretty close to the wind, and any tardiness in the arrival of any part of our income was sure to cause some inconvenience."

An "interview" with a Presidential hopeful, General Grant, reported by Mark Twain.

THE MADDEST VANITY FAIR

How Mark Twain saw postwar Washington was put into *The Gilded Age,* a novel he wrote a few years later with his Hartford neighbor, Charles Dudley Warner: "Washington was . . . the maddest Vanity Fair one could conceive. It seemed . . . a feverish, unhealthy atmosphere in which lunacy would be easily developed. Everybody attached to himself an exaggerated importance, from the fact of being at the national capital, the center of political influence, the fountain of patronage, preferment, jobs, and opportunities.

"People were introduced to each other as from this or that state, not from cities or towns, and this gave a largeness to their representative feeling. All the women talked politics as naturally and glibly as they talk fashion or literature elsewhere. There was always some exciting topic at the Capitol, or some huge slander was rising up like a miasmatic exhalation from the Potomac, threatening to settle no one knew exactly where. Every other person was an aspirant for a place, or, if he had one, for a better place, or more pay; almost every other one had some claim or interest or remedy to urge; even the women were all advocates for the advancement of some person, and they violently espoused or denounced this or that measure as it would affect some relative, acquaintance, or friend.

Thaddeus Stevens, the Republican Radical Congressman from Pennsylvania who helped shape Reconstruction policies.

"Love, travel, even death itself, waited on the chances of the dies daily thrown in the two Houses, and the committee-rooms there. If the measure went through, love could afford to ripen into marriage, and longing for foreign travel would have fruition; and it must have been only eternal hope springing in the breast that kept alive numerous old claimants who for years and years had besieged the doors of Congress, and who looked as if they needed not so much an appropriation of money as six feet of ground. And those who stood so long waiting for success to bring them death were usually those who had a just claim."

NOTES FROM CAPITOL HILL

Wandering over Capitol Hill, Mark's eye made vivid note of personalities and scenes: "Thad. Stevens—Very deep eyes, sunken unshaven cheeks, thin lips, long and strong mouth, long, large, sharp nose—whole face sunken and sharp, full of inequalities—dark wavy hair—Indian—club-footed—ablest man."

"Ben Butler—forward part of his bald skull looks raised like a water-blister—its boundaries at the sides and at its base in front is marked by deep creases—fat face—small dark moustache—considerable hair behind and on the sides—one reliable eye. Is short and pursy—fond of standing up with hands in pants pockets and looking around to each speaker with the air of a man who has half a mind to crush them and yet is rather too indifferent. Butler is dismally and drearily homely and when he smiles it is like the breaking up of a hard winter."

"How insignificant a Senator or an M.C. is in N.Y. —and how great a personage he is in Washington.

"We should have a much better sort of legislation if we had these swollen country jakes in N.Y. as their capital. Congress OUGHT to sit in a big city.

"I remember how those pigmy Congressmen used to come into the Arlington breakfast room with a bundle of papers and letters—you could see by their affection for it and their delight in this sort of display that out in the woods where they came from they weren't used to much mail matter.

"They always occupied their seats at table a level hour after breakfast, to be looked at, though they wore a weak pretense of settling the affairs of empires, over their mail—contracting brows, etc.

"How N.Y. would squeeze the conceit out of those poor little Congressmen."

"The Congregational graveyard at Washington—stones even for ex-members of Congress buried elsewhere. Chuckle-headed vanity of brief grandeur can no further go. Congressman is the trivialest distinction for fullgrown man."

Benjamin Butler of Massachusetts, Civil War general and postwar politician.

ON CONGRESSIONAL INVESTIGATIONS

The speculative fever that seized the country as the Civil War ended had its counterpart in the halls of Congress. The log-rolling and back-scratching for private interests observed by Twain are satirized in his explanation (in *The Gilded Age*) of how Congressional investigations are conducted: "'I think Congress always tries to do as near right as it can, according to its lights. A man can't ask any fairer than that. The first preliminary it always starts out on, is to clear itself, so to speak. It will arraign two or three dozen of its members, or maybe four or five dozen, for taking bribes to vote for this and that and the other bill last winter.

"'Well, after they have finished the bribery cases, they will take up cases of members who have bought their seats with money. That will take another four weeks.

"'Next they will try each other for various smaller irregularities, like the sale of appointments to West Point cadetships, and that sort of thing—mere trifling pocket-money enterprises that might better be passed over in silence, perhaps; but then one of our Congresses can never rest easy till it has thoroughly purified itself of all blemishes—and that is a thing to be applauded.'

"'How long does it take to disinfect itself of these minor impurities?'

"'Well, about two weeks, generally.'

"'So Congress always lies helpless in quarantine ten weeks of a session. That's encouraging. Doesn't it occur to you that by the time it has expelled all its impure members there may not be enough members left to do business legally?'

"'Why, I did not say Congress would expel anybody.'

"'Well, won't it expel anybody?'

"'Not necessarily. Did it last year? It never does. That would not be regular.'

"'Then why waste all the session in that tomfoolery of trying members?'

"'It is usual; it is customary; the country requires it.'

"'Then the country is a fool, I think.'

"'Oh, no. The country thinks somebody is going to be expelled.'

"'Well, when nobody is expelled, what does the country think then?'

"'By that time, the thing has strung out so long that the country is sick and tired of it and glad to have a change on any terms. But all that inquiry is not lost. It has a good moral effect.'

An indication of what Mark covered in his Washington newsletters. To the *Alta*'s readers he reported his toast to "Woman" and suggested, "The women of San Francisco ought to send me a medal, or a doughnut, or something, for I had them chiefly in my mind in this eulogy."

"'Who does it have a good moral effect on?'

"'Well—I don't know. On foreign countries, I think. We have always been under the gaze of foreign countries. There is no country in the world, sir, that pursues corruption as inveterately as we do. There is no country in the world whose representatives try each other as much as ours do, or stick to it as long on a stretch. I think there is something great in being a model for the whole civilized world, Washington.'

"'You don't mean a model; you mean an example.'

"'Well, it's all the same; it's just the same thing. It shows that a man can't be corrupt in this country without sweating for it, I can tell you that.'

"'Hang it, Colonel, you just said we never punish anybody for villainous practices.'

" 'But, good God! we try them, don't we? Is it nothing to show a disposition to sift things and bring people to a strict account? I tell you it has its effect.'

" 'Oh, bother the effect!—What is it they do do? How do they proceed? You know perfectly well—and it is all bosh, too. Come, now, how do they proceed?'

" 'Why they proceed right and regular—and it ain't bosh. They appoint a committee to investigate, and that committee hears evidence three weeks, and all the witnesses on one side swear that the accused took money or stock or something for his vote. Then the accused stands up and testifies that he may have done it, but he was receiving and handling a good deal of money at the time and he doesn't remember this particular circumstance—at least with sufficient distinctness to enable him to grasp it tangibly. So of course the thing is not proven—and that is what they say in the verdict. They don't acquit, they don't condemn. They just say, "Charge not proven." It leaves the accused in a kind of shaky condition before the country, it purifies Congress, it satisfies everybody, and it doesn't seriously hurt anybody. It has taken a long time to perfect our system, but it is the most admirable in the world now.'

" 'So one of those long stupid investigations always turns out in that lame silly way. Yes, you are correct. I thought maybe you viewed the matter differently from other people. Do you think a Congress of ours could convict the devil of anything if he were a member?'

" 'My dear boy, don't let these damaging delays prejudice you against Congress. Don't use such strong language; you talk like a newspaper. Congress has inflicted frightful punishments on its members—now you know that. When they tried Mr. Fairoaks, and a cloud of witnesses proved him to be—well, you know what they proved him to be—and his own testimony and his own confession gave him the same character, what did Congress do then?—come!'

" 'Well, what did Congress do?'

" 'You know what Congress did, Washington. Congress intimated plainly enough, that they considered him almost a stain upon their body; and without waiting ten days, hardly, to think the thing over, they rose up and hurled at him a resolution declaring that they disapproved of his conduct! Now you know that, Washington.'

" 'It was a terrific thing—there is no denying that. If he had been proven guilty of theft, arson, licentiousness, infanticide, and defiling graves, I believe they would have suspended him for two days.'

" 'You can depend on it, Washington. Congress is vindictive, Congress is savage, sir, when it gets waked up once. It will go to any length to vindicate its honor at such a time.' "

At a stag dinner of the Correspondents Club, given January 11, 1868, Mark delivered a toast to "Woman" which the Washington *Star* thought worth printing in full. Mark bragged to his family that Speaker of the House Schuyler Colfax said it was "the best dinner-table speech he had ever heard at a banquet."

The Trouble Begins at 8...

Joseph Keppler, founder of the comic periodical *Puck*, draws Mark Twain on the lecture platform.

"After about four or five months [in Hawaii] I returned to California to find myself about the best-known honest man on the Pacific coast. Thomas McGuire, proprietor of several theaters, said that now was the time to make my fortune—strike while the iron was hot—break into the lecture field! I did it. I announced a lecture on the Sandwich Islands, closing the advertisement with the remark: 'Admission one dollar; doors open at half past seven, the trouble begins at eight.' A true prophecy. The trouble certainly did begin at eight, when I found myself in front of the only audience I had ever faced, for the fright which pervaded me from head to foot was paralyzing. It lasted two minutes and was as bitter as death; the memory of it is indestructible but it had its compensations, for it made me immune from timidity before audiences for all time to come."

With his first New York lecture scheduled for May 6, 1867, Mark began to feel a bit nervous. To his mother he wrote: "Everything looks shady, at least, if not dark; I have a good agent; but now, after we have hired the Cooper Institute, and gone to an expense in one way or another of $500, it comes out that I have got to play against Speaker Colfax at Irving Hall, Ristori, and also the double troop of Japanese jugglers, the latter opening at the great Academy of Music—and with all this against me I have taken the largest house in New York and cannot back water. Let her slide! If nobody else cares, I don't."

Reporting the lecture to the *Alta*, Mark's tone changed: "I had a first-rate success myself at the Cooper Institute the other night, but I am not going to say much about that, because you can get it out of the newspapers. The Californians worked the thing up, and got about twenty-five hundred people into the house—which was well, because on my own merits I could not have accomplished it, perhaps. I lectured once in Brooklyn afterwards, and here again last night, and came out handsomely, notwithstanding I managed to get everything wrong end foremost and hopelessly tangled in the matter of announcing last night's performance. Governor Nye promised to introduce me to my audience at Cooper Institute, and I published it; but he was not at his hotel when the carriage went for him, has not been seen since, and has never sent a word of explanation. However, it is a matter of no consequence. I introduced myself as well as he could have done it—that is, without straining himself."

Right: Daily *Alta California,* Dec. 10, 1866.

Far right: Daily *Alta California,* Oct. 2, 1866.

110

TWAIN ON DICKENS

Mark heard Charles Dickens read at Steinway Hall in New York on January 2 or 3, 1868. A week later he described his reactions in a letter to the *Alta California*, referring parenthetically to the special nature of the occasion—his first date with his wife-to-be, Livy Langdon:

"Promptly at 8 P.M., unannounced, and without waiting for any stamping or clapping of hands to call him out, a tall, 'spry,' (if I may say it,) thin-legged old gentleman, gotten up regardless of expense, especially as to shirt-front and diamonds with a bright red flower in his button-hole, gray beard and moustache, bald head, and with side hair brushed fiercely and tempestuously forward, as if its owner were sweeping down before a gale of wind, the very Dickens came! He did not emerge upon the stage—that is not the word—that is rather too deliberate a word—he strode. He strode—in the most English way and exhibiting the most English general style and appearance—straight across the stage, heedless of everything, unconscious of everybody, turning neither to the right nor the left—but striding eagerly straight ahead, as if he had seen a girl he knew turn the next corner. He brought up handsomely in the centre and faced the opera glasses. His pictures are hardly handsome, and he, like everybody else, is less handsome than his pictures. That fashion he has of brushing his hair and goatee so resolutely forward gives him a comical Scotch-terrier look about the face, which is rather heightened than otherwise by his portentous dignity and gravity. But that queer old head took on a sort of beauty, bye and bye, and a fascinating interest, as I thought of the wonderful mechanism within it, the complex but exquisitely adjusted machinery that could create men and women, and put the breath of life into them and alter all their ways and actions, elevate them, degrade them, murder them, marry them, conduct them through good and

Charles Dickens (caricatured by André Gill) created a sensation when he read to American audiences from his best sellers.

evil, through joy and sorrow, on their long march from the cradle to the grave, and never lose its godship over them, never make a mistake! I almost imagined I could see the wheels and pulleys work. This was Dicken–Dickens. There was no question about that, and yet it was not right easy to realize it. Somehow this puissant god seemed to be only a man, after all. How the great do tumble from their high pedestals when we see them in common human flesh, and know that they eat pork and cabbage and act like other men!

"Mr. Dickens had a table to put his book on, and on it he had also a tumbler, a fancy decanter and a small bouquet. Behind him he had a huge red screen—a bulkhead—a sounding-board, I took it to be—and overhead in front was suspended a long board with reflecting lights attached to it, which threw down a glory upon the gentleman, after the fashion in use in the picture-galleries for bringing out the best effects of great paintings. Style!—There is style about Dickens, and style about all his surroundings.

"He read *David Copperfield*. He is a bad reader, in one sense—because he does not enunciate his words sharply and distinctly—he does not cut the syllables cleanly, and therefore many and many of them fell dead before they reached our part of the house. (I say 'our' because I am proud to observe that there was a beautiful young lady with me—a good deal disappointed in Mr. Dickens' reading—I will go further and say, a great deal disappointed.) The *Herald* and *Tribune* critics must have been carried away by their imaginations when they wrote their extravagant praises of it. Mr. Dickens' reading is rather monotonous, as a general thing; his voice is husky; his pathos is only the beautiful pathos of his language—there is no heart, no feeling in it—it is glittering frostwork; his rich humor cannot fail to tickle an audience into ecstasies save when he reads to himself."

Twain often drafted his own advertising copy. The "quaint remarks" were a hit with audience and press in his New York debut.

A BIG GUN IN THE LYCEUM SYSTEM

In a year on the platform (1868–69) Mark earned eight or nine thousand dollars, but, he wrote his mother, "I most cordially hate the lecture field. And, after all, I shudder to think that I may never get out of it." In his autobiography he recalls how the lyceum system worked: "I began as a lecturer in 1866 in California and Nevada; in 1867 lectured in New York once and in the Mississippi Valley a few times; in 1868 made the whole Western circuit; and in the two or three following seasons added the Eastern circuit to my route.

"The 'lyceum system' was in full flower in those days and James Redpath's Bureau in School Street, Boston, had the management of it throughout the Northern States and Canada. Redpath farmed out the lectures in groups of six or eight to the lyceums all over the country at an average of about $100 a night for each lecture. His commission was 10 per cent; each lecture appeared about 110 nights in the season. There were a number of good drawing names in his list: Henry Ward Beecher; Anna Dickinson; John B. Gough; Horace Greeley; Wendell Phillips; Petroleum V. Nasby; Josh Billings; Hayes, the Arctic explorer; Vincent, the English astronomer; Parsons, Irish orator; Agassiz; et al. He had in his list twenty or thirty men and women of light consequence and

limited reputation who wrought for fees ranging from twenty-five dollars to fifty dollars. Their names have perished long ago. Nothing but art could find them a chance on the platform. Redpath furnished that art. All the lyceums wanted the big guns and wanted them yearningly, longingly, strenuously. Redpath granted their prayers—on this condition; for each house-filler allotted them they must hire several of his house-emptiers. This arrangement permitted the lyceums to get through alive for a few years, but in the end it killed them all and abolished the lecture business."

James Redpath, above, ex-newspaperman and abolitionist, ran the Boston Lyceum Bureau and took Mark Twain under his wing when press notices like the one above showed what a hit the man was. Redpath earned his ten per cent commission, as this 1871 letter of Mark's proves:

"DEAR RED,—I am different from other women; my mind changes oftener. People who have no mind can easily be steadfast and firm, but when a man is loaded down to the guards with it, as I am, every heavy sea of foreboding or inclination, maybe of indolence, shifts the cargo. See? Therefore, if you will notice, one week I am likely to give rigid instructions to confine me to New England; next week, send me to Arizona; the next week withdraw my name; the next week give you full untrammelled swing; and the week following modify it. You must try to keep the run of my mind, Redpath, it is your business being the agent, and it always was too many for me. It

THE LYCEUM COMMITTEEMAN'S DREAM

A cartoonist for *Harper's Weekly* drew 19 of the day's popular lecturers in character.
The jester at bottom center is Mark Twain.

appears to me to be one of the finest pieces of mechanism I have ever met with. Now about the West, this week, I am willing that you shall retain all the Western engagements. But what I shall want next week is still with God.

"Let us not profane the mysteries with soiled hands and prying eyes of sin.

Yours,

MARK."

GUEST OF THE VILLAGE

A portrait of the lionized lecturer was painted by Mark in a letter to his fiancée, Olivia Langdon, sent from Clinton, Massachusetts, on November 15, 1869:

"LIVY DARLING—I had to submit to the customary & exasperating drive around town in a freezing open buggy this morning (at Norwich) to see the wonders of the village. (Mem.—They always consist of the mayor's house; the ex-mayor's house; the house of a State Senator; house of an ex-governor; house of a former member of Congress; the public school with its infernal architecture; the female seminary; paper mill or factory of some kind or other; the cemetery; the court house; the plaza; the place where the park is going to be—& I must sit & shiver & stare at a melancholy grove of skeleton trees & listen while

my friend gushes enthusiastic statistics & dimensions. All towns are alike—all have the same stupid trivialities to show, & all demand an impossible interest at the suffering stranger's hands. Why won't these insane persecutors believe me when I protest pleadingly that I *don't* care two cents for all the thrilling wonders the village can boast.—

"(How I gloat in secret when one of those people regrets that I cannot 'remain over' & see his accursed village! And how unblushingly I repeat the threadbare lie that I am sorry!

"(After the natural wonders are all visited, then we have to call on other inanimated wonders with dull faces, but with legs to them that show them to be human: the mayor; the richest man; the wag of the village (who instantly assails me with old stale jokes & humorous profanity); the village editor—& a lot more of people I take no possible interest in & don't want to see. And when by some divine accident one of them isn't at home what a fervent prayer of thankfulness rises up in my heart!)

"I only have to submit to these inflictions when I am the guest of somebody & cannot refuse to suffer in return for his hospitality. When I am paying my own bills at a hotel, I talk out & say No Sir—not any village wonders for the subscriber, if you please.

"Here I am in a hotel—the Clinton House—& a villainous one it is—shabby bed, shabby room, shabby furniture, dim lights—everything shabby & disagreeable."

William Dean Howells, novelist, critic, editor. He became Mark's close friend and literary counselor.

The old *Atlantic Monthly* office, 124 Tremont Street, in Boston, where Twain and Howells first met.

LITERARY LUNCH IN BOSTON

A Boston audience—"4,000 critics," Mark called them —was a major hurdle for lecturers. Mark's first Boston trial occurred on November 10, 1869, and was "a handsome success," he reported to Livy. Here he met William Dean Howells, and a lifelong friendship began. This is Howells recalling that first encounter:

"It was in the little office of James T. Fields, over the book-store of Ticknor & Fields, at 124 Tremont Street, Boston, that I first met my friend of now forty-four years, Samuel L. Clemens. Mr. Fields was then the editor of *The Atlantic Monthly,* and I was his proud and glad assistant, with a pretty free hand as to manuscripts, and an unmanacled command of the book-notices at the end of the magazine. I wrote nearly all of them myself, and in 1869 I had written rather a long notice of a book just winning its way to universal favor. In this review I had intimated my reservations concerning the *Innocents Abroad,* but I had the luck, if not the sense, to recognize that it was such fun as we had not had before. I forget just what I said in praise of it, and it does not matter; it is enough that I praised it enough to satisfy the author.

"At the time of our first meeting, which must have been well toward the winter, Clemens (as I must call him instead of Mark Twain, which seemed always somehow to mask him from my personal sense) was wearing a sealskin coat, with the fur out, in the satisfaction of a caprice, or the love of strong effect which he was apt to indulge through life. I do not know what droll comment was in Fields' mind with respect to this garment, but probably he felt that here was an original who was not to be brought to any Bostonian book in the judgment of his vivid qualities. With his crest of dense red hair, and the wide sweep of his flaming mustache, Clemens was not discordantly clothed in that sealskin coat, which afterward, in spite of his own warmth in it, sent the cold chills through me when I once accompanied it down Broadway, and shared the immense publicity it won him.

"There is a gap in my recollections of Clemens, which I think is of a year or two, for the next thing I remember of him is meeting him at a lunch in Boston given us by that genius of hospitality, the tragically destined Ralph Keeler, author of the most unjustly forgotten book *Vagabond Adventure,* a true bit of picaresque autobiography. Keeler never had any money, to the general knowledge, and he never borrowed, and he could not have had credit at the restaurant where he invited us to feast at his expense.

114

The sealskin coat that made Mark an "original" in Boston's eyes.

James T. Fields, *Atlantic Monthly* editor.

Ralph Keeler, a Californian Mark met again in the East. Adopted by Boston's writers, he became an *Atlantic* contributor. Mark liked to have him along for company while lecturing. Keeler disappeared mysteriously from a boat en route to Cuba.

There was T. B. Aldrich, there was J. T. Fields, much the oldest of our company, who had just freed himself from the trammels of the publishing business, and was feeling his freedom in every word; there was Bret Harte, who had lately come East in his princely progress from California; and there was Clemens. Nothing remains to me of the happy time but a sense of idle and aimless and joyful talk-play, beginning and ending nowhere, of eager laughter, of countless good stories from Fields, of a heat-lightning shimmer of wit from Aldrich, of an occasional concentration of our joint mockeries upon our host, who took it gladly; and amid the discourse, so little improving, but so full of good fellowship, Bret Harte's fleering dramatization of Clemens's mental attitude toward a symposium of Boston illuminates. 'Why, fellows,' he spluttered, 'this is the dream of Mark's life,' and I remember the glance from under Clemens's feathery eyebrows which betrayed his enjoyment of the fun. We had beefsteak with mushrooms, which in recognition of their shape Aldrich hailed as shoe-pegs, and to crown the feast we had an omelette souffle, which the waiter brought in as flat as a pancake, amid our shouts of congratulations to poor Keeler, who took them with appreciative submission. It was in every way what a Boston literary lunch ought not to have been in the popular ideal which Harte attributed to Clemens."

Thomas Bailey Aldrich. "When it came to making fun of a folly, a silliness, a windy pretense, a wild absurdity, Aldrich was a master," said Twain. But vain? —"as vain as I am myself, which is saying all that can be said under that head without being extravagant."

PETROLEUM V. NASBY AND
JOSH BILLINGS

Twain and Petroleum V. Nasby (David R. Locke) were often together in Boston. In July, 1869, Mark described Nasby for the readers of the *Alta:* "Nasby is about thirty-five years old. He is compact, solid, heavy. He weighs a hundred and seventy or eighty, perhaps. There is nothing of a dainty look about him, but, on the contrary, he is as burly and vigorous as a theatrical blacksmith. His energy is invincible. After traveling all day and lecturing every night for months together, he was as fresh as ever. His attire is unfashionable, but he cares nothing for that. It does not fit, but that does not concern him. He is not graceful on the stage, but that does not distress him. He is not as handsome as I am, but more picturesque.

Bret Harte, caricatured by "Spy."

"Nasby has achieved a great success, and did it without other help than the talents that were born with him. His newspaper has a prodigious circulation; his letters take well; his books sell well; his lecture-field is the whole country. His lecture is the best thing he has written. It is a very unvarnished narrative of the Negro's career, from the flood to the present day, and bristles with satire. For instance, the interpolating of the word white in State Constitutions existing under a great general Constitution which declares all men to be equal, is neatly touched by a recommendation that the Scriptures be so altered, at the same time, as to make them pleasantly conform to men's notions—thus: 'Suffer little white children to come unto me, and forbid them not!' The lecture is a fair and logical argument against slavery, and is the pleasantest to listen to I have ever heard upon that novel and interesting subject. It is necessarily severe upon the Democracy, but not more so than one would expect from Nasby. The wonder is that anybody should expect anything else. But they do. In half the places I have lectured in Pennsylvania, Indiana, Iowa, Michigan, Illinois, and other states, I heard people talking acrimoniously about Nasby having given them an offensive political lecture instead of one upon some inoffensive subject. I wonder what on earth they did expect Nasby to talk about? Poetry, no doubt. Well, Nasby is a good fellow, and companionable, and we sat up till daylight reading Bret Harte's Condensed Novels and talking over Western lecturing experiences. But lecturing experiences, deliciously toothsome and interesting as they are, must be recounted only in secret session, with closed doors. Otherwise, what a telling magazine article one could make out of them. I lectured all over the States, during the entire winter and far into the spring, and I am sure that my salary of twenty-six hundred dollars a month was only about half of my pay—the rest was jolly experiences. I am not sure but that Nasby will go with me when I start to California about the first of August."

A few months later, in the Buffalo *Express*, Mark puffed Josh Billings (Henry Wheeler Shaw) and his new *Almanac:*

"Joshua is still lecturing hereabouts in the New England towns. Lately he took a contract to deliver eight lectures in various cities, for the benefit of a young colored man, a protege of the gentleman who contracted for the lectures. Billings says this is a benevolent object, the idea being to raise means to give the young colored fellow an education, and if the thing proves a success he thinks of delivering a course of lectures in his own behoof and devoting the proceeds to acquiring a knowledge of how to spell in a little more elegant and hostile manner.

"His last literary venture, the *Farmer's Allminax,* is a pleasant conceit and happily executed. It exhibits a marvellous facility in the handling of the signs of the zodiac and in the construction of poetry suited to any latitude and to all climatic and geographical diversities and peculiarities. The pamphlet is selling handsomely and profitably."

PORTRAIT OF BRET HARTE

Friends in California, Twain and Bret Harte met again in the East when fame brought both into Boston's inner circle. The friendship went awry; after Harte's death Mark wrote this biographical sketch:

"Bret Harte was one of the pleasantest men I have ever known. He was also one of the unpleasantest men I have ever known. He was showy, meretricious, insincere; and he constantly advertised these qualities in his dress. He was distinctly pretty, in spite of the fact that his face was badly pitted with smallpox. In the days when he could afford it—and in the days he couldn't—his clothes always exceeded the fashion by a shade or two. He was always conspicuously a little more intensely fashionable than the fashionablest of the rest of the community. He had good taste in clothes. With all his conspicuousness there was never anything really loud nor offensive about them. They always had a single smart little accent, effectively located, and that accent would have distinguished Harte from any other of the ultrafashionables. Oftenest it was his necktie. Always it was of a single color, and intense. Most frequently, perhaps, it was crimson—a flash of flame under his chin; or it was indigo blue and as hot and vivid as if one of those splendid and luminous Brazilian butterflies had lighted there. Harte's dainty self-complacencies extended to his carriage and gait. His carriage was graceful and easy, his gait was of the mincing sort but was the right gait for him, for an unaffected one would not have harmonized with the rest of the man and the clothes.

"He hadn't a sincere fiber in him. I think he was incapable of emotion, for I think he had nothing to feel with. I think his heart was merely a pump and had no other function. I am almost moved to say I know it had no other function. I knew him intimately in the days when he was private secretary on the second floor and I a fading and perishing reporter on the third, with Smiggy McGlural looming doomfully in the near distance. I knew him intimately when he came east five years later in 1870 to take the editorship of the proposed Lakeside Monthly in Chicago, and crossed the continent through such a prodigious blaze of national interest and excitement that one might have supposed he was the Viceroy of India on a progress, or Halley's comet come again after seventy-five years of lamented absence.

Swinging around Redpath's New England lecture circuit in the 1870's, three of the country's most popular humorists paused for a self-conscious portrait. *From the left:* Petroleum V. Nasby, Mark Twain, and Josh Billings.

"I knew him pretty intimately thenceforth until he crossed the ocean to be consul, first at Crefeldt in Germany and afterwards in Glasgow. He never returned to America. When he died in London, he had been absent from America and from his wife and daughters twenty-six years.

"This is the very Bret Harte whose pathetics, imitated from Dickens, used to be a godsend to the farmers of two hemispheres on account of the freshets of tears they compelled. He said to me once with a cynical chuckle that he thought he had mastered the art of pumping up the tear of sensibility. The idea conveyed was that the tear of sensibility was oil, and that by luck he had struck it.

"The higher passions were left out of Harte; what he knew about them he got from books. When he put them into his own books they were imitations; often good ones, often as deceptive to people who did not know Harte as are the actor's simulation of passions on the stage when he is not feeling them but is only following certain faithfully studied rules for their artificial reproduction."

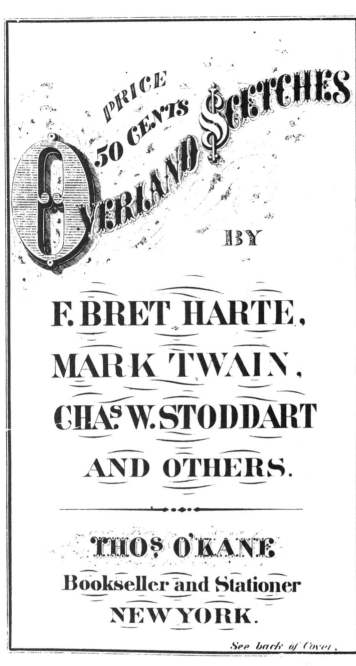

This collection of sketches by Western writers appeared in New York in August, 1868, shortly after Mark returned from his California lecture tour.

The "Jumping Frog" poster advertising a Mark Twain lecture.

MY PERSONAL APPEARANCE

What did Mark Twain look like on the platform? To a Chicago reporter he was "a thin man of five foot ten, thirty-five, eyes that penetrate like a new gimlet, nasal prow projecting and pendulous, carrotty, curly hair and mustache, arms that are always in the way, ex-

pression dreadfully melancholy, he stares inquisitively here and there, and cranes, and cranes his long neck around the house like a bereaved voter who was just coming from the deathbed of his mother-in-law and is looking for a sexton."

Mark defended himself in his autobiography: "The first critic that ever had occasion to describe my personal appearance littered his description with foolish and inexcusable errors whose aggregate furnished the result that I was distinctly and distressingly unhandsome. That description floated around the country in the papers and was in constant use and wear for a quarter of a century. It seems strange to me that apparently no critic in the country could be found who could look at me and have the courage to take up his

A British review of a Twain lecture.

pen and destroy that lie. That lie began its course on the Pacific coast in 1864 and it likened me in personal appearance to Petroleum V. Nasby, who had been out there lecturing. For twenty-five years afterward, no critic could furnish a description of me without fetching in Nasby to help out my portrait. I knew Nasby well and he was a good fellow, but in my life I have not felt malignantly enough about any more than three persons to charge those persons with resembling Nasby. It hurts me to the heart, these things. To this day it hurts me to the heart and it had long been a distress to my family—including Susy—that the critics should go on making this wearisome mistake year after year, when there was no foundation for it. Even when a critic wanted to be particularly friendly and complimentary to me, he didn't dare to go beyond my clothes. He did not venture beyond that frontier. When he had finished with my clothes he had said all the kind things, the pleasant things, the complimentary things he could risk. Then he dropped back on Nasby.''

The placards for Mark Twain's lectures in England were as conservative as his audiences. A London artist caught the contrast between Mark's solemn delivery and the surprised hilarity of his listeners. In the fall of 1873 he entertained the Britishers with his old Sandwich Island lecture and the newer "Roughing It on the Silver Frontier." He was an immense success.

Mr. Samuel L. Clemmens, more popularly known by his pseudonym of "Mark Twain," gave a new lecture at the Hanover Square Rooms on Monday, under the title of "Roughing it on the Silver Frontier." Although not, perhaps, equal to his previous one on "The Sandwich Islands," his quaint discourse, which related to the wonders of Nevada, was full of that graphic description and dryness of humour that lend such peculiar charms to his delivery. The whole State of Nevada, which, when first explored by miners in 1859, was called "Washoe," is one vast silver mine, and "Mark Twain," who was at one time editor of the Enterprise, a daily paper, published in the city of Virginia, had some curious tales to tell of the difficulties of journalism, in a place where to wield a pen it was necessary to handle a revolver. His description of a native cantankerous pony called "A Mexican Plug," which has the knack of throwing its rider into the air, and a propensity for devouring all linen hung out to dry upon clothes-lines, was the means of keeping a crowded audience uproariously mirthful for some time. A fair specimen of those travellers' tales, which may be suspected of a little exaggeration, might be cited in his account of the Nevada "zephyr," which—"when on business"—blows a hurricane. In one instance Mr. Mark Twain stated the wind blew a man's hair entirely off his head, and when the disconsolate traveller wished to know what was to become of him under the circumstances, the reply came, "Well, Sir, I guess you are a slim, light figure, and easy to handle, and my advice is to chalk your smooth, bald head, and let yourself out at so much an hour as a billiard-cue, and I'm darned if you don't make your fortune here in a month." It is now definitely settled that the new theatre built within the walls of "The Criterion," in Piccadilly, will be opened in February, under the management of Mr. H. J. Byron. The programme is to consist only of farce, vaudeville, and ballet, and the entertainments commencing at eight are to terminate before eleven.

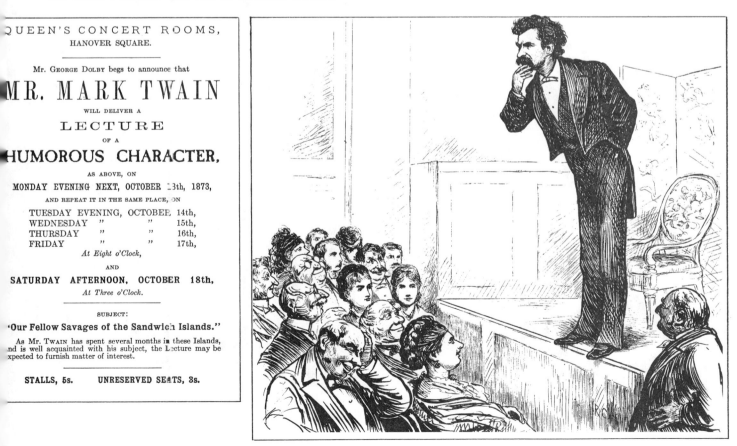

QUEEN'S CONCERT ROOMS,
HANOVER SQUARE.

Mr. George Dolby begs to announce that

MR. MARK TWAIN

WILL DELIVER A

LECTURE

OF A

HUMOROUS CHARACTER,

AS ABOVE, ON

MONDAY EVENING NEXT, OCTOBER 13th, 1873,

AND REPEAT IT IN THE SAME PLACE, ON

TUESDAY EVENING, OCTOBER 14th,
WEDNESDAY " " 15th,
THURSDAY " " 16th,
FRIDAY " " 17th,
At Eight o'Clock,

AND

SATURDAY AFTERNOON, OCTOBER 18th,
At Three o'Clock.

SUBJECT:

'Our Fellow Savages of the Sandwich Islands.''

As Mr. Twain has spent several months in these Islands, and is well acquainted with his subject, the Lecture may be expected to furnish matter of interest.

STALLS, 5s.   UNRESERVED SEATS, 3s.

Lewis Carroll.

Robert Browning.

Henry Stanley.

Ivan Turgenev.

An 1873 photo of Twain, taken in London.

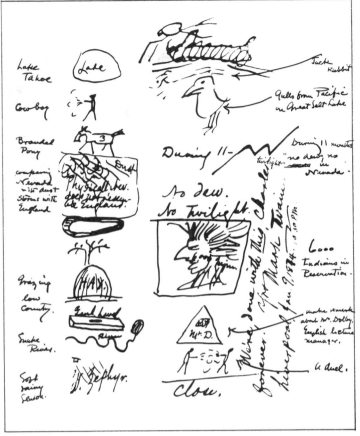

These sketches are Mark's notes for a *Roughing It* lecture given in Liverpool in 1874. Obscure to others, the scratchings made sense to him. In the margins are notes of an expert on the Mark Twain West, deciphering the sketches.

In Edinburgh, the Twains became warm friends of Dr. John Brown (*seated*), their physician and the author of *Rab and His Friend*. Year-old Susy Clemens is seated on her nurse's lap.

LONDON TRIUMPH

Mark Twain made his first trip to England in the summer of 1872 and was royally received by literary London. Six months later he was back again, this time with his family. They stayed abroad from May to October of 1873, with Mark making his first platform appearance in the last week of their visit. In November he was once again in England, delivering his popular lectures until January. Both *Roughing It* and *The Gilded Age* were published, and Mark was honored everywhere as a uniquely American writer. Celebrated figures such as Robert Browning, Lewis Carroll ("the shyest full-grown man, except Uncle Remus, I ever met"), Charles Kingsley, Wilkie Collins, Charles Reade, Ivan Turgenev, and the explorer Henry Stanley sought him out; select clubs made him an honorary member; and *Punch* deigned to quote him.

The Langdon mansion in Elmira, New York, where Mark Twain came courting "that wonderful miracle of humanity, little Miss Livy."

Mr. & Mrs. S. L. Clemens.

Wedding card of Olivia Langdon and Mark Twain.

Olivia Langdon. She was ten years younger than Mark.   Mark Twain was 34 in 1870, the year he married Livy.

Family Life

"MR. AND MRS. SAMUEL LANGHORNE CLEMENS"

It was at the St. Nicholas Hotel in New York on December 27, 1867, that Mark Twain first met the girl he was to marry. He had come up from Washington to spend the Christmas holidays with *Quaker City* friends. Charlie Langdon and his family were in town, too, and Mark was introduced to the original of the ivory miniature he had seen in the Bay of Smyrna. On New Year's day he dropped in on Olivia Langdon's family at ten in the morning, and left thirteen hours later. On their first date he took Livy and her family to hear Dickens read at Steinway Hall. "Beautiful girl," he wrote his mother and sister. "I am going to spend a few days with the Langdons in Elmira, New York, as soon as I get time."

But covering Capitol Hill, getting started on *The Innocents,* and lecturing on the West Coast interfered, and it was late August before Elmira welcomed him. The Langdons lived in a big house that took up a whole city block. Livy's father, Jervis Langdon, had risen from country store clerk to wealthy coal dealer. Livy, now twenty-two, had slowly been recovering from a partial paralysis caused by a fall on the ice at sixteen. A genteel girl of the Victorian period, she felt nervous about entertaining an unmarried man, a man ten years her senior, a man known as the Wild Humorist of the Pacific Slope, a man who had written a book. Would he be funny all the time? Would he expect her to be?

The first visit did not turn out to be an ordeal. For two weeks, with Livy and her young cousin Hattie, Mark rode, walked, sang, and entertained them in that lazy drawl that delighted everyone. Before he left he asked the all-important question—and was turned down. Livy would simply be his "sister."

A heavy lecture schedule took Mark away but letters streamed back and forth and he managed to squeeze in two brief visits. By the end of November he could report to a friend that Livy said she "was *glad* and *proud* she loved me!" A day or two later Mark's sister was let in on the news: "I love—I *worship*—Olivia L. Langdon

On this page in the family Bible Mark recorded his marriage.

of Elmira—& she loves me. When I am permanently *settled*—& when I am a Christian—& when I have *demonstrated* that I have a good, steady reliable character, her parents will withdraw their objection, & she *may* marry me—I say she *will*—I intend she *shall.* . . ."

Now the problem was to assure Jervis Langdon that Livy's choice had a blameless past and that he could support Livy in the proper style. The character witnesses summoned by Mark almost wrecked his plans. One wrote, "Clemens is a humbug," and another predicted Mark "would fill a pauper's grave." But against this sour evidence Jervis Langdon said, "I'll be your friend myself. Take the girl. I know you better than they do."

On February 4, 1869, Mark and Livy were formally engaged. Almost a year later—February 2, 1870—they were married.

The Reverend Thomas K. Beecher of the Park Church, Elmira. With the Reverend Joseph Twichell of Hartford, he performed the ceremonies at Mark Twain's marriage. Thomas was as eloquent a preacher as his famous brother Henry Ward, but he also served his congregation as carpenter, painter, and paper hanger. Like his wife, who bobbed her hair in 1857, he had little respect for convention, money, or fame. His was a "home church" where Christians of all creeds or no creed could feel they belonged.

MARK ON LIVY

A few weeks after his marriage, Mark wrote to a Nevada mining friend:

"If all of one's married days are as happy as these new ones have been to me, I have deliberately fooled away thirty years of my life. If it were to do over again I would marry in early infancy instead of wasting time cutting teeth & breaking crockery."

Thirty-six years later—it was two years after Livy's death—Mark paid this tribute to his wife:

"In the beginning of February 1870 I was married to Miss Olivia L. Langdon, and I took up my residence in Buffalo, New York.

"I saw her first in the form of an ivory miniature in her brother Charley's stateroom in the steamer Quaker City in the Bay of Smyrna, in the summer of 1867, when she was in her twenty-second year. I saw her in the flesh for the first time in New York in the following December. She was slender and beautiful and girlish—and she was both girl and woman. She remained both girl and woman to the last day of her life. Under a grave and gentle exterior burned inextinguishable fires of sympathy, energy, devotion, enthusiasm and absolutely limitless affection. She was always frail in body and she lived upon her spirit, whose hopefulness and courage were indestructible.

"Perfect truth, perfect honesty, perfect candor, were qualities of my wife's character which were born with her. Her judgments of people and things were sure and accurate. Her intuitions almost never deceived her. In her judgments of the characters and acts of both friends and strangers there was always room for charity, and this charity never failed. I have compared and contrasted her with hundreds of persons and my conviction remains that hers was the most perfect character I have ever met. And I may add that she was the most winningly dignified person I have ever known. Her character and disposition were of the sort that not only invite worship but command it.

"She was always cheerful; and she was always able to communicate her cheerfulness to others. During the nine years that we spent in poverty and debt she was always able to reason me out of my despairs and find a bright side to the clouds and make me see it. In all that time I never knew her to utter a word of regret concerning our altered circumstances, nor did I ever know her children to do the like. For she had taught them and they drew their fortitude from her. The love which she bestowed upon those whom she loved took the form of worship, and in that form it was returned— returned by relatives, friends, and the servants of the household.

"It was a strange combination which wrought into one individual, so to speak, by marriage—her disposition and character and mine. She poured out her prodigal affections in kisses and caresses and in a vocabulary of endearments whose profusion was always an astonishment to me. I was born reserved as to endearments of speech, and caresses, and hers broke upon me as the summer waves break upon Gibraltar. I was reared in that atmosphere of reserve. As I have already said, I never knew a member of my father's family to kiss another member of it except once, and that at a deathbed. And our village was not a kissing community. The kissing and caressing ended with courtship—along with the deadly piano-playing of that day.

"She had the heart-free laugh of a girl. It came seldom, but when it broke upon the ear it was as inspiring as music. I heard it for the last time when she had been occupying her sick bed for more than a year and I made a written note of it at the time—a note not to be repeated."

Mr. and Mrs. Jervis Langdon, Livy's parents. The Langdons were liberals; they led Elmira abolitionists out of the Presbyterian Church in 1846 in a conflict over slavery and formed the Park Congregational Church. Runaway slaves heading north found shelter at the Langdons' and men like Garrison, Phillips, and Fred Douglass were always welcome. Livy's background was Victorian, but hardly orthodox.

125

The whole wedding party accompanied Mark and Livy to Buffalo. Instead of moving into a boardinghouse, Mark was surprised by a grand gift from his father-in-law: this house, completely furnished, on fashionable Delaware Avenue.

Main Street in the Buffalo of Mark's day. Muddy street, meat hanging on hooks outside the butcher shop, sofas for sale on the sidewalk.

BUFFALO EDITOR

On a quick lobbying expedition to Washington in July, 1870, Mark spent an hour at Mathew Brady's studio and had this picture taken. On Mark's right is his friend David Gray, poet-editor of the Buffalo *Courier;* the other man is George Alfred Townsend, journalist.

Although he was a successful lecturer and the author of a best-seller, Mark felt marriage required a more solid financial base. He bought a third interest in the Buffalo *Express,* borrowing $12,500 from Jervis Langdon. In August, 1869, he took up his duties as roving editor, introducing himself in a Salutatory:

"Being a stranger, it would be immodest and unbecoming of me to suddenly and violently assume the associate editorship of the Buffalo Express without a single explanatory word of comfort or encouragement to the unoffending patrons of the paper, who are about to be exposed to constant attacks of my wisdom and learning. But this explanatory word shall be as brief as possible. I only wish to assure parties having a friendly interest in the prosperity of the journal, that I am not going to hurt the paper deliberately and intentionally at any time. I am not going to introduce any startling reforms, or in any way attempt to make trouble. I am simply going to do my plain, unpretending duty, when I cannot get out of it; I shall work diligently and honestly and faithfully at all times and upon all occasions, when privation and want shall compel me to do it; in writing, I shall always confine myself strictly to the truth, except when it is attended with inconvenience; I shall witheringly rebuke all forms

THE BUFFALO EXPRESS

SEPT. 17 1869

PEOPLE AND THINGS.

-Oranges are ripe in Florida.

-Jeff. Davis is back in London again.

-Pion-Plon is forty-seven

-Elder Parsons, one of Brigham's "Twelve Apostles," is dead.

-Barnum is going to the Sandwich Islands.

-The venerable Lucretia Mott has been visiting her birthplace, Nantucket.

-Jem Mace, the pugilist, is our latest distinguished English visitor.

-The Boston *Post* cruelly calls Elizabeth Cady Stanton a pantaloonatic.

-Bishop Kingsley sailed for China last Saturday.

-Saratoga lake is suggested for the next Harvard-Oxford boat race.

-Paris fashions are now Worthless, for Worth is dead.

-Julius Janin is sinking under an overweight of fat.

-A Kentucky cigar maker has no ears, and he listens with his mouth. His name

-"C-c-can that p-p-pup-parrot t-ter-talk?" asked a stuttering man of a German. "Suppose he no can talk so moche' better as that what you talk, I chop he dam head off," was his reply. *E.C.*

-Another trifling mistake by Judge Lynch : " The negro found hanging near Dresden, Tennessee, a few days ago, and who was supposed to have been hung for committing a rape on a small girl, has proved not to be the right person."

-A frightful zest was lately given to one of the bull fights at Madrid, by a bull which tossed a man, killed him in an instant, and ran about the circus with his entrails twisted about the horns. Nobody, of course, thought of stopping the performance, which went on for three hours afterward.

-It is a touching little anecdote, that which Sherman told of General Rawlins, who, at the decoration of the soldiers' graves at Arlington, last Spring, heard the exquisite requiem beginning:

For the *Express* Mark wrote editorials, gossip columns and satires, often spending 12 or 15 hours at his desk. He took a hand in everything, urging his reporters "to modify the adjectives, curtail their philosophical reflections and leave out the slang," and toning down the thunder-and-lightning typography to give the paper a more respectable look. The son of slaveholders and the ex-Confederate was now becoming "de-Southernized," as his antilynching editorial reproduced here shows. Meeting Frederick Douglass, he admired the Negro leader's fight against segregation in the schools. He wrote editorials denouncing injustice wherever he found it and never hesitated to name the wrongdoers, no matter how prominent.

That first year in Buffalo began well, but disaster soon struck. Mr. Langdon fell ill of cancer. His death in August, 1870, crushed Livy, who was now an expectant mother. A visiting school friend was downed by typhoid fever and died in September. The shocks brought about the premature birth of Livy's first child, Langdon. Plunged into deep melancholy, Mark tried to relieve the strain by "half-insane tempests and cyclones of humor."

---

of crime and misconduct, except when committed by the party inhabiting my own vest; I shall not make use of slang or vulgarity upon any occasion or under any circumstances, and shall never use profanity except in discussing house-rent and taxes. Indeed, upon second thought, I will not even use it then, for it is unchristian, inelegant and degrading—though to speak truly I do not see how house-rent and taxes are going to be discussed worth a cent without it. I shall not often meddle with politics, because we have a political editor who is already excellent, and only needs to serve a term in the penitentiary in order to be perfect. I shall not write any poetry, unless I conceive a spite against the subscribers.

"Such is my platform. I do not see any earthly use in it, but custom is law, and custom must be obeyed, no matter how much violence it may do to one's feelings."

THE BUFFALO EXPRESS
THURSDAY, AUGUST 26, 1869.

ONLY A NIGGER.

A dispatch from Memphis mentions that, of two negroes lately sentenced to death for murder in that vicinity, one named Woods has just confessed to having ravished a young lady during the war, for which deed another negro was hung at the time by an avenging mob, the evidence that doomed the guiltless wretch being a hat which Woods now relates that he stole from its owner and left behind, for the purpose of misleading. Ah, well! Too bad, to be sure! A little blunder in the administration of justice by Southern mob-law; but nothing to speak of. Only "a nigger" killed by mistake—that is all. Of course, every high toned gentleman whose chivalric impulses were so unfortunately misled in this affair, by the cunning of the miscreant Woods, is as sorry about it as a high toned gentleman can be expected to be sorry about the unlucky fate of "a nigger." But mistakes will happen, even in the conduct of the best regulated and most high toned mobs, and surely there is no good reason why Southern gentlemen should worry themselves with useless regrets, so long as only an innocent "nigger" is hanged, or roasted or knouted to death, now and then. What if the blunder of lynching the wrong man does happen once in four or five cases! Is that any fair argument against the cultivation and indulgence of those fine chivalric passions and that noble Southern spirit which will not brook the slow and cold formalities of regular law, when outraged white womanhood appeals for vengeance? Perish the thought so unworthy of a Southern soul! Leave it to the sentimentalism and humanitarianism of a cold-blooded Yankee civilization! What are the lives of a few "niggers" in comparison with the preservation of the impetuous instincts of a proud and fiery race? Keep ready the halter, therefore, oh chivalry of Memphis! Keep the lash knotted; keep the brand and the faggots in waiting, for prompt work with the next "nigger" who may be suspected of any damnable crime! Wreak a swift vengeance upon him, for the satisfaction of the noble impulse, that animate knightly hearts, and then leave time and accident to discover, if they will, whether he was guilty or no.

Mark Twain in 1871, his last year in Buffalo.

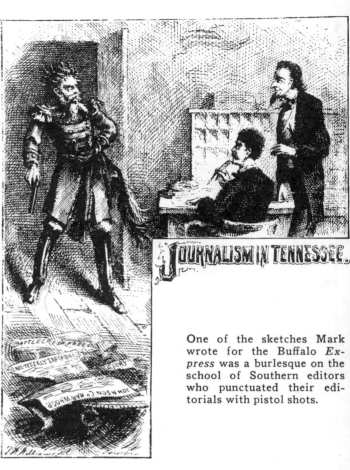

One of the sketches Mark wrote for the Buffalo *Express* was a burlesque on the school of Southern editors who punctuated their editorials with pistol shots.

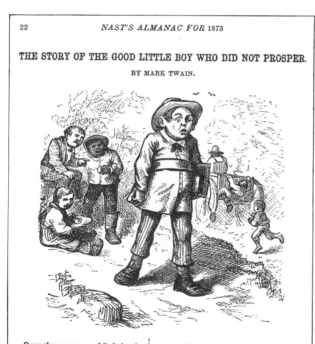

THE STORY OF THE GOOD LITTLE BOY WHO DID NOT PROSPER.

BY MARK TWAIN.

ONCE there was a good little boy by the name of Jacob Blivens. He always obeyed his parents, no matter how absurd and unreasonable their demands were; and he always learned his book, and never was late at Sabbath-school. He would not play hookey, even when his sober judgment told him it was the most profitable thing he could do. None of the other boys could ever make that boy out, he acted so strangely. He wouldn't lie, no matter how convenient it was. He just said it was wrong to lie, and that was sufficient for him. And he was so honest that he was simply ridiculous. The curious ways that Jacob had surpassed every thing. He wouldn't play at marbles on Sunday, he wouldn't rob birds' nests, he wouldn't give hot pennies to organ-grinders' monkeys; he didn't seem to take any interest in any kind of rational amusement. So the other boys used to try to reason it out, and come to an understanding of him, but they couldn't arrive at any satisfactory conclusion; as I said

JOURNALIST AND AUTHOR

Mark Twain was considered a great catch for the *Galaxy*, a magazine for which he agreed to write a monthly "Memoranda" column. They paid him $2,000 a year, and let him write what he pleased. This was 1870–71, the year his new family suffered so many misfortunes, and he found it hard to be funny on demand. In the very first column he blistered the renowned minister, De Witt Talmage, for urging that workmen be kept out of fashionable pews because common people didn't smell good. "We have reason to believe," wrote Mark, "that there will be laboring men in heaven; and also a number of Negroes, and Esquimaux, and Terra del Fuegans, and Arabs, and a few Indians, and possibly even some Spaniards and Portuguese. All things are possible with God. We shall have all these sorts of people in Heaven; but, alas! in getting them we shall lose the society of Dr. Talmage. Which is to say, we shall lose the company of one who

In Mark's 1870 study of pious little Jacob Blivens he tied a string of firecrackers to the Victorian myth of the Sunday school boy whose virtue was always rewarded. Thomas Nast, *Harper's* great cartoonist, reprinted it in his *Almanac*.

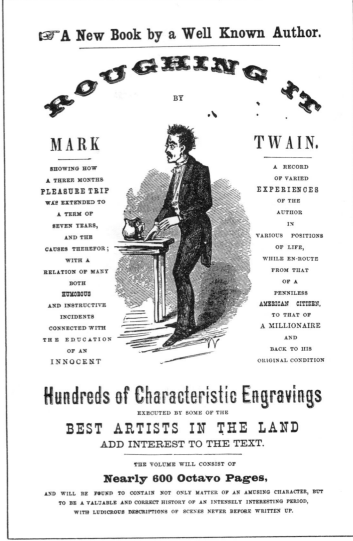

could give more real 'tone' to celestial society than any other contribution Brooklyn could furnish. And what would eternal happiness be without the Doctor? Blissful, unquestionably—we know that well enough—but would it be distingué, would it be recherché without him?"

In another column he teased his editor's predilection for printing portraits of celebrities by drawing his own "portrait" of William III, with scholarly annotations. And he hoaxed his readers with an imaginary British review of his own *Innocents Abroad,* another of his hoaxes which everyone took seriously, to his disgust. In April, 1871, he gave up the *Galaxy* and sold his interest in the *Express,* losing $10,000. It was the end of his career in journalism. With Livy and the baby he moved to Elmira, to Quarry Farm, where he spent the summer completing *Roughing It,* the story of his adventures in the West. Early in 1872 the book was published, and its advance sales promised to be as handsome as *The Innocents'.* From now on, Mark's profession was author.

129

A spinster cousin of Mark Twain, Xantippe Saunders, painted this portrait of him in 1873.

THE HANDSOMEST TOWN

Hartford was to be Mark Twain's first "permanent home" after almost twenty years of wandering. The Connecticut town won his favor instantly on his first visit, January 21, 1868. He came up to drive a bargain for *The Innocents* with the American Publishing Company. He stayed with John and Isabella Beecher Hooker. She was Henry Ward Beecher's sister and an ardent champion of women's rights. She and John, the "Puritanical Wag," were leaders of the town's intellectual life. In *Alta* letters, Mark recorded his first impressions of Hartford:

"I think this is the best-built and the handsomest town I have ever seen. They call New England the land of steady habits, and I see the evidence about me that it was not named amiss. As I came along the principal street, today—smoking, of course—I noticed that of the 200 men in sight at one time only two were smoking beside myself. I had to walk two blocks to find a cigar store. I saw no drinking saloons on that street—but I was not looking for any. I hear no swearing here; I see no one chewing tobacco. I have found nobody drunk. What a singular country this is.

"At the hospitable mansion where I am a guest, I have to smoke surreptitiously when all are in bed, to save my reputation, and then draw suspicion upon the cat when the family detect the unfamiliar odor. I never was so absurdly proper in the broad light of day in my life as I have been for the last day or two. So far, I am safe; but I am sorry to say that the cat has lost caste. She has steadily decreased in popularity since I made my advent here. She has achieved a reputation for smoking, and may be regarded as a degraded, a dishonored, a ruined cat.

"They have the broadest, straightest streets in Hartford that ever led a sinner to destruction; and the dwelling-houses are the simplest in size, and the shapelyest, and have the most capacious ornamental grounds about them. But I would speak of other things. This is the center of Connecticut wealth. Hartford dollars have a place in half the great moneyed enterprises in the union. All those Phoenix and Charter Oak insurance companies, whose gorgeous chromo-lithographic showcards it has been my delight to study in far-away cities, are located here.

"The Sharps' rifle factory is here; the great silk factory of this section is here; the heaviest subscription publishing houses in the land are here; and last, and greatest, the Colt's revolver manufactory is a Hartford institution."

The Hooker house in Hartford, where Mark was a guest on his first visit to the city in 1868. In October, 1871, he rented it and his family lived in it until their own house was ready in April, 1874.

The Hartford house of Elisha Bliss, Jr., publisher of *The Innocents Abroad*. Here Mark often stayed while working on the book.

MARK TWAIN'S HOUSE

BUILT 1874   EDWARD TUCKERMAN POTTER, ARCHITECT

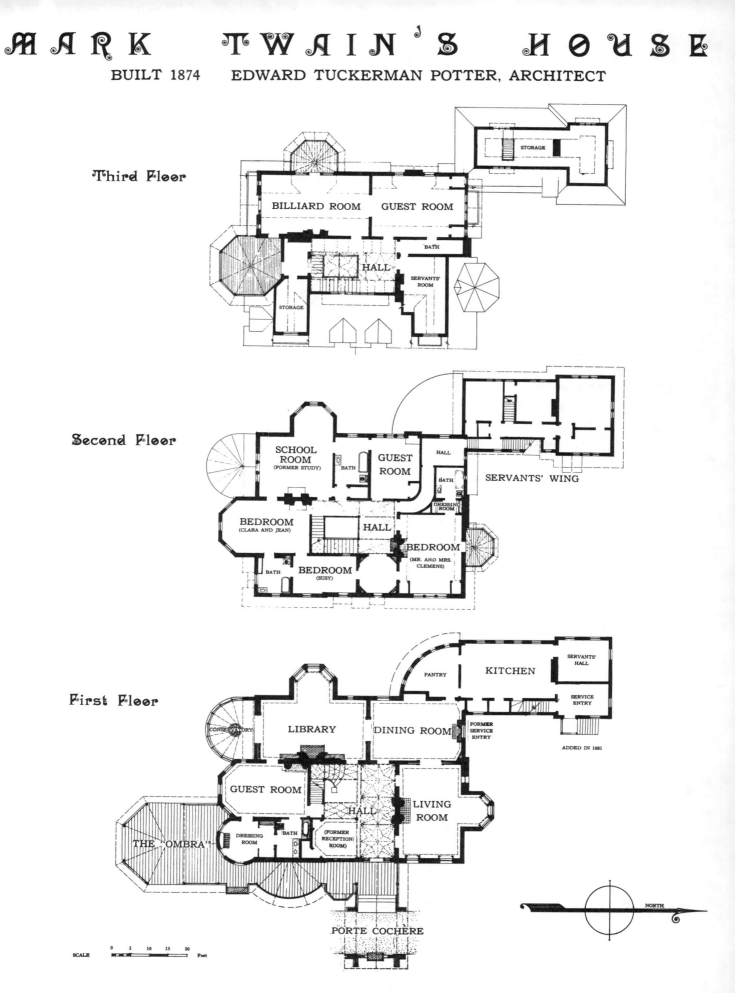

Third Floor

BILLIARD ROOM   GUEST ROOM

STORAGE

BATH

HALL

SERVANTS' ROOM

STORAGE

Second Floor

SCHOOL ROOM (FORMER STUDY)

BATH

GUEST ROOM

HALL

BATH

DRESSING ROOM

SERVANTS' WING

BEDROOM (CLARA AND JEAN)

HALL

BEDROOM (MR. AND MRS. CLEMENS)

BATH

BEDROOM (SUSY)

First Floor

PANTRY

KITCHEN

SERVANTS' HALL

SERVICE ENTRY

CONSERVATORY

LIBRARY

DINING ROOM

FORMER SERVICE ENTRY

ADDED IN 1881

GUEST ROOM

HALL

LIVING ROOM

DRESSING ROOM

BATH

(FORMER RECEPTION ROOM)

THE "OMBRA"

PORTE COCHÈRE

NORTH

SCALE   0   5   10   15   20   Feet

The Mark Twain house. It was the oddest and most elaborate home in Hartford, with 19 large rooms and five baths. Mark spent $31,000 for the five acres, $21,000 for furniture, and $70,000 for the house. With Gothic turrets, a balcony like a pilothouse, a porch like a river-boat deck, and lookouts commanding the best views, it was a bizarre departure that shocked Hartford for a while. The house was built for hospitality. Most of Mark's writing was done not here but at the summer farm, Quarry Farm, in Elmira. The family lived in this house from 1874 to 1891, and sold it in 1903. Today it is a Mark Twain museum.

MARK TWAIN'S HOUSE

Mark's feeling for the home in which he had raised his family is conveyed in this letter he wrote Livy in 1895. The family had been living in Europe since 1891, struggling to climb out of bankruptcy:

"Livy darling, when I arrived in town I did not want to go near the house, & I didn't want to go anywhere or see anybody. I said to myself, 'If I may be spared it I will never live in Hartford again.'

"But as soon as I entered this front door I was seized with a furious desire to have us all in this house again & right away, & never go outside the grounds any more forever—certainly never again to Europe.

"How ugly, tasteless, repulsive, are all the domestic interiors I have ever seen in Europe compared with the perfect taste of this ground floor, with its delicious dream of harmonious color, & its all-pervading spirit of peace & serenity & deep contentment. You did it all, & it speaks of you & praises you eloquently & unceasingly. It is the loveliest home that ever was. I had no faintest idea of what it was like. I supposed I had, for I have seen it in its wraps & disguises several times in the past three years; but it was a mistake; I had wholly forgotten its olden aspect. And so, when I stepped in at the front door—was suddenly confronted by all its richness & beauty minus wraps & concealments, it almost took my breath away. Katy had every rug & picture and ornament & chair exactly where they had always belonged, the place was bewitchingly bright & splendid & homelike & natural, & it seemed as if I had burst awake out of a hellish dream, & had never been away, & that you would come drifting down out of those dainty upper regions with the little children tagging after you."

Susy Clemens, Mark's second child, born in 1872.

On the back of this photo Mark wrote: "Miss Jean Clemens (17 months) listening to admonitions & moral teachings from her father. Hartford, Christmas, 1881."

FAMILY LIFE

Six months after the move to Hartford, Susy Clemens was born. Mark's first child, Langdon, died only ten weeks later and Susy became the center of attention. "Like other children," Mark wrote in his autobiography, "Susy was blithe and happy, fond of play; unlike the average of children, she was at times much given to retiring within herself and trying to search out the hidden meanings of the deep things that make the puzzle and pathos of human existence and in all the ages have baffled the inquirer and mocked him. As a little child aged seven she was oppressed and perplexed by the maddening repetition of the stock incidents of our race's fleeting sojourn here, just as the same thing has oppressed and perplexed maturer minds from the beginning of time. A myriad of men are born; they labor and sweat and struggle for bread; they squabble and scold and fight; they scramble for little mean advantages over each other. Age creeps upon them; infirmities follow; shames and humiliations bring down their prides and their vanities. Those they love are taken from them and the joy of life is turned to aching grief. The burden of pain, care, misery, grows heavier year by year. At length ambition is dead; pride is dead; vanity is dead; longing for

Mark's three girls. *From the left:* Clara (born in 1874), Jean, and Susy.

134

The Twains on their steamboat deck porch.

release is in their place. It comes at last—the only unpoisoned gift earth ever had for them—and they vanish from a world where they were of no consequence; where they achieved nothing; where they were a mistake and a failure and a foolishness; where they have left no sign that they have existed—a world which will lament them a day and forget them forever. Then another myriad takes their place and copies all they did and goes along the same profitless road and vanishes as they vanished—to make room for another and another and a million other myriads to follow the same arid path through the same desert and accomplish what the first myriad and all the myriads that came after it accomplished—nothing!

"'Mamma, what is it all for?' asked Susy, preliminarily stating the above details in her own halting language, after long brooding over them alone in the privacy of the nursery.

"When Susy was thirteen and was a slender little maid with plaited tails of copper-tinged brown hair down her back and was perhaps the busiest bee in the household hive, by reason of the manifold studies, health exercises and recreations she had to attend to, she secretly and of her own motion and out of love added another task to her labors—the writing of a biography of me. She did this work in her bedroom at night and kept her record hidden. After a little the mother discovered it and filched it and let me see it; then told Susy what she had done and how

pleased I was and how proud. I remember that time with a deep pleasure. I had had compliments before but none that touched me like this; none that could approach it for value in my eyes. It has kept that place always since. I have had no compliment, no praise, no tribute from any source that was so precious to me as this one was and still is. As I read it now, after all these many years, it is still a king's message to me and brings me the same dear surprise it brought me then—with the pathos added of the thought that the eager and hasty hand that sketched it and scrawled it will not touch mine again—and I feel as the humble and unexpectant must feel when their eyes fall upon the edict that raises them to the ranks of the noble.

"It is quite evident that several times, at breakfast and dinner, in those long-past days, I was posing for the biography. In fact, I clearly remember that I was doing that—and I also remember that Susy detected it. I remember saying a very smart thing with a good deal of an air, at the breakfast table one morning and that Susy observed to her mother privately a little later that papa was doing that for the biography."

Clara, Jean, and Susy with their dog, Flash.

An 1887 photo of the Clemens girls and their Langdon cousins. *From the left:* Julia Langdon, Clara and Jean Clemens, Jervis and Ida Langdon, and Susy Clemens. On the back of the photo someone noted little Ida's overheard comment: "Julia is grinning—Clara is sober—Jervis is cross—Jean is sweet—and Susy and I are beautiful!"

Patrick McAleer, "the brisk and electric young coachman" who began working for the Twains in Buffalo and stayed with them for 25 years. "As the children grew up," Mark wrote, "he was their guide. He was all honor, honesty and affection—my idea of a perfect gentleman."

Katy Leary, who worked for the Twains for over 30 years. Mark Twain "was a very affectionate father," she wrote after his death. "I have never known a happier household."

John Lewis worked for the Twains for 29 years, and was retired on a pension. Once he stopped a runaway horse and saved the lives of Livy's sister-in-law, and her daughter and nursemaid.

During Christmas week of 1884 the neighborhood children surprised Mark with a production of the play based on *The Prince and the Pauper*. When Susy read the line, "Fathers be alike, mayhap; mine hath not a doll's temper," it brought the house down. Above is a scene from the play. Sometimes Mark himself played Miles Hendon.

SUSY LOOKS AT MARK

The biography of Mark Twain that Susy began in 1885, when her father was forty-nine and she thirteen, is a delightful sketch Mark quoted from in his own autobiography:

"We are a very happy family. We consist of Papa, Mamma, Jean, Clara and me. It is papa I am writing about, and I shall have no trouble in not knowing what to say about him, as he is a very striking character.

"Papa's appearance has been described many times, but very incorrectly. He has beautiful gray hair, not any too thick or any too long, but just right; a Roman nose, which greatly improves the beauty of his features; kind blue eyes and a small mustache. He has a wonderfully shaped head and profile. He has a very good figure—in short, he is an extraordinarily fine looking man. All his features are perfect, except that he hasn't extraordinary teeth. His complexion is very fair, and he doesn't ware a beard. He is a very good man and a very funny one. He has got a temper, but we all of us have in this family. He is the loveliest man I ever saw or ever hope to see— and oh, so absent-minded. He does tell perfectly delightful stories. Clara and I used to sit on each arm of his chair and listen while he told us stories about the pictures on the wall.

"Papa's favorite game is billiards, and when he is tired and wishes to rest himself he stays up all night and plays billiards, it seems to rest his head. He smokes a great deal almost incessantly. He has the mind of an author exactly, some of the simplest things he can't understand.

"Papa has a peculiar gait we like, it seems to sute him, but most people do not; he always walks up and down the room while thinking and between each coarse at meals.

"Papa is very fond of animals particularly of cats, we had a dear little gray kitten once that he named 'Lazy' (papa always wears gray to match his hair and eyes) and he would carry him around on his shoulder, it was a mighty pretty sight! the gray cat sound asleep against papa's gray coat and hair. The names that he has given our different cats, are realy remarkably funny, they are namely Stray Kit, Abner, Motley, Fraeulein, Lazy, Bufalo Bill, Soapy Sall, Cleveland, Sour Mash, and Pestilence and Famine.

"Papa said the other day, 'I am a mugwump and a mugwump is pure from the marrow out.' (Papa knows that I am writing this biography of him, and he said this for it.) He doesn't like to go church at all, why I never understood, until just now, he told us the other day that he couldn't bear to hear any one talk but himself, but that he could listen to himself talk for hours without getting tired, of course he said this in joke, but I've no dought it was founded on truth.

Saturday was family theater day in the Twain home. The children staged scenes from plays they liked or wrote their own scripts. Neighbors and servants often took part. This scene from a Greek play shows, *from the left,* Clara, Margaret Warner, Jean, Susy, and Fanny Freese.

An 1891 photo of Susy, Jean, and Clara Clemens.

"One of papa's latest books is *The Prince and the Pauper* and it is unquestionably the best book he has ever written, some people want him to keep to his old style, some gentleman wrote him, 'I enjoyed Huckleberry Finn immensely and am glad to see that you have returned to your old style.' That enoyed me that enoyed me greatly, because it trobles me [Susy was troubled by that word, and uncertain; she wrote a u above it in the proper place, but reconsidered the matter and struck it out] to have so few people know papa, I mean realy know him, they think of Mark Twain as a humorist joking at everything; 'And with a mop of reddish brown hair which sorely needs the barbars brush a roman nose, short stubby mustache, a sad care-worn face, with maney crow's feet,' etc. That is the way people picture papa, I have wanted papa to write a book that would reveal something of his kind sympathic nature, and *The Prince and the Pauper* partly does it. The book is full of lovely charming ideas, and oh the language! It is perfect. I think that one of the most touching scenes in it, is where the pauper is riding on horseback with his nobles in the 'recognition procession' and he sees his mother oh and then what followed! How she runs to his side, when she sees him throw up his hand palm outward, and is rudely pushed off by one of the King's officers, and then how the little pauper's consceince troubles him when he remembers the shameful words that were falling from his lips, when she was turned from his side 'I know you not woman' and how his grandeurs were stricken valueless, and his pride consumed to ashes. It is a wonderfully beautiful and touching little scene, and papa has described it so wonderfully. I never saw a man with so much

variety of feeling as papa has; now the *Prince and the Pauper* is full of touching places, but there is most always a streak of humor in them somewhere. Now in the coronation—in the stirring coronation, just after the little king has got his crown back again papa brings that in about the Seal, where the pauper says he used the Seal "to crack nuts with." Oh it is so funny and nice! Papa very seldom writes a passage without some humor in it somewhere, and I don't think he ever will."

"Our varius occupations [at Quarry Farm in Elmira] are as follows. Papa rises about ½ past 7 in the morning, breakfasts at eight, writes, plays tennis with Clara and me and tries to make the donkey go, in the morning; does varius things in P.M., and in the evening plays tennis with Clara and me and amuses Jean and the donkey.

"Mama rises about ¼ to eight, breakfasts at eight, teaches Jean German reading from 9-10, reads German with me from 10-11. Then she reads studdies or visits with aunt Susie for a while, and then she reads to Clara and I till lunch time things connected with English history (for we hope to go to England next summer) while we sew. Then we have lunch. She studdies for about half an hour or visits with aunt Susie, then reads to us an hour or more, then studdies writes reads and rests till supper time. After supper she sits out on the porch and works till eight o'clock, from eight o'clock to bedtime she plays whist with papa and after she has retired she reads and studdies German for a while.

"Clara and I do most everything from practicing to donkey riding and playing tag. While Jean's time is spent in asking mama what she can have to eat.

"When we are all alone at home nine times out of ten he talks about some very earnest subject (with an occasional joke thrown in), and he a good deal more often talks upon such subjects than upon the other kind.

"He is as much of a philosopher as anything, I think. I think he could have done a great deal in this direction if he had studied while young, for he seems to enjoy reasoning out things, no matter what; in a great many such directions he has greater ability than in the gifts which have made him famous."

SUSY ON HUCK

"Ever since papa and mama were married papa has written his books and then taken them to mama in manuscript, and she has expergated them. Papa read *Huckleberry Finn* to us in manuscript, just before it came out, and then he would leave parts of it with mama to expergate, while he went off to the study to work, and sometimes Clara and I would be sitting with mama while she was looking the manuscript over, and I remember so well, with what pangs of regret we used to see her turn down the leaves of the pages, which meant that some delightfully terrible part must be scratched out. And I remember one part perticularly which was perfectly fascinating it was so terrible, that Clara and I used to delight in and oh, with what despair we saw mama turn down the leaf on which it was written, we thought the book would almost be ruined without it. But we gradually come to think as mama did."

Jean Clemens.   Clara Clemens at 16.

Saturday Morning Club.

LECTURES,

1876 — 1877.

··•··

COMMITTEE.

Miss EMILY H. PERKINS.   Miss ANNIE E. TRUMBULL.

1. THOMAS HOOD,	. . . .	Mr. J. T. Fields.
2. POTTERY AND PORCELAIN,	. .	Dr. W. C. Prime
3. THE AMERICAN REVOLUTION,	. .	Mrs. H. E. Burton.
4. NAMES,	. . . .	Rev. S. J Andrews.
5. JOHN SEBASTIAN BACH,	. .	Rev. W. L. Gage.
6. LIFE OF LORD MACAULAY,	. .	Mr. S. L. Clemens.
7. THANKFUL BLOSSOM: A Story,	.	Mr. F. Bret Harte.
8. WORK FOR THE POOR,	. .	Mrs. S. G. Sluyter.
9. HOW EDWARD STURM MET HIS DESTINY: A Story,	. . .	Prof. H. H. Boyesen.
10. EGYPT,	. .	Mr. C. D. Warner.
11. MUSIC,	. . .	Mrs. C. D. Warner.
12. MOORISH CIVILIZATION,	. .	Dr. J. H. Trumbull.
13. THE WAR OF THE REBELLION,	.	Rev. J. H. Twichell.
14. SUFFRAGE,	. . . .	Hon. H. C. Robinson.
15. HEALTH,	. . . .	Mrs. R. Gleason.
16. MENDELSSOHN,	. . .	Rev. W. L. Gage.
17. THE WAR OF THE REBELLION,	.	Gen. J. R. Hawley.

Mark Twain organized a Saturday Morning Club for girls 16 to 20. They met at his home to hear talks by guest speakers. Number 7 on the program above was especially memorable because it was written by Bret Harte, inspired by a bottle of Scotch, the night before he read it to the club.

SUSY ON SOLITAIRE

"Clara sprained her ankle a little while ago by running into a tree when coasting, and while she was unable to walk with it she played solotaire with cards a great deal. While Clara was sick and papa saw her play solotaire so much he got very much interested in the game, and finally began to play it himself a little; then Jean took it up, and at last MAMA even played it occasionally; Jean's and papa's love for it rapidly increased, and now Jean brings the cards every night to the table and papa and mama help her play, and before dinner is at an end papa has gotten a separate pack of cards and is playing alone, with great interest. Mama and Clara next are made subject to the contagious solotaire, and there are four solotarireans at the table, while you hear nothing but 'Fill up the place,' etc. It is dreadful!"

139

NOOK FARM

Nook Farm, scene of Mark Twain's happiest and most productive years, was a 100-acre tract, heavily wooded, lying on the western edge of Hartford. The Hookers began developing it in the 1850s; by the end of a decade several of their relatives and friends had built large, comfortable homes there. The select society kept open house, and conversation about literature and politics flourished. By 1871 the circle included the Warners, Stowes and Twains. Soon the literary lions of Boston and New York found Hartford a very congenial stopping place. Large dinners at the Warners' or Twains' "produced an incomparable hilarity" and sometimes the party was up till dawn, enjoying ale, wit and parlor tricks. Mark liked to dance, sing and tell stories for the guests. "M.T. *never was* so funny as this time," wrote Joe Twichell after one dinner. "The perfect art of a certain kind of story telling will die with him."

Whist, skating and sleighing, picnics, long drives in the carriage, billiards, hikes, bicycling, excursions on the river—these were the recreations of Nook Farm. Servants eased the chores of hospitality but the continuous social life made creative work difficult.

"Work?" Mark wrote a friend in 1881—"One *can't* you know, to any purpose. I don't really get anything done worth speaking of except during the three or four months that we are away in the summer. I keep three or four books on the stocks all the time, but I seldom add a satisfactory chapter to one of them if home."

As the expense and strain of maintaining a lavish scale of living mounted, Mark confided to Howells, "A life of don't-care-a-damn in a boarding house is what I have asked for in many a secret prayer."

But the social round went on (Mark's living expenses in one year soared to $100,000) and won applause from friends who enjoyed it. "You must know," Reverend Thomas K. Beecher told Livy, "that yours is one of the few *restful* homes in which intelligence, culture, luxury and company combine to the compounding of a pleasure which every visitor longs to taste again."

A glimpse of the writer at home is furnished by a reporter who came by for an interview: "I called at the door of his astonishing residence in the outskirts of the city. The domestic informed me that I would find Mr. Clemens in the back yard. When I approached the celebrated humorist he was sitting on an inverted washtub, trying to teach a frowsy little terrier to catch crackers in its mouth. Twain had his hat full of oyster

Isabella Beecher Hooker in 1904. After her death three years later, Mark said of his eccentric feminist neighbor that she had helped win the only revolution for the emancipation of half a nation that cost no blood.

Reverend Joseph H. Twichell, about 1875. He was Mark Twain's closest friend for 40 years. A brigade chaplain in the Civil War, Twichell became pastor of Asylum Hill church, a congregation of professional and business men. Mark called it the "Church of the Holy Speculators." The Twain-Twichell debate over religion and politics was endless but affectionate.

Harriet Beecher Stowe. The author of *Uncle Tom's Cabin* lived next door to the Twains, and designed their conservatory. In her last forgetful years in Nook Farm she was a gentle wraith wandering in and out of the Twain household.

The house of Charles and Susan Warner, another landmark in the literary colony.

crackers. The dog stood on its hind legs and snapped, with much perseverance, but with only a moderate degree of skill, at the bits tossed by the master. To set a good example, Twain tossed every third or fourth cracker up into the air, catching it in his own mouth as it descended, and never missing. I complimented him upon his surprising dexterity.

" 'Oh,' said he, carelessly, 'a great deal can be accomplished by long practice.'

"He led the way into his study, and carefully locked the door. It is a strange apartment. The floor was littered up with a confusion of newspapers, newspaper cuttings, books, children's toys, pipes, models of machinery, and cigar ends. Twain's method is to drop everything when he's done using it, but he will let nobody else interfere with the arrangements of his study. 'I am naturally lazy,' he says, 'and I wish to conquer the detestable habit by imposing on myself a certain amount of domestic work. I take care of the room myself.' In one corner stood a stack of his patent self-gumming scrapbooks. This invention, I am told, is the source of a considerable income to Mr. Clemens. On the mantel, where the bust of Calvin stood until Mark destroyed it with a poker in a moment of religious frenzy, I noticed a pitcher that looked as if it contained beer. On the table were many manuscript sheets of Mr. Clemens' unfinished historical work, 'The Mother-in-Law in All Ages.' "

Charles Dudley Warner, editor of the Hartford *Courant* and of *Harper's*. He was a warm friend of Twain's and collaborated with him on *The Gilded Age*. His travel books, essays and fiction were popular in his day.

Mark Twain's Lecture.

One of the largest and finest audiences of the season was present at the Opera House last evening to hear Mark Twain deliver his lecture on "Old Pioneering Times in the Silver Mining Region." The lecturer began by a description of the overland trip to Nevada, in a stage coach, then dwelt at length upon the characteristics of the mountainous region and the plains, narrating some personal experiences at Virginia City, including a duel, and giving a graphic picture of the lawless state of society there eleven or twelve years ago. He concluded with some facts about the famous bonanza of the Comstock lode, and an irresistibly funny story of his experiences with a Mexican "plug." The lecture abounded in graphic description and amusing anecdote, and was delivered in the remarkably comical manner which is peculiar to Mark Twain. No lecture that we have ever heard has been more provocative of mirth. The audience were kept the whole evening in one perpetual burst of laughter. No newspaper report could begin to reproduce its genuine and wholesome humor, or indicate how extraordinarily funny were some of its incidents. The lecture is without doubt the best Mr. Clemens has yet delivered in this city. The audience testified their approbation by frequent and hearty applause. Colt's full band performed a number of selections before the lecture, in an admirable manner, and the "The Last Rose of Summer" with a cornet solo received the compliment of an encore. The cornet playing was excellent. The band also played a quickstep after the lecture. Altogether the entertainment was a remarkable one in the amusement season of 1875. The people of Hartford owe Mr. Clemens the heartiest thanks for his generosity in thus contributing to the relief of the city's poor. Colt's band are also entitled to thanks for volunteering their services, as also Mr. Rathbun for his excellent management of the affair. The receipts were over $1200, all of which will be placed in Father Hawley's hands for the benefit of his "clients" as Mr. Clemens calls them.

Hartford prosperity was widespread but the city had its slums and poverty. Hard times were eased by charity bazaars and fairs. Mark Twain was among the most generous with time and money. This 1875 lecture raised $1,200.

William Gillette, actor and dramatist. Mark gave his young neighbor a start in the theater with a bit part in Twain's play version of *The Gilded Age*. Then he loaned young Gillette $3,000 to finance a theatrical career. The stage was taboo to respectable Hartford until Mark's prestige destroyed the Puritanical prejudice.

J. Hammond Trumbull, Twain's antiquarian neighbor. The most learned man in Hartford, he could swear in 27 languages. He added the exotic mottoes that adorn the chapter heads of *The Gilded Age*. With Calvin Stowe and Horace Bushnell he founded the Monday Evening Club for discussion of social, political, and literary subjects. It served Mark Twain as a trial forum for his serious ideas.

SPORTS AND SPELLING

Twain and Twichell often took ten-mile walks from which they returned jaw-weary but not footsore. In November, 1874, inspired by the walking fever that had swept the country's sport arenas, they started out to walk the hundred miles from Hartford to Boston. They had made only twenty-eight miles when blisters and lameness forced them to board a train for Boston where Redpath and Howells provided supper and an audience for the abortive adventure.

After pedestrianism came the bicycling craze. Mark and Joe bought high-wheelers and got up at 5:00 A.M. to take headers on Farmington Avenue. All the new bicycle profanity that later came into general use Mark always bragged he had invented during these lessons.

Baseball provided a spectator sport for Mark. (Once, when a small boy stole Mark's umbrella from beneath the bleachers, Mark offered a five-dollar reward for the umbrella and two hundred dollars for the boy's remains.) Spelling bees exercised his mind. Mark was a big drawing card at the "orthographical solemnities" (as he called them) which livened Twichell's church festivals. "I don't see any use in having a uniform and arbitrary way of spelling words," Mark told the audience. "We might as well make all clothes alike and cook all dishes alike. Sameness is tiresome; variety is pleasing. Kow spelled with a large K is just as good as with a small one. It is better. It gives the imagination a broader field, a wider scope. It suggests to the mind a grand, vague, impressive new kind of a cow." A natural-born speller, Mark said he was. He didn't win the prize that night.

In Twain's day, Hartford society made the tour of Europe every few years. The fashion piled up household bric-a-brac and swept away provincialism. In August, 1878, Twain, with Twichell as his guest, tramped through the Black Forest and the Alps, sometimes switching to train, raft, or donkey cart. *A Tramp Abroad,* published in 1880, was patched together from the experiences of this trip. In it Twichell figures as Harris. The drawings on this page are from the book and depict some of the pair's adventures.

These pipes were Mark Twain's. They are now in the Twain Museum at Hannibal, Missouri.

ONE CIGAR AT A TIME

Mark had only one temperance rule: never to smoke but one cigar at a time. In a letter to Reverend Twichell, he discussed his struggle to overcome the smoking habit: "Smoke? I always smoke from 3 till 5 Sunday afternoons—and in New York the other day I smoked a week, day and night. But when Livy is well I smoke only those two hours on Sunday. I'm 'boss' of the habit, now, and shall never let it boss me any more. Originally, I quit solely on Livy's account, (not that I believed there was the faintest *reason* in the matter, but just as I would deprive myself of sugar in my coffee if she wished it, or quit wearing socks if she thought them immoral,) and I stick to it yet on Livy's account, and shall always continue to do so, without a pang. But somehow it seems a pity that *you* quit, for Mrs. T. didn't mind it if I remember rightly. Ah, it is turning one's back upon a kindly Providence to spurn away from us the good creature he sent to make the breath of life a *luxury* as well as a necessity, *enjoyable* as well as useful, to go and quit smoking when there ain't any sufficient excuse for it! Why, my old boy, when they used to tell me I would shorten my life ten years by smoking, they little knew the devotee they were wasting their puerile word upon —they little knew how trivial and valueless I would regard a decade that had no smoking in it! But I won't persuade you, Twichell—I won't until I see you again —but *then* we'll smoke for a week together, and then shut off again."

In 1885, Mark came to his 50th birthday, and *The Critic* printed tributes from the country. Among them was this from Dr. Holmes, greeted by the Twain family with "electrical surprise and gratitude and exaltation."

MARK TWAIN'S SEMI-CENTENNIAL.

Some Birthday Letters of Congratulations and Condolence.

[The Critic.]

Mark Twain will be half-a-hundred years old on Monday. Within the past half-century he has done more than any other man to lengthen the lives of his contemporaries by making them merrier, and it looks as if he was going to do even more good in this way within the next fifty years than in those just ended. We print below a few letters of condolence from writers whose pens, like his, have increased 'the stock of human pleasures,' and whom we have reminded of the approach of Mr. Clemens's first semi-centennial.

TO MARK TWAIN
(On his fiftieth birthday.)

Ah Clemens, when I saw thee last,—
  We both of us were younger,—
How fondly mumbling o'er the past
  Is Memory's toothless hunger!

So fifty years have fled, they say,
  Since first you took to drinking,—
I mean in Nature's milky way,
  Of course no ill I'm thinking.

But while on life's uneven road
  Your track you've been pursuing,
What fountains from your wit have flowed—
  What drinks you have been brewing!

I know whence all your magic came,—
  Your secret I've discovered,—
The source that fed your inward flame—
  The dreams that round you hovered:

Before you learned to bite or munch
  Still kicking in your cradle,
The Muses mixed a bowl of punch
  And Hebe seized the ladle.

Dear babe, whose fiftieth year to-day
  Your ripe half-century rounded,
Your books the precious draught betray
  The laughing Nine compounded.

So mixed the sweet, the sharp, the strong,
  Each finds its faults amended,
The virtues that to each belong
  In happier union blended.

And what the flavor can surpass
  Of sugar, spirit, lemons?
So while one health fills every glass
Mark Twain for Baby Clemens!
                    OLIVER WENDELL HOLMES.

Leaving Heilbronn.

During their 1878 tour of Germany, Twichell and Twain took a carriage ride on the Heidelberg road. Mark made this drawing of it for *A Tramp Abroad,* adding this comment: "I made a sketch of the turn-out. It is not a Work, it is only what artists call a 'study'—a thing to make a finished picture from. This sketch has several blemishes in it; for instance, the wagon is not traveling as fast as the horse is. This is wrong. Again, the person trying to get out of the way is too small; he is out of perspective, as we say. The two upper lines are not the horse's back, they are the reins; —there seems to be a wheel missing—this would be corrected in a finished Work, of course. The thing flying out behind is not a flag, it is a curtain. That other thing up there is the sun, but I didn't get enough distance on it. I do not remember, now, what that thing is that is in front of the man who is running, but I think it is a haystack or a woman. This study was exhibited in the Paris Salon of 1879, but did not take any medal; they do not give medals for studies."

Mark Twain's opinions were freely expressed in Hartford. Before the Monday Evening Club he advocated woman's suffrage, attacked the license of the press, mocked blind loyalty to the Republican Party. For the young ladies of the Saturday Morning Club he ranged over temperance, plagiarism, the Knights of Labor, and mind-reading. In the press he was equally vocal. The *Courant* was always ready to print his views, as these typical headlines show.

QUARRY FARM

The quiet, secluded hours he needed for his best writing Mark found in summers spent at Quarry Farm. It was the home of Livy's sister, Mrs. Theodore Crane; built on a hill, it overlooked Elmira and the Chemung River. To the children Quarry Farm was a grand playground, and to Livy, a refuge from Hartford's heavy social duties. For himself, Mark had a study shaped like a pilothouse. In letters to friends he conveys his delight in the place:

"Susie Crane has built the loveliest study for me, you ever saw. It is octagonal, with a peaked roof, each octagon filled with a spacious window, and it sits perched in complete isolation on top of an elevation that commands leagues of valley and city and retreating ranges of distant blue hills. It is a cosy nest, with just room in it for a sofa and a table and three or four chairs—and when the storms sweep down the remote valley and the lightning flashes above the hills beyond, and the rain beats upon the roof over my head, imagine the luxury of it! It stands 500 feet above the valley and 2½ miles from it.

"On hot days I spread the study wide open, anchor my papers down with brickbats and write in the midst of the hurricanes, clothed in the same thin linen we make shirts of. The study is nearly on the peak of the hill; it is right in front of the little perpendicular wall of rock left where they used to quarry stones. On the peak of the hill is an old arbor roofed with bark and covered with the vine you call the 'American Creeper' —its green is almost bloodied with red. The study is 30 yards below the old arbor and 100 yards above the dwelling-house—it is remote from all noises.

"Now isn't the whole thing pleasantly situated?

"In the picture of me in the study you glimpse (through the left-hand window) the little rock bluff that rises behind the pond, and the bases of the little trees on top of it. The small square window is over the fireplace; the chimney divides to make room for it. Without the stereoscope it looks like a framed picture. All the study windows have Venetian blinds; they long ago went out of fashion in America but they have not been replaced with anything half as good yet.

"The study is built on top of a tumbled rock-heap that has morning-glories climbing about it and a stone stairway leading down through and dividing it."

The pictures on these pages show the main house at Quarry Farm and Mark's octagonal study. The photo at top left is from a stereoscopic view made in 1874. The other pictures of Mark relaxing are from a series made in 1903.

Writer at Work

AN AUTHOR FOR 20 YEARS, AND AN ASS FOR 55

In a fragment of a letter written in 1891 to an unknown correspondent, Mark Twain tells why he considers himself trained for the writing trade: "I confine myself to life with which I am familiar when pretending to portray life. But I confined myself to the boy-life out on the Mississippi because that had a peculiar charm for me, and not because I was not familiar with other phases of life. I was a soldier two weeks once in the beginning of the war, and was hunted like a rat the whole time. Familiar? My splendid Kipling himself hasn't a more burnt-in, hard-baked, and unforgettable familiarity with that death-on-the-pale-horse-with-hell-following-after, which is a raw soldier's first fortnight in the field—and which, without any doubt, is the most tremendous fortnight and the vividest he is ever going to see.

"Yes, and I have shoveled silver tailings in a quartz-mill a couple of weeks, and acquired the last possibilities of culture in that direction. And I've done 'pocket-mining' during three months in the one little patch of ground in the whole globe where Nature conceals gold in pockets—or did before we robbed all of those pockets and exhausted, obliterated, annihilated the most curious freak Nature ever indulged in. There are not thirty men left alive who, being told there was a pocket hidden on the broad slope of a mountain, would know how to go and find it, or have even the faintest idea of how to set about it; but I am one of

the possible 20 or 30 who possess the secret, and I could go and put my hand on that hidden treasure with a most deadly precision.

"And I've been a prospector, and know pay rock from poor when I find it—just with a touch of the tongue. And I've been a silver miner and know how to dig and shovel and drill and put in a blast. And so I know the mines and the miner interiorly as well as Bret Harte knows them exteriorly.

"And I was a newspaper reporter four years in cities, and so saw the inside of many things; and was reporter in a legislature two sessions and the same in Congress one session, and thus learned to know personally three sample bodies of the smallest minds and the selfishest souls and the cowardliest hearts that God makes.

"And I was some years a Mississippi pilot, and familiarly knew all the different kinds of steamboat-men—a race apart, and not like other folk.

"And I was for some years a traveling 'jour' printer, and wandered from city to city—and so I know that sect familiarly.

"And I was a lecturer on the public platform a number of seasons and was a responder to toasts at all the

148

different kinds of banquets—and so I know a great many secrets about audiences—secrets not to be got out of books, but only acquirable by experience.

"And I watched over one dear project of mine for years, spent a fortune on it, and failed to make it go—and the history of that would make a large book in which a million men would see themselves as in a mirror; and they would testify and say, Verily, this is not imagination; this fellow has been there—and after would cast dust upon their heads, cursing and blaspheming.

"And I have been an author for 20 years and an ass for 55.

"Now then; as the most valuable capital or culture or education usable in the building of novels is personal experience I ought to be well equipped for that trade.

"I surely have the equipment, a wide culture, and all of it real, none of it artificial, for I don't know anything about books."

But seventeen years later, writing an autobiographical passage, Mark looks back into his past from another angle, seeing most of it as a lifetime of delightful idleness: "From the time that my father died, March 24, 1847, when I was past eleven years old, until the end of 1856, or the first days of 1857, I worked—not diligently, not willingly, but fretfully, lazily, repiningly, complainingly, disgustedly, and always shirking the work when I was not watched. The statistics show that I was a worker during about ten years. I am approaching seventy-three and I believe I have never done any work since—unless I may call two or three years of lazy effort as reporter on the Pacific Coast by that large and honorable name—and so I think I am substantially right in saying that when I escaped from the printing office fifty or fifty-one years ago I ceased to be a worker and ceased permanently.

"Piloting on the Mississippi River was not work to me; it was play—delightful play, vigorous play, adventurous play—and I loved it; silver mining in the Humboldt Mountains was play, only play, because I did not do any of the work; my pleasant comrades did it and I sat by and admired; my silver mining in Esmeralda was not work, for Higbie and Robert Howland did it and again I sat by and admired. I accepted a job of shoveling tailings in a quartz mill there, and that was really work and I had to do it myself, but I retired from that industry at the end of two weeks, and not only with my own approval but with the approval of the people who paid the wages. These mining experiences occupied ten months and came to an end toward the close of September, 1862.

"I then became a reporter in Virginia City, Nevada, and later in San Francisco, and after something more than two years of this salaried indolence I retired from my position on the Morning Call, by solicitation. Solicitation of the proprietor. Then I acted as San Franciscan correspondent of the Virginia City Enterprise for two or three months; next I spent three months in pocket-mining at Jackass Gulch with the Gillis boys; then I went to the Sandwich Islands and corresponded thence for the Sacramento Union five or six months; in October, 1866, I broke out as a lecturer, and from that day to this I have always been able to gain my living without doing any work; for the writing of books and magazine matter was always play, not work. I enjoyed it; it was merely billiards to me."

Mark Twain made jottings in notebooks from the time he started to learn the Mississippi River. But he was never able to maintain the routine of a journal. "If you wish to inflict a heartless and malignant punishment upon a young person," he advises in *The Innocents Abroad*, "pledge him to keep a journal a year. At certain periods it becomes the dearest ambition of a man to keep a faithful record of his performances in a book; and he dashes at this work with an enthusiasm that imposes on him the notion that keeping a journal is the veriest pastime in the world, and the pleasantest. But if he only lives twenty-one days, he will find out that only those rare natures that are made up of pluck, endurance, devotion to duty for duty's sake, and invincible determination, may hope to venture upon so tremendous an enterprise as the keeping of a journal and not sustain a shameful defeat."

A suggestion to writers from Mark Twain: "How to get the most work done."

THE LITERARY SHIPYARD

"There has never been a time in the past thirty-five years," wrote Mark Twain in 1906, "when my literary shipyard hadn't two or more half-finished ships on the ways, neglected and baking in the sun; generally there have been three or four; at present there are five. This has an unbusiness-like look but it was not purposeless, it was intentional. As long as a book would write itself I was a faithful and interested amanuensis and my industry did not flag, but the minute that the book tried to shift to my head the labor of contriving its situations, inventing its adventures and conducting its conversations, I put it away and dropped it out of my mind. Then I examined my unfinished properties to see if among them there might not be one whose interest in itself had revived through a couple of years' restful idleness and was ready to take me on again as amanuensis.

"It was by accident that I found out that a book is pretty sure to get tired along about the middle and refuse to go on with its work until its powers and its interest should have been refreshed by a rest and its depleted stock of raw materials reinforced by lapse of time. It was when I had reached the middle of *Tom Sawyer* that I made this invaluable find. At page 400 of my manuscript the story made a sudden and determined halt and refused to proceed another step. Day after day it still refused. I was disappointed, distressed and immeasurably astonished, for I knew quite well that the tale was not finished and I could not understand why I was not able to go on with it. The reason was very simple—my tank had run dry; it was empty; the stock of materials in it was exhausted; the story could not go on without materials; it could not be wrought out of nothing.

"When the manuscript had lain in a pigeonhole two years I took it out one day and read the last chapter that I had written. It was then that I made the great discovery that when the tank runs dry you've only to leave it alone and it will fill up again in time, while you are asleep—also while you are at work at other things and are quite unaware that this unconscious and profitable cerebration is going on. There was plenty of material now and the book went on and finished itself without any trouble.

"Ever since then, when I have been writing a book I have pigeonholed it without misgivings when its tank ran dry, well knowing that it would fill up again without any of my help within the next two or three years, and that then the work of completing it would be simple and easy. *The Prince and the Pauper* struck work in the middle because the tank was dry, and I

Puck's comment on Mark Twain's humor.

did not touch it again for two years. A dry interval of two years occurred in *A Connecticut Yankee in King Arthur's Court*. A like interval had occurred in the middle of other books of mine."

I HAVE ALWAYS PREACHED

"Within the compass of these forty years wherein I have been playing professional humorist before the public, I have had for company seventy-eight other American humorists. Each and every one of the seventy-eight rose in my time, became conspicuous and popular, and by and by vanished.

"Why have they perished? Because they were merely humorists. Humorists of the 'mere' sort cannot survive. Humor is only a fragrance, a decoration. Often it is merely an odd trick of speech and of spelling, as in the case of Ward and Billings and Nasby and the 'Disbanded Volunteer,' and presently the fashion passes and the fame along with it. There are those who say a novel should be a work of art solely and you must not preach in it, you must not teach in it. That may be true as regards novels but it is not true as regards humor. Humor must not professedly teach and it must not professedly preach, but it must do both if it would live forever. By forever, I mean thirty years. With all its preaching it is not likely to outlive so long a term as that. The very things it preaches about and which are novelties when it preaches about them can cease to be novelties and become commonplaces in thirty years. Then that sermon can thenceforth interest no one.

"I have always preached. That is the reason that I have lasted thirty years. If the humor came of its own accord and uninvited I have allowed it a place in my sermon, but I was not writing the sermon for the sake of the humor. I should have written the sermon just the same, whether any humor applied for admission or not. I am saying these vain things in this frank way because I am a dead person speaking from the grave. Even I would be too modest to say them in life. I think we never become really and genuinely our entire and honest selves until we are dead—and not then until we have been dead years and years. People ought to start dead and then they would be honest so much earlier."

Mark Twain's right hand—the nemesis of palmists.

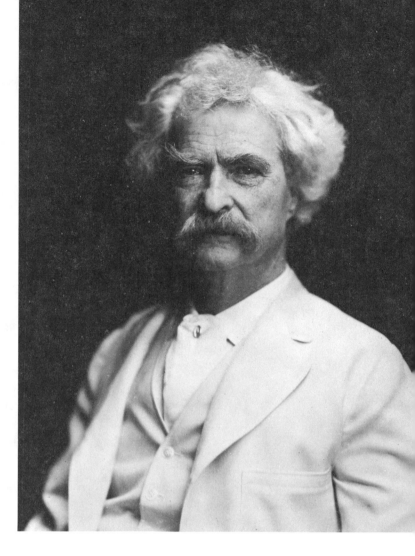

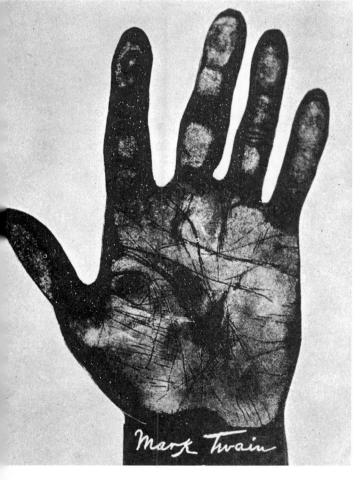

Mark Twain

NO SENSE OF HUMOR

Mark Twain was reared in an atmosphere of faith in phrenologists and palmists. Later he took pleasure in testing their art, sometimes, as this passage shows, with the help of such friends as George Harvey, president of Harper and Brothers: "Two years ago Col. Harvey took prints of my two hands and sent them to six professional palmists of distinguished reputation here in New York City; and he, also, withheld my name and asked for estimates. History repeated itself. The word humor occurred only once in the six estimates and then it was accompanied by the definite remark that the possessor of the hands was destitute of the sense of humor. Now then, I have Fowler's estimate; I have the estimates of Stead's six or seven palmists; I have the estimates of Harvey's half-dozen: the evidence that I do not possess the sense of humor is overwhelming, satisfying, convincing, incontrovertible—and at last I believe it myself."

A MAN OF MARK.

LITERARY PIRACY

The popular writers of Twain's day suffered from international literary piracy. Theft of a writer's work was common on both sides of the Atlantic. Thieves and bribers were used to snatch proof sheets from the printing houses and binderies of publishers in other countries. To insure Canadian copyright of *The Prince and the Pauper* Mark went to Canada for two weeks in December, 1881. He found authors had to register their works with the Ministry of Agriculture, which gave Thomas Nast a chance to be funny at his friend's expense. Mark never let up on his fight for copyright reform at home and abroad. He took fantastically elaborate precautions to prevent piracy of his own work and even had the name "Mark Twain" registered as a trade-mark in the hope of protecting his by-line after expiration of book copyright.

MY WRITING HABITS

In an unmailed letter of 1887, Mark described his working habits and commented on his productivity: "It is my habit to keep four or five books in process of erection all the time and every summer add a few courses of bricks to two or three of them, but I cannot forecast which of the two or three it is going to be. It takes seven years to complete a book by this method but still it is a good method: gives the public a rest. I have been accused of rushing into print prematurely, moved thereto by greediness for money, but

in truth I have never done that. Do you care for trifles of information? Well, then, *Tom Sawyer* and *The Prince and the Pauper* were each on the stocks two or three years, and *Old Times on the Mississippi* eight. One of my unfinished books has been on the stocks sixteen years, another seventeen. This latter book could have been finished in a day, at any time during the past five years. But as in the first of these two narratives all the action takes place in Noah's ark, and as in the other the action takes place in heaven, there seemed to be no hurry and so I have not hurried. Tales of stirring adventure in those localities do not need to be rushed to publication lest they get stale by waiting. In twenty-one years, with all my time at my free disposal, I have written and completed only eleven books, whereas with half the labor that a journalist does I could have written sixty in that time. I do not greatly mind being accused of a proclivity for rushing into print but at the same time I don't believe that the charge is really well founded. Suppose I did write eleven books, have you nothing to be grateful for? Go to—remember the forty-nine which I didn't write."

Twenty-two years later, finding the letter had never been sent, Mark added these notes on the subject: "I still have the habit of keeping unfinished books lying around years and years, waiting. I have four or five novels on hand at present in a half-finished condition and it is more than three years since I have looked at any of them. I have no intention of finishing them. I could complete all of them in less than a year, if the impulse should come powerfully upon me. Long, long ago money-*necessity* furnished that impulse once, (*Following the Equator*), but mere desire for money has never furnished it so far as I remember. Not even money-necessity was able to overcome me on a couple of occasions when perhaps I ought to have allowed it to succeed. While I was bankrupt and in debt two offers were made me for weekly literary contributions to continue during a year and they would have made a debtless man of me, but I declined them, with my wife's full approval, for I had no instance where a man had pumped himself out once a week and failed to run 'emptyings' before the year was finished.

"As to that 'Noah's Ark' book, I began it in Edinburgh in 1873; I don't know where the manuscript is now. It was a Diary, which professed to be the work of Shem but wasn't. I began it again several months ago, but only for recreation; I hadn't any intention of carrying it to a finish—or even to the end of the first chapter, in fact.

"As to the book whose action 'takes place in Heaven.' That was a small thing, *Captain Stormfield's Visit to Heaven*. It lay in my pigeon-holes 40 years, then I took it out and printed it in *Harper's Monthly* last year."

INNOCENCE ABROAD (IN SEARCH OF A COPYRIGHT).

"'Then a sentimental passion of a vegetable fashion must excite your languid spleen—
An attachment à la Plato for a bashful young potato, or a not-too-French French bean!
Though the Philistines may jostle, you will rank as an apostle in the high æsthetic band,
If you walk down Piccadilly with a poppy or a lily in your mediæval hand.
          And every one will say,
          As you walk your flowery way,
'If he's content with a vegetable love, which would certainly not suit *me*,
Why, what a most particularly *pure young man this pure young man must be!*'"—PATIENCE.

Thomas Nast

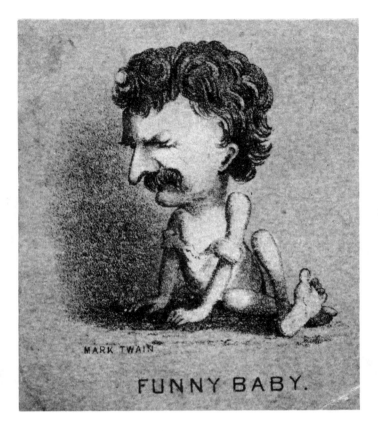

MARK TWAIN

FUNNY BABY.

THE VERFLUCHTETE PROOFS

After the agony of writing the book comes the fresh agony of proofing it. When Howells offered to help out with *Huck Finn,* Mark replied: "It took my breath away, and I haven't recovered it yet, entirely—I mean the generosity of your proposal to read the proofs of Huck Finn.

"Now if you mean it, old man—if you are in earnest—proceed, in God's name, and be by me forever blest. I cannot conceive of a rational man deliberately piling such an atrocious job upon himself; but if there is such a man and you be that man, why then pile it on. It will cost me a pang every time I think of it, but this anguish will be eingebusst to me in the joy and comfort I shall get out of the not having to read the verfluchtete proofs myself. But if you have repented of your augenblichlicher Tobsucht and got back to calm cold reason again, I won't hold you to it unless I find I have got you down in writing somewhere. Herr, I would not read the proof of one of my books for any fair and reasonable sum whatever, if I could get out of it.

"The proof-reading on the P & P cost me the last rags of my religion."

FINISHING A BOOK

Mark finished his *Joan of Arc* in 1895. "Possibly the book may not sell," he wrote a friend, "but that is nothing—it was written in love." In a memorandum jotted down at the time, he told what the writer feels when a large piece of work is finally done:

"Do you know that shock? I mean when you come at your regular hour into the sick-room where you have watched for months and find the medicine-bottles all gone, the night-table removed, the bed stripped, the furniture set stiffly to rights, the windows up, the room cold, stark, vacant—& you catch your breath & realize what has happened.

"Do you know that shock?

"The man who has written a long book has that experience the morning after he has revised it for the last time & sent it away to the printer. He steps into his study at the hour established by the habit of months—& he gets that little shock. All the litter and confusion are gone. The piles of dusty reference-books are gone from the chairs, the maps from the floor; the chaos of letters, manuscripts, note-books, paper-knives, pipes, matches, photographs, tobacco-jars, & cigar-boxes is gone from the writing-table, the furniture is back where it used to be in the long-ago. The house-maid, forbidden the place for five months, has been there & tidied it up & scoured it clean & made it repellent & awful.

"I stand here this morning contemplating this desolation, & I realize that if I would bring back the spirit that made this hospital home-like & pleasant to me I must restore the aids to lingering dissolution to their wonted places & nurse another patient through & send it forth for the last rites, with many or few to assist there, as may happen; & that I will do."

I HUNTED BIGGER GAME

A Connecticut Yankee in King Arthur's Court, published in 1889, did not win favor in England. Some of the critics said the book was not fit for the cultivated class. To his British friend Andrew Lang, Mark wrote this comment on his goal as a writer: "Indeed I have been misjudged, from the very first. I have never tried in even one single instance, to help cultivate the cultivated classes. I was not equipped for it, either by native gifts or training. And I never had any ambition in that direction, but always hunted for bigger game—the masses. I have seldom deliberately tried to instruct them, but have done my best to entertain them. To simply amuse them would have satisfied my dearest

HARPER'S WEEKLY
JOURNAL OF CIVILIZATION

VOL. L.   *New York, Saturday, December 22, 1906*   NO. 2609

Writing his autobiography.

ambition at any time; for they could get instruction elsewhere, and I had two chances to help to the teacher's one: for amusement is a good preparation for study and a good healer of fatigue after it. My audience is dumb, it has no voice in print, and so I cannot know whether I have won its approbation or only got its censure."

A few years earlier, he had said:

"My books are water; those of the great geniuses are wine. Everybody drinks water."

THE

GILDED AGE

A TALE OF TO-DAY

BY
MARK TWAIN
(SAMUEL L. CLEMENS)
AUTHOR OF "INNOCENTS ABROAD," "ROUGHING IT," ETC.
AND
CHARLES DUDLEY WARNER
AUTHOR OF "MY SUMMER IN A GARDEN," "BACK LOG STUDIES," ETC.

FULLY ILLUSTRATED FROM NEW DESIGNS
BY HOPPIN, STEPHENS, WILLIAMS, WHITE, ETC., ETC.

SOLD BY SUBSCRIPTION ONLY.

*

HARTFORD:
AMERICAN PUBLISHING COMPANY.
W. E. BLISS & CO., TOLEDO, OHIO.
1874.

Mark Twain in 1873. He got mad when some newspapers charged that Warner really wrote *The Gilded Age* and he had only added his name to the title page to give it a large sale. Other editors criticized him for washing the country's dirty linen in public.

Twain and Warner each made $18,000 out of the book. Sold by subscription, not through bookstores, it rolled through three editions in a month. By the end of 1874, 58,000 copies had been sold.

THE GILDED AGE

"Chas. Dudley Warner & I have been belting away every day on a *partnership novel*," Mark wrote his friend Mrs. Fairbanks in April, 1873. "I have worked 6 days a week—good full days—& laid myself up, once. Have written many chapters twice, & some of them three times—have thrown away 300 clean pages of MS & still there's havoc to be made when I enter on final polishing. Warner has been more fortunate—he won't lose 50 pages.

"Three more chapters will end the book. I laid out the plan of the *boss* chapter, the climax chapter, yesterday, & Warner will write it up today; I wrote it up yesterday, & shall work & trim & polish at it today —& tonight we shall read, & the man who has written it best is all right—the other man's MS will be torn up. If *neither* succeeds, we'll both write the chapter over again."

The Gilded Age was the product of the partnership. It started in the winter of 1873, when the Twains were living in the Hooker house in Hartford. At dinner with the Warners one night, the husbands gibed at the novels the wives were reading. Challenged to do better, Twain and Warner set to work.

Mark had wanted for some time to build a story around James Lampton, his mother's cousin; perhaps the offer of collaboration was what he needed to push him into his first attempt at a novel. By the end of April the book was done. Warner "has worked up the fiction," Mark said, "and I have hurled in the facts."

The Gilded Age raked the incredible Grant era to the bone and named it for posterity. The book is uneven, mixing Warner's sentimental melodrama with Twain's savage satire and burlesque. But it was the only contemporary novel to attack the fevered speculation and expose the political muck of its day. The lobbyists, the Wall Street financiers, Washington's political hacks, the boom towns of the West, the railroad builders, the vulgar new aristocracy of wealth, "the great putty-hearted public" that tolerated the plunder—all fall beneath the axe Twain had been sharpening since that winter of 1867 when he had watched Capitol Hill in action.

If penetrating social satire is half the novel's achievement, the other half is the creation of Colonel Beriah Sellers out of cousin James Lampton and Mark's genius. Here is the Colonel improvising a splendid new world for young Washington Hawkins:

" 'I intend to look out for you, Washington, my boy. I hunted up a place for you yesterday, but I am not referring to that, now—that is a mere livelihood—mere bread and butter; but when I say I mean to look out for you I mean something very different. I mean to put things in your way that will make a mere livelihood a trifling thing. I'll put you in a way to make more money than you'll ever know what to do with. You'll be right here where I can put my hand on you when anything turns up. I've got some prodigious operations on foot; but I'm keeping quiet; mum's the word; your old hand don't go around pow-wowing and letting everybody see his k'yards and find out his little game. But all in good time, Washington, all in good time. You'll see. Now, there's an operation in corn that looks well. Some New York men are trying to get me to go into it—buy up all the growing crops and just boss the market when they mature—ah, I tell you it's a great thing. And it only costs a trifle; two millions or two and a half will do it. I haven't exactly promised yet—there's no hurry—the more indifferent I seem, you know, the more anxious those fellows will get. And then there is the hog speculation—that's bigger still. We've got quiet men at work,' (he was very impressive here,) 'mousing around, to get propositions out of all the farmers in the whole West and Northwest for the hog crop, and other

Colonel Sellers blowing bubbles for Washington Hawkins, who was patterned on Mark's brother, Orion Clemens.

agents quietly getting propositions and terms out of all the manufactories—and don't you see, if we can get all the hogs and all the slaughter-houses into our hands on the dead quiet—whew! it would take three ships to carry the money. I've looked into the thing—calculated all the chances for and all the chances against, and though I shake my head and hesitate and keep on thinking, apparently, I've got my mind made up that if the thing can be done on a capital of six millions, that's the horse to put up money on! Why, Washington —but what's the use of talking about it—any man can see that there's whole Atlantic oceans of cash in it, gulfs and bays thrown in. But there's a bigger thing than that, yet—a bigger . . .

" 'Why Washington, my boy, these things are nothing. They look large—of course they look large to a novice, but to a man who has been all his life accustomed to large operations—shaw! They're well enough to while away an idle hour with, or furnish a bit of employment that will give a trifle of idle capital a chance to earn its bread while it is waiting for something to do, but— now just listen a moment—just let me give you an idea of what we old veterans of commerce call "business." Here's the Rothschilds' proposition—this is between you and me, you understand . . .

" ' . . . for I wouldn't have it get out for a fortune. They want me to go in with them on the sly—agent was here two weeks ago about it—go in on the sly' (voice down to an impressive whisper, now) 'and buy up a hundred and thirteen wildcat banks in Ohio, Indiana, Kentucky, Illinois, and Missouri—notes of these banks are at all sorts of discount now—average discount of the hundred and thirteen is forty-four per cent—buy them all up, you see, and then all of a sudden let the cat out of the bag! Whiz! the stock of every one of those wildcats would spin up to a tremendous premium before you could turn a handspring—profit on the speculation not a dollar less than forty millions!' (An eloquent pause, while the marvelous vision settled into W.'s focus). 'Where's your hogs now! Why, my dear innocent boy, we would just sit down on the front doorsteps and peddle banks like lucifer matches!

" 'I have a small idea that may develop into something for us both, all in good time. Keep your money close and add to it. I'll make it breed. I've been experimenting (to pass away the time) on a little preparation for curing sore eyes—a kind of decoction nine-tenths water and the other tenth drugs that don't cost more than a dollar a barrel; I'm still experimenting; there's one ingredient wanted yet to perfect the thing, and somehow I can't just manage to hit upon the thing that's necessary, and I don't dare talk with a chemist, of course. But I'm progressing, and before many weeks I wager the country will ring with the fame of Beriah Sellers' Infallible Imperial Oriental Optic Liniment and Salvation for Sore Eyes—the Medical Wonder of the Age! Small bottles fifty cents, large ones a dollar. Average cost, five and seven cents for the two sizes. The first year sell, say, ten thousand bottles in Missouri, seven thousand in Iowa, three thousand in Arkansas, four thousand in Kentucky, six thousand in Illinois, and say twenty-five thousand in the rest of the country. Total, fifty-five thousand bottles; profit clear of all expenses, twenty thousand dollars at the very lowest calculation. All the capital needed is to manufacture the first two thousand bottles—say a hundred and fifty dollars—then the money would begin to flow in. The second year, sales would reach 200,000 bottles—clear profit, say, $75,000—and in the meantime the great factory would be building in St. Louis, to cost, say $100,000. The third year we could easily sell 1,000,000 bottles in the United States and——'

" 'O, splendid!' said Washington. 'Let's commence right away—let's——'

" '—1,000,000 bottles in the United States—profit at least $350,000—and then it would begin to be time to turn our attention toward the real idea of the business.'

" 'The real idea of it! Ain't $350,000 year a pretty real——'

" 'Stuff! Why, what an infant you are, Washington—what a guileless, short-sighted, easily-contented innocent you are, my poor little country-bred know-nothing! Would I go to all that trouble and bother for the poor crumbs a body might pick up in this country? Now do I look like a man who—does my history suggest that I am a man who deals in trifles, contents himself with the narrow horizon that hems in the common herd, sees no further than the end of his nose? Now, you know that that is not me—couldn't be me. You ought to know that if I throw my time and abilities into a patent medicine, it's a patent medicine whose field of operations is the solid earth! its clients the swarming nations that inhabit it! Why what is the republic of America for an eye-water country? Lord bless you, it is nothing but a barren highway that you've got to cross to get to the true eye-water market! Why, Washington, in the Oriental countries people swarm like the sands of the desert; every square mile of ground upholds its thousands upon thousands of struggling human creatures—and every separate and individual devil of them's got the ophthalmia! It's as natural to them as noses are—and sin. It's born with them, it stays with them, it's all that some of them have left when they die. Three years of introductory trade in the Orient and what will be the result? Why, our headquarters would be in Constantinople and our hind-quarters in Further India! Factories and warehouses in Cairo, Ispahan, Bagdad, Damascus, Jerusalem, Yedo, Peking, Bangkok, Delhi, Bombay, and Calcutta! Annual income—well, God only knows how many millions and millions apiece!' "

Male lobbyist: $3,000.

Female lobbyist: $3,000.

High moral Senator: $3,000.

Chairman of Committee: $10,000.

LEGISLATION IS EXPENSIVE

Mark has an old Washington hand in *The Gilded Age* explain how an appropriations bill is put through Congress:

"Why the matter is simple enough. A Congressional appropriation costs money. Just reflect, for instance. A majority of the House committee, say $10,000 apiece—$40,000; a majority of the Senate committee, the same each—say $40,000; a little extra to one or two chairmen of one or two such committees, say $10,000 each—$20,000; and there's $100,000 of the money gone, to begin with. Then, seven male lobbyists, at $3,000 each—$21,000; one female lobbyist, $3,000; a high moral Congressman or Senator here and there—the high moral ones cost more, because they give tone to a measure—say ten of these at $3,000 each, is $30,000; then a lot of small-fry country members who won't vote for anything whatever without pay—say twenty at $500 apiece, is $10,000 altogether; lot of jimcracks for Congressmen's wives and children—those go a long way—you can't spend too much money in that line—well, those things cost in a lump, say $10,000—along there somewhere;—and then comes your printed documents—your maps, your tinted engravings, your pamphlets, your illuminated show cards, your advertisements in a hundred and fifty papers at ever so much a line—because you've got to keep the papers all right or you are gone up, you know. Oh, my dear sir, printing bills are destruction itself. Ours, so far amount to—let me see—10; 52; 22; 13;—and then there's 11; 14; 33—well, never mind the details, the total in clean numbers foots up $118,254.42 thus far!"

Lobbyist Laura Hawkins petitioning Congress.

Colonel Sellers uses fork, pipe, shears, snuffer, and everything else within reach to show his wife the route his dream railroad will take. The map and the other illustrations on these pages are from the first edition of *The Gilded Age*.

FROM ST. LOUIS TO CORRUPTIONVILLE

"Tell me about the railroad," says Mrs. Sellers to her husband. She was feeling a bit blue and needed to hear that tongue let go on the future dead moral certainties:

" 'Now, then—there you are!' [The Colonel, mapping out the road on the tablecloth.] 'It's a beautiful road, beautiful. Jeff Thompson can out-engineer any civil engineer that ever sighted through an aneroid, or a theodolite, or whatever they call it—he calls it sometimes one and sometimes the other—just whichever levels off his sentence neatest, I reckon. But ain't it a ripping road, though? I tell you, it'll make a stir when it gets along. Just see what a country it goes through. There's your turnip country all around Doodleville— bless my life, what fortunes are going to be made there when they get that contrivance perfected for extracting olive oil out of turnips—if there's any in them; and I reckon there is, because Congress has made an appropriation of money to test the thing, and they wouldn't have done that just on conjecture, of course. And now we come to the Brimstone region—cattle raised there till you can't rest—and corn, and all that sort of thing. Then you've got a little stretch along through Belshazzar that don't produce anything now—at least nothing but rocks—but irrigation will fetch it. Then from Catfish to Babylon it's a little swampy, but there's dead loads of peat down under there somewhere. Next is the Bloody Run and Hail Columbia country—tobacco enough can be raised there to support two such railroads. Next is the sassparilla region. I reckon there's enough of that truck along in there on the line of the pocket-knife, from Hail Columbia to Hark-from-the-Tomb to fat up all the consumptives in all the hospitals from Halifax to the Holy Land. It just grows like weeds! I've got a little belt of sassparilla land in there just tucked away unobstrusively waiting for my little Universal Expectorant to get into shape in my head. And I'll fix that, you know. One of these days I'll have all the nations of the earth expecto——'

" 'But Beriah, dear——'

" 'Don't interrupt me, Polly—I don't want you to lose the run of the map—well, take your toy-horse, James Fitz-James, if you must have it—and run along with you. Here, now—the soap will do for Babylon. Let me see—where was I? Oh yes—now we run down

A Brady photo of Samuel C. Pomeroy, the corrupt Senator from Kansas who was the model for Senator Dilworthy in *The Gilded Age*.

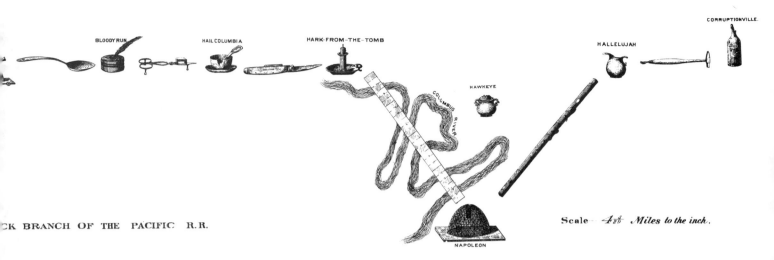

BLOODY RUN   HAIL COLUMBIA   HARK-FROM-THE-TOMB   HALLELUJAH   CORRUPTIONVILLE.

HAWKEYE

COLUMBUS RIVER

NAPOLEON

Scale —— Miles to the inch.

to Napoleon. Beautiful road. Look at that, now. Perfectly straight line—straight as the way to the grave. And see where it leaves Hawkeye—clear out in the cold, my dear, clear out in the cold. That town's as bound to die as—well if I owned it I'd get its obituary ready, now, and notify the mourners. Polly, mark my

The illustrator did not bother to disguise Senator Pomeroy when drawing Senator Dilworthy serving up a choice piece of hypocrisy to the Sunday school audience.

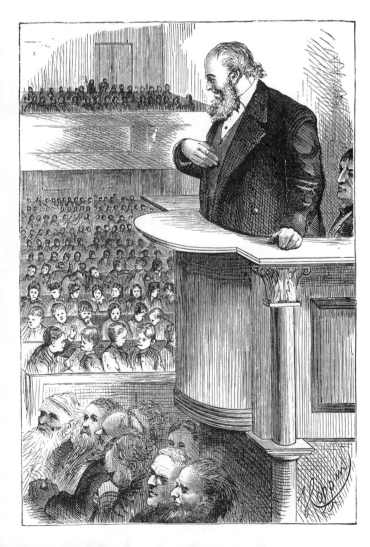

words—in three years from this, Hawkeye'll be a howling wilderness. You'll see. And just look at that river—noblest stream that meanders over the thirsty earth!—calmest, gentlest artery that refreshes her weary bosom! Railroad goes all over it and all through it—wades right along on stilts. Seventeen bridges in three miles and a half—forty-nine bridges from Hark-from-the-Tomb to Stone's Landing altogether—forty-nine bridges, and culverts enough to culvert creation itself! Hadn't skeins of thread enough to represent them all—but you get an idea—perfect trestle-work of bridges for seventy-two miles. Jeff Thompson and I fixed all that, you know; he's to get the contracts and I'm to put them through on the divide. Just oceans of money in those bridges. It's the only part of the railroad I'm interested in,—down along the line—and it's all I want, too. It's enough, I should judge. Now here we are at Napoleon. Good enough country—plenty good enough—all it wants is population. That's all right—that will come. And it's no bad country now for calmness and solitude, I can tell you—though there's no money in that, of course. No money, but a man wants rest, a man wants peace—a man don't want to rip and tear around all the time. And here we go, now, just as straight as a string for Hallelujah—it's a beautiful angle—handsome upgrade all the way—and then away you go to Corruptionville, the gaudiest country for early carrots and cauliflowers that ever—good missionary field, too. There ain't such another missionary field outside the jungles of Central Africa. And patriotic?—why, they named it after Congress itself. Oh, I warn you, my dear, there's a good time coming, and it'll be right along before you know what you're about, too. That railroad's fetching it. You see what it is as far as I've got, and if I had enough bottles and soap and bootjacks and such things to carry it along to where it joins onto the Union Pacific, fourteen hundred miles from here, I should exhibit to you in that little internal improvement a spectacle of inconceivable sublimity.' "

161

Tom Sawyer. Frontispiece of first edition of the book.

THE ADVENTURES

OF

TOM SAWYER

BY

MARK TWAIN.

THE AMERICAN PUBLISHING COMPANY,
HARTFORD, CONN.: CHICAGO, ILL.: CINCINNATI, OHIO.
A. ROMAN & CO., SAN FRANCISCO, CAL.
1876.

Title page of first edition. The illustrations on this and facing page are all from this edition.

THE ADVENTURES OF TOM SAWYER

"*Tom Sawyer* is simply a hymn," its author said, "put into prose to give it a worldly air." It was Mark's first solo flight in fiction. Published in December, 1876, in an edition of 5,000 copies, by 1904 it had sold over two million and today is still the most popular of Twain's books. It quickly became a children's classic, but as Mark hoped, its appeal has been as great for adults who enjoy its reminder of what they like to think they were once like themselves.

Tom's beginnings go back to 1870 when Mark explored in diary form the boyhood adventures of a Billy Rogers. Two years later, in another false start, he experimented with Tom in a play. Then in April, 1874, in his new study at Quarry Farm, he got the story moving fast. All summer he worked on it, producing fifty pages of manuscript a day, so wrapped up in his dream of boyhood he was dead to anything else.

When the inspiration tank ran dry, Mark put Tom aside to write the *Colonel Sellers* play and the Mississippi articles for the *Atlantic*. In Hartford, in 1875, he felt Tom flowing again and by July had finished the nostalgic idyll. He copied the manuscript on a type-writer—the new invention he had first seen in a Boston store window—asserting later that he was the first person in the world to apply the machine to literature. Sent off to Howells, *Tom Sawyer* won his approval as "altogether the best boy's story I ever read. It will be an immense success."

And when it appeared in December, 1876, it was.

Mark Twain in the 1870's, during the writing of *Tom Sawyer*.

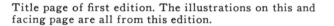

162

The whitewashing of the fence, one of the best-known scenes in Mark Twain.

The three pirates on their raft: Tom Sawyer, the Black Avenger of the Spanish Main, Huck Finn the Red-Handed, and Joe Harper, the Terror of the Seas.

Tom's brother Sid.

Huckleberry Finn.

Becky Thatcher, Tom's girl.

Tom's Aunt Polly.

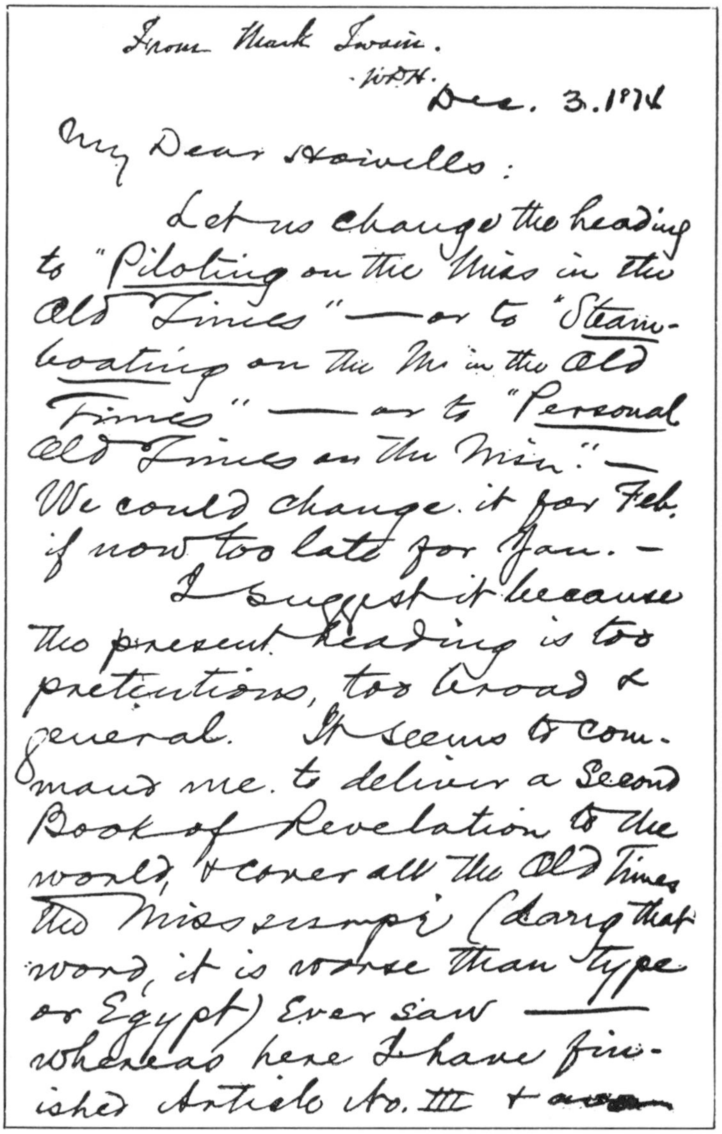

Twain writes Howells, editor of the *Atlantic,* to suggest a new title for the magazine series on the Mississippi.

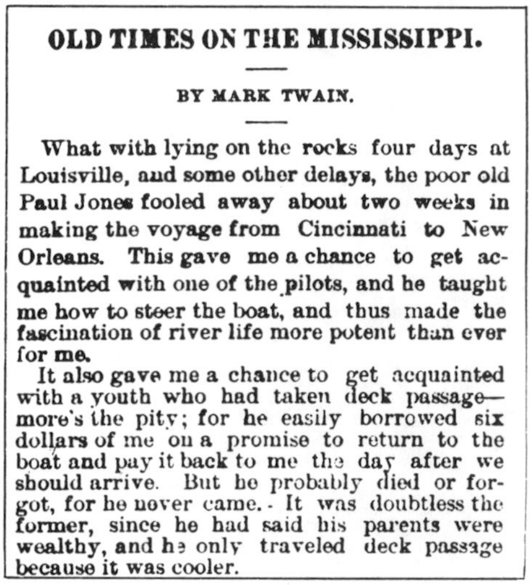

OLD TIMES ON THE MISSISSIPPI

Mark Twain's first contribution to the *Atlantic Monthly* (November, 1874) was "A True Story," taken down from a Negro cook at Quarry Farm who had been twice sold as a slave in Virginia. For it Mark was paid sixty dollars. It was the highest price the magazine had ever given anyone, but although Mark had received much higher rates, he was delighted to find himself in the august *Atlantic.* Urged to contribute again, he replied to editor Howells:

"I take back the remark that I can't write for the Jan. number. For Twichell and I have had a long walk

OLD TIMES ON THE MISSISSIPPI.

BY MARK TWAIN.

What with lying on the rocks four days at Louisville, and some other delays, the poor old Paul Jones fooled away about two weeks in making the voyage from Cincinnati to New Orleans. This gave me a chance to get acquainted with one of the pilots, and he taught me how to steer the boat, and thus made the fascination of river life more potent than ever for me.

It also gave me a chance to get acquainted with a youth who had taken deck passage—more's the pity; for he easily borrowed six dollars of me on a promise to return to the boat and pay it back to me the day after we should arrive. But he probably died or forgot, for he never came. It was doubtless the former, since he had said his parents were wealthy, and he only traveled deck passage because it was cooler.

As soon as Mark's pieces appeared in the *Atlantic,* newspapers—including Mark's Hartford *Courant,* shown here—"borrowed" them.

in the woods and I got to telling him about old Mississippi days of steamboating glory and grandeur as I saw them (during 5 years) from the pilot-house. He said 'What a virgin subject to hurl into a magazine!' I hadn't thought of that before. Would you like a series of papers to run through 3 months or 6 or 9?—or about 4 months, say?"

The answer was yes, and the first experimental chapter soon arrived in Boston. "Cut it, scarify it, reject it," he wrote. But Howells knew it was superb, and begged for chapters he could run every month. In ten days Mark had written three more. "And yet," he noted, "I have spoken of nothing but of piloting as a science so far: and I doubt if I ever get beyond that portion of my subject. And I don't care to. Any muggins can write about Old Times on the Miss. of 500 different kinds, but I am the only man alive that can scribble about the piloting of that day—and no man ever has tried to scribble about it yet. Its newness pleases me all the time—and it is about the only new subject I know of. If I were to write fifty articles they would all be about pilots and piloting."

Old Times on the Mississippi appeared in the *Atlantic* from January to July, 1875. The chapters were immediately picked up by newspapers, and pirated in book form in Canada. They were a concrete, vivid, picture of an apprenticeship to a trade. "I am powerfully moved to write," Mark told Howells. "Which is natural enough, since I am a person who would quit anything in a minute to go piloting, if the madam would stand it." Mark found the new *Atlantic* audience "the only one I can sit down before in perfect security (for the simple reason that it doesn't require a 'humorist' to

The *Baton Rouge,* Horace Bixby, Captain, carried Mark Twain up the river from New Orleans in 1882 as he hunted for material to complete the Mississippi book.

paint himself striped and stand on his head every fifteen minutes.)" The seven-page articles brought him twenty dollars a page, a rate he deplored. "However," he comforted himself, "the awful respectability of the magazine makes up" for it.

In between writing sessions he relaxed on the December ice with the neighborhood girls, informing a friend "there would be a power of fun in skating if you could do it with somebody else's muscles." By January he reported "the piloting material has been uncovering itself by degrees, until it has exposed such a huge hoard

to my view that a whole book will be required to contain it if I use it. So I have agreed to write the book for Bliss."

To get more material for the book he proposed to Howells a trip down the Mississippi, with their wives along. But the plan was abandoned when Howells couldn't get away.

It was April, 1882, before Mark was ready to take up the unfinished business of the Mississippi River book. With his publisher, James R. Osgood, and a stenographer to take notes, he caught the steamer *Gold*

Captain Horace E. Bixby, the Mississippi pilot who trained Mark Twain.

James R. Osgood. Mark was fond of the Boston publisher in spite of his trade.

165

LIFE ON THE MISSISSIPPI

BY

MARK TWAIN

AUTHOR OF "THE INNOCENTS ABROAD," "ROUGHING IT," "THE PRINCE AND THE PAUPER," ETC.

WITH MORE THAN 300 ILLUSTRATIONS

Mississippi Steamboat of Fifty Years Ago.

[SOLD BY SUBSCRIPTION ONLY.]

BOSTON
JAMES R. OSGOOD AND COMPANY
1883

Title page of the first edition. The illustrations on this and facing page are from this edition.

The pilothouse, "a sumptuous temple."

Dust at St. Louis and drifted down the river. Early the first morning he went on deck to see if he could recognize the old landmarks. But it was a strange river; he couldn't recall anything. He clung to the pilothouse, reliving the happy and carefree dream life of twenty years before. At New Orleans he met Joel Chandler Harris, author of *Uncle Remus*, and George W. Cable, the novelist, and the three writers browsed through the French Quarter for days. His old river teacher was there

The cub learning the river.

The cocky apprentice sporting a toothpick.

The pilot points out landmarks.

too, and Mark made the trip north to St. Louis with Captain Horace Bixby in his new steamboat, *City of Baton Rouge*. Later Mark wrote Bixby, "Twenty years have not added a month to your age or taken a fraction from your loveliness."

At Hannibal, Mark stopped off to look around, and noted down: "Alas! everything was changed in Hannibal—but when I reached Third or Fourth street the tears burst forth, for I recognized the mud. It at least was the same—the same old mud—the mud that Annie Macdonald got stuck in.

"The romance of boating is gone now. In Hannibal the steamboatman is no longer a god. The youth don't talk river slang any more. Their pride is apparently railways—which they take a peculiar vanity in reducing to initials—an affectation which prevails all over the West. They roll these initials as a sweet morsel under the tongue."

To Livy he wrote: "I have spent three delightful days in Hannibal, loitering around all day long, examining the old localities and talking with the grey-heads who were boys and girls with me 30 or 40 years ago. It has been a moving time. I spent my nights with John and Helen Garth, three miles from town, in their spacious and beautiful house. They were children with me, and afterwards schoolmates. Now they have a daughter

The pre-war river pilots had their union, the Pilots' Benevolent Association. Here two pilots meet and give the sign of membership. Mark tells the story of their union in Chapter XV.

The leadsman measures the river's depth.

19 or 20 years old. Spent an hour, yesterday, with A. W. Lamb, who was not married when I saw him last. He married a young lady whom I knew. And now I have been talking with their grown-up sons and daughters. Lieutenant Hickman, the spruce young handsomely-uniformed volunteer of 1846, called on me—a grisly elephantine patriach of 65 now, his grace all vanished.

"That world which I knew in its blossoming youth is old and bowed and melancholy, now; its soft cheeks are leathery and wrinkled, the fire is gone out in its eyes, and the spring from its step. It will be dust and ashes when I come again. I have been clasping hands with the moribund—and usually they said, 'It is for the last time.' "

Life on the Mississippi appeared in 1883. It was really two books, not one. The *Atlantic* articles are chapters IV to XX; they are the marvelous memory of his four prewar years on the river. The last forty chapters are the record of how the river and its towns looked to Mark twenty years later. This part is crammed with statistics, yarns, scenery, essays, a chapter from the unfinished *Huck Finn*, an attack on Sir Walter Scott for starting the Civil War, and material lifted hastily from books and newspapers in order to fill out the book on schedule.

167

The young reader of the 1870's was caught between two huge waves of literature—the dime novels and the Sunday school tracts. The flood of extremes raised danger signals in some quarters, as this 1882 cartoon from *Puck* shows. Both Mark Twain's *Tom Sawyer* and Thomas Bailey Aldrich's *Story of a Bad Boy* were reactions against the school of piety.

HUCKLEBERRY FINN

In a casual letter to Howells in August, 1876, Mark mentions that he has begun "another boy's book—more to be at work than anything else. I have written 400 pages on it—therefore it is very nearly half done. It is Huckleberry Finn's Autobiography. I like it only tolerably well, as far as I have got, and may possibly pigeonhole it or burn the MS when it is done.'

Huck was soon dropped in favor of *1601,* a piece of Elizabethan ribaldry Mark wrote originally as a letter to Reverend Twichell, who enjoyed it immensely. Then came the diversion of the Hayes-Tilden Presidential campaign and collaboration with Bret Harte on a comedy.

Huck stirred briefly to life in 1880, then subsided. The trip into the Mississippi country in 1882 freshened Mark's interest in the little river rat's adventures. By August, 1883, he could tell Howells:

"I have written eight or nine hundred manuscript pages in such a brief space of time that I mustn't name the number of days; I shouldn't believe it myself, and of course couldn't expect you to. I used to restrict myself to four and five hours a day and five days in the week, but this time I have wrought from breakfast till 5.15 P.M. six days in the week, and once or twice I smouched a Sunday—when the boss wasn't looking. Nothing is half so good as literature hooked on Sunday, on the sly."

In the spring of 1884, proofs of *Huck* were coming from the printer. "My days are given up to cursings, both loud and deep," Mark wrote Howells, "for I am reading the *Huck Finn* proofs. They don't make a very great many mistakes but those that do occur are of a nature that make a man swear his teeth loose." Generously going over the proofs, Howells commented, "If I had written half as good a book as *Huck Finn* I shouldn't ask anything better than to read the proofs."

The December and January issues of the *Century* magazine printed chapters from the book. In February the canvassers were able to rush 40,000 copies of *Huck* to customers who had ordered in advance.

Mark Twain in 1880, the beginning of his happiest and most fertile five years. Out of it came *Huck, The Prince and the Pauper,* and *Life on the Mississippi.*

over the water, was a kind of dull line—that was the woods on t'other side—you couldn't make nothing else out; then a pale place in the sky; then more paleness, spreading around; then the river softened up, away off, and warn't black any more, but gray; you could see little dark spots drifting along ever so far away—trading scows, and such things; and long black streaks—rafts; sometimes you could hear a sweep creaking; or jumbled up voices, it was so still, and sounds come so far; and by-and-by you could see a streak on the water which you know by the look of the streak that there's a snag there in a swift current which breaks on it and makes the streak look that way; and you see the mist curl up off of the water, and the east reddens up, and the river, and you make out a log cabin in the edge of the woods away on the bank on t'other side of the river, being a woodyard, likely, and piled by them cheats so you can throw a dog through it anywheres; then the nice breeze springs up, and comes fanning you from over there, so cool and fresh, and sweet to smell, on account of the woods and the flowers; but sometimes not that way, because they've left dead fish laying around, gars, and such, and they do get pretty rank; and next you've got the full day, and everything smiling in the sun, and the song-birds just going it!

ON THE RIVER

"You don't know me without you have read a book by the name of *The Adventures of Tom Sawyer,* but that ain't no matter." With these first words from Huckleberry Finn the reader enters a stream of delightful language that floats him through a score of picaresque adventures shared by the boy and the runaway slave Jim. Twain's radical use of the vernacular and his fresh vision of landscape are caught in Huck's report of life on a river raft:

"Two or three days and nights went by; I reckon I might say they swum by, they slid along so quiet and smooth and lovely. Here is the way we put in the time. It was a monstrous big river down there—sometimes a mile and a half wide; we run nights, and laid up and hid day-times; soon as night was most gone, we stopped navigating and tied up—nearly always in the dead water under a tow-head; and then cut young cotton-woods and willows and hid the raft with them. Then we set out the lines. Next we slid into the river and had a swim, so as to freshen up and cool off; then we set down on the sandy bottom where the water was about knee deep, and watched the daylight come. Not a sound, anywheres—perfectly still—just like the whole world was asleep, only sometimes the bull-frogs a-cluttering, maybe. The first thing to see, looking away

The original design for the book's cover.

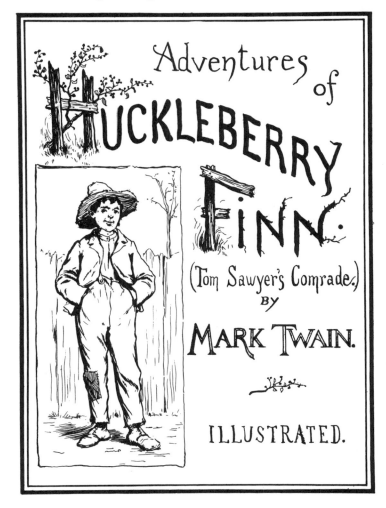

"A little smoke couldn't be noticed, now, so we would take some fish off of the lines, and cook up a hot breakfast. And afterwards we would watch the lonesomeness of the river, and kind of lazy along, and by-and-by lazy off to sleep. Wake up, by-and-by, and look to see what done it, and maybe see a steamboat, coughing along up stream, so far off towards the other side you couldn't tell nothing about her only whether she was a stern-wheel or side-wheel; then for about an hour there wouldn't be nothing to hear nor nothing to see—just solid lonesomeness. Next you'd see a raft sliding by, away off yonder, and maybe a galoot on it chopping, because they're most always doing it on a raft; you'd see the ax flash, and come down—you don't hear nothing; you see that ax go up again, and by the time it's above the man's head, then you hear the *k'chunk!* —it had took all that time to come over the water. So we would put in the day, lazying around, listening to the stillness. Once there was a thick fog, and the rafts and things that went by was beating tin pans so the steamboats wouldn't run over them. A scow or a raft went by so close we could hear them talking and cussing and laughing—heard them plain; but we couldn't see no sign of them; it made you feel crawly, it was like spirits carrying on that way in the air. Jim said he believed it was spirits; but I says:

"'No, spirits wouldn't say, "dern the dern fog."'

"Soon as it was night, out we shoved; when we got her out to about the middle, we let her alone, and let her float wherever the current wanted her to; then we lit the pipes, and dangled our legs in the water and talked about all kinds of things—we was always naked, day and night, whenever the mosquitos would let us— the new clothes Buck's folks made me was too good to be comfortable, and besides I didn't go much on clothes, nohow.

"Sometimes we'd have that whole river all to our-

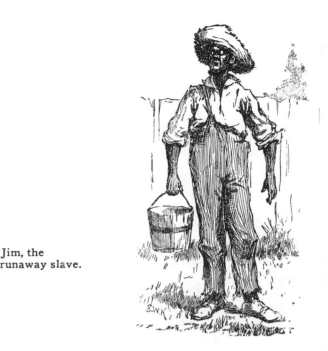

Jim, the runaway slave.

selves for the longest time. Yonder was the banks and the islands, across the water; and maybe a spark— which was a candle in the cabin window—and sometimes on the water you could see a spark or two—on a raft or a scow, you know; and maybe you could hear a fiddle or a song coming over from one of them crafts. It's lovely to live on a raft. We had the sky, up there, all speckled with stars, and we used to lay on our backs and look up at them, and discuss about whether they was made, or only just happened—Jim he allowed they was made, but I allowed they happened; I judged it would have took too long to *make* so many. Jim said the moon could a *laid* them; well, that looked kind of reasonable, so I didn't say nothing against it, because I've seen a frog lay most as many, so of course it could be done. We used to watch the stars that fell, too, and see them streak down. Jim allowed they'd got spoiled and was hove out of the nest.

"Once or twice of a night we would see a steamboat slipping along in the dark, and now and then she would belch a whole world of sparks up out of her chimbleys, and they would rain down in the river and look awful pretty; then she would turn a corner and her lights would wink out and her pow-wow shut off and leave the river still again; and by-and-by her waves would get to us, a long time after she was gone, and joggle the raft a bit, and after that you wouldn't hear nothing for you couldn't tell how long, except maybe frogs or something.

"After midnight the people on shore went to bed, and then for two or three hours the shores was black— no more sparks in the cabin windows. These sparks was our clock—the first one that showed again meant morning was coming, so we hunted a place to hide and tie up, right away."

Pappy Finn, Huck's father.

HUCK AND JIM

The right-and-wrong morality of the old South provided Mark Twain with material for savage satire. After Huck helps the slave Jim to run away toward freedom, he listens to Jim's plans:

"Jim talked out loud all the time while I was talking to myself. He was saying how the first thing he would do when he got to a free State he would go to saving up money and never spend a single cent, and when he got enough he would buy his wife, which was owned on a farm close to where Miss Watson lived; and then they would both work to buy the two children, and if their master wouldn't sell them, they'd get an Ab'litionist to go and steal them.

"It most froze me to hear such talk. He wouldn't ever dared to talk such talk in his life before. Just see what a difference it made in him the minute he judged he was about free. It was according to the old saying, 'give a nigger an inch and he'll take an ell.' Thinks I, this is what comes of my not thinking. Here was this nigger which I had as good as helped to run away, coming right out flat-footed and saying he would steal his children—children that belonged to a man I didn't know; a man that hadn't ever done me no harm."

Mark Twain as Huck Finn. The caricaturist put a gun under Huck's arm to symbolize Mark's deadly fire on injustice.

Jim disguises Huck in a calico gown in preparation for a scouting expedition on shore.

The slave code Huck was raised on forces a moral crisis on the boy which is dramatized in one of the best scenes in the novel. Huck's conscience pushes him into writing a letter informing Miss Watson where she can find her runaway slave, Jim. Then Huck thinks:

"I felt good and all washed clean of sin for the first time I had ever felt so in my life, and I knowed I could pray now. But I didn't do it straight off, but laid the paper down and set there thinking—thinking how good it was all this happened so, and how near I come to being lost and going to hell. And went on thinking. And got to thinking over our trip down the river; and I see Jim before me, all the time, in the day, and in the night-time, sometimes moonlight, sometimes storms, and we a floating along, talking, and singing, and laughing. But somehow I couldn't seem to strike no places to harden me against him, but only the other kind. I'd see him standing my watch on top of his'n, stead of calling me, so I could go on sleeping; and see him how glad he was when I come back out of the fog; and when I come to him again in the swamp, up there where the feud was; and such-like times; and would always call me honey, and pet me, and do everything he could think of for me, and how good he always was; and at last I struck the time I saved him by telling the men we had small-pox aboard, and he was so grateful, and said I was the best friend old Jim ever had in the world, and the *only* one he's got now; and then I happened to look around, and see that paper.

"It was a close place. I took it up, and held it in my hand. I was a trembling, because I'd got to decide, forever, betwixt two things, and I knowed it. I studied a minute, sort of holding my breath, and then says to myself:

"'All right, then I'll *go* to hell'—and tore it up."

The Duke and the King, the two rascals
who invade Huck's and Jim's raft.

COLONEL SHERBURN AND
THE LYNCHERS

After Colonel Sherburn has killed the drunken Boggs,
a mob swarms up to the Colonel's house, bent on lynching him. Huck watches the Colonel step out on the roof
of his porch, a shotgun in his hand, to look down on
the crowd. Then—in the only place in the book where
he drops Huck's voice—Twain speaks through the
Colonel to condemn the mob:

" 'The idea of *you* lynching anybody! It's amusing.
The idea of you thinking you had pluck enough to lynch
a *man!* Because you're brave enough to tar and feather
poor friendless cast-out women that come along here,
did that make you think you had grit enough to lay
your hands on a *man?* Why, a *man's* safe in the hands
of ten thousand of your kind—as long as it's daytime
and you're not behind him.

" 'Do I know you? I know you clear through. I was
born and raised in the South, and I've lived in the
North; so I know the average all around. The average
man's a coward. In the North he lets anybody walk
over him that wants to, and goes home and prays for
a humble spirit to bear it. In the South one man, all
by himself, has stopped a stage full of men, and robbed
the lot. Your newspapers call you a brave people so
much that you think you *are* braver than any other
people—whereas you're just *as* brave, and no braver.
Why don't your juries hang murderers? Because they're
afraid the man's friends will shoot them in the back,
in the dark—and it's just what they *would* do.

" 'So they always acquit; and then a *man* goes in the
night, with a hundred masked cowards at his back, and
lynches the rascal. Your mistake is, that you didn't
bring a man with you; that's one mistake, and the other
is that you didn't come in the dark, and fetch your
masks. You brought *part* of a man—Buck Harkness,
there—and if you hadn't had him to start you, you'd
a taken it out in blowing.

" 'You didn't want to come. The average man don't
like trouble and danger. *You* don't like trouble and
danger. But if only *half* a man—like Buck Harkness,
there—shouts "Lynch him, lynch him!" you're afraid
to back down—so you raise a yell, and hang yourselves
onto that half-a-man's coat tail, and come raging up
here, swearing what big things you're going to do. The
pitifulest thing out is a mob; that's what an army is—
a mob; they don't fight with courage that's born in
them, but with courage that's borrowed from their mass,
and from their officers. But a mob without any *man* at
the head of it, is *beneath* pitifulness. Now the thing for
you to do, is to droop your tails and go home and crawl
in a hole. If any real lynching's going to be done, it will
be done in the dark, Southern fashion; and when they
come they'll bring their masks, and fetch a *man* along.
Now *leave*—and take your half-a-man with you'—toss-
ing his gun up across his left arm and cocking it, when
he says this.

"The crowd washed back sudden, and then broke all
apart, and went tearing off every which way, and Buck
Harkness he heeled it after them, looking tolerable
cheap. I could 'a' staid, if I wanted to, but I didn't
want to."

CENSORS AND CRITICS

Huckleberry Finn got the greatest advance publicity of any book of Twain's up to that time. Mark couldn't agree with his old publishers on a contract for *Huck* and the rupture became news. The *Century* and some newspapers ran chapters in advance. Mark promoted the book by readings from it on his tour with Cable. When an engraving was suggestively tampered with, the prospectus containing it had to be recalled with much attendant hullabaloo. Then Mark sued a Boston firm for undercutting the canvasser's price. Finally—and most advantageously for the book's sale—the Concord Library in Massachusetts banned the book because it was morally injurious to the young. The press, taking sides in the censorship fight, put *Huck* on the front

Huck is censored again: the New York *Times*, Sept. 12, 1957. Earlier, in 1905, *Huck* and *Tom* were both removed from the children's room of the Brooklyn Public Library because they were "bad examples for ingenuous youth."

Continued on Page 20, Column 1

'Huck Finn' Barred As Textbook by City

By LEONARD BUDER

The Board of Education has quietly dropped Mark Twain's "The Adventures of Huckleberry Finn" from the approved textbook lists for the city's elementary and junior high schools.

The book can still be purchased for school libraries, but it can no longer be bought for wide distribution to pupils as a textbook, except in the high schools. Even in these schools, Huck Finn's days may be numbered.

"Huckleberry Finn," which tells the story of boyhood in the Mississippi Valley in the Eighteen Forties, has been criticized by some Negroes as "racially offensive." A central figure in the book, which was written in dialect, is "Miss

Continued on Page 29, Column 2

page. "A rattling tiptop puff" from Concord's "moral icebergs," Mark commented. "They have expelled *Huck* from their library as 'trash suitable only for the slums.' That will sell 25,000 copies for us sure." On the other end of the town's seesaw the Concord Free Trade Club promptly elected Mark an honorary member.

So the book was off to a great sale. But the critics were indifferent or cold. The *Century* was the only magazine to review it; none of the country's major newspapers did. Some of the papers editorialized that Mark's day as a writer was done. *Huck Finn*, Mark Twain's masterpiece and one of the world's great novels, was too vulgar, coarse and inelegant for the critics of the genteel age.

When *Huck* was finally completed, Mark saw in *Life* magazine the comic drawings of a young man named E. W. Kemble and commissioned him to illustrate the novel. Kemble was delayed by the exigencies of moving and sent the sketch on this page as evidence. Mark thought his pictures "most rattling good. They please me exceedingly." Kemble had never been South and used a New York boy as model not only for Huck but all the characters, regardless of age, sex or color. So truthful did his drawings seem that he was besieged with commissions to illustrate the work of Southern writers. *Huck* had made him famous and prosperous overnight.

A faint idea of my conditi
Very truly.
E W Kemble

173

PLAYWRIGHT AND PERFORMER

"He was the most consummate public performer I ever saw," wrote Howells of Mark Twain, "and it was an incomparable pleasure to hear him lecture; on the platform he was the great and finished actor which he probably would not have been on the stage." Lecturing for the author-half of Twain was perdition, said Howells. For the actor-half, it was paradise.

Mark loved the theater from his first sight of the itinerant players who strayed downriver into Hannibal. His own debut on the stage took place in Hartford on April 26, 1876, in an amateur production of *Loan of a Lover*. He played Peter Spyk, "an irresistibly comical model blockhead," a part he rewrote as his performance proceeded. Private theatricals and charades he never gave up, amusing his family and friends with them into his seventies.

Mark's first successful playwrighting was his adaptation of *The Gilded Age*. "I worked a month on my play," he wrote Howells, "and launched it in New York last Wednesday. I believe it will go. The newspapers have been complimentary. It is simply a *setting* for one character, Col. Sellers. As a play I guess it will not bear critical assault in force. . . .

"Many persons regarded Colonel Sellers as a fiction, an invention, an extravagant impossibility, and did me the honor to call him a 'creation'; but they were mistaken. I merely put him on paper as he was; he was not

Mark tried *Tom Sawyer* as a play in 1872. Aunt Winny, the character on this first manuscript page, became Aunt Polly in the novel.

A year after *Roughing It* was published, Augustin Daly distilled from it a "totally original, strikingly picturesque, and absorbingly interesting Kaleidoscopic Drama in 4 Acts, Eleven Tableaux and a Transformation." Or at least out of Mark's title, for none of the characters listed are in the book. The playbill does mention Mark Twain twice, however.

a person who could be exaggerated. [Sellers was Mark's mother's favorite cousin, James Lampton.] The incidents which looked most extravagant, both in the book and on the stage, were not inventions of mine, but were facts of his life; and I was present when they were developed. John T. Raymond's audiences used to come near to dying with laughter over the turnip-eating scene; but, extravagant as the scene was, it was faithful to the facts in all its absurd details. The thing happened in Lampton's own house and I was present. In fact, I was myself the guest who ate the turnips. In the hands of a great actor that piteous scene would have dimmed any manly spectator's eyes with tears and racked his ribs apart with laughter at the same time. But Raymond was great in humorous portrayal only. In that he was superb, he was wonderful—in a word, great; in all things else he was a pygmy of pygmies. The real Colonel Sellers, as I knew him in James Lampton, was a pathetic and beautiful spirit, a manly man, a straight and honorable man, a man with a big, foolish, unselfish heart in his bosom, a man born to be loved; and he was loved by all his friends, and by his family worshiped. It is the right word. To them he was but little less than a god. The real Colonel Sellers was never on the stage. Only half of him was there. Raymond could not play the other half of him; it was above his level. That half was made up of qualities of which Raymond was wholly destitute. For Raymond was not a manly man, he was not an honorable man nor an honest man, he was empty and selfish and vulgar and ignorant and silly, and there was a vacancy in him where his heart should have been.

"One man who could have played the whole of Colonel Sellers . . . was Frank Mayo."

Mark, of course, had his own Colonel Sellers nature, although he preferred to believe the true model was solely James Lampton. Raymond was a great hit in the Sellers role, playing it for over a thousand performances. He shared the profits equally with Twain; they divided well over a hundred thousand dollars.

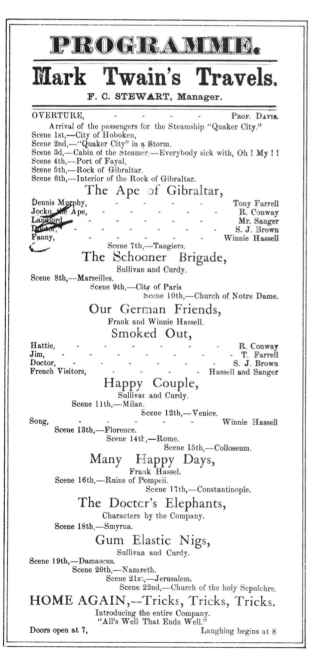

PROGRAMME.
Mark Twain's Travels.
F. C. STEWART, Manager.

OVERTURE, - - - - Prof. Davis.
Arrival of the passengers for the Steamship "Quaker City."
Scene 1st,—City of Hoboken,
Scene 2nd,—"Quaker City" in a Storm.
Scene 3d,—Cabin of the Steamer.—Everybody sick with, Oh ! My ! !
Scene 4th,—Port of Fayal,
Scene 5th,—Rock of Gibraltar.
Scene 6th,—Interior of the Rock of Gibraltar.

The Ape of Gibraltar,
Dennis Murphy, - - - - Tony Farrell
Jocko, the Ape, - - - - R. Conway
Landlord, - - - - - Mr. Sanger
Doctor, - - - - - S. J. Brown
Fanny, - - - - - Winnie Hassell
Scene 7th,—Tangiers.

The Schooner Brigade,
Sullivan and Curdy.
Scene 8th,—Marseilles.
Scene 9th,—City of Paris
Scene 10th,—Church of Notre Dame.

Our German Friends,
Frank and Winnie Hassell.

Smoked Out,
Hattie, - - - - - R. Conway
Jim, - - - - - T. Farrell
Doctor, - - - - - S. J. Brown
French Visitors, - - - Hassell and Sanger

Happy Couple,
Sullivan and Curdy.
Scene 11th,—Milan.
Scene 12th,—Venice.
Song, - - - - - Winnie Hassell
Scene 13th,—Florence.
Scene 14th,—Rome.
Scene 15th,—Colloseum.

Many Happy Days,
Frank Hassel.
Scene 16th,—Ruins of Pompeii.
Scene 17th,—Constantinople.

The Doctor's Elephants,
Characters by the Company.
Scene 18th,—Smyrna.

Gum Elastic Nigs,
Sullivan and Curdy.
Scene 19th,—Damascus.
Scene 20th,—Nazareth.
Scene 21st,—Jerusalem.
Scene 22nd,—Church of the holy Sepulchre.

HOME AGAIN,--Tricks, Tricks, Tricks.
Introducing the entire Company.
"All's Well That Ends Well."
Doors open at 7,   Laughing begins at 8

A playbill for *Colonel Sellers*, in the second year of its success.

Another probably unauthorized exploitation of Mark Twain, this time of his *Quaker City* voyage to Europe and the Holy Land. Since the *Innocents Abroad* title is not used, the production may have been rushed to the stage before the book was out.

Mark Twain congratulates John T. Raymond, who played Colonel Sellers in Twain's version of *The Gilded Age*. The firm handshake is the product of publicity, not affection.

Poster issued during the run of the Twain-Harte play at the National Theatre in Washington in 1877.

NATIONAL THEATRE--TO-NIGHT
"AH SIN"
THE HEATHEN CHINEE.

MARK TWAIN AND BRET HARTE'S NEW PLAY.
CHAS. T. PARSLOE - - as - - AH SIN.
Toueli Bros., Printers and Engravers, 181 W. Baltimore street, Baltimore.

FROM AH SIN TO HAMLET

In the fall of 1876, Bret Harte proposed that he and Mark should write a play together. Harte came to Hartford; Twain described their collaboration: "The next morning after his arrival we went to the billiard room and began work upon the play. I named my characters and described them; Harte did the same by his. Then he began to sketch the scenario, act by act and scene by scene. He worked rapidly and seemed to be troubled by no hesitations or indecisions; what he accomplished in an hour or two would have cost me several weeks of painful and difficult labor and would have been valueless when I got through. But Harte's work was good and usable; to me it was a wonderful performance.

"Then the filling in began. Harte set down the dialogue swiftly, and I had nothing to do except when one of my characters was to say something; then Harte told me the nature of the remark that was required, I furnished the language and he jotted it down. After this fashion we worked two or three or four hours every day for a couple of weeks and produced a comedy that was good and would act. His part of it was the best part of it but that did not disturb the critics; when the piece was staged they praised my share of the work with a quite suspicious prodigality of approval and gave Harte's share all the vitriol they had in stock. The piece perished."

The comedy was *Ah Sin,* the story of a Chinese laundryman on the Western frontier; "hurled" at the Washington public May 7, 1877, it made no great stir. When it opened in New York in August, one critic wrote: "Few plays can be mentioned whose literary execution is so bad, whose construction is so ramshackle, whose texture is so barren of true wit, good taste and the peculiar American humor for which both these authors are justly celebrated." Mark himself confessed it was "full of incurable defects: to wit, Harte's deliberate thefts and plagiarism and my own unconscious ones."

But even while *Ah Sin* was staggering toward cheerful disaster, Mark was writing a new play, *Simon Wheeler, the Amateur Detective.* "I have a good opinion of the chief character in it," he wrote Mollie Fairbanks. "I want to play it myself, in New York or London, but the madam won't allow it." Like Colonel Sellers, he speculated gloriously that "if the play's a success it's worth $50,000 or more—if it fails it's worth nothing and even the worst of failures can't rob me of the 6½ days of booming pleasure I have had in writing it." It never had the chance to fail; no one would produce it. Looking it over two years later, Mark found it "dreadfully witless and flat."

Mark's delight in playwriting infected Howells, who came to Hartford in 1883 to work with Mark on a sequel to *Sellers*. "We cracked our sides laughing at it as we went along," Howells said. Raymond and other actor-managers refused to do the play. Finally an elocutionist agreed to try it on the road. It died in a week, but not Mark's hopes for it. Howells, less deluded, said, "I believe the thing will fail, and it would be a disgrace to have it succeed."

That same year, 1883, Mark dramatized both *The Prince and the Pauper* and *Tom Sawyer* in a few weeks. No one had faith in these either. Other playwrights were able to adapt Mark's work for commercial success, but his stagecraft wasn't equal to the task. As late as 1898 he was still trying futilely, this time collaborating with a Vienna journalist.

In 1888 Mark became one of the founders of The Players club in New York, joining with such stars as

David Belasco directed Mrs. Richardson's play version of Twain's novel. Three special performances for the Hartford folks were announced on the playbill.

HARTFORD MARCH 3, 4, 5.

BROADWAY THEATRE,
41st Street and Broadway, New York.
The Handsomest and Safest Theatre in the World.
FRANK W. SANGER, - - - MANAGER.

Commencing Monday, January 20, 1890.
EVERY EVENING AT 8 O'CLOCK.
MATINEES WEDNESDAYS AND SATURDAYS.

DANIEL FROHMAN'S PRODUCTION
A play which every child should see.—*N. Y. Spirit of the Times.*

The sweetest, rarest, and prettiest of all the plays since "Little Lord Fauntleroy." Mark Twain was right when he said the performance of this play was the realization of a fifteen years' dream.—N. Y. Herald.

—OF—

THE PRINCE AND THE PAUPER,
(WITH ELSIE LESLIE.)
Dramatized from MARK TWAIN'S Story
—BY—
ABBY SAGE RICHARDSON.
UNDER THE STAGE DIRECTION OF DAVID BELASCO.

The popular actor, Frank Mayo, dramatized Mark's novel and played it profitably for over 20 years.

Edwin Booth, John Drew, and Joseph Jefferson. Nothing daunted by his own playwrighting failures, Mark tried intermittently for nine years to improve *Hamlet* by the addition of a burlesque character who strolls through the action making funny comments on it. Not long before his death Mark decided that that ignorant actor, Will Shakespeare, couldn't have written those plays, and added his own book—*Is Shakespeare Dead?*—to the arsenal of the Baconians.

177

Bayard Taylor (*top*) and Murat Halstead (*bottom*) sailed to Europe with the Twain family in April, 1878. Taylor, a poet bound for a new post as minister to Germany, was, in Mark's eyes, "a genial, lovable, simple-hearted soul," who outlived his voluminous verse. Mark thought it crazily unfair that Halstead, a Cincinnati editor, "was condemned to sixty years of editorial slavery and I let off with a lifetime of delightful idleness."

ROBERT INGERSOLL'S MUSIC

The Twains returned from a seventeen-month stay in Europe in September, 1879. As usual, Mark was promptly caught up in a round of grand banquets and private dinner parties. The high points were his November speech in Chicago when General Grant was honored, and his tribute to Dr. Oliver Wendell Holmes at a breakfast in Boston. Emerson, Longfellow, Whittier, Julia Ward Howe, Harriet Beecher Stowe, Francis Parkman, all joined in homage to Holmes. At home in Hartford a rich creative period began, but it did not interfere with Mark's brilliant evenings. His literary friends Howells and Aldrich, the actors Edwin Booth and Sir Henry Irving, the Civil War heroes Sheridan and Sherman, were typical of the distinction that crowded Twain's table.

It was at the banquet for Ulysses Grant that Mark heard Robert Ingersoll speak.

"I doubt if America has ever seen anything quite equal it," Mark wrote Howells. "I am well satisfied I shall not live to see its equal again. How pale those speeches are in print, but how radiant, how full of color, how blinding they were in the delivery! Bob Ingersoll's music will sing through my memory always as the divinest that ever enchanted my ears. And I shall always see him, as he stood that night on a dinner-table, under the flash of lights and banners, in the midst of seven hundred frantic shouters, the most beautiful human creature that ever lived. 'They fought, that a mother might own her child.' The words look like any other print, but, Lord bless me! he borrowed the very accent of the angel of mercy to say them in, and you should have seen that vast house rise to its feet; and you should have heard the hurricane that followed. That's the *only* test! People may shout, clap their hands, stamp, wave their napkins but none but the master can make them *get up on their feet*."

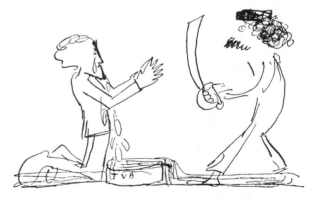

The sculptor Augustus Saint-Gaudens sends Mark a sketch apologizing for a broken engagement.

Colonel Robert G. Ingersoll, whose speeches Mark admired so much he used to read them to the girls in his Saturday Morning Club.

Robert Louis Stevenson, author of *Treasure Island*.

UNCLE REMUS

A newspaper item in 1906 revived in Mark's mind memories of his old friendship for Joel Chandler Harris, creator of the *Uncle Remus* stories: "It is just a quarter of a century since I have seen Uncle Remus. He visited us at our home in Hartford and was reverently devoured by the big eyes of Susy and Clara, for I made a deep and awful impression upon the little creatures—who knew his book by heart through my nightly declamation of its tales to them—by revealing to them privately that he was the real Uncle Remus whitewashed so that he could come into people's houses the front way.

"He was the bashfulest grown person I have ever met. When there were people about he stayed silent and seemed to suffer until they were gone. But he was lovely nevertheless, for the sweetness and benignity of the immortal Remus looked out from his eyes and the graces and sincerities of his character shone in his face."

ROBERT LOUIS STEVENSON

Robert Louis Stevenson once wrote Mark Twain that he had read *Huck Finn* four times, "and am quite ready to begin again tomorrow." In December, 1887, Mark visited Stevenson, a victim of tuberculosis, at his hotel in Greenwich Village. Years later, recalling their talk, Twain wrote: "It was on a bench in Washington Square that I saw the most of Louis Stevenson. It was an outing that lasted an hour or more and was very pleasant and sociable. I had come with him from his house, where I had been paying my respects to his family. His business in the square was to absorb the sunshine. He was most scantily furnished with flesh, his clothes seemed to fall into hollows as if there might be nothing inside but the frame for a sculptor's statue. His long face and lank hair and dark complexion and musing and melancholy expression seemed to fit these details justly and harmoniously, and the altogether of it seemed especially planned to gather the rags of your observation and focalize them upon Stevenson's special distinction and commanding feature, his splendid eyes. They burned with a smoldering rich fire under the penthouse of his brows and they made him beautiful."

Joel Chandler Harris. He wrote his animal legends, reflecting Negro folk life, while working as editorial writer for the Atlanta *Constitution*.

MARK TWAIN—MASTER OF YALE

The first honorary degree conferred upon the self-educated Twain was Yale's Master of Arts, given him in 1888. The solemn honor did not inhibit the new M.A. Speaking to the college he said:

"I was sincerely proud and grateful to be made a Master of Arts by this great and venerable University. . . . Along at first, say for the first month or so, I did not quite know how to proceed because of my not knowing just what authorities and privileges belonged to the title which had been granted me, but after that I consulted some students of Trinity—in Hartford—and they made everything clear to me. It was through them that I found out that my title made me head of the Governing Body of the University, and lodged in me very broad and severely responsible powers.

"I was told that it would be necessary to report to you at this time, and of course I comply, though I would have preferred to put it off till I could make a better showing; for indeed I have been so pertinaciously hindered and obstructed at every turn by the faculty that it would be difficult to prove that the University is really in any better shape now than it was when I first took charge. By advice, I turned my earliest attention to the Greek department. I told the Greek professor I had concluded to drop the use of Greek-written character because it is so hard to spell with, and so impossible to read after you get it spelt. Let us draw the curtain there. I saw by what followed that nothing but early neglect saved him from being a very profane man.

"I ordered the professor of mathematics to simplify the whole system, because the way it was I couldn't understand it, and I didn't want things going on in the college in what was practically a clandestine fashion. I told him to drop the conundrum system; it was not suited to the dignity of a college, which should deal in facts, not guesses and suppositions; we didn't want any more cases of IF A and B stand at opposite poles of earth's surface and C at the equator of Jupiter, at what variations of angle will the left limb of the moon appear to these different parties?—I said you just let that thing alone; it's plenty of time to get in a sweat about it when it happens; as like as not it ain't going to do any harm, anyway. His reception of these instructions bordered on insubordination, insomuch that I felt obliged to take his number and report him.

"I found the astronomer of the University gadding around after comets and other such odds and ends—tramps and derelicts of the skies. I told him pretty plainly that we couldn't have that. I told him it was no economy to go on piling up and piling up raw material in

The founders of "The Players" autograph the back of Mark's menu at the luncheon which gave birth to the club. Mark's signature is missing, but the line at the top is his note. At the bottom is the smallest autograph: "W. T. Sherman, General."

the way of new stars and comets and asteroids that we couldn't ever have any use for till we had worked off the old stock. At bottom I don't really mind comets so much, but somehow I have always been down on asteroids. There is nothing mature about them; I wouldn't sit up nights the way that man does if I could get a basketful of them. He said it was the best line of goods he had; he said he could trade them to Rochester for comets, and trade the comets to Harvard for nebulae, and trade the nebulae to the Smithsonian for flint hatchets. I felt obliged to stop this thing on the spot; I said we couldn't have the University turned into an astronomical junkshop.

"And while I was at it I thought I might as well make the reform complete; the astronomer is extraordinarily mutinous, and so, with your approval, I will transfer him to the law department and put one of the law students in his place. A boy will be more biddable, more tractable, also cheaper. It is true he cannot be intrusted with important work at first, but he can comb the skies for nebulae till he gets his hand in. I have other changes in mind, but as they are in the nature of surprises I judge it politic to leave them unspecified at this time."

A year later Johns Hopkins fell into line:

"A few months ago I was told that the Johns Hopkins University had given me a degree. I naturally supposed this constituted me a Member of the Faculty,

A few years after his meeting with Mark Twain, Kipling married an American and settled in Vermont for four years. There he wrote four of his children's books. This portrait engraving of Kipling was made in 1902, the year he wrote his American publisher: "I love to think of the great and godlike Clemens. He is the biggest man you have on your side of the water by a damn sight, and don't you forget it. Cervantes was a relation of his."

and so I started in to help what I could there. I told them I believed they were perfectly competent to run a college as far as the higher branches of education are concerned, but what they needed was a little help here and there from a practical commercial man. I said the public is sensitive to little things and they wouldn't have full confidence in a college that didn't know how to spell John."

THE STRANGER, RUDYARD KIPLING

An unknown young journalist, Rudyard Kipling, was touring America in 1889, writing travel letters home to an Indian newspaper. One summer day he showed up in Elmira to interview the world-renowned writer, Mark Twain. The extraordinary impression he left was recalled by Mark seventeen years later: "Kipling came down that afternoon and spent a couple of hours with me, and at the end of that time I had surprised him as much as he had surprised me, and the honors were easy. I believed that he knew more than any person I had ever met before, and I knew that he knew I knew less than any person he had met before —though he did not say it and I was not expecting that he would. When he was gone, Mrs. Langdon wanted to know about my visitor. I said, 'He is a stranger to me but he is a most remarkable man—and I am the other one. Between us, we cover all knowl-

edge; he knows all that can be known and I know the rest.'

"He was a stranger to me and to all the world and remained so for twelve months, then he became suddenly known and universally known. From that day to this he has held this unique distinction; that of being the only living person, not head of a nation, whose voice is heard around the world the moment it drops a remark, the only such voice in existence that does not go by slow ship and rail but always travels first-class —by cable."

Kipling, too, recorded that visit in his letter to India:

"You are a contemptible lot over yonder. Some of you are Commissioners and some are Lieutenant-Governors, and some have the V.C., and a few are privileged to walk about the Mall arm in arm with the Viceroy; but I have seen Mark Twain this golden morning, have shaken his hand and smoked a cigar —no, two cigars—with him, and talked with him for more than two hours! Understand clearly that I do not despise you; indeed, I don't. I am only very sorry for you, from the Viceroy downward.

"A big, darkened drawing-room; a huge chair; a man with eyes, a mane of grizzled hair, a brown mustache covering a mouth as delicate as a woman's, a strong, square hand shaking mine, and the slowest, calmest, levelest voice in all the world.

"The thing that struck me first was that he was an elderly man; yet, after a minute's thought, I perceived that it was otherwise, and in five minutes, the eyes looking at me, I saw that the gray hair was an accident of the most trivial. He was quite young. I was shaking his hand. I was smoking his cigar, and I was hearing him talk—this man I had learned to love and admire fourteen thousand miles away.

"Reading his books, I had striven to get an idea of his personality, and all my preconceived notions were wrong and beneath the reality. Blessed is the man who finds no disillusion when he is brought face to face with a revered writer."

Twain's friend Edwin Booth, in whose home The Players club is housed.

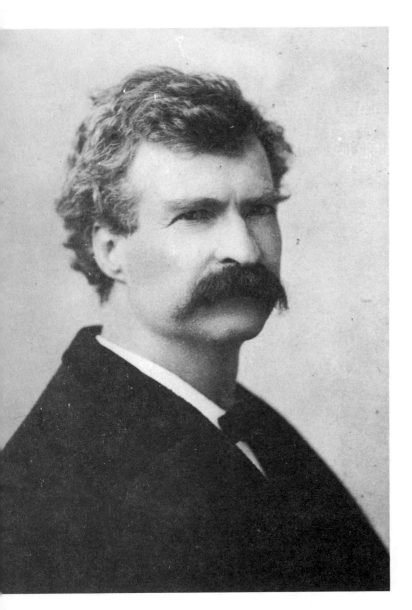

IN THE 1880'S

In New York, about 1880.

How this happened to be posed is
unknown. Date: probably 1883.

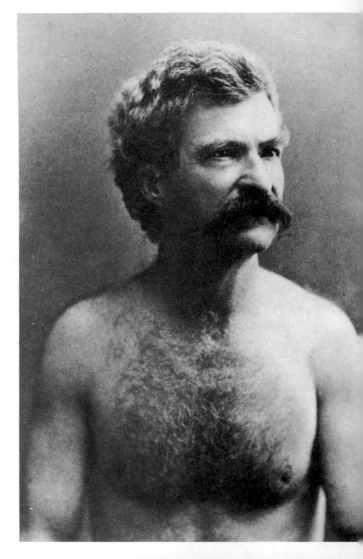

182

Studio portraits made at the same sitting in 1885.

The "bright and jolly" company that gathered at Onteora in the Catskills in the summer of 1890. Mark Twain is second from the right. Seated at far left is Carroll Beckwith, another Hannibal boy who made good. He painted Mark's portrait shown on facing page. Standing in center, hat in hand, is Brander Matthews, the drama critic. Mary Mapes Dodge, editor of *St. Nicholas*, is seated sixth from the left. The mustachioed Laurence Hutton is seated in front of Mrs. Dodge. Everybody autographed the print.

A SUMMER IN THE CATSKILLS

In the summer of 1890 the Twain family came to Tannersville in the Catskills, to the literary colony of the Onteora Club. Susy and Clara, now eighteen and sixteen, co-starred with their father in the pantomimes and charades while eleven-year-old Jean amused herself riding a pony and going barefoot. Mark's troublesome business interests dragged him back to New York frequently that summer. Rheumatism crept into his arm and shoulder, interfering with his writing. In October his mother died, at eighty-seven, and only a month later, Livy's mother. That December, ending a business letter, Mark wrote: "Merry Christmas to you —and I wish to God I could have one myself before I die."

A verse and sketch Mark dedicated that summer to his friend Larry Hutton.

184

The Last Meeting, & Final Parting

When I meet you I shall know you,
By your halo I shall know you
    Thus shall know you, blameless man;
And you'll know me also, Larry,
When we meet but may not tarry —
    Yes, alas, alas, you'll know me by my fan.

Onteora, July 5, 1890.

Mark Twain

Portrait of Mark Twain smoking his corncob pipe, painted by Carroll Beckwith at Onteora in the summer of 1890.

Mark Twain on Laurence Hutton's porch at Onteora, photographed by James Mapes Dodge.

Twain and Hutton match cigars and profiles in a vaudeville pose at Onteora.

"TWINS OF GENIUS"—ON TOUR

"Cable has been here, creating worshipers on all hands," Twain wrote Howells in 1882. "He is a marvelous talker on a deep subject. I do not see how even Spencer could unwind a thought more smoothly or orderly, and do it in a cleaner, clearer, crisper English.

Mark Twain of Missouri and George W. Cable of Louisiana, billed as the "Twins of Genius," during their 1884–85 tour. They were the first major Southern writers to portray the Negro sympathetically in their fiction.

The evening's bill usually lasted two hours. Frequently Cable sang Creole songs in his sweet tenor. Both authors promoted their new work on the tour: *Dr. Sevier* was just published and *Huck Finn* was about to be.

He astounded Twichell with his faculty. You know when it comes down to moral honesty, limpid innocence, and utterly blemishless piety, the Apostles were mere policemen to Cable, so with this in mind you must imagine him at a midnight dinner in Boston the other night, where we gathered around the board of the Summerset Club; Osgood, full, Boyle O'Reilly, full, Fairchild responsively loaded, and Aldrich and myself possessing the floor, and properly fortified. Cable told Mrs. Clemens when he returned here, that he seemed to have been entertaining himself with horses, and had a dreamy idea that he must have gone to Boston in a cattle-car. It was a very large time. He called it an orgy. And no doubt it was, viewed from his standpoint."

When the two writers met for the first time, Twain was world-famous as a humorist, lecturer and novelist. Cable had just come out of obscurity with his two books of Louisiana life, *Old Creole Days* and *The Grandissimes*. Their friendship was immediate. Cable was looking to the platform to help support his family and in the winter of 1883–84 stayed with the Twains while giving public readings in Hartford.

Mark wanted to include Cable in a menagerie of lecturing literary lions with Howells, Aldrich, Warner, and Harris. But the grand plan for a cross-country picnic in a private railway car shrank to the tour with Cable. Mark hired Cable for $450 weekly and expenses, with Major James B. Pond to be "boss and head ringmaster." The tour began in November, 1884, and moved from Washington to Toronto and west to Minnesota. They were on the road for four months, taking only ten days off, for Christmas family festivities.

Mark had never tried reading before, and it was ten years since he had lectured.

"It was ghastly!" he recalled. "At least in the beginning. I had selected my readings well enough but had not studied them. I supposed it would only be necessary to do like Dickens—get out on the platform and read from the book. I did that and made a botch of it. Written things are not for speech; their form is literary; they are stiff, inflexible and will not lend themselves to happy and effective delivery with the tongue—where their purpose is to merely entertain, not instruct; they have to be limbered up, broken up, colloquialized and turned into the common forms of unpremeditated talk—otherwise they will bore the house, not entertain it. After a week's experience with the book I laid it aside and never carried it to the platform again; but meantime I had memorized those pieces, and in delivering them from the platform they soon transformed themselves into flexible talk, with all their obstructing precisenesses and formalities gone out of them for good."

The tour excited great public interest. The crowds were large and rewarding, the press interviews unrelenting, the applause stirringly satisfying. The incongruous pair—Twain vivid, sociable, profane; Cable mousy, prim, pious—had an immense time. "You should have seen that alert and radiant mass of well-dressed humanity," Mark wrote Livy from Chicago. "Last night I was the greatest triumph we have ever made. It just went with a long roll of artillery—laughter all down the line, interspersed with Congreve rockets and bomb shell explosions from the first word to the last."

But there were tensions in the four-month tour. Cable turned out to be fanatically parsimonious and pious. He refused to travel on Sunday, and swiftly had to be discouraged from reading his Bible aloud to Mark.

"Livy dear," Mark wrote in February, "you cannot imagine anything like this idiotic Sunday superstition of Cable's. I would throttle a baby that had it. It is the most beggarly disease, the pitiful, the most contemptible mange that ever a grown creature was afflicted withal. The only time the man ever grows nervous, the only time he ever shows trepidation, is when some quarter of a minute of his detestable Sabbath seems threatened. Since I have been with this paltry child, I have imbibed a venomous & unreasoning detestation of the very name of the Sabbath.

"He is in many ways fine & great, & splendid; & in others paltriness itself. In Napoleon resided a god & a little mere man.

"I have modified Cable's insulting & insolent ways with servants, but have not cured them; may-be they cannot be cured. Pond says the servants of the Everett House all hate him. Says that when C. is paying his own expenses, he starves himself; & when somebody else is paying them his appetite is insatiable. O, do you know, that for a year or two he was longing to hear Beecher, but would not cross the river on Sunday? He wouldn't cross the *bridge* on Sunday.

"Do you know, that infernal Night Ride of Mary's has grown from 6 minutes (in New Haven) to *fifteen!* And it is in every program. This pious ass allows an 'entirely new program' to be announced from the stage & in the papers, & then comes out without a wince or an apology & jerks that same old Night Ride on the audience again. He did it 5 times in Chicago; but even that was not as bad as doing it 3 times in a little place like Indianapolis. He keeps his program strung out to one hour, in spite of all I can do. I am thinking of cutting another of his pieces out of the program."

The advertisement in the *Tribune* for the first New York appearance.

Twain and Cable reached Quincy, Illinois, on January 12, 1885, and stayed with Mark's relatives by marriage, the widow of Erasmus Mason Moffett and her daughters. The celebrities posed for a family photo. *From left:* Twain, Lizzie Moffett, the widow Moffett, Ella Moffett, Lizzie's husband Valentine Surghor, and Cable.

The Twain-Cable debut at Chickering Hall brought a page-one review from the New York *Sun* on November 19, 1884.

Mark used his notebook during the tour. These pages block out his own material on the left, and the program's timing on the right. By January, Mark had got Cable to go on for 15 minutes while the audience was filing in. "Only half the house hears C's first piece," he confided to Livy, "so there isn't too much of C any more—whereas heretofore there has been a thundering sight too much of him."

HOME TO HANNIBAL

In January, 1885, the tour brought Mark home to Hannibal for the first time in three years. "Such slathers of ancient friends, & such worlds of talk, & such deep enjoyment of it!" he wrote Livy. "This visit to Hannibal—you can never imagine the infinite great deeps of pathos that have rolled their tides over me. I shall never see another such day. I have carried my heart in my mouth for twenty-four hours. And at the last moment came Tom Nash—cradle-mate, baby-mate, little-boy mate—deaf & dumb, now, for near 40 years, & nobody suspecting the deep & fine nature hidden behind his sealed lips—& hands me this letter, & wrings my hand, & gives me a devouring look or two, & walks shyly away. I kept it, & read it half an hour ago—& of course, although it was past midnight & I had not written to you yet, I sat down at once & answered it."

The next night they were in Keokuk, where Mark's mother, his brother Orion, and Orion's wife, Mollie, were living. They all came to the Opera House to revel in Mark's fame and later that night eighty-one-year-old Jane Clemens showed her sons she could still

166 THE ADVENTURES OF HUCKLEBERRY FINN.

out and say so? Do you want to spread it all over?"

"Well," says I, a blubbering, "I've told everybody before, and then they just went away and left us." [fellows.]

"Poor devil, there's something in that. We are right down sorry for you, but we—well, hang it, we don't want the small-pox, you see. Look here, I'll tell you what to do. Don't you try to land by yourself, or you'll smash everything to pieces. You float along down about twenty miles and you'll come to a town on the left-hand side of the river. It will be long after sun-up, then, and when you ask for help, you tell them your folks are all down with chills and fever. Don't be a fool again, and let people guess what is the matter. Now we're trying to do you a kindness; so you just put twenty miles between us, that's a good boy. It wouldn't do any good to land yonder where the light is—it's only a wood-yard. Say—I reckon your father's poor, and I'm bound to say he's in pretty hard luck. Here—I'll put a twenty dollar gold piece on this board, and you get it when it floats by. I feel mighty mean to leave you, but my kingdom! it won't do to fool with small-pox, don't you see?"

"Hold on, Parker," says the other man, "here's a twenty to put on the board for me. Good-bye,

to fur as I can see, a consarnce is put in you just to object to whatever you do

THE ADVENTURES OF HUCKLEBERRY FINN. 167

do, don't make difference what it is.

boy, you do as Mr. Parker told you, and you'll be all right."

"That's so, my boy—good-bye, good-bye. If you see any runaway niggers, you get help and nab them, and you can make some money by it."

"Good-bye, sir," says I, "I won't let no runaway niggers get by me if I can help it."

They went off and I got aboard the raft, feeling bad and low, because I knowed very well I had done wrong, and I see it warn't no use for me to try to learn to do right; a body that don't get *started* right when he's little, ain't got no show—when the pinch comes there ain't nothing to back him up and keep him to his work, and so he gets beat. Then I thought a minute, and says to myself, hold on,—s'pose you'd a done right and give Jim up; would you felt better than what you do now? No, says I, I'd feel bad—I'd feel just the same way I do now. Well, then, says I, what's the use you learning to do right, when it's troublesome to do right and ain't no trouble to do wrong, and the wages is just the same? I was stuck. I couldn't answer that. So I reckoned I wouldn't bother no more about it, but after this always do whichever come handiest at the time.

I went into the wigwam; Jim warn't there. I looked all around; he warn't anywhere. I says:

---

dance as lightly as a girl. "A beautiful evening with Ma," Mark wrote, "& she is her old beautiful self; a nature of pure gold—one of the purest & finest & highest this land has produced."

As the tour neared its end in February, Mark summed up to Howells his feelings about Cable: "It has been a curious experience. It has taught me that Cable's gifts of mind are greater and higher than I had suspected. But—

"That 'But' is pointing toward his religion. You will never, never know, never divine, guess, imagine, how loathsome a thing the Christian religion can be made until you come to know and study Cable daily and hourly. Mind you, I like him; he is pleasant company; I rage and swear at him sometimes, but we do not quarrel; we get along mighty happily together; but in him and his person I have learned to hate all religions. He has taught me to abhor and detest the Sabbath-day and hunt up new and troublesome ways to dishonor it."

After all expenses were deducted, the tour earned $16,000 for Twain, $5,000 for Cable and $3,000 for Major Pond. But it did more than that for the "Twins of Genius." Mark helped loosen up Cable's morals. Soon he would be able to enjoy the theater, tolerate card-players, drink Scotch, and travel on Sundays. Like Mark, Cable never gave up his hatred of social injustice. He was forced to move from the South because of his subversive defense of the Negro's civil rights. With Twain he shared the distinction of pioneering in the literature of Southern realism. Perhaps the brilliant mind that produced the dramatic novels and the fearless essays (*The Silent South* and *The Negro Question*) exposing the social and moral problems of his region helped shape Mark's thinking in that brief but intense association. The beauty and strength of *Huck Finn* may owe something to George Cable.

Thanksgiving was spent with cartoonist Thomas Nast's family in Morristown, New Jersey. Mark rose in the night to stop the clocks that were interfering with his sleep. The amused Nast sent him this cartoon in remembrance.

Patents, Publishing, and the Paige

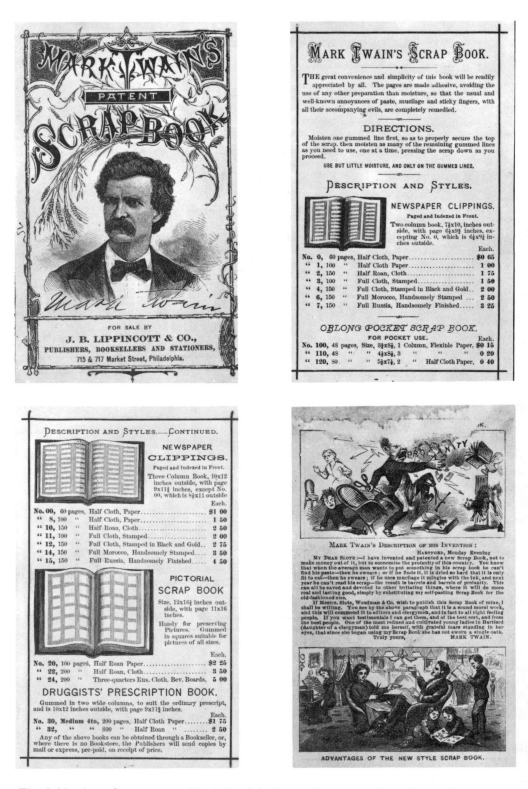

The folder issued to promote *Mark Twain's Patent Scrapbook*. Dan Slote, his *Quaker City* roommate, manufactured the invention Mark expected would wipe out the paste-pot. As in most of Mark's unhappy financial dealings, he came to suspect chicanery and was inexorably certain he had been swindled. His wrath against the real or imagined wrongdoers was violently vindictive.

A CHARMING MACHINE

"Livy darling," Mark wrote one day in 1889, "I have seen a charming machine to-day. You could put it in my study at the farm & have room around it for chairs for the spectators. It makes envelops—9,000 an hour. You place 500 sheets of paper in its grip, & then stand aside & let it alone. That is *all* you ever have to do. It gums them, prints them, counts them, & passes them out in packages of 25 with a paper band around them. It oils itself, it attends to its own glue & ink. If you steal an envelop from it, it won't count that one. I enclose a specimen of its work."

Mark's fascination for another man's invention must have given his wife a chill. The Colonel Sellers in him made him see millions in almost any gadget brought to his attention. The speculative fever that seized him in the Comstock never really left him. He was ready to invest his money and his time in the promotion of a bewildering variety of inventions—a patent steam generator, a steam pulley, an engraving process, a cash register, a marine telegraph, a mechanical organ, a carpet-pattern machine, a synthetic food for invalids called "plasmon," a brass-founding process—the list runs over a hundred.

Like Colonel Sellers, too, he was always falling just short of a smashing success. Young Mr. Alexander Graham Bell offered him stock in a new device to carry the human voice on an electric wire.

"I declined. I said I didn't want anything more to do with wildcat speculation. Then he (Bell) offered the stock to me at twenty-five. I said I didn't want it at any price. He became eager; insisted that I take five hundred dollars' worth. He said he would sell me as much as I wanted for five hundred dollars; offered to let me gather it up in my hands and measure it in a plug hat; said I could have a whole hatful for five hundred dollars. But I was the burnt child, and I resisted all these temptations—resisted them easily; went off with my check intact, and next day lent five thousand of it, on an unindorsed note, to a friend who was going to go bankrupt three days later."

Mark couldn't see the telephone as a sound risk but he thought his own creation of a self-pasting scrapbook was a "great humanizing and civilizing invention. If I do say it myself, it was the only rational scrapbook the world has ever seen. I patented it and put it in the hands of that old particular friend of mine who had originally interested me in patents and he made a good deal of money out of it. But by and by, just when I was about to begin to receive a share of the money myself, his firm failed. I didn't know his firm was going to fail—he didn't say any-

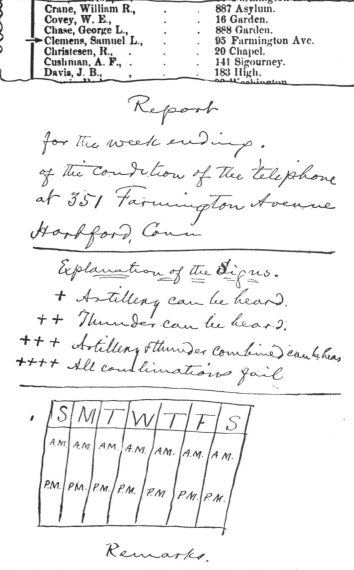

Report for the week ending. of the condition of the telephone at 351 Farmington Avenue Hartford, Conn

Explanation of the Signs.
+ Artillery can be heard.
++ Thunder can be heard.
+++ Artillery & thunder combined can be heard
++++ All combinations fail

S	M	T	W	T	F	S
A.M.	A.M.	A.M.	A.M.	A.M.	A.M.	A.M.
P.M.	P.M.	P.M.	P.M.	P.M.	P.M.	P.M.

Remarks.

Shortly after Mark turned down Bell, he put in a telephone wire from his house to the Hartford *Courant* office—"the only telephone wire in town, and the *first* one that was ever used in a private house in the world," he bragged. *Top:* His 1879 listing in the Hartford directory. (Subscribers were called by name then, not number.) The phone didn't work too well, and Mark designed this chart to record his troubles with the instrument. There seems to be no symbol for profanity. In 1877 Mark used the telephone as a literary symbol in a short story—probably the first writer to do so.

thing about it. One day he asked me to lend the firm five thousand dollars and said he was willing to pay seven per cent. As security he offered the firm's note. I asked for an endorser. He was much surprised and said that if endorsers were handy and easy to get at he wouldn't have to come to me for the money, he could get it anywhere. That seemed reasonable and so I gave him the five thousand dollars. They failed inside of three days—and at the end of two or three years I got back two thousand dollars of the money."

The first of three patents granted Mark Twain. It was designed to help a man with his shirts, vests, drawers, and pantaloons. There's no evidence that any but the patent model was ever made.

BJUYT KIOP M LKJHGFDSA:QWERTYUIOP:˛-98V&6432QW RT
HA

HARTFORD, DEC. 9.

DEAR BROTHER:

I AM TRYING T TO GET THE HANG OF THIS NEW F
FANGLED WRITING MACHINE, BUT AM NOT MAKING
A SHINING SUCCESS OF IT.   HOWEVER THIS IS THE
FIRST ATTEMPT I EVER HAVE MADE, & YET I PER-
CEIVETHAT I SHALL SOON & EASILY ACQUIRE A FINE
FACILITY IN ITS USE.   I SAW THE THING IN BOS-
TON THE OTHER DAY & WAS GREATLY TAKEN WI:TH
IT.   SUSIE HAS STRUCK THE KEYS ONCE OR TWICE,
& NO DOUBT HAS PRINTED SOME LETTERS WHICH DO
NOT BELONG WHERE SHE PUT THEM.
THE HAVING BEEN A COMPOSITOR IS LIKELY TO BE
A GREAT HELP TO ME, SINCE O NE CHIEFLY NEEDS
SWIFTNESS IN BANGING THE KEYS. THE MACHINE COSTS
125 DOLLARS. THE MACHINE HAS SEVERAL VIRTUES
I BELIEVE IT WILL PRINT FASTER THAN I CAN WRITE.
ONE MAY LEAN BACK IN HIS CHAIR & WORK IT.   IT
PILES AN AWFUL STACK OF WORDS ON ONE PAGE.
IT DONT MUSS THINGS OR SCATTER INK BLOTS AROUND.
OF COURSE IT SAVES PAPER.

                    SUSIE IS GONE,
NOW, & I FANCY I SHALL MAKE BETTER PROGRESS.
WORKING THIS TYPE-WRITER REMINDS ME OF OLD
ROBERT BUCHANAN, WHO, YOU REMEMBER, USED TO
SET UP ARTICLES AT THE CASE WITHOUT PREVIOUS-
LY PUTTING THEM IN THE FORM OF MANUSCRIPT: I
WAS LOST IN ADMIRATION OF SUOH MARVELOUS
INTELLECTUAL CAPACITY.

                    LOVE TO MOLLIE.
          YOUR BROTHER,
                    SAM.

Mark's first attempt at typing—an 1874 letter to brother Orion.

Mark's own Hammond typewriter of 1880, the second machine he bought, and mastered. It is in the Hannibal museum.

Mark's second patented invention, the scrapbook, did make money for a while, chiefly because of his personal promotion. It was manufactured in 26 different versions over a twenty-year period.

192

The Game Apparatus was Mark's Memory-Builder, developed originally as an open-air game to teach his children history dates painlessly. He couldn't sleep as his mind projected the game into a vast scheme that would sweep millions into his pockets. By the time fantasy stopped, the game looked like a cross between an income tax form and a table of logarithms.

DISCOVERY—THE NOBLEST DELIGHT

The marvelous intellectual capacity that created the new machines of the nineteenth century; the wide diffusion of wealth they promised; their potential for controlling nature, for easing man's burdens, for extending his happiness—these as well as the dream of personal wealth were what fascinated Mark Twain about his business ventures. In *The Innocents Abroad* he pays this tribute to the creators:

"What is it that confers the noblest delight? What is that which swells a man's breast with pride above that which any other experience can bring to him? Discovery! To know that you are walking where none others have walked; that you are beholding what human eye has not seen before; that you are breathing a virgin atmosphere. To give birth to an idea—to discover a great thought—an intellectual nugget, right under the dust of a field that many a brain-plow had gone over before. To find a new planet, to invent a new hinge, to find the way to make the lightnings carry your messages. To be the first—that is the idea. To do something, say something, see something, before anybody else—these are the things that confer a pleasure compared with which other pleasures are tame and commonplace, other ecstasies cheap and trivial. Morse, with his first message, brought by his servant, the lightning; Fulton, in that long-drawn century of suspense, when he placed his hand upon the throttle-valve, and lo, the steamboat moved; Jenner, when his patient with the cow's virus in his blood, walked through the small-pox hospitals unscathed; Howe, when the idea shot through his brain that for a hundred and twenty generations the eye had been bored through the wrong end of the needle; the nameless lord of art who laid down his chisel in some old age that is forgotten now, and gloated upon the finished Laocoön; Daguerre, when he commanded the sun, riding in the zenith, to print the landscape upon his insignificant

MARK TWAIN'S MEMORY-BUILDER.
A Game for Acquiring and Retaining All Sorts of FACTS and DATES.

silvered plate, and he obeyed; Columbus, in the Pinta's shrouds, when he swung his hat above a fabled sea and gazed abroad upon an unknown world! These are the men who have really lived—who have actually comprehended what pleasure is—who have crowded long lifetimes of ecstasy into a single moment."

Mark could flame with enthusiasm over any gadget that might make a chore lighter. "The damned human race" would be saved by the accordion letter-file, the fountain pen, or the stylographic pen—"a genuine God's blessing" that "the dullest ass gets the hang of." He would pioneer the use of any tool to ease the author's work. He spent $125 on a Remington in 1874. Even an ex-compositor had trouble with the primitive typewriter; it was ruining his morals, he said, foisting it on Howells.

The "sudden and frantic impulse" which turned him from one rash enterprise to another had its effect. "Life has come to be a very serious matter with me," he wrote his mother in 1881. "I have a badgered, harassed feeling a good part of my time. It comes mainly from business responsibilities and annoyances."

Mark Twain, about 1880.

Charles L. Webster. He married Mark's niece, Annie Moffett, and became Mark's business agent and publisher.

MARK TWAIN: PUBLISHER

That "badgered feeling" Mark complained of to his mother came out of a year—1881—in which he paid out over $100,000. About $40,000 of it was sucked into schemes that would never pay off. Another $30,000 went into broader acres and an improved house, and the rest supported an ever more lavish scale of living. Spending more and more, he needed to earn more and more. From writing books he took to publishing books—his own and others. His publisher Bliss had died in 1880, and Mark had taken to financing his books under J. R. Osgood's imprint. By 1884 he had his own publishing house, Charles L. Webster and Company, named for the nephew who managed it.

For many years Mark's books had been sold very profitably by subscription, with "broken-down clergymen, maiden ladies, grass widows and college students" taking the bulky and heavily ornamented volumes into every rural corner of America where they kept company with the Bible on the center table. *Huck Finn* was the new firm's first subscription book and a grand success.

The next book was to make publishing history. It was the *Memoirs* of Ulysses S. Grant, long a friend of Mark's. After serving two terms in the Presidency the General had been swindled out of his own and his family's savings by a Wall Street bucket-shop operator. To meet his housekeeping bills Grant wrote Civil War recollections for the *Century* at $500 an article. Twain undertook to pay Grant seventy per cent of all net profits for a two-volume edition of the *Memoirs;* before Grant had finished writing, Web-

ster's door-to-door canvassers had sold over 100,000 sets.

In a letter to Henry Ward Beecher, Mark Twain recorded these impressions of the dying Grant: "The sick-room brought out the points of Gen. Grant's character—some of them particularly, to wit:

"His patience; his indestructible equability of temper; his exceeding gentleness, kindness, forbearance, lovingness, charity; his loyalty: to friends, to convictions, to promises, half-promises, infinitesimal fractions and shadows of promises; (There was a requirement of him which I considered an atrocity, an injustice, an outrage; I wanted to implore him to repudiate it; Fred Grant said, 'Save your labor, I know him; he is in doubt as to whether he made that half-promise or not—and he will give the thing the benefit of the doubt; he will fulfill that half-promise or kill himself trying;' Fred Grant was right—he did fulfill it;) his aggravatingly trustful nature; his genuineness, simplicity; modesty; diffidence, self-depreciation, poverty in the quality of vanity—and, in no contradiction of this last, his simple pleasure in the flowers and general ruck sent to him by Tom, Dick and Harry from everywhere—a pleasure that suggested a perennial surprise that he should be the object of so much fine attention—he was the most lovable great child in the world; (I mentioned his loyalty: you remember Harrison, the colored bodyservant? the whole family hated him, but that did not make any difference, the General always stood at his back, wouldn't allow him to be scolded; always excused his failures and deficiencies with the one unvarying formula, 'We are responsible for these things in his race—it is not fair to visit our fault upon them—let him alone;' so they did let him alone, under compulsion, until the great heart that was his shield was taken away; then—well they simply couldn't stand him, and so they were excusable for

In his last days, dying from cancer of the throat, General Grant was photographed with his family at Mt. McGregor in the Adirondacks. He stubbornly finished the *Memoirs* he had agreed to write to help his impoverished family, and died a few days after the job was done.

determining to discharge him—a thing which they mortally hated to do, and by lucky accident were saved from the necessity of doing;) his toughness as a bargainer when doing business for other people or for his country (witness his 'terms' at Donelson, Vicksburg, etc.; Fred Grant told me his father wound up an estate for the widow and orphans of a friend in St. Louis—it took several years; at the end every complication had been straightened out, and the property put upon a prosperous basis; great sums had passed through his hands, and when he handed over the papers there were vouchers to show what had been done with every penny) and his trusting, easy, unexacting fashion when doing business for himself (at that same time he was paying out money in driblets to a man who was running his farm for him —and in his first Presidency he paid every one of those driblets again (total $3,000 F. said,) for he hadn't a scrap of paper to show that he had ever paid them before; in his dealings with me he would not listen to terms which would place my money at risk and leave him protected—the thought plainly gave him pain, and he put it from him, waved it off with his hands, as one does accounts of crushings and mutilations—wouldn't listen, changed the subject;) and his fortitude!

"He was under sentence of death last spring; he sat thinking, musing, several days—nobody knows what about; then he pulled himself together and set to work to finish that book, a colossal task for a dying man. Presently his hand gave out; fate seemed to have got him checkmated. Dictation was suggested. No, he never could do that; had never tried it; too old to learn, now. By and by—if he could only do Appomattox—well. So he sent for a stenographer, and dictated 9,000 words at a single sitting!—never pausing, never hesitating for a word, never repeating —and in the written-out copy he made hardly a correction. He dictated again, every two or three days—the intervals were intervals of exhaustion and slow recuperation—and at last he was able to tell me that he had written more matter than could be got into the book. I then enlarged the book—had to. Then he lost his voice. He was not quite done yet, however;—there was no end of little plums and spices to be stuck in, here and there; and this work he patiently continued, a few lines a day, with pad and pencil, till far into July, at Mt. McGregor. One day he put his pencil aside, and said he was done— there was nothing more to do. If I had been there I could have foretold the shock that struck the world three days later."

General Grant's last writing.

The first royalty check on the Grant *Memoirs* paid by Mark's publishing house to Grant's widow. It was for $200,000. Eight months later Mrs. Grant got a second check, for $150,000. It was the largest royalty ever paid an author up to that time.

TOWARDS SURE DESTRUCTION

Mark was as rough on his nephew, Charles Webster, as he was on all his publishers. To young Webster's official duties he added the chores of handyman, errand-boy, banker, broker, detective, lawyer, shopper, and target for sudden rages. The Grant book paid Mrs. Grant about half a million dollars. "I turned out to be a competent prophet," Mark complimented himself, and then slid off into the effect of the success on Webster:

"Webster was in his glory. In his obscure days his hat was number six and a quarter; in these latter days he was not able to get his head into a barrel. He loved to descant upon the wonder of the book. He liked to go into the statistics. He liked to tell that it took thirteen miles of gold leaf to print the gilt titles on the book backs; he liked to tell how many thousand tons the three hundred thousand sets weighed. Of course that same old natural thing happened: Webster thought it was he that sold the book. He thought that General Grant's great name helped but he regarded himself as the main reason of the book's prodigious success. This shows that Webster was merely human and merely a publisher. All publishers are Columbuses. The successful author is their America. The reflection that they—like Columbus—didn't discover what they expected to discover, and didn't discover what they started out to discover, doesn't trouble them. All they remember is that they discovered America; they forgot that they started out to discover some patch or corner of India."

The Grant project had required a vast expansion of the Webster firm. To sustain business a steady flow of profitable books was required. Beecher was signed for his autobiography, with Mark hoping the preacher would "heave in just enough piousness" to produce profits of $350,000. But Beecher died on him too soon. Then came Sandwich Island legends, and a swarm of reminiscences of Union commanders—McClellan, Hancock, Sheridan, Custer, Badeau—which could not counterbalance the sums Mark extracted from the business to finance a typesetting machine. By 1888 his notebook had a desperate ring:

"Sherman (Life of) proves to be unprofitable. Demand a reconstruction of contract placing power in my hands where it belongs. Refused? Go into court. Second: Demand dissolution. Go into court.

196

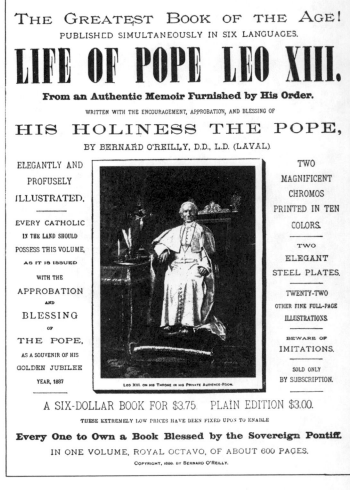

With the Grant *Memoirs* a fantastic success Mark was captivated by the notion that a *Life of Pope Leo XIII* would have a sale limited only by the number of Catholics in Christendom. Even Howells was dazzled by the scheme. The book was issued in six languages simultaneously, but alas, Howells noted, "neither of us saw the total defect in it. We did not consider how often Catholics could not read, how often when they could, they might not wish to read." The book paid, but so poorly Twain's "sanguine soul was utterly confounded."

A notice in the Hartford *Courant*, on April 20, 1894, when the publishing venture collapsed.

Return to S. L. CLEMENS,
HARTFORD, Conn.,
If not delivered within 5 days.

Mr. Charles L. Webster

FAR ROCKAWAY.

[Somewhere off the port of New York, in New Jersey, or New York, or Staten Island, or Hell gate, or one of those other States around there somewhere. Keep on trying: & from time to time, send for more postage.]

This envelope addressed by Mark Twain got to Webster, courtesy of an amused postal service.

Can I be held for debts made beyond the capital? I will buy or sell out.

"Since the spring of 1886, the thing has gone straight down hill, towards sure destruction. It must be brought to an end, February 1, at all hazards. This is final."

Thomas Nast sent this self-portrait to Webster as thanks for something the firm had done for him.

THE DAMN TYPESETTER

Over the billiard table one night, a Hartford jeweler asked Mark Twain to take a little chance on a new typesetting machine being developed at the Colt arms factory. "It is here that the music begins," Mark noted. "An old practical typesetter like myself can perceive the value of the thing." He put $5,000 into James Paige's invention and thought little more about it while busying himself with *Life on the Mississippi* and *Huck Finn.* Five years later Paige dropped in to offer a half interest in return for funds to perfect the machine. "*Now* the damn typesetter is in lucrative shape at last," Mark said. Its possibilities began to flower in his notebook:

"There are 11,000 papers and periodicals in America.

"This typesetter does not get drunk.

"He does not join the printer's union.

"A woman can operate him."

To Charley Webster he wrote, "I know that a paper that once uses this machine in its now perfected shape, will always use it. Three years from now I calculate to have about 1000 of these machines hired out in this country at $2,500,000." It would take ten men, he thought, just to count the profits.

So in this Sellers mood, $30,000 more went into the machine. It lasted a year. The machine had 18,000 separate parts. Some of them always needed a bit more tinkering. Paige came back for more money. By the end of 1887, Mark was writing Pamela: "We go on and on, but the type-setter goes on forever—at $3000 a month." Now $80,000 had been sunk. Pamela was sent only $15 that Christmas.

197

A year later he told Orion, "I have kept this family on very short rations for two years, and they must go on scrimping until the machine is finished, no matter how long it may be." In 1889, his own resources drained, Mark tried peddling stock to pay the master mechanics still struggling for perfection. Investors shrank away, but Mark's faith was undimmed:

"All the other wonderful inventions of the human brain sink pretty nearly into commonplaces contrasted with this awful mechanical miracle. Telephones, telegraphs, locomotives, cotton-gins, sewing-machines, Babbage calculators, Jacquard looms, perfecting presses, all mere toys, simplicities! The Paige Compositor marches alone and far in the land of human inventions."

He paid little heed to reports of other inventors busy on the same type of machine. Offered a half-interest swap by promoters of the Mergenthaler linotype, Mark casually declined. Through 1890 the "cunning devil" continued to swallow $4,000 a month, now destroying Livy's inheritance too. With Joe Goodman's help Mark tried to interest some Nevada millionaire friends in the Paige, holding up visions of fifty-five million dollars a year. But no one shared his dreams. By February, 1891, $190,000 had been consumed. In April, Charles Webster died. The next month the Twains decided to close the costly Hartford house and go abroad where they could live much less expensively.

But again and again Mark had to return to New York, to try to plug holes in the sinking Paige. Almost frantic from the threat of financial disaster, Mark found help in Henry H. Rogers, a wealthy

A photo taken in the early 1890's. The Twain family moved to Europe in June, 1891, driven to seek cheaper living. Mark made frequent trips back to the States to look after his rapidly declining business fortunes.

The Paige typesetter, the monster whose failure cost **Mark** Twain $300,000. It is now on display in the basement of the Hartford house.

acquaintance who had long been one of his admirers. "Livy darling," Mark wrote her early in 1894, "Yesterday I talked all my various matters over with Mr. Rogers. I never fully laid Webster's disastrous condition before Mr. Rogers until to-night after billiards. I did hate to burden his good heart and over-worked head with it, but he took hold with avidity and said it was no burden to work for his friends, but a pleasure. We discussed it from various standpoints, and found it a sufficiently difficult problem to solve; but he thinks that after he has slept upon it and thought it over he will know what to suggest.

"You must not think I am ever rude with Mr. Rogers, I am not. He is not common clay, but fine —fine and delicate—and that sort do not call out the coarsenesses that are in my sort. I am never afraid of wounding him; I do not need to watch myself in that matter. The sight of him is peace.

"When I arrived in September, lord how black the prospect was—how desperate, how incurably desperate! Webster and Co. had to have a small sum of money or go under at once. I flew to Hartford—to my friends—but they were not moved, not strongly interested, and I was ashamed that I went. It was from Mr. Rogers, a stranger, that I got the money and was by it saved. And then—while still a stranger —he set himself the task of saving my financial life without putting upon me (in his native delicacy) any sense that I was the recipient of a charity, a benevolence—and he has accomplished that task; accomplished it at a cost of three months of wearing and difficult labor. He gave that time to me—time which could not be bought by any man at a hundred thousand dollars a month—no, nor for three times the money."

To Mark, Rogers was "the best and wisest man of the whole Standard Oil group—a multi-millionaire." Rogers took over the burden of the Paige and the publishing problems. By the end of the year, Mark, back in Paris with his family, could write:

"Dear Mr. Rogers,—Notwithstanding your heart is 'old and hard,' you make a body choke up. I know you 'mean every word you say' and I do take it 'in the same spirit in which you tender it.' I shall keep your regard while we two live—that I know; for I shall always remember what you have done for me, and that will insure me against ever doing anything that could forfeit it or impair it. I am 59 years old; yet I never had a friend before who put out a hand and tried to pull me ashore when he found me in deep waters."

Henry H. Rogers, known in the 1890's as the handsomest and most ruthless pirate who ever flew his flag in Wall Street. "The only man I care for in the world; the only man I would give a damn for; the only man who is lavishing his sweat and blood to save me and mine from starvation and shame, is a Standard Oil fiend," Mark confided to Livy when he told her he had refused to publish a muckraker's book on the oil monopolists.

HENRY ROGERS, FRIEND

Shortly after Henry Rogers' death in 1909, Mark Twain paid this tribute to his friend: "All through my life I have been the easy prey of the cheap adventurer. He came, he lied, he robbed and went his way, and the next one arrived by the next train and began to scrape up what was left. I was in the toils of one of these creatures sixteen years ago and it was Mr. Rogers who got me out. We were strangers when we met and friends when we parted, half an hour afterward. The meeting was accidental and unforeseen but it had memorable and fortunate consequences for me. He dragged me out of that difficulty and also out of the next one—a year or two later— which was still more formidable than its predecessor.

He did these saving things at no cost to my self-love, no hurt to my pride; indeed, he did them with so delicate an art that I almost seemed to have done them myself. By no sign, no hint, no word did he ever betray any consciousness that I was under obligations to him. I have never been so great as that and I have not known another who was. I have never approached it; it belongs among the loftiest of human attributes. This is a world where you get nothing for nothing; where you pay value for everything you get and 50 per cent over; and when it is gratitude you owe, you have to pay a thousand. In fact, gratitude is a debt which usually goes on accumulating, like blackmail; the more you pay, the more is exacted. In time you are made to realize that the kindness done you is become a curse and you wish it had not happened."

Mark Twain's financial troubles, like everything else about him, were news. The New York *Herald* launched a public relief fund for him but Twain gratefully declined the help offered.

As H. H. Rogers was negotiating a settlement with Mark Twain's creditors, Mark took time off to visit the laboratory of the electrical inventor Nikola Tesla. This flashlight photo was taken on March 3, 1894, as Mark tried one of Tesla's experiments with an incandescent lamp. Despite the sorrows they brought him, Mark couldn't root up his love for inventions. In 1899 he wrote John Hay about a postal check he had devised, predicting "the government officials would probably not care to buy it as soon as they found they couldn't kill Christians with it."

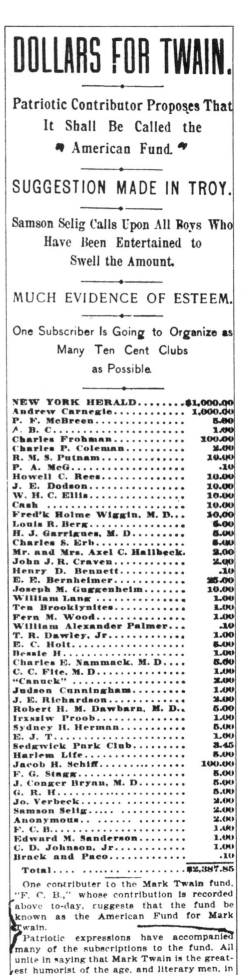

DOLLARS FOR TWAIN.

Patriotic Contributor Proposes That It Shall Be Called the ❦ American Fund. ❦

SUGGESTION MADE IN TROY.

Samson Selig Calls Upon All Boys Who Have Been Entertained to Swell the Amount.

MUCH EVIDENCE OF ESTEEM.

One Subscriber Is Going to Organize as Many Ten Cent Clubs as Possible.

NEW YORK HERALD	$1,000.00
Andrew Carnegie	1,000.00
P. F. McBreen	5.00
A. B. C.	1.00
Charles Frohman	100.00
Charles P. Coleman	2.00
R. M. S. Putnam	10.00
P. A. McG.	.10
Howell C. Rees	10.00
J. E. Dodson	10.00
W. H. C. Ellis	10.00
Cash	10.00
Fred'k Holme Wiggin, M. D.	10.00
Louis R. Berg	5.00
H. J. Garrigues, M. D.	5.00
Charles S. Erb	5.00
Mr. and Mrs. Axel C. Hallbeck	2.00
John J. R. Craven	2.00
Henry D. Bennett	.10
E. E. Bernheimer	25.00
Joseph M. Guggenheim	10.00
William Lang	1.00
Ten Brooklynites	1.00
Fern M. Wood	1.00
William Alexander Palmer	.10
T. R. Dawley, Jr.	1.00
E. C. Holt	5.00
Bessie H	1.00
Charles E. Nammack, M. D.	5.00
C. C. Fite, M. D.	1.00
"Canuck"	2.00
Judson Cunningham	1.00
J. E. Richardson	2.00
Robert H. M. Dawbarn, M. D.	5.00
Irxszlw Proob	1.00
Sydney H. Herman	5.00
E. J. T.	1.00
Sedgwick Park Club	3.45
Harlem Life	5.00
Jacob H. Schiff	100.00
F. G. Stagg	5.00
J. Conger Bryan, M. D.	5.00
G. R. H.	5.00
Jo. Verbeck	2.00
Samson Selig	2.00
Anonymous	2.00
F. C. B.	1.00
Edward M. Sanderson	1.00
C. D. Johnson, Jr.	1.00
Brack and Paco	.10
Total	$2,387.85

One contributer to the Mark Twain fund. "F. C. B.," whose contribution is recorded above to-day, suggests that the fund be known as the American Fund for Mark Twain.

Patriotic expressions have accompanied many of the subscriptions to the fund. All unite in saying that Mark Twain is the greatest humorist of the age, and literary men, in interviews and letters that have been pub-

Commodore Cornelius Vanderbilt,
a target for Twain.

A Pen Warmed Up
in Hell

THE MORALIST OF THE MAIN

With the same gusto he gave to his get-rich-quick speculations, Mark Twain heaved bricks at the Vanderbilts, Rockefellers, and Wanamakers. He liked success and he delighted in the comforts wealth provided, but he could not abide the worship of money, nor the sacrifice of human values to the getting of it. His earliest readers on the frontier tagged him The Wild Humorist of the Pacific Slope, but they recognized him also as The Moralist of the Main. He was both clown and satirist all along, but in his first fame the serious side was too often overlooked. The genteel guardians of literature could not take a funny man seriously, and besides, his work was too popular to be good. *The Gilded Age,* with its harsh satire on politics and society, changed Mark's standing with the critics. As more and more work came from his pen in the seventies and eighties, his scorn of pretense and his hatred of injustice found even fuller voice. Beneath the laughter listeners could hear the rage.

A few months after his public attack on Vanderbilt, Mark wrote Livy about his meeting with a man at the opposite end of the social and economic scale —Frederick Douglass, the Negro who had escaped from slavery to become the spokesman for his race: "Had a talk with Fred Douglass, to-day, who seemed exceedingly glad to see me—& I certainly was glad to see him for I do so admire his 'spunk.' He told the history of his child's expulsion from Miss Tracy's school, & his simple language was very effective. Miss Tracy said the pupils did not want a colored child among them—which he did not believe, & challenged the proof. She put it at once to a vote of the school,

OPEN LETTER TO COM. VANDERBILT

HOW my heart goes out in sympathy to you! how I do pity you, Commodore Vanderbilt! Most men have at least a few friends, whose devotion is a comfort and a solace to them, but you seem to be the idol of only a crawling swarm of small souls, who love to glorify your most flagrant unworthinesses in print; or praise your vast possessions worshippingly; or sing of your unimportant private habits and sayings and doings, as if your millions gave them dignity; friends who applaud your superhuman stinginess with the same gusto that they do your most magnificent displays of commercial genius and daring, and likewise your most lawless violations of commercial honor —for these infatuated worshippers of dollars not their own, seem to make no distinctions, but swing their hats and shout hallelujah every time you do *anything*, no matter what it is I do pity you. I would pity any man with such friends as these

better to be a mean *live* man than a s . . . . a gold-headed stick. And now my lesson is done. It is bound to refresh you and make you feel good; for you must necessarily get sick of puling flattery and sycophancy sometimes, and sigh for a paragraph of honest criticism and abuse for a change. And in parting, I say that, surely, standing as you do upon the pinnacle of moneyed magnificence in America you must certainly feel a vague desire in you sometimes to do some splendid deed in the interest of commercial probity, or of human charity, or of manly honor and dignity, that shall flash into instant celebrity over the whole nation, and be rehearsed to ambitious boys by their mothers a century after you are dead. I say you must feel so sometimes, for it is only natural, and therefore I urge you to congeal that thought into an act. Go and surprise the whole country by doing something right. Cease to do and say unworthy things, and excessively *little* things, for those reptile friends of yours to magnify in the papers. Snub them thus, or else throttle them. Yours truly, MARK TWAIN.

202

Mark blistered the Commodore in
Packard's Monthly for March, 1869.

and asked 'How many of you are willing to have this colored child be with you?' And they all held up their hands! Douglass added: 'The children's hearts were right.' There was pathos in the way he said it. I would like to hear him make a speech. Has a grand face."

Mark's feeling for Douglass deepened. In 1881, he wrote President-elect Garfield, asking him to retain Douglass as Marshal of the District of Columbia: "I offer this petition with peculiar pleasure and strong desire, because I so honor this man's high and blemishless character and so admire his brave, long crusade for the liberties and elevation of his race.

"He is a personal friend of mine, but that is nothing to the point, his history would move me to say these things without that, and I feel them too."

Garfield appointed Douglass Recorder of Deeds, instead, a post the Negro held for four years. Twain also paid the way of Negro students through Yale Law School. It was a long step from the Southerner who had worn the Confederate gray. In 1898 he could say, "I think I have no color prejudices nor caste prejudices nor creed prejudices. Indeed I know it. I can stand any society. All I care to know is that a Man is a human being, and that is enough for me; he can't be any worse."

Frederick Douglass.

This "galaxy of persons of distinction" who had visited California was widely distributed in 1876 by the San Francisco photographers Bradley & Rulofson. Mark Twain is encircled.

ODE TO WHISKY

In *Life on the Mississippi* Mark paused for a moment to deliberate on the prime mover of progress: "How solemn and beautiful is the thought that the earliest pioneer of civilization, the van-leader of civilization is never the steamboat, never the railroad, never the newspaper, never the Sabbath-school, never the missionary—but always whisky! Such is the case. Look

"The 'Brains' "—Thomas Nast's best-known caricature of Boss Tweed, leader of the Tammany political ring which milked New York of some two hundred million dollars.

history over; you will see. The missionary comes after the whisky—I mean he arrives after the whisky has arrived; next comes the poor immigrant, with axe and hoe and rifle; next, the trader; next, the miscellaneous rush; next, the gambler, the desperado, the highwayman, and all their kindred in sin of both sexes; and next, the smart chap who has bought up an old grant that covers all the land; this brings the lawyer tribe; the vigilance committee brings the undertaker. All these interests bring the newspaper; the newspaper starts up politics and a railroad; all hands turn to and build a church and a jail—and behold! civilization is established forever in the land. But whisky, you see, was the van-leader in this beneficent work. It always is. It was like a foreigner —and excusable in a foreigner—to be ignorant of this great truth, and wander off into astronomy to borrow a symbol. But, if he had been conversant with the facts, he would have said:

" 'Westward the Jug of Empire takes its way.' "

204

THE REVISED CATECHISM.

First class in modern Moral Philosophy stand up and recite:

What is the chief end of man?

A. To get rich.

In what way?

A. Dishonestly if we can; honestly if we must.

Who is God, the one only and true?

A. Money is God. Gold and greenbacks and stock —father, son, and the ghost of the same—three persons in one: these are the true and only God, mighty and supreme; and William Tweed is his prophet.

Name the twelve disciples.

A. St. Ass's Colt Hall, whereon the prophet rode into Jerusalem; St. Connolly, the beloved disciple; St. Matthew Carnochan, that sitteth at the receipt of customs; St. Peter Fisk, the belligerent disciple; St. Paul Gould, that suffereth many stripes and glorieth in them; St. Iscariot Winans; St. Jacob Vanderbilt, the essteamed disciple; St. Garvey, the chair-itable; St. Ingersoll, of the holy carpets; St. N. Y. Printing Co., the meek and lowly, that letteth not its right hand know what its left hand taketh; St. Peter Hoffman, that denied his (Irish) master when the public cock had crowed six or seven times; St. Barnard, the wise judge, who imparteth injunctions in time of trouble, whereby the people are instructed to their salvation.

How shall a man attain the chief end of life?

A. By furnishing imaginary carpets to the Court-House, apocryphal chairs to the armories, and invisible printing to the city.

Are there other ways?

A: Yea. By purchasing the quarantine apostle for a price; by lightering shipmen of all they possess; by proceeding through immigrants from over sea; by burying the moneyless at the public charge and transhipping the rest 10 miles at $40 a head. By testing iron work for buildings. By furnishing lead and iron gas-pipes to the Court-House and. then conveying the impression in the bill that they were constructed of gold and silver and set with diamonds. By taking care of the public parks at $5 an inch. By loafing around gin mills on a salary under the illusion that you are imparting impetus to a shovel on the public works.

Are these sufficient? If not, what shall a man do else, to be saved?

A. Make out his bill for ten prices and deliver nine of them into the hands of the prophet and the holy family. Then shall he be saved.

Who were the models the young were taught to emulate in former days?

A. Washington and Franklin.

Whom do they and should they emulate now in this era of larger enlightenment?

A. Tweed, Hall, Connolly, Carnochan, Fisk, Gould, Barnard, and Winans.

What works were chiefly prized for the training of the young in former days?

A. Poor Richard's Almanac, the Pilgrim's Progress, and the Declaration of Independence.

What are the best prized Sunday-school books in this more enlightened age?

A. St. Hall's Garbled Reports, St. Fisk's Ingenious Robberies, St. Carnochan's Guide to Corruption, St. Gould on the Watering of Stock, St. Barnard's Injunctions, St. Tweed's Handbook of Morals, and the Court-House edition of the Holy Crusade of the Forty Thieves.

Do we progress?

A. You bet your life!

Yours truly,   MARK TWAIN.

Corruption in government, whether he found it in Nevada, San Francisco, Washington, or New York, evoked from Mark Twain loud and public indictments. This clipping from the New York *Tribune* of September 27, 1871, shows how he pilloried the Tweed ring.

"Jay Gould's Private Bowling Alley"—An Opper cartoon in *Puck*, March 29, 1882.

JAY GOULD—THE MIGHTIEST DISASTER

One of the Gilded Age's most notorious financial manipulators was Jay Gould. With "Jubilee Jim" Fisk he ruined thousands in the Wall Street Black Friday incident of 1869. The two shared with Tweed in the staggering Erie Railroad swindles. Gould died in 1892, at 56, leaving seventy-two million dollars, but even death did not diminish Mark Twain's acid contempt:

"Jay Gould was the mightiest disaster which has ever befallen this country. The people had *desired* money before his day, but *he* taught them to fall down and worship it. They had respected men of means before his day, but along with this respect was joined the respect due to the character and industry which had accumulated it. But Jay Gould taught the entire nation to make a god of the money and the man, no matter how the money might have been acquired. In my youth there was nothing resembling a worship of money or of its possessor, in our region. And in our region no well-to-do man was ever charged with having acquired his money by shady methods.

"The gospel left behind by Jay Gould is doing giant work in our days. Its message is 'Get money.

Get it quickly. Get it in abundance. Get it in prodigious abundance. Get it dishonestly if you can, honestly if you must.' "

AGE OF PROGRESS

The fruits of progress Twain discussed in a speech he made to a gathering of Americans in London on the Fourth of July, 1872:

"This is an age of progress, and ours is a progressive land. A great and glorious land, too—a land which has developed a Washington, a Franklin, a William M. Tweed, a Longfellow, a Motley, a Jay Gould, a Samuel C. Pomeroy, a recent Congress which has never had its equal (in some respects), and a United States Army which conquered sixty Indians in eight months by tiring them out—which is much better than uncivilized slaughter, God knows. We have a criminal jury system which is superior to any in the world; and its efficiency is only marred by the difficulty of finding twelve men every day who don't know anything and can't read. And I may observe that we have an insanity plea that would have saved Cain. I think I can say, and say with pride, that we have some legislatures that bring higher prices than any in the world."

CONSCIENCE FIRST, THE PARTY SECOND

The Presidential contest of 1884 between James Blaine and Grover Cleveland brought Mark Twain into political campaigning for the third time. Eight years earlier Rutherford Hayes' advocacy of civil service reform had swung Mark into an election for the first time. He had made a speech in Hartford, rallying literary men to come out of their studies and work for Hayes. In 1880 he spoke again, to win votes for Garfield. But now, in 1884, he bolted the Republicans because he couldn't stomach their candidate. His friend Howells, however, refused to mugwump with Mark for the Democratic nominee, Cleveland. "My dear Howells," Mark wrote him, "Somehow I can't seem to rest quiet under the idea of your voting for Blaine. I believe you said something about the country and the party. Certainly allegiance to these is well; but as certainly a man's first duty is to his own conscience and honor—the party or the country come second to that, and never first. I don't ask you to vote at all—I only urge you to not soil yourself by voting for Blaine.

"When you wrote before, you were able to say the charges against him were not proven. But you know now that they are proven, and it seems to me that that bars you and all other honest and honorable men (who are independently situated) from voting for him.

"It is not necessary to vote for Cleveland; the only necessary thing to do, as I understand it, is that a man shall keep himself clean, (by withholding his vote for an improper man) even though the party and the country go to destruction in consequence. It is not parties that make or save countries or that build them to greatness—it is clean men, clean ordinary citizens, rank and file, the masses. Clean masses are not made by individuals standing back till the rest become clean.

"As I said before, I think a man's first duty is to his own honor; not to this country and not to his party. Don't be offended; I mean no offence. I am not so concerned about the rest of the nation, but —well, good-bye."

Scandals dirtied the names of both candidates in the Presidential race of 1884. In this cartoon Grover Cleveland tells the truth about his private life; Blaine hides his sins. Mark Twain advocated an independent candidate to permit the unhappy voters of both major parties to voice their protest, but nothing came of it.

"First Annual Picnic of the 'Knights of Labor'—More Fun for the Spectators than for the Performers." A *Puck* cartoon of June 21, 1882.

THE NEW DYNASTY

The "squalid want, criminal woe, wretchedness and suffering" he saw in the slums of the great cities made Mark Twain question the morality of this world during his earliest travels about the country. He tolerated neither the hypocrisy that claimed poverty was a blessing in disguise nor the calumny that poverty was the fault of the poor. He had no faith that employers would voluntarily introduce such reforms as the eight-hour day or better working conditions. In *Life on the Mississippi* he told how the river pilots organized a closed shop union in 1861 and won higher pay. Labor journals reprinted his chapter and praised him for his "powerful contribution to labor's struggle for justice."

As the Knights of Labor rose to strength in the 1880s, a move to outlaw the industrial union as a lawless, violent and subversive organization swung into action. In March, 1886, Mark made a stirring defense of unionism before the Monday Evening Club in a speech called "Knights of Labor—The New Dynasty." The unionized workman, he told the Hartford audience, "is here and he will remain. He is the greatest birth of the greatest age the nations of the world have known. You cannot sneer at him—that time has gone by. He has before him the most righteous work that was ever given into the hand of man to do; and he will do it. Yes, he is here; and the question is not—as it has been heretofore during a thousand ages—What shall we do with him? For the first time in history we are relieved of the necessity of managing his affairs for him. He is not a broken dam this time—he is the Flood!"

207

Hank, the Connecticut Yankee. A foreman in Colt's arms factory in Hartford, he was knocked on the head and woke up in the England of King Arthur's ancient day. Here he is depicted in his 19th-century clothes.

Above: Henry George, author of *Progress and Poverty,* 1879. *Below:* Edward Bellamy, whose 1888 novel of Utopia, *Looking Backward,* Mark thought a "fascinating book." These were among the books that molded William Dean Howells' socialism and, together with Twain's *Connecticut Yankee,* were great stimulants to progressive thought in the late 19th century.

A CONNECTICUT YANKEE

Six months after Mark's Knights of Labor speech he informed Mrs. Fairbanks that he was busy on a new novel. "The story isn't a satire peculiarly," he wrote, "it is more especially a *contrast.* It merely exhibits under high lights, the daily life of the time & that of today; & necessarily the bringing them into this immediate juxtaposition emphasizes the salients of both." It was the life of medieval England that had absorbed him ever since Cable had put a copy of Malory's *Morte d'Arthur* into his hands on their lecture tour. "I am only after the *life* of that day, that is all: to picture it; to try to get into it; to see how it feels & seems." Three years later, after the usual gaps in interest, Mark could tell Howells: "Well, my book is written—let it go. But if it were only to write over again there wouldn't be so many things left out. They burn in me; & they keep multiplying & multiplying; but now they can't ever be said. And besides, they would require a library—and a pen warmed up in Hell."

What was not left out of *A Connecticut Yankee in*

King Arthur's Court was Mark's loathing of the inhumanity and ignorance of medieval Europe, and his powerful championing of a Jacksonian brand of democracy. These themes he had struck before—in 1881, in *The Prince and the Pauper*. There he had used the mechanism of switched identities to ridicule the pretenses of royalty while setting in opposition the humanism of democracy.

Now, he made an even more fervent attack upon privilege: "The blunting effects of slavery upon the slaveholder's moral perceptions are known and conceded the world over," says his Yankee, "and a privileged class, an aristocracy, is but a band of slaveholders under another name." In another passage the Yankee shows how his creator has changed in the sixteen years since he had shown contempt for popular suffrage in *The Gilded Age*. "Men write many fine and plausible arguments in support of monarchy, but the fact remains that where every man in a state has a vote, brutal laws are impossible."

The fierce independence that made Mark a Mugwump in the 1884 elections is expressed again in the *Yankee*:

"You see my kind of loyalty was loyalty to one's country, not to its institutions, or its office-holders. The country is the real thing, the substantial thing,

Hank is shown as Sir Boss in King Arthur's court.

the eternal thing; it is the thing to watch over, and care for, and be loyal to; institutions are extraneous, they are its mere clothing, and clothing can wear out, become ragged, cease to be comfortable, cease to protect the body from winter, disease, and death. To be loyal to rags, to shout for rags, to worship rags, to die for rags—this is a loyalty to unreason, it is pure animal; it belongs to monarchy, was invented by monarchy; let monarchy keep it.

"I was from Connecticut, whose Constitution declares 'that all political power is inherent in the people, and all free governments are founded on their authority and instituted for their benefits; and that they have at all times an undeniable and indefeasible right to alter their form of government in such a manner as they may think expedient.'

"Under that gospel, the citizen who thinks he sees that the commonwealth's political clothes are worn out, and yet holds his peace and does not agitate for a new suit, is disloyal; he is a traitor. That he may be the only one who thinks he sees decay, does not excuse him; it is his duty to agitate anyway, and it is the duty of the others to vote him down if they do not see the matter as he does."

To the Yank not kings but commoners are the real nation: "To subtract them would have been to subtract the Nation and leave behind some dregs, some refuse, in the shape of a king, nobility and gentry, idle, unproductive, acquainted mainly with the arts of wasting and destroying, and of no sort of use or value in any rationally controlled world."

As for the "damned human race," the Yankee says, "A man *is* a man, at bottom. Whole ages of abuse and oppression cannot crush the manhood clear out of him. There is plenty good enough material for a republic in the most degraded people that ever existed—even the Russians—even the Germans—if one could but force it out of its timid and suspicious privacy, to overthrow and trample in the mud every throne that was ever set up and any nobility that ever supported it."

The humorist and the satirist were, as almost always, intermingled in the *Yankee*. The book delighted its readers at home but infuriated most of the English reviewers. They resented a "low comedian" vaulting into "the charmed circle of Arthurian romance." Some were repelled by the satire while others were appalled by what they considered to be vulgar burlesque and extravaganza. The *Yankee*, Mark said angrily to his British publishers, "was not written for America; it was written for England. So many Englishmen have done their sincerest best to tell us something for our betterment that it seems to me high time that some of us should substantially recognize the good intent by trying to pry up the English nation to a little higher level of mankind in turn."

209

Daniel Carter Beard, illustrator for *A Connecticut Yankee*. The drawings on these pages are from the first edition. The book was Mark Twain's first in five years. He wanted to make it handsome and profitable. He liked the drawings by Dan Beard in *Cosmopolitan* and sent for the artist. "I am not going to tell you what to draw," he said. "If a man comes to me and says, 'Mr. Clemens, I want you to write me a story,' I'll write it for him; but if he undertakes to tell me what to write I'll say, 'Go hire a typewriter.'"

Beard used as his model a real Connecticut Yankee who happened to be experimenting next door to Beard's studio on Fifth Avenue. Other models (real or photographic) included Queen Victoria, a French waiter, Annie Russell, Sarah Bernhardt, a panhandler, the King of England, the Prince of Wales, the German Emperor, Jay Gould, and himself. Beard, whose politics were socialist, relished the assignment and finished his work in less than two months, after which he took to his bed for several weeks. This photo of Beard was taken about ten years after his work on the *Yankee*. Later Beard became president of the Society of Illustrators and founder of the American Boy Scouts.

KING ARTHUR'S COURT

"A tree is known by its fruits."

The armored knight rides to battle on a bicycle.

The church, the king, the nobleman, and the freeman. "All pictures of this type were expurgated from later editions," Dan Beard, the artist, noted.

A chapter heading from the *Yankee*. Sir Boss introduced soap as a civilizing influence into Camelot. "Many a small thing has been made large by the right kind of advertising," he said.

The *Yankee* is set in 6th century England. Actually, the time Mark writes about is nearer the 12th or 13th century.

From *Life* magazine, 1903.

The Brave Sir Mark

A Yankee Writer at King Arthur's Court

PUDD'N HEAD WILSON

A TALE BY MARK TWAIN

THERE is no character, howsoever good and fine, but it can be destroyed by ridicule, howsoever poor and witless. Observe the ass, for instance: his character is about perfect, he is the choicest spirit among all the humbler animals, yet see what ridicule has brought him to. Instead of feeling complimented when we are called an ass, we are left in doubt.—*Pudd'nhead Wilson's Calendar.*

A WHISPER TO THE READER.

A PERSON who is ignorant of legal matters is always liable to make mistakes when he tries to photograph a court scene with his pen; and so I was not willing to let the law chapters in this book go to press without first subjecting them to rigid and exhausting revision and correction by a trained barrister—if that is what they are called. These chapters are right, now, in every detail, for they were rewritten under the immediate eye of William Hicks, who studied law part of a while in southwest Missouri thirty-five years ago and then came over here to Florence for his health and is still helping for exercise and board in Macaroni Vermicelli's horse-feed shed which is up the back alley as you turn around the corner out of the Piazza del Duomo just beyond the house where that stone that Dante used to sit on six hundred years ago is let into the wall when he let on to be watching them build Giotto's campanile and yet always got tired looking as soon as Beatrice passed along on her way to get a chunk of chestnut cake to defend herself with in case of a Ghibelline outbreak before she got to school, at the same old stand where they sell the same old cake to this day and it is just as light and good as it was then, too, and this is not flattery, far from it. He was a little rusty on his law, but he rubbed up for this book; and those two or three legal chapters are right and straight, now. He told me so himself.

Given under my hand this second day of January, 1893, at the Villa Viviani, village of Settignano, three miles back of Florence, on the hills—the same certainly affording the most charming view to be found on this planet, and with it the most dream-like and enchanting sunsets to be found in any planet or even in any solar system—and given, too, in the swell room of the house, with the busts of Cerretani senators and other grandees of this line looking approvingly down upon me as they used to look down upon Dante, and mutely asking me to adopt them into my family, which I do with pleasure, for my remotest ancestors are but spring chickens compared with these robed and stately antiques, and it will be a great and satisfying lift for me, that six hundred years will.

Mark Twain.

CHAPTER I.

TELL the truth or trump—but get the trick.—*Pudd'nhead Wilson's Calendar.*

THE scene of this chronicle is the town of Dawson's Landing, on the Missouri side of the Mississippi, half a day's journey, per steamboat, below St. Louis.

In 1830 it was a snug little collection of modest one- and two-story frame dwellings whose whitewashed exteriors were almost con-stood wooden boxes containing moss-rose plants and terra-cotta pots in which grew a breed of geranium whose spread of intensely red blossoms accented the prevailing pink tint of the rose-clad house-front like an explosion of flame. When there was room on the ledge outside of the pots and boxes for a cat, the cat was there—in sunny weather—stretched at full length, asleep and blissful, with her furry belly to the sun and a paw curved over her nose. Then that house was complete, and its content-

---

The opening page of the serialized novel, from the *Century* of December, 1893. When the chapters were finished, Mark's publishing house, Webster and Company, had failed. The book was issued in 1894 by the American Publishing Company, his old Hartford friends.

PUDD'NHEAD WILSON

A story Mark Twain began as a "howling farce" turned out to be one of his most daring and significant books. *Pudd'nhead Wilson* seems to have been as chaotically produced as most of his works—started on one tack, rushed ahead, abruptly dropped, turned in an opposite direction, drastically rewritten, sliced by a fourth, packed off to a publisher with the casual hope, "It'll furnish me cash for a while, I reckon." He wrote *Pudd'nhead* in Europe in 1892–93. *Century* magazine bought serial rights for $6,500 and ran it through five issues.

Pudd'nhead is about slavery, and the complex morality of its society. The Dawson's Landing of this story, like St. Petersburg and Obedstown, is the Hannibal of Twain's childhood. Again he uses the device of switched identities—the white boy raised as a slave, and the slave raised as a white. In the slave Roxana, one-sixteenth colored, he created a Negro character with far more human reality than any writer had done before him—and most writers since.

Each chapter of the book begins with a cynical aphorism from "Pudd'nhead Wilson's Calendar." They are Mark Twain's utterances, of course. When *Following the Equator* appeared in 1897, he added to the collection. Calendars featuring the maxims were published until long after Twain's death. This sampling is from them:

"Training is everything. The peach was once a bitter almond; cauliflower is nothing but cabbage with a college education."

"Let us endeavor so to live that when we come to die even the undertaker will be sorry."

"Why is it that we rejoice at birth and grieve at a funeral? It is because we are not the person involved."

"As to the Adjective; when in doubt, strike it out."

"When I reflect upon the number of disagreeable people who I know have gone to a better world, I am moved to lead a different life."

"October. This is one of the peculiarly dangerous months to speculate in stocks in. The others are July, January, September, April, November, May, March, June, December, August, and February."

"Nothing so needs reforming as other people's habits."

"If you pick up a starving dog and make him prosperous, he will not bite you. This is the principal difference between a dog and a man."

"April 1. This is the day upon which we are reminded of what we are on other three hundred and sixty-four."

"October 12, *the Discovery*. It was wonderful to find America, but it would have been more wonderful to miss it."

"A man may have no bad habits and have worse."

"Noise proves nothing. Often a hen who has merely laid an egg cackles as if she had laid an asteroid."

"He was as shy as a newspaper is when referring to its own merits."

"Truth is the most valuable thing we have. Let us economize it."

"Everything human is pathetic. The secret source of Humor itself is not joy but sorrow. There is no humor in heaven."

"When in doubt, tell the truth."

"Truth is stranger than fiction, but it is because fiction is obliged to stick to possibilities; truth isn't."

"It is by the goodness of God that in our country we have those three unspeakably precious things: freedom of speech, freedom of conscience, and the prudence never to practice either of them."

"'Classic.' A book which people praise and don't read."

"Man is the Only Animal that Blushes. Or needs to."

"The universal brotherhood of man is our most precious possession, what there is of it."

"Let us be thankful for the fools. But for them the rest of us could not succeed."

"When people do not respect us we are sharply offended; yet deep down in his private heart no man much respects himself."

"The man with a new idea is a Crank until the idea succeeds."

"There are several good protections against temptations, but the surest is cowardice."

"Prosperity is the best protector of principle."

"By trying we can easily learn to endure adversity. Another man's, I mean."

"It takes your enemy and your friend, working together, to hurt you to the heart; the one to slander you and the other to get the news to you."

"Let me make the superstitions of a nation and I care not who makes its laws or its songs either."

"In statesmanship get the formalities right, never mind about the moralities."

"Every one is a moon, and has a dark side which he never shows to anybody."

"The very ink with which all history is written is merely fluid prejudice."

"There isn't a Parallel of Latitude but thinks it would have been the Equator if it had had its rights."

A ROYAL FLUSH

On June 6, 1891, Mark Twain and his family sailed for Europe, leaving their Hartford home, never to live in it again. They planned a long stay abroad, hoping to find health and lower living costs in Europe. Both Mark and Livy were disabled by rheumatism, and Livy suffered from a heart ailment too. Mark had experimented with dictation into a phonograph, in order to finish *The American Claimant*. Before sailing, he was able to syndicate it for $12,000, and to contract for a series of six European letters, at $1,000 each.

Travel and the European baths might benefit Susy too, who had fallen ill in her first year at Bryn Mawr.

For nine years the Twains made their home abroad, moving restlessly through France, Germany, Italy, Switzerland, Austria, England, and Sweden. For the first few years Mark ferried back and forth across the Atlantic, hoping that the Paige typesetter would miraculously rescue his sinking publishing business. The 1893 depression was the final disaster. Now nothing but his pen and his voice—not inconsiderable assets—would support his family.

In their European rovings Mark's popularity, as always, attracted brilliant and amusing company. His widely translated books were read everywhere. The royal courts, the embassies, the universities, the press sought him out in every city.

When the German Emperor invited him to dinner, Mark's daughter Jean said, "Papa, the way things are going, pretty soon there won't be anybody left for you to get acquainted with but God."

Mark, who thoroughly enjoyed his celebrity, had this to say about royalty worship:

"We are all alike—on the inside. Also we are exteriorly all alike, if you leave out Carnegie. Scoffing democrats as we are, we do dearly love to be noticed by a duke, and when we are noticed by a monarch we have softening of the brain for the rest of our lives. We try our best to keep from referring to these precious collisions, and in time some of us succeed in keeping our dukes and monarchs to ourselves; it costs us something to do this but in time we accomplish it. In my own case, I have so carefully and persistently trained myself in this kind of self-denial that today I can look on calm and unmoved when a returned American is casually and gratefully playing the earls he has met; I can look on, silent and unexcited, and never offer to call his hand, although I have three kings and a pair of emperors up my sleeve."

Roving Ambassador

As Max Beerbohm saw Mark Twain.

Carmen Sylva, Queen of Rumania, who became a friend of Mark Twain in Vienna in 1898. "I owe you," she wrote him once, "days and days of forgetfulness of self, and troubles, and the intensest of all joys—hero-worship!"

Emperor Francis Joseph, of Austria. Invited to meet the Emperor in 1899, Mark had concocted a one-sentence speech of eighteen German words. But he forgot it. He thought Francis Joseph "most kind-hearted, with a great deal of plain, good, attractive human nature about him. Necessarily he must have or he couldn't have unbent to me as he did. I couldn't unbend if I were an emperor."

The Emperor and Empress of Germany. Mark Twain was guest of honor at a dinner given for him by William II in Berlin in 1892. "The guests stood in awe of him," Mark reported, "and naturally they conferred that feeling upon me, for, after all, I am only human, although I regret it. The Emperor was used to all this atmosphere, and it did not chill his blood; maybe it was an inspiration to him, for he was alert, brilliant, and full of animation; also he was most gracefully and felicitously complimentary to my books—and I will remark here that the happy phrasing of a compliment is one of the rarest of human gifts and the happy delivery of it another."

215

"Below the Mark"—Spy's caricature of Mark Twain in *Vanity Fair*.

ANOTHER THRONE GONE DOWN

Mark could savor the society of kings while detesting the institution of monarchy. Not long before the beginning of his nine-year residence abroad, the report came that the Brazilian monarchy had fallen. Echoing his Connecticut Yankee, Mark wrote this letter to a Boston newspaperman:

"Another throne has gone down, and I swim in oceans of satisfaction. I wish I might live fifty years longer; I believe I should see the thrones of Europe selling at auction for old iron. I believe I should really see the end of what is surely the grotesquest of all the swindles ever invented by man—monarchy. It is enough to make a graven image laugh, to see apparently rational people, away down here in this wholesome and merciless slaughter-day for shams, still mouthing empty reverence for those moss-backed frauds and scoundrelisms, hereditary kingship and so-called 'nobility.' It is enough to make the monarchs and nobles themselves laugh—and in private they do; there can be no question about that. I think there is only one funnier thing, and that is the spectacle of these bastard Americans—Hamersleys and Huntingtons and such—offering cash, uncumbered by themselves, for rotten carcases and stolen titles. When our great brethren and disenslaved Brazilians frame their Declaration of Independence, I hope they will insert this missing link: 'We hold these truths to be self-evident: that all monarchs are usurpers, and descendants of usurpers; for the reason that no throne was ever set up in this world by the will, freely exercised, of the only body possessing the legitimate right to set it up—the numerical mass of the nation.'

"Have you noticed the rumor that the Portuguese throne is unsteady, and that the Portuguese slaves are getting restive? Also, that the head slave-driver of Europe, Alexander III, has so reduced his usual monthly order for chains that the Russian foundries are running on only half time now? Also that other rumor that English nobility acquired an added stench the other day—and had to ship it to India and the continent because there wasn't any more room for it at home? Things are working. By and by there is

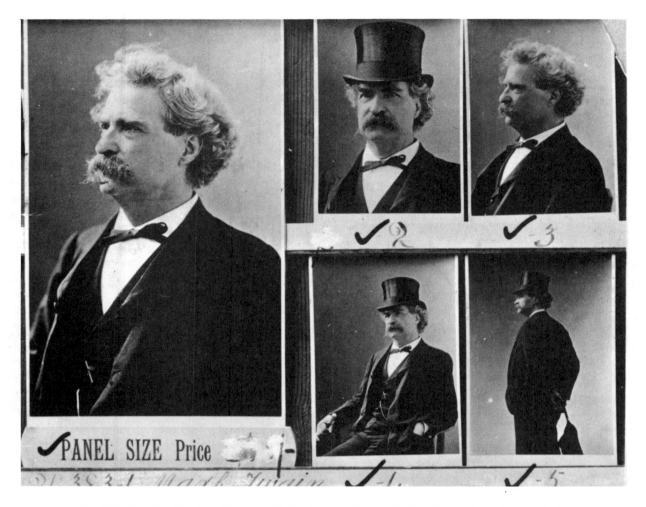

In 1895–97, the Twains lived at 23 Tedworth Square in London, where he worked on his last travel book, *Following the Equator*. He took time off one day to visit a photographer's studio. This is a proof sheet with the five pictures he checked off.

going to be an emigration, may be. Of course we shall make no preparation; we never do. In a few years from now we shall have nothing but played-out kings and dukes on the police, and driving the horse-cars, and whitewashing fences, and in fact over-crowding all the avenues of unskilled labor; and then we shall wish, when it is too late, that we had taken common and reasonable precautions and drowned them at Castle Garden."

In the fall of 1891 Mark decided on a little trip down the Rhone in a flat-bottomed boat. The lazy, drifting days rested his spirit. But now and then he saw something which struck a chord that was to dominate him more and more:

"Livy darling, I didn't write yesterday. We left La Voulte in a driving storm of cold rain—couldn't write in it—and at 1 p.m. when we were not thinking of stopping, we saw a picturesque and mighty ruin on a high hill back of a village, and I was seized with a desire to explore it; so we landed at once and set out with rubbers and umbrella, sending the boat ahead to St. Andeol, and we spent 3 hours clambering about those cloudy heights among those worn and vast and idiotic ruins of a castle built by two crusaders 650 years ago. The work of these asses was full of interest, and we had a good time inspecting, examining and scrutinizing it. All the hills on both sides of the Rhone have peaks and precipices, and each has its gray and wasted pile of mouldy walls and broken towers. The Romans displaced the Gauls, the Visigoths displaced the Romans, the Saracens displaced the Visigoths, the Christians displaced the Saracens, and it was these pious animals who built these strange lairs and cut each other's throats in the name and for the glory of God, and robbed and burned and slew in peace and war; and the pauper and the slave built churches, and the credit of it went to the Bishop who racked the money out of them. These are pathetic shores, and they make one despise the human race."

217

MOMMSEN, WAGNER, AND THE JUBILEES

Wintering in Berlin in 1891–92, Mark attended a mighty beerfest given by a thousand students in honor of Virchow and Helmholtz, two of Germany's greatest scientists. In one of his syndicated newsletters to America, Twain describes the moment when Mommsen, the historian and archeologist, unexpectedly joined the celebration:

"There seemed to be some signal whereby the students on the platform were made aware that a professor had arrived at the remote door of entrance, for you would see them suddenly rise to their feet, strike an erect military attitude, then draw their swords; the swords of all their brethren standing guard at the innumerable tables would flash from the scabbard and be held aloft—a handsome spectacle. Three clear bugle-notes would ring out, then all these swords would come down with a crash, twice repeated, on the tables and be uplifted and held aloft again; then in the distance you would see the gay uniforms and uplifted swords of a guard of honor clearing the way and conducting the guest down to his place. The songs were stirring, and the immense outpour from young life and young lungs, the crash of swords, and the thunder of the beer-mugs gradually worked a body up to what seemed to be the last possible summit of excitement. It surely seemed to me that I had reached that summit, that I had reached my limit, and that there was no higher lift devisable for me. When apparently the last eminent guest had long ago taken his place, again those three bugle-blasts rang out, and once more the swords leaped from their scabbards. Who might this late comer be? Nobody was interested to inquire. Still, indolent eyes were turned toward the distant entrance, and we saw the silken gleam and the lifted sword of a guard of honor plowing through the remote crowds. Then we saw that end of the house rising to its feet; saw it rise abreast the advancing guard all along like a wave. This supreme honor has been offered to no one before. There was an excited whisper at our table—'Mommsen!'—and the whole house rose—rose and shouted and stamped and clapped and banged the beer-mugs. Just simply a storm! Then the little man with his long hair and Emersonian face edged his way past us and took his seat. I could have touched him with my hand—Mommsen!—think of it!

"This was one of those immense surprises that can happen only a few times in one's life. I was not dreaming of him; he was to me only a giant myth, a world-shadowing specter, not a reality. The surprise of it all can be only comparable to a man's suddenly coming upon Mont Blanc, with its awful form towering into the sky, when he didn't suspect he was in its neighborhood. I would have walked a great many miles to get a sight of him, and here he was, without trouble, or tramp, or cost of any kind. Here he was, clothed in a titanic deceptive modesty which made him look like other men. Here he was, carrying the Roman world and all the Caesars in his hospitable skull, and doing it as easily as the other luminous vault, and the skull of the universe, carries the Milky Way and the constellations."

Mark's introduction to the music of Richard Wagner occurred during these years in Europe:

"Another time, we went to Mannheim and attended a shivaree—otherwise an opera—the one called 'Lohengrin.' The banging and slamming and booming and crashing were something beyond belief. The racking and pitiless pain of it remains stored up in my memory alongside the memory of the time that I had my teeth fixed. There were circumstances which made it necessary for me to stay through the four hours to the end, and I stayed; but the recollection of that long, dragging, relentless season of suffering is indestructible. To have to endure it in silence, and sitting still, made it all the harder. I was in a railed compartment with eight or ten strangers, of the two sexes, and this compelled repression; yet at times the pain was so exquisite that I could hardly keep the tears back. At those times, as the howlings and wailings and shriekings of the singers, and the ragings and roarings and explosions of the vast orchestra rose higher and higher, and wilder and wilder, and fiercer and fiercer, I could have cried if I had been alone. Those strangers would not have been surprised

Theodor Mommsen, the German scholar. "Been taken for Mommsen twice," Mark said. "We have the same hair, but on examination it was found the brains were different."

The Fisk Jubilee Singers. It was this group Mark Twain first met in London in the 1870's. One of them was still with the Singers when Mark heard them again in Switzerland, 24 years later. Twain loved the Jubilees, and sang them beautifully for his family and friends.

to see a man do such a thing who was being gradually skinned, but they would have marvelled at it here, and made remarks about it no doubt, whereas there was nothing in the present case which was an advantage over being skinned.

"Each sang his indictive narrative in turn, accompanied by the whole orchestra of sixty instruments; and when this had continued for some time, and one was hoping they might come to an understanding and modify the noise, a great chorus composed entirely of maniacs would suddenly break forth, and then during two minutes, and sometimes three, I lived over again all that I had suffered the time the orphan asylum burned down.

"I have since found out that there is nothing the Germans like so much as an opera. They like it, not in a mild and moderate way, but with their whole hearts. This is a legitimate result of habit and education. Our nation will like the opera, too, by-and-by, no doubt. One in fifty of those who attend our operas likes it already, perhaps, but I think a good many of the other forty-nine go in order to learn to like it, and the rest in order to be able to talk knowingly about it. The latter usually hum the airs while they are being sung, so that their neighbors may perceive that they have been to operas before. The funerals of these do not occur often enough."

In Lucerne, in the summer of 1897, the Twains ran across another group of Americans. "The other night," Mark wrote Joe Twichell, "we had a detachment of the Jubilee Singers—6. I had known one of them in London 24 years ago. Three of the 6 were born in slavery, the others were children of slaves. How charming they were—in spirit, manner, language, pronunciation, enunciation, grammar, phrasing, matter, carriage, clothes—in every detail that goes to make the real lady and gentleman, and welcome guest. We went down to the village hotel and bought our tickets and entered the beer-hall, where a crowd of German and Swiss men and women sat grouped at round tables with their beer mugs in front of them —self-contained and unimpressionable looking people, an indifferent and unposted and disheartened audience —and up at the far end of the room sat the Jubilees in a row. The Singers got up and stood—the talking and glass jingling went on. Then rose and swelled out above those common earthly sounds one of those rich chords the secret of whose make only the Jubilees possess, and a spell fell upon that house. It was fine to see the faces light up with the pleased wonder and surprise of it. No one was indifferent any more; and when the singers finished, the camp was theirs. It was a triumph. It reminded me of Launcelot riding in Sir Kay's armor and astonishing complacent Knights who thought they had struck a soft thing. The Jubilees sang a lot of pieces. Arduous and painstaking cultivation has not diminished or artificialized their music, but on the contrary—to my surprise—has mightily reinforced its eloquence and beauty. Away back in the beginning—to my mind—their music made all other vocal music cheap; and that early notion is emphasized now. It is utterly beautiful, to me; and it moves me infinitely more than any other music can. I think that in the Jubilees and their songs America has produced the perfectest flower of the ages; and I wish it were a foreign product, so that she would worship it and lavish money on it and go properly crazy over it."

219

SOCIETY'S FAVORITE

Society's hunger for Mark Twain was just as great in New York during his frequent business trips home as in the capitals of Europe. "I am already way behind again with my correspondence—which consists mainly of declining all conceivable kinds of entertainments," he wrote Livy in 1894. "Dr. Rice said last night that my welcome to New York has been phenomenal, & that the manifest affection of the people for me was the sort of fame that was worth having; & Mr. Rogers said the other day to Rice or to Archbold that other people's successes in this world were made over broken hearts or at the cost of other people's feelings or food, but that my fame had cost no one a pang or a penny. And this morning down stairs some one read a remark in an English magazine that there was a curious fact that had been observed —to wit, that the most fleetest & evanescent of fames was that of the second-rate humorist, while the most substantial & permanent was that of the first-rate humorist; & said he believed I was a first-rate. All this is pleasant. I can stand considerable petting. Born so."

That he didn't say no every time is clear from this next letter:

"Livy dear, last night I played billiards with Mr. Rogers until 11, then went to Robert Reid's studio and had a most delightful time until 4 this morning. No ladies were invited this time. Among the people present were—

Coquelin;
Richard Harding Davis;
Harrison, the great out-door painter;
Wm. H. Chase, the artist;
Bettini, inventor of the new phonograph.
Nikola Tesla, the world-wide illustrious electrician; see article about him in Jan. or Feb. Century.
John Drew, actor;
James Barnes, a marvelous mimic; my, you should see him!
Smedley the artist;
Zorn the artist;
Zogbaum the artist;
Reinhart the artist;
Metcalf the artist;
Ancona, head tenor at the Opera;

"Oh, a great lot of others. Everybody there had done something and was in his way famous.

"Somebody welcomed Coquelin in a nice little French speech; John Drew did the like for me in English, and then the fun began. Coquelin did some excellent French monologues—one of them an un-

This ink sketch was done by J. T. McCutcheon in 1905.

grammatical Englishman telling a colorless historiette in French. It nearly killed the fifteen or twenty people who understood it.

"I told a yarn, Ancona sang half a dozen songs, Barnes did his darling imitations, Harding Davis sang the hanging of Danny Deever, which was of course good, but he followed it with that most fascinating (for what reason I don't know) of all Kipling's poems, 'On the Road to Mandalay,' sang it tenderly, and it searched me deeper and charmed me more than the Deever.

"Young Gerrit Smith played some ravishing dance-music and we all danced about an hour. There couldn't

ER PLOT

Given by
other.

etailed P an
onfessed
acy.

15.—The t al
d with b ing
Gov. Go bel.
Youtsey vas
tion as st
ened and his
id hearir g of
tnesses ere
lld be h rd
ollow, m in-
to be sit ing

he testim ny
he dead Gov-
jail the ay
en said:
Ir. Yout ey's
Youtsey, Col.
and tol me
and I h e
ne what y u
r it is t e,
estions.'
Mr. G ebel,
ell is t. e.'
low, I ould
t getting the
Powers, nd
going to ee
o see Taylor
iere you got
oceeded and
npbell, I had
onday morn-
vas ready to
Caleb Pow-
ld he told me
to John Pow-
e the key. I
ld him that
the shooting.
not to come
been exnect-

MARK TWAIN HOME AGAIN

Writer Reaches America After His Prolonged Stay Abroad.

GREETED BY MANY FRIENDS

Talks Freely of His Travels, His Experiences, and His Triumphs—In the Best of Health.

Mark Twain returned to America yesterday on the Atlantic Transport Line steamship Minnehaha.

As is well known, Mark Twain registers at hotels and signs checks under the name of Samuel M. Clemens, but it was the writer and lecturer, Mark Twain, who attracted to the pier so many friends and associates of former days.

Mr. Clemens never looked better, was in a splendid humor, and greeted his friends with the most affectionate cordiality.

As soon as the author had finished with the salutations of his friends, he was surrounded by a large number of newspaper men, and asked for a story of what he had been doing during all the nine years of his absence from his native land.

"Now, that's a long story, but I suppose I must give you something, even if it is in a condensed form," he said. "I left America June 6, 1891, and went to Aix-les-Bains, France, where I spent the Fall and Winter. After that I went to Berlin, where I lectured, giving readings from my works. After this my next stop was the Riviera, where I remained for three months, going from there to the baths near Frankfort, where I remained during the cholera season.

"Most of 1892 I spent at Florence, where I rented a home. While there I wrote 'Joan of Arc' and finished up 'Puddin-head Wilson.' For the next two years I was in France. I can't speak French yet. In the Spring of 1895 I came to the United States for a brief stay, crossing the continent from New York to San Francisco, lecturing every night. In October of that

When the Twain family finally returned home in 1900, the welcome was affectionate and universal. They had been abroad for nine years.

be a pleasanter night than that one was. Some of those people complained of fatigue but I don't seem to know what the sense of fatigue is."

He reveled in his crowded calendar, perhaps partly because it might have taken his mind off his intolerable financial worries: "I am too busy," he wrote Clara, "to attend to the photo-collecting right, because I have to live up to the name which Jamie Dodge has given me—the 'Belle of New York'—and it just keeps me rushing. Yesterday I had engagements to breakfast at noon, dine at 3, and dine again at 7. I got away from the long breakfast at 2 P.M., went and excused myself from the 3 o'clock dinner, then lunched

with Mrs. Dodge in 58th Street, returned to the Players and dressed, dined out at 7, and was back at Mrs. Dodge's at 10 P.M. where we had magic-lantern views of a superb sort, and a lot of yarns until an hour after midnight, and got to bed at 2 this morning—a good deal of a gain on my recent hours. But I don't get tired; I sleep as sound as a dead person, and always wake up fresh and strong—usually at exactly 9.

"I was at breakfast lately where people of seven separate nationalities sat and the seven languages were going all the time. At my side sat a charming gentleman who was a delightful and active talker, and interesting. He talked glibly to those folks in all those seven languages—and still had a language to spare! I wanted to kill him, for very envy."

Everybody who was anybody must have wanted Mark Twain at his table. The letters read like a gossip column: "When I go anywhere to dinner on invitation, I go in evening dress, of course. When I drop in at either of three places—Rice's, Laffan's & Hutton's on my own invitation, it is always on a sudden notion & there's no time to dress. I go as I am. It is the clear understanding. My place is ready for me—to occupy when I please. I have never dropped in at Hutton's in this way—it is only accident that I haven't—but various times Mrs. Hutton has ordered Larry to bring me & he has done it & there was no other guest there & no occasion for evening dress & we didn't wear it.

"Now while I think of it I'll run out & leave cards at Chas. A. Dana's. I declined a dinner there for day before yesterday. I love you with all my heart, & I keep your commandments better than I give myself credit for, my darling.

"P.S. Mind you, it rains invitations, but I don't accept them. I am attending strictly to business, & to private dinners where there are no speeches. To-night, dinner at R. U. Johnson's—don't want to go, but can't properly decline; Tuesday, 1 P.M., at Mrs. Carroll Beckwith's—luncheon—she's playing me as a card, & will have a large company—but she has been treating me very handsomely, & so I'm perfectly willing to spin yarns if her guests want them; Monday 7:30 P.M., dinner with Stanford White the architect, up in his quarters in the Tower of Madison Square Garden—Abbey the artist & other artists are to be there. I shall enjoy it. But I decline all of the banquets, now. I made such a big hit at Brander Matthews' banquet—without expecting it—that I'm going to keep what I've gained, & make no more speeches."

MARK TWAIN—ON EVERYTHING

"The New York papers," Mark Twain once said, "have long known that no large question is ever really settled until I have been consulted; it is the way they feel about it, and they show it by always sending to me when they get uneasy."

As the headlines on these pages indicate, hardly a day passed without a reporter seeking his opinions. At home, on the street, on train or ship, at work or on holiday, it made no difference; the man who had become, in the words of the *Evening Mail,* "a kind of

Mark Twain shortly after his return to New York in 1900.

joint Aristides, Solon and Themistocles of the American metropolis" must always have his wit and wisdom on tap for a thirsty public.

He must have given hundreds and hundreds of interviews, but he was rarely satisfied with the results. "What I say in an interview loses its character in print —all its life and personality. The reporter realizes this himself, and tries to improve upon me, but he doesn't help matters any."

Once Edward Bok interviewed Mark in Hartford, and sent him a draft for approval. Back came this letter:

"MY DEAR MR. BOK,—No, no. It is like most interviews, pure twaddle and valueless.

"For several quite plain and simple reasons, an 'interview' must, as a rule, be an absurdity, and chiefly for this reason—It is an attempt to use a boat on land or a wagon on water, to speak figuratively. Spoken speech is one thing, written speech is quite another. Print is the proper vehicle for the latter, but it isn't for the former. The moment 'talk' is put into print you recognize that it is not what it was when you heard it; you perceive that an immense something has disappeared from it. That is its soul. You have nothing but a dead carcass left on your hands. Color, play of feature, the varying modulations of the voice, the laugh, the smile, the informing inflections, everything that gave that body warmth, grace, friendliness and charm and commended it to your affections—or, at least, to your tolerance—is gone and nothing is left but a pallid, stiff and repulsive cadaver.

"Such is 'talk' almost invariably, as you see it lying in state in an 'interview.' The interviewer seldom tries to tell one how a thing was said; he merely puts in the naked remark and stops there. When one writes for print his methods are different. He follows forms which have but little resemblance to conversation, but they make the reader understand what the writer is trying to convey. And when the writer is making a story and finds it necessary to report some of the talk of his characters observe how cautiously and anxiously he goes at that risky and difficult thing.

"So painfully aware is the novelist that naked talk in print conveys no meaning that he loads, and often overloads, almost every utterance of his characters with explanations and interpretations. It is a loud confession that print is a poor vehicle for 'talk'; it is a recognition that uninterpreted talk in print would result in confusion to the reader, not instruction.

"Now, in your interview, you have certainly been most accurate; you have set down the sentences I uttered as I said them. But you have not a word of explanation; what my manner was at several points is not indicated. Therefore, no reader can possibly know where I was in earnest and where I was joking; or whether I was joking altogether or in earnest alto-

MARK TWAIN COMING TO RUN FOR PRESIDENT.

"I Am in Favor of Everything Everybody Is in Favor Of—Temperance and Intemperance, Gold Standard and Free Silver. I Will Satisfy the Whole Nation and Not Be Half a President," He Says.

MARK TWAIN ON LYING

SAYS IT IS THE RESOURCE OF PRIMITIVE INTELLIGENCE.

Refuses to Consider It as an Art—Believes That Telling the Truth Properly Is Greatest Evidence of Mental Culture, and That All Educated People Resort to It, When They Think of It.

MARK TWAIN TALKS

Says His Chief Desire Is Not to Be Told to Move On.

TIRED OF KNOCKING AROUND

In Politicks He Is a Mugwump, and Would Vote for the Candidate Who Had the Best Morals—Now Claims Connection with Leisure Class.

WOULDN'T WORK 30 MINUTES FOR $500.

In Declining The World's Offer Mark Twain Says He Hates Labor.

'THE LAZIEST MAN ALIVE'

Declares That He Only Does Work When It Is an Absolute Necessity.

HAD PLANNED TO GO TO SLEEP.

Would Rather Go to Bed Early and Lose $500 than Miss a Chance to Rest.

SURE MARK TWAIN'S IN A CROOKED GAME.

Housekeeper at No. 14 East Tenth Street Annoyed by Inquiries for Him.

HE'S AT NO. 14 WEST.

MARK TWAIN ON MEDICINE

He Discusses the Progress Made in the Science.

Justice Woodward, Another Guest at Medical Jurisprudence Society Dinner, Deals with Expert Testimony.

TWAIN FLEES FROM A WOMAN'S CLUB

Humorist Takes Advantage of a Distribution of Sandwiches to Regain His Liberty.

WIT ENLIVENED DEBATE

Heard a Solemn Proposition to Boycott Light Literature and Gravely Approved of It.

NATION'S GRAMMAR IS BAD

Finds That Professors Are Very Prone to Use Slipshod English in Conversation.

MARK TWAIN IS STAR OF THE DAY

He Reads Shelley's "Ode to a Skylark" at the Waldorf to an Impressionable Audience.

JULIA MARLOWE RECITES

MARK TWAIN BESTS A GRASPING CABMAN.

Declares Also that All Good Citizens Should Do Likewise.

PUBLIC'S FAULT, HE SAYS

gether. Such a report of a conversation has no value. It can convey many meanings to the reader, but never the right one. To add interpretations which would convey the right meaning is a something which would require—what? An art so high and fine and difficult that no possessor of it would ever be allowed to waste it on interviews.

"No; spare the reader and spare me; leave the whole interview out; it is rubbish. I wouldn't talk in my sleep if I couldn't talk better than that.

"If you wish to print anything print this letter; it may have some value, for it may explain to a reader here and there why it is that in interviews, as a rule, men seem to talk like anybody but themselves."

223

MARK TWAIN TONIGHT!

The year 1894 ended with both the publishing house and the Paige machine dead and buried. Mark had lost $60,000 in his Webster Company and Livy $65,000. The company owed ninety-six creditors about $1,000 apiece. The Panic of '93 had cut off Livy's income from her inheritance; Mark's royalties had almost vanished. To celebrate their silver wedding anniversary, Mark could give Livy only a five-franc piece. He pushed on with his newest book, *Joan of Arc,* and finished it in Paris. "Possibly the book may not sell," he wrote his benefactor Rogers, "but that is nothing —it was written for love." (It was the only book he dedicated to Livy.) With Rogers' help, Harper's arranged to take over the serial and book publication of *Joan.*

Mark and Livy, sick over the debts, determined to pay back every cent. Major Pond suggested another lecture tour. Hadn't it worked when he needed money in 1872 and 1884? Mark went him one better—a lecture circuit of the world, with a book to come out of it as an extra dividend.

The family went back to America in May, 1895 to rest at Quarry Farm and prepare for the tour. But bad luck still rode Twain. A huge carbuncle confined him for seven weeks and made the trip's beginning an agonizing experience. He hated to make the tour alone; Livy and Clara decided to go with him, while Susy and Jean were to stay with their aunt in Elmira. On July 14, their train—with Major and Mrs. Pond aboard to accompany them to the West Coast—drew out of Elmira, leaving Susy alone on the platform, waving good-bye.

224

(CORRECTED JULY 26).

MARK TWAIN'S TOUR
AROUND THE WORLD,

Beginning in Cleveland, Ohio, July 15th, 1895

Closing in London, May, 1896

ROUTE IN AMERICA.

JULY

Mon.	15.	Cleveland, Ohio	Stillman House
Tues.	16.	" "	"
Wed.	17.	*Travel on Steamer.*	
Thur.	18.	Sault Ste., Mich	Hotel Iroquois
Fri.	19.	Mackinac	Grand Hotal
Sat.	20.	Petoskey, Mich	Arlington Hotel
SUN.	21.	Mackinac	Grand Hotel
Mon.	22.	Duluth, Minn	Spalding, Hotel
Tues.	23.	Minneapolis, Minn	Hotel West
Wed.	24.	St. Paul, Minn.	Hotel Ryan
Thur	25.	*Travel.*	
Fri.	26.	Winnipeg	The Manitoba
Sat.	27.	'	"
SUN.	28.	"	"
Mon.	29.	Crookston, Minn	Crookston Hotel
Tues.	30.	*Travel.*	
Wed.	31.	Great Falls, Mont.	Park Hotel

AUGUST

Thur.	1.	Butte, Montana	The Butte Hotel
Fri.	2.	Anaconda, Mont	The Montana
Sat.	3.	Helena, Mont	Hotel Helena
SUN.	4.	"	"
Mon.	5.		
Tues.	6.	*Travel.*	
Wed.	7.	Spokane, Wash	The Spokane
Thur.	8.	*Travel.*	
Fri.	9.	Portland, Oregon	The Portland
Sat.	10.	Olympia, Wash	The Olympia
SUN.	11.	" "	"
Mon.	12.	Tacoma, Wash	The Tacoma
Tues.	13.	Seattle, Wash	The Rainier-Grand
Wed.	14.	New Whatcom, Wash	
Thur.	15.	Vancouver, B.C.	Hotel Vancouver
Fri.	16.	*Sails from Vancouver for Australia.*	

ADDRESS ALL COMMUNICATIONS TO

MAJOR J. B. POND,
EN ROUTE.

The lecture tour announcement for the U.S. and Canada.

As Theodore Wust saw Mark Twain on the platform.

Friends see Mark and Livy off at the Winnepeg station on July 29, 1895. Livy is in black, facing Mark. This picture and those on following pages were taken by Major Pond during the tour.

Mark Twain amuses Mrs. Henry Ward Beecher and Senator Wilbur F. Sanders of Montana, at the Missoula station, August 5, 1895. They met by chance on the train.

In Seattle on August 13, Mark was a dinner guest on the U.S.S. *Mohican*. He was photographed in the clothes he wore for the lecture at the opera house that night.

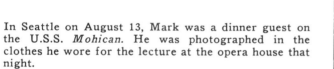

Out of bed early on July 30 to catch the train at Crookston, Minnesota, Mark had Major Pond carry out his contractual obligation to keep him moving. Livy looked on while Clara snapped the Kodak.

"The best interview I ever had," Mark said of this 12-minute meeting on August 10 with Mr. Pease, of the Portland *Oregonian*. The reporter made a two-column story of the brief talk.

Mark having breakfast in his hotel room at Olympia, Washington.

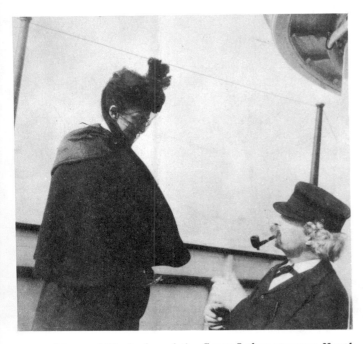

Livy and Mark aboard the Great Lakes steamer *Northland*, during a trip on Lake Huron early in the tour.

At Great Falls, Montana, Twain and Pond visited the Norwegian shanties. The little girl is debating whether to sell Mark her kitten.

DEATH OF SUSY

The grand tour that had begun in Cleveland ended in Capetown, South Africa. "We lectured and robbed and raided for thirteen months," Mark said. "I sent the lecture money to Mr. Rogers as fast as we captured it. He banked it and saved it up for the creditors straightway." By the end of 1898—adding book earnings to

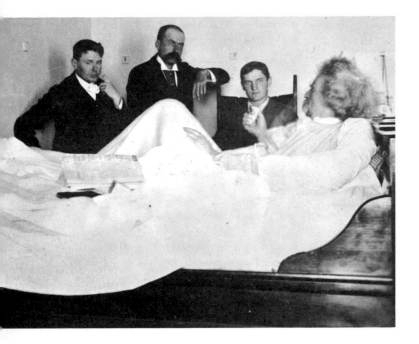

This seems to have been Twain's turn to interview the reporters. He talked to them from his hotel bed in Vancouver on August 18, 1895. "From my reception thus far on my lecturing tour," he told them, "I am confident that if I live I can pay off the last debt within four years. After which, at the age of 64, I can make a fresh and unencumbered start in life."

the pot—the creditors had all been paid a hundred cents on the dollar.

The lecture campaign was hard work, especially with Mark crippled by carbuncles. For readings he relied mainly on *Roughing It* and *Innocents Abroad,* sometimes throwing in *Tom* and *Huck.* The "Golden Arm" tale was usually the climax of the evening. Everywhere —Australia, New Zealand, Ceylon, India, South Africa —packed houses and records broken. At Johannesburg for eight nights running, crowds jammed the hall, overran the stage and fought to get through the closed doors.

Exactly a year after they had left Elmira they sailed from South Africa for England. Hardly three weeks later, on August 18, 1896, as Mark wrote, "I was standing in our dining-room, thinking of nothing in particular, when a cablegram was put into my hand. It said, 'Susy was peacefully released to-day.'

"It is one of the mysteries of our nature that a man, all unprepared, can receive a thunder-stroke like that and live. There is but one reasonable explanation of it. The intellect is stunned by the shock and but gropingly gathers the meaning of the words. The power to realize their full import is mercifully wanting. The mind has a dumb sense of vast loss—that is all. It will take mind and memory months and possibly years to gather together the details and thus learn and know the whole extent of the loss. A man's house burns down. The smoking wreckage represents only a ruined home that was dear through years of use and pleasant associations. By and by, as the days and weeks go on, first he misses this, then that, then the other thing. And when he casts about for it he finds that it was in that house. Always it is an essential—there was but one of its kind. It cannot be replaced. It was in that house. It is irrevocably lost. He did not realize that it was an essential when he had it; he only discovers it now when he finds himself balked, hampered, by its absence. It will be years before the tale of lost essentials is complete, and not till then can he truly know the magnitude of his disaster."

To his dearest friend, Joe Twichell, Mark wrote: "Ah, well, Susy died at *home.* She had that privilege. Her dying eyes rested upon nothing that was strange to them, but only upon things which they had known & loved always & which had made her young years glad; & she had you & Sue & Katie & John & Ellen. This was happy fortune—I am thankful that it was vouchsafed to her. If she had died in another house—well, I think I could not have borne that. To us our house was not unsentient matter—it had a heart & a soul & eyes to see us with, & approvals & solicitudes & deep sympathies; it was of us, & we were in its confidence, & lived in its grace & in the peace its face did not light up &

The Twains—Mark, Clara and Livy—say good-by to Major and Mrs. Pond from the deck of the *Warrimoo.* It sailed from Victoria for Australia on August 23. In 38 days Mark had given 24 lectures in 22 cities.

Mark lecturing in Melbourne, Australia.

speak out its eloquent welcome—& we could not enter
it unmoved. And could we now? oh, now, in spirit we
should enter it unshod."

One day, after Susy's death, Mark picked up the
notebook in which Susy had been writing his biography,
and saw her unfinished last sentence. The depth of his
sorrow is in his comment:

"When I look at the arrested sentence that ends the
little book it seems as if the hand that traced it cannot
be far—it is gone for a moment only, and will come
again and finish it. But that is a dream; a creature of
the heart, not of the mind—a feeling, a longing, not a
mental product; the same that lured Aaron Burr, old,
gray, forlorn, forsaken, to the pier day after day, week
after week, there to stand in the gloom and the chill of
the dawn, gazing seaward through veiling mists and sleet
and snow for the ship which he knew was gone down,
the ship that bore all his treasure—his daughter."

The Belle of New York

The three photos on these pages were made on the same day in 1901.

Amended Obituaries

To the Editor:

SIR,—I am approaching seventy; it is in sight; it is only three years away. Necessarily, I must go soon. It is but matter-of-course wisdom, then, that I should begin to set my worldly house in order now, so that it may be done calmly and with thoroughness, in place of waiting until the last day, when, as we have often seen, the attempt to set both houses in order at the same time has been marred by the necessity for haste and by the confusion and waste of time arising from the inability of the notary and the ecclesiastic to work together harmoniously, taking turn about and giving each other friendly assistance—not perhaps in fielding, which could hardly be expected, but at least in the minor offices of keeping game and umpiring; by consequence of which conflict of interests and absence of harmonious action a draw has frequently resulted where this ill-fortune could not have happened if the houses had been set in order one at a time and hurry avoided by beginning in season, and giving to each the amount of time fairly and justly proper to it.

In setting my earthly house in order I find it of moment that I should attend in person to one or two matters which men in my position have long had the habit of leaving wholly to others, with consequences often most regrettable. I wish to speak of only one of these matters at this time: Obituaries. Of necessity, an Obituary is a thing which cannot be so judiciously edited by any hand as by that of the subject of it. In such a work it is not the Facts that are of chief importance, but the light which the obituarist shall throw upon them, the meanings which he shall dress them in, the conclusions which he shall draw from them, and the judgments which he shall deliver upon them. The Verdicts, you understand: that is the danger-line.

In considering this matter, in view of my approaching change, it has seemed to me wise to take such measures as may be feasible, to

N.B. I cannot make a good mouth, therefore leave it out. There is enough without it anyway. Done with the best ink. M.T.

acquire, by courtesy of the press, access to my standing obituaries, with the privilege—if this is not asking too much—of editing, not their Facts, but their Verdicts. This, not for pres-

ent profit, further than as concerns my family, but as a favorable influence usable on the Other Side, where there are some who are not friendly to me.

With this explanation of my motives, I will now ask you of your courtesy to make an appeal for me to the public press. It is my desire that such journals and periodicals as have obituaries of me lying in their pigeon-holes, with a view to sudden use some day, will not wait longer, but will publish them now, and kindly send me a marked copy. My address is simply New York city—I have no other that is permanent and not transient.

I will correct them—not the Facts, but the Verdicts—striking out such clauses as could have a deleterious influence on the Other Side, and replacing them with clauses of a more judicious character. I should, of course, expect to pay double rates for both the omissions and the substitutions; and I should also expect to pay quadruple rates for all obituaries which proved to be rightly and wisely worded in the originals, thus requiring no emendations at all.

It is my desire to leave these Amended Obituaries neatly bound behind me as a perennial consolation and entertainment to my family, and as an heirloom which shall have a mournful but definite commercial value for my remote posterity.

I beg, sir, that you will insert this Advertisement (1t-eow, agate, inside), and send the bill to

Yours very respectfully,

MARK TWAIN.

P. S.—For the best Obituary—one suitable for me to read in public, and calculated to inspire regret—I desire to offer a Prize, consisting of a Portrait of me done entirely by myself in pen and ink without previous instruction. The ink warranted to be the kind used by the very best artists.

A letter to the editor of *Harper's Weekly,* printed on November 15, 1902. Several readers responded to the offer.

ST. LOUIS POST-DISPATCH

THE ONLY ST. LOUIS NEWSPAPER WITH THE ASSOCIATED PRESS DAY DISPATCHES.
TEN PAGES.

VOL. 54, NO. 282.   ST. LOUIS, FRIDAY EVENING, MAY 30, 1902.   PRICE | In St. Louis, One Cent. / Outside St. Louis, Two Cent.

MARK TWAIN SEES THE HOME OF HIS BOYHOOD

Viewed the Old House Where He Lived at Hannibal and Talked With Old Time Chums—Visited Cemetery Where His Parents Are Buried.

BY ROBERTUS LOVE.

Special to the Post-Dispatch.

HANNIBAL, Mo., May 30.—Mark Twain at 10:30 o'clock visited and identified the old house on Hill street where most of his boyhood was passed.

"Yes, this is the house," he said, while a large crowd of adults and children gathered about him.

"I couldn't recognize the picture, but I recognize the house." He tarried only long enough for a photographer to preserve the incident to posterity's eyes, then entered a carriage with Mrs. John H. Garth, widow of an old-time chum, and was driven to Mt. Olivet Cemetery, where he saw the graves of his parents and brother.

Mr. Clemens did not emerge from his room until 9 o'clock, clad in a fresh suit of clothes to match his hair and a real Panama hat of the circular type. He walked down stairs, remarking that he had slept unusually well. He had remained in his room 16 hours. This afternoon he will attend the Memorial Day exercises at the Presbyterian Church and tonight he will present diplomas to 15 girl graduates and 3 boys of the Hannibal High School class of

THREE POSSIBLE "HUCKS."
CHARLES W. CURTS, aged 70
WILLIA...
EI...

The *Post-Dispatch* covered every moment of Mark's last visit to Missouri. The reporter noted that there were more originals of Huck, Tom, and Becky in Hannibal since Mark's arrival "than one would expect to meet in a staid old town with 23 respectable Sunday schools and a Salvation Army."

The first morning in town Mark visited his old home on Hill Street and was photographed at the front door with the townsfolk looking on.

RETURN TO MISSOURI

An invitation from the University of Missouri to be honored with an LL.D. at the June commencement in 1902 brought Mark Twain home to Missouri for the last time. He stopped first at St. Louis, then was off to Hannibal. To Livy went a midnight report of the first day's events:

"Livy darling, I slept pretty well the second night on the train, & was up at 6 in the morning well rested; shaved & put on a white shirt; breakfasted in my room & was at the same time interviewed by a St. Louis reporter who had mounted the train after midnight.

"Jim Clemens & his cousin a Mr. Cates met me at the station & took me to the Planters, where I stood in the lobby from 8 till noon talking with reporters & hundreds of people; then went to the Pilots' Rooms with Bixby & talked half an hour with the old stagers —several of whom I knew 45 years ago; then to the Merchants' Exchange with its President, & made a 5-minute speech.

"Then back to the hotel & sat or stood & talked with people (& Bryan Clemens) until 2:15; then to the station with Jim & Cates, & started for Hannibal. In the train was accosted by a lady who required me to name her. I said I was sure I could do it. But I had the wit to say that if she would tell me her name I would tell her whether I had guessed correctly or not. It was the widow of Mr. Lakenan. I had known her as a child. We talked 3 hours.

"Arrived at Hannibal 5:30, P.M., I went to the hotel & was in bed in an hour—leaving word that I was not to be disturbed. I read & smoked until 10:30; then to sleep; awoke at 8 this morning; got a hot bath; shaved; put on a fresh white shirt & the lightest gray suit; breakfasted; went & stood in the door of the old house I lived in when I whitewashed the fence 53 years ago; (a big crowd) was photographed, with a crowd looking on.

"Then drove with Mrs. Garth & her daughter to the Cemetery & visited the graves of my people.

"Back to the hotel by 12:30; rested till 2:15 & was driven to the Presbyterian Church & sat on the platform 3½ hours listening to Decoration-Day addresses; made a speech myself.

"Back to the hotel & jumped into evening dress & a fresh white shirt, & was at Mrs. Garth's before 6:30, in

MARK TWAIN DINES WITH HIS SWEETHEART OF OLD TIME DAYS

Sam Clemens and Laura Hawkins Guests at the Costly Mansion of Mrs. Helen Garth—Tears in the Humorist's Eyes at Memorial Meeting.

"MARK TWAIN WEPT AS HE BADE "FAREWELL"

Pathetic Climax of the Humorist's Visit to His Old Home in Hannibal--Men and Women Shed Tears With Him as He Spoke.

DR. MARK TWAIN AT A SMOKE TALK

The LL. D. Entertained by His Cousin,

ALSO VISITED ST. LOUIS CLUB

TAKING AN EXCURSION TODAY ON A BOAT NAMED FOR HIM.

MARK TWAIN AT THE PILOT WHEEL

GREAT HUMORIST BIDS FARE-WELL TO THE MISSISSIPPI.

BOAT NAMED IN HIS HONOR

TWAIN AT UNIVERSITY CLUB

Says His Joy Has Been Made Perfect by the Handshaking of Missourians.

Dr. Samuel H. Clemens showed his appreciation of his new title Friday night in his remarks at the University Club, whose guest he was.

Dr. David S. H. Smith introduced him as Dr. Clemens, and was thanked by the humorist for observing the proprieties. "If I am not called at least 'Doc' from now on," said Mark Twain, "there will be a decided coolness.

"This is a university club. No ignorant person can enter here. You are my collegiate colleagues—perhaps I may say col-

Mark dined with his old schoolmate Laura Hawkins Frazer (the Becky Thatcher of *Tom Sawyer*) and had their picture taken.

time to dine. Laura Hawkins present (schoolmate 62 years ago). Smoked & talked, & was ready at 8 to go to the Opera House & deliver diplomas. (It was High-School Commencement.) Entered by the stage door & sat at the base of a great pyramid of girls dressed in white (the audience not visible, the curtain being down.) When it went up, it rose upon a packed house, & there was great enthusiasm. I listened to the essays 3 hours; then spoke 15 minutes; delivered the diplomas, & shook hands with that crowd of girls & other people an hour—then home.

"In the afternoon (forgot to mention it) the church was crowded; I was speaker No. 3, & when I stepped forward the entire house rose; & they applauded so heartily & kept it up so long, that when they finished I had to stand silent a long minute till I could speak without my voice breaking. At the close I shook hands with everybody. It had been a rushing day, but I have felt no fatigue & feel none now. I love you dearly."

At the Hannibal station, where Mark recognized Tom Nash approaching him. "He was old and white-headed, but the boy of 15 was still visible in him. He came up to me, made a trumpet of his hands at my ear, nodded his head towards the citizens and said confidentially— in a yell like a fog horn—'same damned fools, Sam!'"

The Hannibal High School class of 1902 was unexpectedly favored with a brief commencement address from Mark Twain. A delegation of graduates of the year before—known as the Mark Twain Class because the commencement program dealt with the native son —visited Mark at his hotel to present him with a souvenir spoon engraved with the picture of his house on Hill Street. The girl third from the right later became principal of the town's Mark Twain School.

Stopping again at St. Louis on his way back home, Mark Twain was welcomed aboard the city's harbor boat, named after him, and took the wheel to show he still knew a thing or two about piloting. As the deckhand shouted out the river's depth, the celebrated pilot sang back "Mark Twain—good enough water for anyone; you couldn't improve it without a little whisky."

On June 4, 1902, Twain received his Doctor of Laws degree from the University of Missouri. He led the procession and awarded the diplomas. "If I am not called at least 'Doc' from now on," he said, "there will be a decided coolness." Twain and the men honored with him that day—*first row:* Robert S. Brookings and Twain; *back row:* Secretary of Interior Ethan Allen Hitchcock, Secretary of Agriculture James Wilson, and Beverly Galloway.

INSTRUCTIONS IN ART

That thing in the Right Hand is not a Skillet; it is a Tambourine.

Mark Twain was not just America's foremost writer. Not in his own eyes. He liked to think he was an artist too, especially in portraiture. His first efforts appeared in his brother Orion's Hannibal newspaper in 1852, when he carved those engravings to illustrate his own squibs. How seriously he took this talent is seen in this self-illustrated piece he did for the *Metropolitan* magazine in 1903.

"The great trouble about painting a whole gallery of portraits at the same time is, that the housemaid comes and dusts, and does not put them back the way they were before, and so when the public flock to the studio and wish to know which is Howells and which is Depew and so on, you have to dissemble, and it is very embarrassing at first. Still, you know they are there, and this knowledge presently gives you more or less confidence, and you say sternly, '*This* is Howells,' and watch the visitor's eye. If you see doubt there, you correct yourself and try another. In time you find one that will satisfy, and then you feel relief and joy, but you have suffered much in the meantime; and you know that this joy is only temporary, for the next inquirer will settle on another Howells of a quite different aspect, and one which you suspect is Edward VII or Cromwell, though you keep that to yourself, of course. It is much better to label a portrait when you first paint it, then there is no uncertainty in your mind and you can get bets out of the visitor and win them.

"I believe I have had the most trouble with a portrait which I painted in instalments—the head on one canvas and the bust on another.

"The housemaid stood the bust up sideways, and now I don't know which way it goes. Some authorities think it belongs with the breastpin at the top, under the man's chin; others think it belongs the reverse way, on account of the collar, one of these saying, "A person can wear a breastpin on his stomach if he wants to, but he can't wear his collar anywhere he dern

pleases." There is a certain amount of sense in that view of it. Still, there is no way to determine the matter for certain; when you join the instalments, with the pin under the chin, that seems to be right; then when you reverse it and bring the collar under the chin it seems as right as ever; whichever way you fix it the lines come together snug and convincing, and either way you do it the portrait's face looks equally surprised and rejoiced, and as if it wouldn't be satisfied to have it any way but just that one; in fact, even if you take the bust away altogether the face seems surprised and happy just the same—I have never seen an expression before, which no vicissitudes could alter. I wish I could remember who it is. It looks a little like Washington, but I do not think it can be Washington, because he had as many ears on one side as the other. You can always tell Washington by that; he was very particular about his ears, and about having them arranged the same old way all the time.

"By and by I shall get out of these confusions, and then it will be plain sailing; but first-off the confusions were natural and not to be avoided. My reputation came very suddenly and tumultuously when I published my own portrait, and it turned my head a little, for indeed there was never anything like it. In a single day I got orders from sixty-two people not to paint their portraits, some of them the most distinguished persons in the country—the President, the Cabinet, authors, governors, admirals, candidates for office on the weak side—almost everybody that was anybody, and it would really have turned the head of nearly any beginner to get so much notice and have it come with such a frenzy of cordiality. But I am growing calm and settling down to business, now; and pretty soon I shall cease to be flurried, and then when I do a portrait I shall be quite at myself and able on the

The Head on One Canvas—

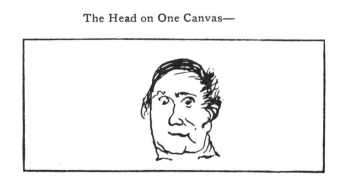

And the Bust on Another.

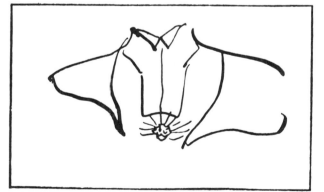

instant to tell it from the others and pick it out when wanted.

"I am living a new and exalted life of late. It steeps me in a sacred rapture to see a portrait develop and take soul under my hand. First, I throw off a study— just a mere study, a few apparently random lines— and to look at it you would hardly ever suspect who it was going to be; even I cannot tell, myself. Take the fourth picture, for instance:

"First you think it's Dante; next you think it's Emerson; then you think it's Wayne MacVeagh. Yet it isn't any of them; it's the beginnings of Depew. Now you wouldn't believe Depew could be devolved out of that; yet the minute it is finished, here you have him to the life, and you say, yourself, 'if that isn't Depew it isn't anybody.'

"Some would have painted him speaking, but he isn't always speaking, he has to stop and think sometimes.

"That is a *genre* picture, as we say in the trade, and differs from the encaustic and other schools in various ways, mainly technical, which you wouldn't understand if I should explain them to you. But you

First you think it's Dante; next you think it's Emerson; then you think it's Wayne McVeagh. Yet it isn't any of them; it's the beginnings of Depew.

Mr. Depew

will get the idea as I go along, and little by little you will learn all that is valuable about Art without knowing how it happened, and without any sense of strain or effort, and then you will know what school a picture belongs to, just at a glance, and whether it is an animal picture or a landscape. It is then that the joy of life will begin for you.

"When you come to examine my portraits of Mr. Howells, Mr. Joe Jefferson and the rest, in the next number of this periodical, your eye will have become measurably educated by that time, and you will recognize at once that no two of them are alike. I will close the present article with an example of the nude, for your instruction.

"The marine picture [on page 239] is intended to educate the eye in the important matters of perspective and foreshortening. The mountainous and bounding waves in the foreground, contrasted with the tranquil ship fading away as in a dream the other side of the fishing-pole convey to us the idea of space and distance as no words could do. Such is the miracle wrought by that wondrous device, perspective.

"The portrait reproduces Mr. Joseph Jefferson, the common friend of the human race. He is fishing, and is not catching anything. This is finely expressed by the moisture in the eye and the anguish of the mouth. The mouth is holding back words. The pole is bamboo, the line is foreshortened. This foreshortening, together with the smoothness of the water away out there where the cork is, gives a powerful impression of distance, and is another way of achieving a perspective effect.

"We now come to the next portrait, which is either Mr. Howells or Mr. Laffan, I cannot tell which, because the label is lost. But it will do for both, because the features are Mr. Howells's, while the expression is Mr. Laffan's. This work will bear critical examination.

"The fourth picture is part of an animal, but I do not know the name of it. It is not finished. The front end of it went around a corner before I could get to it.

"We will conclude with the portrait of a lady, in the style of Raphael. Originally I started it out for Queen Elizabeth, but was not able to do the lace hopper her head projects out of, therefore I tried to turn it into Pocahontas, but was again baffled, and was compelled to make further modifications, this time achieving success. By spiritualizing it and turning it into the noble mother of our race and throwing into the countenance the sacred joy which her first tailor-made outfit infuses into her spirit, I was enabled to add to my gallery the best and most winning and eloquent portrait my brush has ever produced.

"The most effective encouragement a beginner can have is the encouragement which he gets from noting

The portrait reproduces Mr. Joseph Jefferson, the common friend of the human race.

map lying on a table, and step aside, hoping it would attract German soldiers—which it did. They examined it, right side up and upside down, and in other ways, with rising emotion, and discussed it, not in a spirit of calm inquiry, as they should have done, but with lurid violence—which showed that they did not understand it. Upon the average soldier it had the effect of forty-two beers, and was an economy. I could make a very different kind of a map now, if I wanted to. My drawing of the map explains itself. The idea of this map is not original with me, but is borrowed from the great metropolitan journals.

"I claim no other merit for this production (if I may so call it) than that it is accurate. The main blemish of the city paper maps, of which it is an imitation, is that in them more attention seems paid to artistic picturesqueness than geographical reliability.

"Inasmuch as this is the first time I ever tried to draft and engrave a map, or attempted anything in my

his own progress with an alert and persistent eye. Save up your works and date them; as the years go by, run your eye over them from time to time, and measure your advancing stride. This will thrill you, this will nerve you, this will inspire you as nothing else can.

"It has been my own course, and to it I owe the most that I am to-day in Art. When I look back and examine my first effort and then compare it with my latest, it seems unbelievable that I have climbed so high in thirty-one years. Yet so it is. Practice—that is the secret. From three to seven hours a day. It is all that is required. The results are sure; whereas indolence achieves nothing great.

"My first work was a map of Paris. I made it during the Franco-Prussian war. It wrung praises from the most reluctant; I have given them here—read them for yourself. Yet that map has defects in it which anyone can see now; now that Art has progressed so far. For one thing, it lacks delicacy of touch; for another, it lacks spirituality; finally, it merely compels emotion, it furnishes none of its own. I could make twice as good a map now. In Berlin beerhalls, in those days, American students used to leave this

Either Mr. Howells or Mr. Laffan, I cannot tell which, because the label is lost.

It seems unbelievable that I have climbed so high in thirty-one years.

"The reader will comprehend at a glance that that piece of river with the 'High Bridge' over it got left out to one side by reason of a slip of the graving-tool, which rendered it necessary to change the entire course of the River Seine, or else spoil the map. After having spent two days in digging and gouging at the map, I would have changed the course of the Atlantic Ocean before I would lose so much work.

"I never had so much trouble with anything in my life as I had with this map. I had heaps of little fortifications scattered all around Paris at first, but every now and then my instrument would slip and fetch away whole miles of batteries, and leave the vicinity as clean as if the Prussians had been there.

"The reader will find it well to frame this map for future reference, so that it may aid in dispelling the widespread ignorance of the day.

"OFFICIAL COMMENDATIONS.

" 'It is the only map of the kind I ever saw.'

U. S. GRANT.

" 'It places the situation in an entirely new light.'

BISMARCK.

line of art, the commendations the work has received and the admiration it has excited among the people have been very grateful to my feelings. And it is touching to reflect that by far the most enthusiastic of these praises have come from people who knew nothing at all about Art.

"By an oversight, I have engraved the map so that it reads wrong end first, except to left-handed people. I forgot that, in order to make it right in print, it should be drawn and engraved upside down. However, let the student who desires to contemplate the map stand on his head, or hold it before a looking-glass. That will bring it right.

The best and most winning and eloquent portrait my brush has ever produced.

The front end went around a corner before I could get to it.

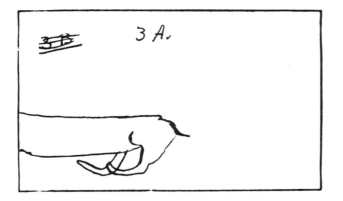

My first work was a map of Paris. I made it during the Franco-Prussian war.

" 'I cannot look upon it without shedding tears.'
BRIGHAM YOUNG.

" 'It is very nice large print.' · NAPOLEON.

" 'My wife was for years afflicted with freckles, and, though everything was done for her relief that could be done, all was in vain. But, sir, since her first glance at your map, they have entirely left her. She has nothing but convulsions now.' J. SMITH.

" 'If I had had this map, I could have got out of Metz without any trouble.' BAZAINE.

" 'I have seen a great many maps in my time, but none that this one reminds me of.' TROCHU.

" 'It is but fair to say that in some respects it is a truly remarkable map.' W. T. SHERMAN.

" 'I said to my son Frederick William, "If you could only make a map like that, I should be perfectly willing to see you die—even anxious."' WILLIAM II.

"This creation, which appears at the beginning of this article, is different from any of the other works. The others are from real life, but this is an example of still-life; so called because it is a portrayal of a fancy only, a thing which has no actual and active existence. The purpose of a still-life picture it to concrete to the eye the spiritual, the intangible, a something which we feel, but cannot see with the fleshly vision—such as joy, sorrow, resentment, and so on. This is best achieved by the employment of that treatment which we call the impressionist, in the trade. The present example is an impressionist picture, done in distemper, with a chiaroscuro motif modified by monochromatic technique, so as to secure tenderness of feeling and spirituality of expression. At a first glance it would seem to be a Botticelli, but it is not that; it is only a humble imitation of that great master of longness and slimness and limbfulness.

"The work is imagined from Greek story, and represents Proserpine or Persepolis, or one of those other Bacchantes doing the solemnities of welcome before the altar of Isis upon the arrival of the annual shipload of Athenian youths in the island of Minos to be sacrificed in appeasement of the Dordonian Cyclops.

"The figure symbolizes solemn joy. It is severely Greek, therefore does not call details of drapery or other factitious helps to its aid, but depends wholly upon grace of action and symmetry of contour for its effects. It is intended to be viewed from the south or south-east, and I think that that is best; for while it expresses more and larger joy when viewed from the east or the north, the features of the face are too much foreshortened and wormy when viewed from that point. That thing in the right hand is not a skillet: it is a tambourine.

"This creation will be exhibited at the Paris Salon in June, and will compete for the *Prix de Rome."*

241

Mark Twain and his wife on the lawn at Dollis Hill House, their home outside London, in the summer of 1900. "Dollis Hill comes nearer to being a paradise than any other home I ever occupied," Twain wrote.

AND NOW SHE IS DEAD . . .

Summers were spent out of town, as usual: 1901 in Saranac, and the next at York Harbor, Maine, where they were conveyed in grand style by Henry Rogers' yacht. In August, 1902, Livy, never well, became critically ill from complications of her goiter and heart disease. She was moved gently back to Riverdale in Oc-

tober, so sick Mark's company was allowed her only a few minutes on some days. Sickness took further toll of the family that winter when pneumonia, followed by measles, attacked Jean and bronchitis put Mark to bed. In the spring Livy picked up a little; they were able to take her to Quarry Farm for her last summer there. In October, 1903, the family sailed for Italy, to live in the Villa di Quarto, in Florence. But the Tuscan winter was miserable and Livy grew worse.

The Twain home in Riverdale, New York, overlooking the Hudson. They lived here from October, 1901, until June, 1903.

242

On Sunday evening, June 5, 1904, Livy seemed bright and cheerful again as Mark sat by her bedside for a half hour. Then he went back to his room, his heart feeling strangely light after the twenty-two months of watching over Livy's suffering: "Then that uplift came again, and grew to an exaltation; and under its influence I did a thing which I have hardly done since we lost our incomparable Susy eight years ago, whose death made a wound in her mother's heart which never healed—I went to the piano and sang the old songs, the quaint Negro hymns which no one cared for when I sang them, except Susy and her mother. When I sang them Susy always came and listened; when she died, my interest in them passed away; I could not put force and feeling into them without the inspiration of her approving presence. But now the force and feeling were all back, in full strength, and I was all alive, and it was as if eight years had fallen from me. In the midst of 'My Lord He call me! He call me by the thunder!' Jean crept into the room and sat down, to my astonishment and—embarrassment; and I stopped, but when she asked me to go on, only the astonishment remained, and it was a pleasant one and inspiring. With great difficulty I brought up little by little the forgotten words of many songs, and Jean remained until a servant came and called her out. After a little I went to my room, and it was now getting toward time to go downstairs and say good-night; for it was quarter past nine, and I must not go later than half-past. At that moment Livy was breathing her last!

"At the head of the stairs I met Miss Lyons, who had come for me.

"Livy was sitting up in bed, with her head bent forward—she had not been able to lie down for seven

Mark and Livy.

months—and Katy was on one side of the bed and the nurse on the other, supporting her; Clara and Jean were standing near the foot of the bed, looking dazed. I went around and bent over and looked into Livy's face, and I think I spoke to her, I do not know; but she did not speak to me, and that seemed strange, I could not understand it. I kept looking at her and wondering—and never dreaming of what had happened! Then Clara said, 'But is it true? Katy, is it true? it can't be true!' Katy burst into sobbings, and then for the first time I knew.

"It was twenty minutes past nine. Only five minutes before, she had been speaking. She had heard me and had said to the nurse, 'He is singing a good-night carol for me.' They had had no idea that she was near to death. She was happy and speaking—and in an instant she was gone from this life. How grateful I was that she had been spared the struggle she had so dreaded. And that I, too, had so dreaded for her. Five times in the last four months she spent an hour and more fighting violently for breath, and she lived in the awful fear of death by strangulation. Mercifully she was granted the gentlest and swiftest of deaths—by heart failure—and she never knew, she never knew!

"She was the most beautiful spirit, and the highest and the noblest I have known. And now she is dead."

From the Hartford *Courant*, April 19, 1902. The house was closed in 1891, when the family moved to Europe. The furniture, stored there for 13 years, was moved to 21 Fifth Avenue when Mark took the New York house in the fall of 1904, after Livy's death.

243

A photo made in 1904, after Mark's return from Florence.

I WISH I WERE WITH LIVY . . .

This was written by Mark two hours after Livy's death. The next day he wrote his friend Howells the news:

"Last night at 9.20 I entered Mrs. Clemens' room to say the usual goodnight—and she was dead—tho' no one knew it. She had been cheerfully talking, a moment before. She was sitting up in bed—she had not lain down for months—and Katie and the nurse were supporting her. They supposed she had fainted, and they were holding the oxygen pipe to her mouth, expecting to revive her. I bent over her and looked in her face, and I think I spoke—I was surprised and troubled that she did not notice me. Then we understood, and our hearts broke. How poor we are to-day!

"But how thankful I am that her persecutions are ended. I would not call her back if I could.

"To-day, treasured in her worn old Testament, I

Mark Twain, about March, 1905.

244

The house at 21 Fifth Avenue, on the southeast corner of Fifth and Ninth Street. Mark Twain moved here with his daughter Jean and his housekeeper Katy Leary, after Livy's death. Clara, who had nursed her mother through her long illness, had collapsed and went to a sanitarium for a year's rest. Twain lived in this Greenwich Village landmark from 1904 to 1908. Despite efforts to establish it as a museum, it was torn down in 1954 to make way for an apartment building.

found a dear and gentle letter from you, dated Far Rockaway, Sept. 13, 1896, about our poor Susy's death. I am tired and old; I wish I were with Livy.

"I send my love—and hers—to you all."

Two days after Livy's passing he was trying to think of what to do next. He asked his friends, the family of Richard Watson Gilder, for help:

"I have been worrying and worrying to know what to do: at last I went to the girls with an idea: to ask the Gilders to get us shelter near their summer home. It was the first time they have not shaken their heads. So to-morrow I will cable to you and shall hope to be in time.

"An hour ago the best heart that ever beat for me and mine went silent out of this house, and I am as one who wanders and has lost his way. She who is gone was our head, she was our hands. We are now trying to make plans—we: we who have never made a plan before, nor ever needed to. If she could speak to us she would make it all simple and easy with a word, and our perplexities would vanish away. If she had known she was near to death she would have told us where to go and what to do: but she was not suspecting, neither were we. (She had been chatting cheerfully a moment before, and in an instant she was gone from us and we did not know it. We were not alarmed, we did not know anything had happened. It was a blessed death—she passed away without knowing it.) She was all our riches and she is gone: she was our breath, she was our life and now we are nothing.

"We send you our love—and with it the love of you that was in her heart when she died."

245

Finley Peter Dunne, who created "Mr. Dooley," a popular newspaper commentator whose salty opinions of American life had much in common with Mark Twain's. In Mark's last years, Dunne and Twain had many billiard sessions together; they usually cost Dunne money. Mark chose Dunne to be one of the few select members of his Human Race Luncheon Club, organized to damn the species.

WRITERS HAVE RIGHTS

One of the few things Mark was able to write in the winter after Livy's death was an open letter on the copyright issue. This was another round in the fight to protect authors' rights which he carried on relentlessly all his professional life. He had lobbied for an improved copyright law in both Washington and London; in December, 1906, he joined another such expedition to the Capitol, using his wit and his white flannels to make headlines. With Howells, Edward Everett Hale and Thomas Nelson Page he appeared before the House Copyright Committee. Pointing out that only one author per year produced a book that outlived the then forty-two-year limit, Mark said, "all that the limited copyright can do is to take the bread out of the mouths of the children of that one author per year." He urged extension of copyright life to the author's life and fifty

years afterward. "I think that would satisfy any reasonable author, because it would take care of his children. Let the grandchildren take care of themselves.

"I am aware that copyright must have a limit, because that is required by the Constitution of the United States, which sets aside the earlier Constitution, which we call the decalogue. The decalogue says you shall not take away from any man his profit. I don't like to be obliged to use the harsh term. What the decalogue really says is, 'Thou shalt not steal,' but I am trying to use more polite language.

"The laws of England and America do take it away, do select but one class, the people who create the literature of the land. They always talk handsomely about the literature of the land, always what a fine great, monumental thing a great literature is, and in the midst of their enthusiasm they turn around and do what they can to discourage it.

"I know we must have a limit, but forty-two years is

246

too much of a limit. I am quite unable to guess why there should be a limit at all to the possession of the product of a man's labor. There is no limit to real estate.

"Doctor Hale has suggested that a man might just as well, after discovering a coal mine and working it forty-two years, have the Government step in and take it away.

"What is the excuse? It is that the author who produced that book has had the profit of it long enough, and therefore the Government takes a profit which does not belong to it and generously gives it to the 88,-000,000 of people. But it doesn't do anything of the kind. It merely takes the author's property, takes his children's bread, and gives the publisher double profit. He goes on publishing the book and as many of his confederates as choose to go into the conspiracy do so, and they rear families in affluence.

"And they continue the enjoyment of those ill-gotten gains generation after generation forever, for they never die. In a few weeks or months or years I shall be out of it, I hope under a monument. I hope I shall not be entirely forgotten, and I shall subscribe to the monument myself. But I shall not be caring what happens if there are fifty years left of my copyright. My copyright produces annually a good deal more than I can use, but my children can use it. I can get along; I know a lot of trades. But that goes to my daughters, who can't get along as well as I can because I have carefully raised them as young ladies, who don't know anything and can't do anything. I hope Congress will extend to them the charity which they have failed to get from me."

NORTH AMERICAN REVIEW

No. DLXXVIII.

JANUARY, 1905.

CONCERNING COPYRIGHT.

AN OPEN LETTER TO THE REGISTER OF COPYRIGHTS.

BY MARK TWAIN.

MARK TWAIN IN WHITE AMUSES CONGRESSMEN

Advocates New Copyright Law and Dress Reform.

WEARS LIGHT FLANNEL SUIT

Says at 71 Dark Colors Depress Him—Talks Seriously of Authors' Right to Profits.

Special to The New York Times.

WASHINGTON, Dec. 7.—Mark Twain spent a busy afternoon at the Capitol to-day, and for half an hour entertained the newspaper correspondents with a characteristic talk. Despite the blustering wind which swept down Pennsylvania Avenue, the author wore a suit of white flannels. In the members' gallery, which he first visited to watch the proceedings of the House, he attracted general attention. Later Mr. Clemens visited the Speaker's

A picture taken at Lakewood, New Jersey, in 1907, at a farewell luncheon for William Dean Howells, who was leaving for Italy. *From left:* Howells, Mark Twain, George Harvey, H. M. Alden, David A. Munro, M. W. Hazeltine. In 1903 Mark had signed a contract that put all his books in Colonel Harvey's firm, Harper & Brothers, and guaranteed him $25,000 a year for five years. The arrangement, negotiated by Henry Rogers, always brought Mark more than the minimum, sometimes twice as much.

Helen Keller (*left*) and her teacher, Annie Sullivan, in 1897.

John Hay, poet, novelist, historian, Theodore Roosevelt's Secretary of State, and Mark Twain's friend. Sick of "that sewer, party politics," Mark watched Hay work for Roosevelt's election in 1904 and wrote Joe Twichell: "I am sorry for John Hay; sorry and ashamed. And yet I know he couldn't help it. He wears the collar, and he had to pay the penalty. Certainly he had no more desire to stand up before a mob of confiding human incapables and debauch them than you had. Certainly he took no more real pleasure in distorting history, concealing facts, propagating immoralities, and appealing to the sordid side of human nature than did you; but he was his party's property, and he had to climb away down and do it."

JOE GOODMAN

Joe Goodman, Mark's old *Territorial Enterprise* editor, had succeeded, after many years, in translating the Mayan inscriptions of Yucatan, and when Mark read his important scientific work in 1902, he wrote his friend: "You think you get 'poor pay' for your twenty years? No, oh no. You have lived in a paradise of the intellect whose lightest joys were beyond the reach of the longest purse in Christendom, you have had daily and nightly emancipation from the world's slaveries and gross interests, you have received a bigger wage than any man in the land, you have dreamed a splendid dream and had it come true, and to-day you could not afford to trade fortunes with anybody—not even with another scientist, for he must divide his spoils with his guild, whereas essentially the world you have discovered is your own and must remain so.

"It is all just magnificent, Joe! And no one is prouder or gladder than

　　　　　　　　Yours always　　　MARK."

Thomas B. Reed, Speaker of the House. "Czar Reed" to Congress; poker player to Mark Twain.

WINSTON CHURCHILL

Two great talkers—Winston Churchill and Mark Twain—crossed paths in New York in 1900. This is Mark's recollection of the encounter:

"There was talk of that soaring and brilliant young statesman, Winston Churchill, son of Lord Randolph

Joseph T. Goodman, in 1907.

Churchill and nephew of a duke. I had met him at Sir Gilbert Parker's seven years before, when he was twenty-three years old, and had met him and introduced him to his lecture audience a year later in New York, when he had come over to tell of the lively experiences he had had as a war correspondent in the South African war, and in one or two wars on the Himalayan frontier of India.

"Sir Gilbert Parker said, 'Do you remember the dinner here seven years ago?'

" 'Yes,' I said, 'I remember it.'

" 'Do you remember what Sir William Vernon Harcourt said about you?'

" 'No.'

" 'Well, you didn't hear it. You and Churchill went up to the top floor to have a smoke and a talk, and Harcourt wondered what the result would be. He said that whichever of you got the floor first would keep it to the end, without a break; he believed that you, being old and experienced, would get it and that Churchill's lungs would have a half-hour's rest for the first time in five years. When you two came down, by and by, Sir William asked Churchill if he had had a good time, and he answered eagerly, 'Yes.' Then he asked you if you had had a good time. You hesitated, then said without eagerness, 'I have had a smoke.' "

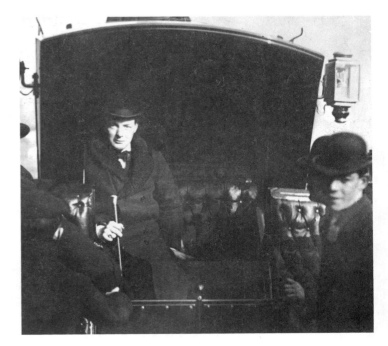

Winston Churchill, catching a cab upon his arrival in New York in 1900.

HELEN KELLER

One Sunday in March, 1895, fourteen-year-old Helen Keller met Mark Twain at Laurence Hutton's. "Mr. Clemens told us many entertaining stories, and it made

Chauncey Depew and his wife. Depew was the Senator from New York whose after-dinner speeches Twain liked to hear.

us laugh till we cried," she wrote a friend. "I think 'Mark Twain' is a very appropriate nom de plume for Mr. Clemens because it has a funny and quaint sound that goes well with his amusing writing, and its nautical significance suggests the deep and beautiful things he has written."

Eighteen months later Mark recorded his impressions of the young girl:

"Helen Keller has been dumb, stone deaf, and stone blind, ever since she was a little baby a year and a half old; and now at sixteen years of age this miraculous creature, this wonder of all ages, passes the Harvard University examination in Latin, German, French history, *belles lettres,* and such things, and does it brilliantly, too, not in a commonplace fashion. She doesn't know merely *things,* she is splendidly familiar with the *meanings* of them. When she writes an essay on a Shakespearean character, her English is fine and strong, her grasp of the subject is the grasp of one who *knows,* and her page is electric with light. Has Miss Sullivan taught her by the methods of India and the American public school? No, oh, no; for then she would be deafer and dumber and blinder than she was before. It is a pity that we can't educate all the children in the asylums."

"It won't do for America to allow this marvelous child to retire from her studies because of poverty," Mark wrote his millionaire friend Rogers. "If she can go with them she will make a fame that will endure in history for centuries." When he asked that funds be raised to finance Helen Keller's education Rogers personally undertook the responsibility.

THE PLUTOCRATS

In Mark Twain's last decade he saw a great deal of Henry Rogers, the Standard Oil chief who had pulled him out of his dollar quicksand. A wolf to his financial rivals, Rogers was a deeply devoted friend to Twain, who delighted in teasing him. "Now, there's Mr. Rogers," Mark said at a banquet, "just out of the affection I bear that man many a time I have given him points in finance that he had never thought of— and if he could lay aside envy, prejudice, and superstition, and utilize those ideas in his business, it would make a difference in his bank account."

Rogers died suddenly in May, 1909, and Mark badly missed the friend who had eased his old age. A few months later he wrote a long tribute to Rogers' "unselfishness where a friend or a cause that was near his heart was concerned."

Mark Twain at Henry Rogers' funeral, May, 1909.

Aboard Henry Rogers' steam yacht, the *Kanawha*, the fastest pleasure craft in the world. Mark joined Rogers' cronies in making many long excursions on the boat. *From left:* Z. S. Freeman (who became a trustee of Twain's estate), Rogers, and Twain. "You see his white mustache and his hair trying to get white?" Mark said of Rogers. "He's always trying to look like me—I don't blame him for that."

ANDREW CARNEGIE

From the time Mark Twain first knew Andrew Carnegie, in the 1890s, he found the little Scottish steelmaster a fascinating study of the "Human Being Unconcealed." The multimillionaire counted Mark one of the most glittering prizes in the Carnegie collection of celebrities and often was generous with him. "For the sake of the future centuries," Mark put down these impressions of Carnegie:

"He has bought fame and paid cash for it; he has deliberately projected and planned out this fame for himself; he has arranged that his name shall be famous in the mouths of men for centuries to come. He has planned shrewdly, safely, securely, and will have his desire. Any town or village or hamlet on the globe can have a public library upon these following unvarying terms; when the applicant shall have raised one-half of the necessary money, Carnegie will furnish the other half, and the library building must permanently bear his name.

"I think that three or four centuries from now Carnegie libraries will be considerably thicker in the world than churches. It is a long-headed idea and will deceive many people into thinking Carnegie a long-headed man in many and many a wise small way—the way of the trimmer, the way of the smart calculator, the way that enables a man to correctly calculate the tides and come in with the flow and go out with the ebb, keeping a permanent place on the top of the wave of advantage while other men as intelligent as he, but more addicted to principle and less to policy, get stranded on the reefs and bars.

"He has never a word of brag about his real achievements; they do not seem to interest him in the least degree; he is only interested—and intensely interested—in the flatteries lavished upon him in the disguise of compliments and in other little vanities which other men would value but conceal. I must repeat he is an astonishing man in his genuine modesty as regards the large things he has done, and in his juvenile delight in trivialities that feed his vanity.

"Mr. Carnegie is not any better acquainted with himself than if he had met himself for the first time day before yesterday. He thinks he is a rude, bluff, independent spirit, who writes his mind and thinks his mind with an almost extravagant Fourth of July independence; whereas he is really the counterpart of the rest of the human race in that he does not boldly speak his mind except when there isn't any danger in it. He thinks he is a scorner of kings and emperors and dukes, whereas he is like the rest of the human race; a slight attention from one of these can make him drunk for a week and keep his happy tongue wagging for seven years."

Once, hearing Mark liked a little Scotch to ease himself into sleep, Carnegie sent him a case of his own preferred brand, direct from Scotland. "Dear St. Andrew," ran Mark's thank-you note, "The whiskey arrived in due course from over the water; last week one bottle of it was extracted from the wood and inserted into me, on the installment plan, with this result: that I believe it to be the best, smoothest whiskey now on the planet. Thanks, oh, thanks! I have discarded Peruna."

Andrew Carnegie at his golf cottage in Westchester, New York. "That foxy, white-whiskered, cunning little face," Mark wrote, which thrilled to "sorrowfully transparent tokens of reverence for his moneybags." In the pre–income tax era Carnegie gleaned 23 million dollars in just one year. His 32,000-acre estate in Scotland was manned by 300 tenants.

On the avenue.

John D. Rockefeller on his way to an investigation of the oil industry. "Satan twaddling sentimental silliness to a Sunday-school," Mark wrote, "could be no burlesque upon John D. Rockefeller and his performances in his Cleveland Sunday-school. When John D. is employed in that way he strikes the utmost limit of grotesqueness. He can't be burlesqued—he is himself a burlesque."

ROCKEFELLER—BIBLE SCHOLAR

"The political and commercial morals of the United States are not merely food for laughter," Mark Twain wrote in 1907, "they are an entire banquet. Like all other nations that worship money and the possessors of it . . . we have the two Roman conditions: stupendous wealth with its inevitable corruptions and moral blight, and the corn and oil pensions—that is to say, vote bribes, which have taken away the pride of thousands of tempted men and turned them into willing alms receivers and unashamed. It is curious—curious that physical courage should be so common in the world, and moral courage so rare."

Morals and commercialism, Mark thought, were strangely combined in that specimen of the new plutocrat, John D. Rockefeller, Jr.:

"One of the standing delights of the American nation in these days is John D. Rockefeller, Junior's Bible Class adventures in theology. Every Sunday young Rockefeller explains the Bible to his class. The next day the newspapers and the Associated Press distribute his

"FROM THE NATURE-FAKER'S GALLERY"

John D. Twain

Mark Rockefeller

John Wanamaker, "The Marvel of Piety." A cartoon from *Puck,* 1889. The department store magnate founded the Bethany Sunday school in 1858. Twain suggested this "butter-mouthed hypocrite" used his "lurid pieties merely as advertisements for his mercantile business." Evidently *Puck's* cartoonist agreed.

explanations all over the continent and everybody laughs. The entire nation laughs, yet in its innocent dullness never suspects that it is laughing at itself. But that is what it is doing.

"Young Rockefeller, who is perhaps thirty-five years old, is a plain, simple, earnest, sincere, honest, well-meaning, commonplace person, destitute of originality or any suggestion of it. And if he were traveling upon his mental merit instead of upon his father's money, his explanations of the Bible would fall silent and not be heard by the public. But his father ranks as the richest man in the world, and this makes his son's theological gymnastics interesting and important. The world believes that the elder Rockefeller is worth a billion dollars. He pays taxes on two million and a half. He is an earnest, uneducated Christian and for years and years has been Admiral of a Sunday school in Cleveland, Ohio. For years and years he has discoursed about himself to his Sunday school and explained how he got his dollars; and during all these years his Sunday school has listened in rapture and has divided its worship between him and his Creator—unequally. His Sunday-school talks are telegraphed about the country and are as eagerly read by the nation as are his son's.

"I have known and liked young John for many years and I have long felt that his right place was in the pulpit. I am sure that the fox fire of his mind would make a proper glow there—but I suppose he must do as destiny has decreed and succeed his father as master of the colossal Standard Oil Corporation."

When Mark Twain incorporated his pen name to protect his copyrights, the New York *World* published this cartoon.

Mark Twain in 1906.

THE DAMNED HUMAN RACE

Twain and Howells, perhaps the country's two most noted literary figures, were seeing a great deal of each other in these days. "We agree perfectly about the Boer War, and the Filipino War, and war generally," Howells told his sister. Manifestos and proclamations designed to arouse the country against the "inhuman methods" the McKinley administration was using against the Filipinos were signed by both men. Twain's anger fired more broadsides against government policy, but most of it went unpublished. In May, 1902, however, the *North American Review* published Twain's "A Defense of General Funston," a savage condemnation of the American military leader's capture of Aguinaldo, the Filipino resistance leader, by a trick. Funston, home from the war to be hailed as a hero, advised his critics to be silent or risk being labeled traitor. Twain argued that Funston couldn't be blamed for his unsavory conduct "because his conscience leaked out through one of his pores when he was little."

THE GOSPEL OF ST. MARK

"I have been reading the morning paper," Mark Twain wrote Howells from Vienna in 1899. "I do it every morning—well knowing that I shall find in it the usual depravities and basenesses and hypocrisies and cruelties that make up civilization, and cause me to put in the rest of the day pleading for the damnation of the human race. I cannot seem to get my prayers answered, yet I do not despair."

Not long after—for New Year's Eve, 1900—Mark sent out to the world this message:

"A salutation-speech from the Nineteenth Century to the Twentieth, taken down in shorthand by Mark Twain:

"I bring you the stately matron named Christendom, returning, bedraggled, besmirched, and dishonored, from pirate raids in Kiao-Chou, Manchuria, South Africa, and the Philippines, with her soul full of meanness, her pocket full of boodle, and her mouth full of pious hypocrisies. Give her soap and towel, but hide the looking-glass."

He was warming up to his favorite subject—the damned human race. It was his searching comment upon what he saw going on in the far corners of the world, where the African, the Filipino, and the Chinese were receiving the blessings of Christianity and the bounty of civilization. Journeying across South Africa in 1896, Mark had sided with the Africans against the English and the Boers, and three years later had stood by the Boers in their resistance to British invasion. When the war with Spain began in 1898, Mark had at

Andrew Carnegie put up $1,000 to reprint this "holy little missal" in a pamphlet disseminated by the Anti-Imperialist League—"the only missionary work," Carnegie said, "I am responsible for."

NORTH AMERICAN REVIEW.

No. DXXXI.

FEBRUARY, 1901.

TO THE PERSON SITTING IN DARKNESS.

BY MARK TWAIN.

General Frederick Funston,
Aguinaldo's captor.

A DEFENCE OF GENERAL FUNSTON.

BY MARK TWAIN.

I.

February 22. To-day is the great Birth-Day; and it was observed so widely in the earth that differences in longitudinal time made curious work with some of the cabled testimonies of respect paid to the sublime name which the date calls up in our minds; for, although they were all being offered at about the same hour, several of them were yesterday to us and several were to-morrow.

There was a reference in the papers to General Funston.

Neither Washington nor Funston was made in a day. It took a long time to accumulate the materials. In each case, the basis or moral skeleton of the man was inborn disposition—a thing which is as permanent as rock, and never undergoes any actual or genuine change between cradle and grave. In each case, the moral flesh-bulk (that is to say, *character*) was built and shaped around the skeleton by training, association and circumstances. Given a crooked-disposition skeleton, no power nor influence in the earth can mould a permanently shapely form around it. Training, association and circumstances can truss it, and brace it, and prop it, and strain it, and crowd it into an artificial shapeliness that can endure till the end, deceiving not only the spectator but the man himself. But there is nothing there but artificiality, and if at any time the props and trusses chance to be removed, the form will collapse into its proper and native crookedness.

Washington did not create the basic skeleton (disposition) that was in him; it was born there, and the merit of its perfection was not his. It—and only It—moved him to seek and prefer associations which were contenting to Its spirit; to welcome influences which pleased It and satisfied It; and to repel or be indif-

Emilio Aguinaldo, head of the Filipino independence movement. He was elected President of the Philippines in 1898.

first supported what he thought was an effort to free Cuba. But early in 1900, with the United States now fighting in the Philippines, he came to feel, as he told the New York *Herald,* that "we do not intend to free but to subjugate the people. We have gone there to conquer, not to redeem. It should, it seems to me, be our pleasure and duty to make those people free and let them deal with their own domestic questions in their own way. And so I am an anti-imperialist. I am opposed to having the eagle put its talons on any other land."

In the case of the Boxer Rebellion, Mark said, "my sympathies are with the Chinese. They have been villainously dealt with by the sceptered thieves of Europe, and I hope they will drive all the foreigners out and keep them out for good. We have no more business in China than in any other country that is not ours."

While Mark's "Greeting" to the twentieth century was being distributed widely on small cards printed by the Anti-Imperialist League, he was hard at work on an article whose appearance in print, Howells said, would make the public want to hang him. It was Twain's "To the Person Sitting in Darkness," and Howells was half right about it. Mark's attack upon the imperialism of all nations brought him both furious condemnation and high praise, showing, Mark said, that "the nation is divided, half-patriots and half-traitors, and no man can tell which is which."

The issue, Twain wrote, is this: *"Shall we?* That is, shall we go on conferring our Civilization upon the peoples that sit in darkness, or shall we give those poor things a rest? Shall we bang right ahead in our old-time, loud, pious way, and commit the new century to the game; or shall we sober up and sit down and think it over first? Would it not be prudent to get our Civilization-tools together, and see how much stock is left on hand in the way of Glass Beads and Theology, and Maxim guns and Hymn Books, and Trade-Gin and Torches of Progress and Enlightenment (patent adjustable ones, good to fire villages with, upon occasion), and balance the books, and arrive at the profit and loss, so that we may intelligently decide whether to continue the business or sell out the property and start a new Civilization Scheme on the proceeds?"

"Can the Missionary Reach This Old Savage?"

KING LEOPOLD'S SOLILOQUY

To the bill of particulars he drew up against the Great Powers for the way they exercised their "unwilling" missions in South Africa, China, and the Philippines, Mark now added the crime of King Leopold's rule in the Congo. The Belgian monarch had taken control of the lives of twenty million Africans. Investigators revealed he had dispossessed the people and built a huge fortune upon their forced labor.

"The royal palace of Belgium," Mark pointed out in 1906, "is still what it has been for fourteen years, the den of a wild beast, King Leopold II, who for money's sake mutilates, murders and starves half a million of friendless and helpless poor natives in the Congo State every year, and does it by the silent consent of all the Christian powers except England, none of them lifting a hand or a voice to stop these atrocities, although thirteen of them are by solemn treaty pledged to the protecting and uplifting of those wretched natives. In fourteen years Leopold has deliberately de-stroyed more lives than have suffered death on all the battlefields of this planet for the past thousand years. In this vast statement I am well within the mark, several millions of lives within the mark. It is curious that the most advanced and most enlightened century of all the centuries the sun has looked upon should have the ghastly distinction of having produced this moldy and piety-mouthing hypocrite, this bloody monster whose mate is not findable in human history anywhere, and whose personality will surely shame hell itself when he arrives there—which will be soon, let us hope and trust.

"The conditions under which the poor lived in the Middle Ages were hard enough, but those conditions were heaven itself as compared with those which have obtained in the Congo State for these past fourteen years."

The 25¢ pamphlet Twain wrote in 1905. Proceeds went to the relief of the Congo people.

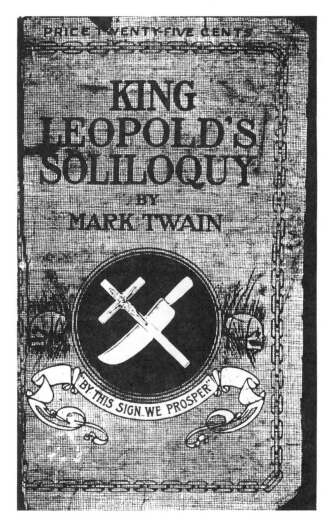

King Leopold of the Belgians, in 1905.

Out of the protests of explorers and missionaries came the Congo Reform Association which asked Mark Twain to lend his voice "for the cause of the Congo natives." *King Leopold's Soliloquy* was his answer, an article which no American magazine would print. It reached the public only as a pamphlet issued by the Congo reform groups in America and England. It was greeted as "a trenchant satire" from "a writer of remarkable courage." Americans with investments in the Congo co-operated with Leopold's agents to suppress editorial comment on and cut distribution of Mark's pamphlet; they even countered with *An Answer to Mark Twain*, accusing him of "an infamous libel." But Mark Twain's voice counted in the worldwide clamor that in 1908 helped bring the Leopoldian atrocities in the Congo to an end.

MR. CLEMENS AND THE MARKED TWAIN.

The London *Daily Chronicle* pays tribute in 1907 to Mark Twain's crusades.

CHRISTIAN SCIENCE.

BY MARK TWAIN.

I.

LET us consider that we are all partially insane. It will explain us to each other; it will unriddle many riddles; it will make clear and simple many things which are involved in haunting and harassing difficulties and obscurities now.

Those of us who are not in the asylum, and not demonstrably due there, are nevertheless, no doubt, insane in one or two particulars. I think we must admit this; but I think that we are otherwise healthy-minded. I think that when we all see one thing alike, it is evidence that, as regards that one thing, our

"Somehow I continue to feel sure of that cult's colossal future . . . I am selling my Lourdes stock already & buying Christian Science trust. I regard it as the Standard Oil of the future." Mark had allowed Christian Science healers to practice on his family. But that did not prevent his seeing humor in some aspects of Mary Baker Eddy's writings. He published several articles such as this in the *North American Review*, chiefly because he feared the growth of any established church as a danger to freedom.

"One of my theories is," Mark Twain wrote in 1901, "that the hearts of men are about alike, all over the world, no matter what their skin-complexions may be." This was a major theme in his work. Above he is seated on the stage of Carnegie Hall, just behind Booker T. Washington, who is speaking. Mark was co-chairman of the 25th anniversary celebration on January 22, 1906, of the founding of Tuskegee Institute.

WHO KILLED CROKER?

When the 1901 municipal election came up in New York, that Mugwump, Mark Twain, happily seized the chance to flay Tammany again. It had been Boss Tweed thirty years ago; now it was Boss Croker. The point was the same, he felt. A handful of corrupt politicians were able to plunge their arms in up to their elbows in the city treasury because the honest voters were unorganized. Mark joined the Acorns, organized to elect Seth Low mayor on a fusion ticket. It was his last political campaign, and it was successful.

TR: POLITICAL TOM SAWYER

Theodore Roosevelt was in the White House during most of Mark Twain's last decade. Despite his reputation as a "trust-buster," TR never impressed Twain. Nor did Roosevelt's office cause Mark to muffle his voice: "Yesterday, for the first time, business was opened to commerce by the Marconi Company and wireless messages sent entirely across the Atlantic, straight from shore to shore; and on that same day the President of the United States for the fourteenth time came within three miles of flushing a bear. As usual he was far away, nobody knew where, when the bear

burst upon the multitude of dogs and hunters and equerries and chamberlains in waiting, and sutlers and cooks and scullions, and Rough Riders and infantry and artillery, and had his customary swim to the other side of a pond and disappeared in the woods. While half the multitude watched the place where he vanished, the other half galloped off, with horns blowing, to scour the State of Louisiana in search of the great hunter. Why don't they stop hunting the bear altogether and hunt the President? He is the only one of the pair that can't be found when he is wanted.

"He was in a skirmish once at San Juan Hill, and he got so much moonshine glory out of it that he has never been able to stop talking about it since. I remember that at a small luncheon party of men at Brander Matthews' house once, he dragged San Juan Hill in three or four times, in spite of all attempts of the judicious to abolish the subject and introduce an interesting one in its place. I think the President is clearly insane in several ways, and insanest upon war and its supreme glories. I think he longs for a big war wherein he can spectacularly perform as chief general and chief admiral, and go down in history as the only monarch of modern times that has served both offices at the same time.

"Mr. Roosevelt is the Tom Sawyer of the political world of the twentieth century; always showing off; always hunting for a chance to show off; in his frenzied imagination the Great Republic is a vast Barnum circus with him for a clown and the whole world for audience; he would go to Halifax for half a chance to show off, and he would go to hell for a whole one."

That was Twain in his autobiography. In a letter to Twichell, in 1905, he had another go at the President, this time from a somewhat different angle:

"I knew I had in me somewhere a definite feeling about the President if I could only find the words to define it with. Here they are, to a hair—from Leonard Jerome: 'For twenty years I have loved Roosevelt the man and hated Roosevelt the statesman and politician.'

"It's mighty good. Every time, in 25 years, that I have met Roosevelt the man, a wave of welcome has streaked through me with the hand-grip; but whenever (as a rule) I meet Roosevelt the statesman and politician, I find him destitute of morals and not respectworthy. It is plain that where his political self and his party self are concerned he has nothing resembling a conscience; that under those inspirations he is naively indifferent to the restraints of duty and even unaware of them; ready to kick the Constitution into the back yard whenever it gets in the way; and whenever he smells a vote, not only willing but eager to buy it, give extravagant rates for it and pay the bill—not out of his own pocket or the party's, but out of the nation's, by cold pillage. As per Order 78 and the appropriation of the Indian trust funds.

Harper's Weekly comments on the President as author.

MARK TWAIN
WILL FIGHT
TAMMANY.

The two opponents square off in a newspaper cartoon.

"But Roosevelt is excusable—I recognize it and (ought to) concede it. We are all insane, each in his own way, and with insanity goes irresponsibility. Theodore the man is sane; in fairness we ought to keep in mind that Theodore, as statesman and politician, is insane and irresponsible.

"Do not throw these enlightenments aside, but study them, let them raise you to higher planes and make you better. You taught me in my callow days, let me pay back the debt now in my old age out of a thesaurus with wisdom smelted from the golden ores of experience.

"Ever yours for sweetness and light."

"TALL OAKS FROM LITTLE
ACORNS GROW."

350 BROADWAY, NEW YORK.

EDMUND BURKE
... ON ...
Croker and Tammany,

By MARK TWAIN,
A Member of the Order of Acorns.

NOTE.—This article, delivered as an address before the Organization Committee of the Acorns, at the Waldorf-Astoria, Thursday evening, October 17, was originally prepared for the "North American Review." Col. G. B. M. Harvey, publisher of the "Review," seeing its great force, agreed that the article should first appear as an address, in order that it reach the citizens of New York before the publication of the November issue of the "North American Review."

GREAT Britain had a Tammany and a Croker a good while ago. This Tammany was in India, and it began its career with the spread of the English dominion after the battle of Plassey. Its first Boss was Clive, a sufficiently crooked person sometimes, but straight as a yardstick when compared with the corkscrew crookedness of the second Boss, Warren Hastings. That old-time

The anti-Tammany group, the Acorns, published Mark's speech which paralleled Burke's impeachment of Hastings. The pamphlet helped defeat Tammany.

"TALL OAKS FROM LITTLE ACORNS GROW."
ORDER OF ACORNS.

APPLICATION BLANK.

I hereby pledge my support to the principles of the Order of Acorns, and express my purpose to register and cast my vote for the Fusion ticket, City and County.

Name St. Clemens

Address Riverdale, New York City

Assembly District

Mark Twain filled out one of these. How about you? The Order of Acorns purposes to restore honesty, decency and common sense to the administration of City Government. Fill out the application blank below, cut it out, and mail it or bring it to our headquarters, 350 Broadway.   THE GREAT OAK.

The Acorns used Mark's great prestige in circulating this pledge.

Seth Low, president of Columbia College, elected Mayor of New York in 1901 on the fusion ticket Mark Twain supported.

Richard Croker, Tammany chief. After Fusion's victory one paper said:
"Who Killed Croker?
I, said Mark Twain,
I killed the Croker,
I, the jolly joker."

Czar Nicholas in his dress uniform. In the "Soliloquy" Twain strips the Emperor of his clothes to reveal the true object of Russian worship.

NORTH AMERICAN REVIEW

No. DLXXX.

MARCH, 1905.

THE CZAR'S SOLILOQUY.

BY MARK TWAIN.

After the Czar's morning bath it is his habit to meditate an hour before dressing himself.—London Times Correspondence.

[*Viewing himself in the pier-glass.*] Naked, what am I? A lank, skinny, spider-legged libel on the image of God! Look at the waxwork head—the face, with the expression of a melon—the projecting ears—the knotted elbows—the dished breast—the knife-edged shins—and then the feet, all beads and joints and bone-sprays, an imitation X-ray photograph! There is nothing imperial about this, nothing imposing, impressive, nothing to invoke awe and reverence. Is it this that a hundred and forty million Russians kiss the dust before and worship? Manifestly not! No one could worship this spectacle, which is Me. Then who is it, what is it, that they worship? Privately, none knows better than I: it is my clothes. Without my clothes I should be as destitute of authority as any other naked person. Nobody could

THE GORKY AFFAIR

Czar Nicholas II was as popular with Mark Twain as King Leopold. Mark was not alone in his contempt for the Russian ruler. Hoping it would help the Russians get rid of their autocracy, many Americans wished for a Japanese victory in the Russo-Japanese War of 1905. The sufferings of political prisoners in Siberia so incensed Twain that he thought lighting a bonfire under the Russian throne to "fry the Czar" would make sense.

"Bloody Sunday"—that January day in 1905 when the Cossacks in St. Petersburg killed and wounded thousands of Russians petitioning before the Winter Palace for food and clothing—brought Mark's passion into the open. He published "The Czar's Soliloquy" in March, calling for revolution in Russia. The negotiated peace saving the Czar from a rout cut short Twain's hope that the Russians would find "the high road to emancipation from an insane and intolerable slavery." He predicted the Czar would now "resume his mediaeval barbarism with a relieved spirit and an immeasurable joy."

When the Revolution of 1905 broke out, young Maxim Gorky, whose international literary reputation had made him a symbol of his suffering people, came to the United States to win financial and moral support for the cause of Russian freedom. His welcome was prepared by the A Club, a group of intellectuals who met at 3 Fifth Avenue, down the block from Mark Twain's home at 21. Mark became chairman of the committee to organize Gorky's U.S. tour, with Howells, Jane Addams, Arthur Brisbane, Finley Peter Dunne, Robert Collier, and S. S. McClure as members. On April 11, 1906, Gorky, dressed in blue peasant blouse and trousers tucked into high boots, was introduced at the A Club by Mark Twain. "Our deepest sympathy," Mark said, "belongs to a people who, as our own ancestors did, are trying to free themselves from an evil oppression. If we keep our hearts in this matter, Russia shall and will be free."

The next morning Gorky toured the city as guest of Hearst's *American,* for whom he was to write exclusive articles, received Twain and Howells in the afternoon, and saw Barnum & Bailey's circus in Madison Square Garden that night. But the next day a headline in the *World*—"GORKY BRINGS ACTRESS HERE AS MME. GORKY"—wrecked the Russian writer's mission. Gorky, who had parted by mutual consent with his first wife, had been living with Mme. Andreyeva of the Moscow Art Theater for three years. She was considered Gorky's completely respectable common-law wife by the Russians, and remained so the rest of his long life, but the Russian Embassy in Washington used the rivalry between Hearst and the *World* to break the exposé. The couple was ousted from several hotels and the furore made Mark Twain feel Gorky was disabled for the work of raising funds. He has made a "bad mistake," Mark said. "Poor fellow, he didn't understand our bigotry. He might as well have come over here in his shirt-tail."

The tour collapsed, but Gorky did not blame "the esteemed Mark Twain" for withdrawing his support from a hopeless effort.

Later that same year, Mark said of Russia: "Cruel and pitiful as was life throughout Christendom in the Middle Ages, it was not as cruel, not as pitiful, as is life in Russia today. In Russia for three centuries the vast population has been ground under the heels, and for the sole and sordid advantage of a procession of crowned assassins and robbers who have all deserved the gallows. Russia's hundred and thirty millions of miserable subjects are much worse off today than were the poor of the Middle Ages whom we so pity. We are accustomed now to speak of Russia as medieval and as standing still in the Middle Ages, but that is flattery. Russia is way back of the Middle Ages; the Middle Ages are a long way in front of her and she is not likely to catch up with them so long as the Czardom continues to exist."

The report of the dinner for Gorky at the A Club. Mark Twain told the press: "I am said to be a revolutionist in my sympathies, by birth, by breeding and by principle. I am always on the side of the revolutionists, because there never was a revolution unless there were some oppressive and intolerable conditions against which to revolute."

Maxim Gorky and Mme. Andreyeva, photographed in New York on their 1906 visit to America. Gorky was 38 then, and popular here through his books, stories, and articles. To many critics he was the new Tolstoy. Mme. Andreyeva had performed in his plays at the Moscow Art Theatre. At the pier, thousands welcomed Gorky with an ovation the *Times* reported "rivaled the welcome given Kossuth and Garibaldi."

Two days after Gorky's arrival, the *World* depicted Mark Twain shoving the Czar off his throne with a push of the pen.

261

THE BANQUETEERING HABIT

Toward the end of 1907, Mark Twain reviewed his social calendar and congratulated himself: "I have been leading a quiet and wholesome life now during two entire banqueteering, speechmaking seasons. These seasons begin in September and last until the end of April; it is half a year. Banquets run late, and by the end of the season the habitual banqueteer is haggard and worn facially, and drowsy in his mind and weak on his legs."

For thirty-six years Twain had kept up the banqueteering habit. Then he tried the tapering-off system used by hard drinkers, but found only the pledge of absolute abstinence would work. As a retired veteran of the table wars he described a typical engagement:

"I wonder what the banquet will be a century from now. If it has not greatly improved by that time it ought to be abolished. It is a dreadful ordeal and in my long experience it has shown not a shade of improvement; I believe it is even worse now than it was a generation ago. The guests gather at half past seven in the evening and stand and chat half an hour and weary themselves with the standing and chatting; then they march out in procession in double file, with the chairman and the chief guest in the lead, and the crashing and deafening clamor of the music breaks out; the guests seat themselves and begin to talk to each other softly, sanely, then a little louder, and a little louder, and still a little louder, each group trying to

Cesare's caricature of Mark Twain teasing Andrew Carnegie at a dinner in "Saint Andrew's" honor in 1907. Carnegie's passion for simplified spelling, said Mark, "is all right enough, but, like chastity, you can carry it too far."

make itself heard above the general din, and before long everybody is shrieking and shouting; knives and forks and plates are clattering, and a man might as well be in pandemonium as far as personal comfort is concerned. This used to continue an hour and a half; then at half past nine the speaking began, and continued for an hour; then the insurrection ceased and the survivors went home.

"Years ago, in order to save my life, I adopted the system of feeding at home, then starting to the banquet in time to reach it when the banquet was over and the speaking ready to begin—say at half past nine; then leaving the place upon one pretext or another as soon as I had emptied my speech upon the assembled sufferers."

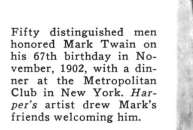

Fifty distinguished men honored Mark Twain on his 67th birthday in November, 1902, with a dinner at the Metropolitan Club in New York. *Harper's* artist drew Mark's friends welcoming him.

THE ART OF SPEECHMAKING

Like many another speechmaker "long accustomed to success and to the delicious intoxication of the applause which follows it," Mark Twain was "fast in the grip of this fell, degrading, demoralizing vice." From time to time he took an oath to never make another speech, resorting even to a money penalty to strengthen his reform. But he never was able to resist the passion for long. In 1884—in an after-dinner speech, of course!—he confided what masters of "the deep art" of speech-making had learned:

"They have learned their art by long observation and slowly compacted experience; so now they know what they did not know at first, that the best and most telling speech is not the actual impromptu one, but the counterfeit of it; they know that that speech is most worth listening to which has been carefully prepared in private and tried on a plaster cast, or an empty chair, or any other appreciative object that will keep quiet until the speaker has got his matter and his delivery limbered up so that they will seem impromptu to an audience. The expert knows that. A touch of indifferent grammar flung in here and there, apparently at random, has a good effect—often restores the confidence of a suspicious audience. He arranges these errors in private; for a really random error wouldn't do any good; it would be sure to fall in the wrong place. He also leaves blanks here and there—leaves them where genuine impromptu remarks can be dropped in, of a sort that will add to the natural aspect of the speech without breaking its line of march. At the banquet he listens to the other speakers, invents happy turns upon remarks of theirs, and sticks these happy turns into his blanks for impromptu use by and by when he shall be called up. When this expert rises to his feet, he looks around over the house with the air

Mark Twain joins a Congress of Writers in toasting Rudyard Kipling in 1898.

Twain amuses his friends at the Lotos Club in New York.

of a man who has just been strongly impressed by something. The uninitiated cannot interpret his aspect; but the initiated can.

"They know what is coming. When the noise of the clapping and the stamping has subsided this veteran says: 'Aware that the hour is late, Mr. Chairman, it was my intention to abide by a purpose which I framed in the beginning of the evening—to simply rise and return my duty and thanks, in case I should be called upon, and then make way for men more able and who have come with something to say. But, sir, I was so struck by General Smith's remark concerning the proneness of evil to fly upward, that'—etc., etc., etc., and before you know it he has slidden smoothly along on his compliment to the general, and out of it and into his set speech, and you can't tell, to save you, where it was nor when it was that he made the connection. And that man will soar along, in the most beautiful way, on the wings of a practiced memory, heaving in a little decayed grammar here, and a little wise tautology there, and a little neatly counterfeited embarrassment yonder, and a little finely acted stumbling and stammering for a word, rejecting this word and that, and finally getting the right one, and fetching it out with ripping effect, and with the glad look of a man who has got out of a bad hobble entirely by accident—and wouldn't take a hundred dollars down for that accident; and every now and then he will sprinkle you in one of those happy turns on something that has previously been said; and at last, with supreme art, he will catch himself, when in the very act of sitting down, and lean over the table and fire a parting rocket, in the way of an afterthought, which makes everybody stretch his mouth as it goes up, and dims the very stars in the heaven when it explodes. And yet that man has been practicing that afterthought and that attitude for about a week."

263

The cover of the menu for the dinner at Delmonico's. George Harvey of *Harper's* arranged it.

THE SEVENTIETH BIRTHDAY

On Mark Twain's seventieth birthday nearly two hundred literary figures gathered to honor America's most distinguished writer and citizen. One after another, his old friends rose to pay loving tribute to Mark Twain. Finally, upon William Dean Howells' introduction, Mark made this speech:

"I have had a great many birthdays in my time. I remember the first one very well, and I always think of it with indignation; everything was so crude, unaesthetic, primeval. Nothing like this at all. No proper appreciative preparation made; nothing really ready. No, for a person born with high and delicate instincts— why, even the cradle wasn't whitewashed—nothing ready at all. I hadn't any hair, hadn't any teeth, I hadn't any clothes, I had to go to my first banquet just like that. Well, everybody came swarming in. It was the merest little bit of a village—hardly that, just a little hamlet, in the backwoods of Missouri, where nothing ever happened, and the people were all interested, and they all came; they looked me over to see if there was anything fresh in my line. Why, nothing ever happened in that village—I—why, I was the only thing that had really happened there for months and months; and although I say it myself that shouldn't, I came the nearest to being a real event that had happened in that village in more than two years. Well, those people came, they came with that curiosity which is so provincial, with that frankness which also is so provincial, and they examined me all around and gave

At the table of the guest of honor sat (*from left*) Kate Douglas Riggs, Mark Twain, Rev. Joseph Twichell, Bliss Carmen, Ruth E. Stuart, Mary E. W. Freeman, Henry Mills Alden, Henry H. Rogers.

their opinion. Nobody asked them, and I shouldn't have minded if anybody had paid me a compliment, but nobody did. Their opinions were all just green with prejudice, and I feel those opinions to this day. Well, I stood that as long as—you know I was courteous, and I stood it to the limit. I stood it an hour, and then the worm turned. I was the worm; it was my turn to turn, and I turned. I knew very well the strength of my position; I knew that I was the only spotlessly pure and innocent person in that whole town, and I came out and said so. And they could not say a word. It was so true. They blushed; they were embarrassed. Well, that was the first after-dinner speech I ever made. I think it was after dinner.

"It's a long stretch between that first birthday speech and this one. That was my cradle song, and this is my swan song, I suppose. I am used to swan songs; I have sung them several times.

"This is my seventieth birthday, and I wonder if you all rise to the size of that proposition, realizing all the significance of that phrase, seventieth birthday.

"The seventieth birthday! It is the time of life when you arrive at a new and awful dignity; when you may throw aside the decent reserves which have oppressed you for a generation and stand unafraid and unabashed upon your seven-terraced summit and look down and teach—unrebuked. You can tell the world how you got there. It is what they all do. You shall never get tired of telling by what delicate arts and deep moralities you climb up to that great place. You will explain the process and dwell on the particulars with senile rapture. I have been anxious to explain my own system this long time, and now at last I have the right.

"I have achieved my seventy years in the usual way: by sticking strictly to a scheme of life which would kill anybody else. It sounds like an exaggeration, but that is really the common rule for attaining old age. When we examine the programme of any of these garrulous old people we always find that the habits which have preserved them would have decayed us; that the way of life which enabled them to live upon the property of their heirs so long, as Mr. Choate says, would have put us out of commission ahead of time. I will offer here, as a sound maxim, this: That we can't reach old age by another man's road.

"I will now teach, offering my way of life to whomsoever desires to commit suicide by the scheme which has enabled me to beat the doctor and the hangman for seventy years. Some of the details may sound untrue, but they are not. I am not here to deceive; I am here to teach.

"We have no permanent habits until we are forty. Then they begin to harden, presently they petrify, then business begins. Since forty I have been regular about going to bed and getting up—and that is one of the main things. I have made it a rule to go to bed when there wasn't anybody left to sit up with; and I have made it a rule to get up when I had to. This has resulted in an unswerving regularity of irregularity. It has saved me sound, but it would injure another person.

"In the matter of diet—which is another main thing —I have been persistently strict in sticking to the things which didn't agree with me until one or the other of us got the best of it. Until lately I got the best of it myself. But last spring I stopped frolicking with mince pie after midnight; up to then I had always believed it wasn't loaded. For thirty years I have taken

Inside, the menu sketched some highlights of Twain's life.

265

DECEMBER

HIS 70TH BIRTHDAY.

Life's cartoonist enjoyed Mark's reference to his elevated taste in cigars.

coffee and bread at eight in the morning, and no bite nor sup until seven-thirty in the evening. Eleven hours. That is all right for me, and is wholesome, because I have never had a headache in my life, but headachy people would not reach seventy comfortably by that road, and they would be foolish to try it. And I wish to urge upon you this—which I think is wisdom—that if you find you can't make seventy by any but an uncomfortable road, don't you go. When they take off the Pullman and retire you to the rancid smoker, put on your things, count your checks, and get out at the first way station where there's a cemetery.

"I have made it a rule never to smoke more than one cigar at a time. I have no other restriction as regards smoking. I do not know just when I began to smoke, I only know that it was in my father's lifetime, and that I was discreet. He passed from this life early in 1847, when I was a shade past eleven; ever since then I have smoked publicly. As an example to others, and not that I care for moderation myself, it has always been my rule never to smoke when asleep, and never to refrain when awake. It is a good rule. I mean, for me; but some of you know quite well that it wouldn't answer for everybody that's trying to get to be seventy.

"I smoke in bed until I have to go to sleep; I wake up in the night, sometimes once, sometimes twice, sometimes three times, and I never waste any of these opportunities to smoke. This habit is so old and dear and precious to me that I would feel as you, sir, would feel if you should lose the only moral you've got—meaning the chairman—if you've got one: I am making no charges. I will grant, there, that I have stopped smoking now and then, for a few months at a time, but it was not on principle, it was only to show off; it was to pulverize those critics who said I was a slave to my habits and couldn't break my bonds.

"To-day it is all of sixty years since I began to smoke the limit. I have never bought cigars with life belts around them. I early found that those were too expensive for me. I have always bought cheap cigars—reasonably cheap, at any rate. Sixty years ago they cost me four dollars a barrel, but my taste has im-

proved, latterly, and I pay seven now. Six or seven. Seven, I think. Yes, it's seven. But that includes the barrel. I often have smoking parties at my house; but the people that come have always just taken the pledge. I wonder why that is?

"As for drinking, I have no rule about that. When the others drink I like to help; otherwise I remain dry, by habit and preference. This dryness does not hurt me, but it could easily hurt you, because you are different. You let it alone.

"Since I was seven years old I have seldom taken a dose of medicine, and have still seldomer needed one. But up to seven I lived exclusively on allopathic medicines. Not that I needed them, for I don't think I did; it was for economy; my father took a drug store for a debt, and it made cod-liver oil cheaper than the other breakfast foods. We had nine barrels of it, and it lasted me seven years. Then I was weaned. The rest of the family had to get along with rhubarb and ipecac and such things, because I was the pet. I was the first Standard Oil Trust. I had it all. By the time the drug store was exhausted my health was established and there has never been much the matter with me since. But you know very well it would be foolish for the average child to start for seventy on that basis. It happened to be just the thing for me, but that was merely accident; it couldn't happen again in a century.

"I have never taken any exercise, except sleeping and resting, and I never intend to take any. Exercise is loathsome. And it cannot be any benefit when you are tired; and I was always tired. But let another person try my way, and see whence he will come out.

"I desire now to repeat and emphasize that maxim: We can't reach old age by another man's road. My habits protect my life, but they would assassinate you.

"I have lived a severely moral life. But it would be a mistake for other people to try that, or for me to recommend it. Very few would succeed: you have to have a perfectly colossal stock of morals; and you can't get them on a margin; you have to have the whole thing, and put them in your box. Morals are an acquirement—like music, like a foreign language, like piety, poker, paralysis—no man is born with them. I wasn't myself, I started poor. I hadn't a single moral. There is hardly a man in this house that is poorer than I was then. Yes, I started like that—the world before me, not a moral in the slot. Not even an insurance moral. I can remember the first one I ever got. I can remember the landscape, the weather, the—I can remember how everything looked. It was an old moral, an old second-hand moral, all out of repair, and didn't fit, anyway. But if you are careful with a thing like that, and keep it in a dry place, and save it for processions, and Chautauquas, and World's Fairs, and so on, and disinfect it now and then, and give it a fresh coat of whitewash once in a while, you will be surprised to see

An artist from *Harper's* made this drawing as Mark Twain was delivering his seventieth birthday speech.

"The previous-engagement plea, which in forty years has cost you so many twinges, you can lay aside forever; on this side of the grave you will never need it again. If you shrink at thought of night, and winter, and the late home-coming from the banquet and the lights and the laughter through the deserted streets—a desolation which would not remind you now, as for a generation it did, that your friends are sleeping, and that you must creep in a-tiptoe and not disturb them, but would only remind you that you need not tiptoe, you can never disturb them more—if you shrink at thought of these things, you need only reply, "Your invitation honors me, and pleases me because you still keep me in your remembrance, but I am seventy; seventy, and would nestle in the chimney corner, and smoke my pipe, and read my book, and take my rest, wishing you well in all affection, and that when you in your turn shall arrive at pier No. 70 you may step aboard your waiting ship with a reconciled spirit, and lay your course toward the sinking sun with a contented heart."

how well she will last and how long she will keep sweet, or at least inoffensive. When I got that mouldy old moral, she had stopped growing, because she hadn't any exercise; but I worked her hard, I worked her Sundays and all. Under this cultivation she waxed in might and stature beyond belief, and served me well and was my pride and joy for sixty-three years; then she got to associating with insurance presidents, and lost flesh and character, and was a sorrow to look at and no longer competent for business. She was a great loss to me. Yet not all loss. I sold her—ah, pathetic skeleton, as she was—I sold her to our Metropolitan Museum, and it was very glad to get her, for without a rag on, she stands 57 feet long and 16 feet high, and they think she's a brontosaur. Well, she looks it. They believe it will take nineteen geological periods to breed her match.

"Morals are of inestimable value, for every man is born crammed with sin microbes, and the only thing that can extirpate these sin microbes is morals. Now you take a sterilized Christian—I mean, you take *the* sterilized Christian, for there's only one. Dear sir, I wish you wouldn't look at me like that.

"Threescore years and ten!

"It is the Scriptural statute of limitations. After that, you owe no active duties; for you the strenuous life is over. You are a time-expired man, to use Kipling's military phrase: You have served your term, well or less well, and you are mustered out. You are become an honorary member of the republic, you are emancipated, compulsions are not for you, nor any bugle call but "lights out." You pay the time-worn duty bills if you choose, or decline if you prefer—and without prejudice—for they are not legally collectable.

Second from left at this 70th birthday table is Finley Peter Dunne ("Mr. Dooley"), third is Owen Johnson, and the last man on the right is George W. Cable.

Richard Watson Gilder is the first man on the left, talking to Mark's daughter Jean Clemens.

Mark asked the artist for the original of this New York *Times* sketch of 1906, calling it "the best one I have ever seen of myself."

Annette Bradshaw in the New York *Journal,* December 18, 1905.

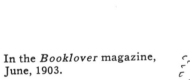

In the *Booklover* magazine, June, 1903.

James Montgomery Flagg's painting, now in the Lotos Club.

Fame is the halo in 1903.

An oil Theodore Wust painted in the 1890's.

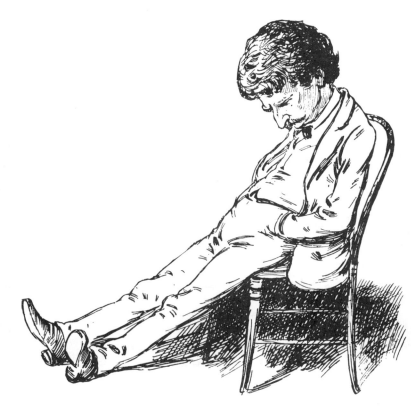

In *Life*, August 9, 1883.

THROUGH THE ARTIST'S EYE

A pastel of Mark Twain at 67, drawn from life by Everett Shinn.

"Mark Twain and His Empire—A Laughing World," 1901.

A page from a notebook: the development of
a Pudd'nhead Wilson maxim.

A memorandum.

IN MARK TWAIN'S HAND

A page of lecture notes.

Suggestion for title page of a book.

Rough copy for a lecture announcement.

A note about some of the autobiographical material intended for posthumous publication.

His memo slate. In the upper right it says: "Leave the cat here. Take the whiskey along."

Figuring out a light-year.

"The billiard-table is better than the doctors," Mark wrote in his thank-you note to the donor, Mrs. Henry Rogers. He often played 9 to 12 hours a day, walking 10 miles around the table. He enjoyed inventing new games and liked to make up the rules as he went along.

Twain and his biographer, Albert Bigelow Paine. They began working together in January, 1906, but billiards often took priority over biography.

"The most remarkable suit seen in New York this sea son," ran the headline over this page-length cartoo The "wondrous white flannels" were more sanita than his old black serge, Mark said, but the reason wore them was just because he wanted to. To Howel Twain's efflorescence in white was "an inspiratic which few men would have had the courage to a upon. . . . It was a magnificent coup, and he dear loved a coup."

THE WONDROUS WHITE SUIT

The New York *Times* interviews Mark Twain about his one-man dress reform. This was at the Congressional hearing on copyright in Washington, December, 1906.

An Advocate of Dress Reform.

While waiting to appear before the committee Mr. Clemens talked to the reporters.

"Why don't you ask why I am wearing such apparently unseasonable clothes? I'll tell you. I have found that when a man reaches the advanced age of 71 years as I have, the continual sight of dark clothing is likely to have a depressing effect upon him. Light-colored clothing is more pleasing to the eye and enlivens the spirit. Now, of course, I cannot compel every one to wear such clothing just for my especial benefit, so I do the next best thing and wear it myself.

"Of course, before a man reaches my years, the fear of criticism might prevent him from indulging his fancy. I am not afraid of that. I am decidedly for pleasing color combinations in dress. I like to see the women's clothes, say, at the opera. What can be more depressing than the sombre black which custom requires men to wear upon state occasions. A group of men in evening clothes looks like a flock of crows, and is just about as inspiring.

"After all, what is the purpose of clothing? Are not clothes intended primarily to preserve dignity and also to afford comfort to their wearer? Now I know of nothing more uncomfortable than the present day clothes of men. The finest clothing made is a person's own skin, but, of course, society demands something more than this.

"The best-dressed man I have ever seen, however, was a native of the Sandwich Islands, who attracted my attention thirty years ago. Now, when that man wanted to don especial dress to honor a public occasion or a holiday, why he occasionally put on a pair of spectacles. Otherwise the clothing with which God had provided him sufficed.

"Of course, I have ideas of dress reform. For one thing, why not adopt some of the women's styles? Goodness knows, they adopt enough of ours. Take the peek-a-boo waist, for instance. It has the obvious advantages of being cool and comfortable, and in addition it is almost always made up in pleasing colors, which cheer and do not depress.

"It is true that I dressed the Connecticut Yankee at King Arthur's Court in a plug hat, but let's see, that was twenty-five years ago. Then no man was considered fully dressed until he donned a plug hat. Nowadays I think that no man is dressed until he leaves it home. Why, when I left home yesterday they trotted out a plug hat for me to wear.

"'You must wear it,' they told me; 'why, just think of going to Washington without a plug hat!' 'But I said no; I would wear a derby or nothing. Why, I believe I could walk along the streets of New York—I never do—but still I think I could—and I should never see a well-dressed man wearing a plug hat. If I did I should suspect him of something. I don't know just what, but I would suspect him.

"Why, when I got up on the second story of that Pennsylvania ferryboat coming down here yesterday, I saw Howells coming along. He was the only man on the boat with a plug hat, and I tell you he felt ashamed of himself. He said he had been persuaded to wear it against his better sense, but just think of a man nearly 70 years old who has not a mind of his own on such matters!"

At the piano, with Clara Clemens and her friend, Miss Nichol.

Off for a ride in Henry Rogers'
automobile, spring, 1906.

With daughter Jean (*left*) on the veranda of the Up-
ton House at Dublin, New Hampshire, in May, 1906.
The dog was Jean's. This was his second summer here,
with much of the time spent in dictating his autobiography.

274

THE MAJESTICAL BED

In his last decade, Mark Twain did a good deal of his reading and writing in bed. It was the magnificent Venetian bed imported to the Hartford home long ago and brought down to 21 Fifth Avenue in 1904. Propped against the pillows he received callers, gave out interviews, dictated memoirs, and pursued his reading. Albert Bigelow Paine, whom Mark had accepted as official biographer, brought in his camera and caught Twain in these natural attitudes.

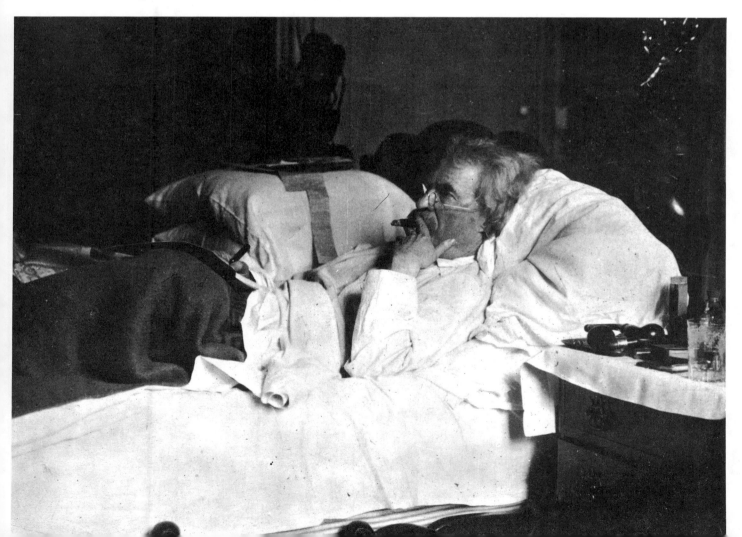

Mark Twain and a young friend, Dorothy Quick, photographed as he returned from a brief winter visit to Bermuda in 1907. Of his companionship with young people in this time, Twain said, "During these years after my wife's death I was washing about on a forlorn sea of banquets and speech-making in high and holy causes, and these things furnished me intellectual cheer and entertainment; but they got at my heart for an evening only, then left it dry and dusty. I had reached the grandfather stage of life without grandchildren, so I began to adopt some."

THE OXFORD PRIZE

In the spring of 1907, Oxford University announced it would give Mark Twain an honorary doctorate of letters on the 26th of June. For two years Mark had been saying his traveling days were over and nothing would ever induce him to cross the ocean again. But for an Oxford degree? "A quite different matter," he wrote in his autobiography. "That is a prize which I would go far to get at any time. To me university degrees are unearned finds, and they bring the joy that belongs with property acquired in that way; and the money-finds and the degree-finds are just the same in number up to date—three: two from Yale and one from Missouri University. It pleased me beyond measure when Yale made me a Master of Arts, because I didn't know anything about art; I had another convulsion of pleasure when Yale made me a Doctor of Literature, because I was not competent to doctor anybody's literature but my own, and couldn't even keep my own in a healthy condition without my wife's help. I rejoiced again when Missouri University made me a Doctor of Laws, because it was all clear profit, I not knowing anything about laws except how to evade them and not get caught. And now at Oxford I am to be made a Doctor of Letters—all clear profit, because what I don't know about letters would make me a multimillionaire if I could turn it into cash.

"Oxford is healing a secret old sore of mine which has been causing me sharp anguish once a year for many, many years. Privately I am quite well aware that for a generation I have been as widely celebrated a literary person as America has ever produced, and I am also privately aware that in my own peculiar line I have stood at the head of my guild during all that time, with none to dispute the place with me; and so it has been an annual pain to me to see our universities confer an aggregate of two hundred and fifty honorary degrees upon persons of small and temporary consequence—persons of local and evanescent notoriety, persons who drift into obscurity and are forgotten inside of ten years—and never a degree offered to me. In these past thirty-five or forty years I have seen our universities distribute nine or ten thousand honorary degrees and overlook me every time. Of all those thousands, not fifty were known outside of America, and not a hundred are still famous in it. This neglect would have killed a less robust person than I am, but it has not killed me; it has only shortened my life and weakened my constitution; but I shall get my strength back now. Out of those decorated and forgotten thousands not more than ten have been decorated by Oxford, and I am quite well aware—and so is America, and so is the rest of Christendom—that an Oxford decoration is a loftier distinction than is conferrable by any other university on either side of the ocean, and is worth twenty-five of any other, whether foreign or domestic.

"Now then, having purged myself of this thirty-five years' accumulation of bile and injured pride, I will drop the matter and smooth my feathers down and talk about something else."

On the steps of the house at Tuxedo, New York, which he took for the summer of 1907.

On the Atlantic crossing, the London *Daily Chronicle* cartoonist Richards accompanied Twain and made this sketch. He labeled it: "How Mark Twain widened his 'Sphere of Influence' while en route for England."

BERNARD SHAW MEETS MARK TWAIN

Bernard Shaw and Mark Twain met at St. Pancras railway station in June, 1907, introduced by Archibald Henderson, Shaw's biographer, who had crossed the Atlantic with Twain. "While I have been waiting," Shaw said to Twain, "the representatives of the press have been asking me whether you were really serious when you wrote *The Jumping Frog*." To a reporter, Shaw said: "Mark Twain is by far the greatest American writer. America has two literary assets—Edgar Allan Poe and Mark Twain. The former they some-

Bernard Shaw, in 1907.

times forget, but Mark Twain does not give them much chance of ignoring him. I am speaking of him rather as a sociologist than as a humorist. Of course he is in very much the same position as myself. He has to put things in such a way as to make people who would otherwise hang him believe he is joking. At one time people believed I was always joking, but now that it is coming to be that I am sometimes serious, they seem to regard me as a sort of archbishop, and the results are just as frightful in this state as in the other. Possibly some day it will dawn upon journalists and others that I am a human being."

Later in the Oxford trip the two writers lunched together; GBS followed it with a note to Twain saying: "I am persuaded that the future historian of America will find your works as indispensable to him as a French historian finds the political tracts of Voltaire. I tell you so because I am the author of a play in which a priest says, 'Telling the truth's the funniest joke in the world,' a piece of wisdom which you helped to teach me."

Twain dictated his impressions of Shaw shortly after he returned home: "Bernard Shaw has not completed his fifty-second year yet, and therefore is merely a lad. The vague and far-off rumble which he began to make five or six years ago is near-by now, and is recognizable as thunder. The editorial world lightly laughed at him during four or five of those years, but it takes him seriously now; he has become a force, and it is conceded that he must be reckoned with. Shaw is a pleasant man; simple, direct, sincere, animated; but self-possessed, sane, and evenly poised, acute, engaging, companionable, and quite destitute of affectations. I liked him. He shows no disposition to talk about himself or his work, or his high and growing prosperities in reputation and the materialities—but mainly—and affectionately and admiringly—devoted his talk to William Morris, whose close friend he had been and whose memory he deeply reveres."

277

MARK TWAIN MAKES $600 BY HIS SILENCE; AMBASSADOR REID SQUELCHES HIS SPEECH

MARK TWAIN "DOING" LONDON IN A BATH ROBE.

The press in Britain and America tried to make humor out of every movement of Mark's. When he crossed from his hotel to a bath club, wearing his bathrobe, the New York *American* embellished the situation with this cartoon.

"MARK TWAIN ARRIVES: ASCOT CUP STOLEN"

On June 8, 1907, exactly forty years from the day he sailed on the *Quaker City*—Mark Twain left for England. When the ship docked at Tilbury, the stevedores roared a welcome that "went to the marrow of me," Mark said. Throngs of visitors and sacks of mail turned his hotel into both royal court and post office. Everyone wanted to meet and honor him. "Surely such weeks as this must be very rare in the world," Mark wrote. "I had seen nothing like them before; I shall see nothing approaching them again!" Coupling two news events, the press entertained London readers with the headline: "MARK TWAIN ARRIVES: ASCOT CUP STOLEN."

Hannibal's pride met Edward VII and Queen Alexandra at the royal garden party at Windsor Castle on June 22. "All that report of my proposal to buy Windsor Castle and its grounds was a false rumor," Mark said. "I started it myself. One newspaper said I patted his Majesty on the shoulder—an impertinence of which I was not guilty. I was reared in the most exclusive circles of Missouri and I know how to behave."

THE CONNECTICUT YANKEE IN KING EDWARD'S COURT.
(It would be very appropriate for King Edward to make Mark Twain a Knight of the Bath.)
From the *Journal* (Minneapolis).

KING FULL ON DEUCES.
(Apropos of Mark Twain's recent enthusiastic reception in England.)
From the *Pioneer Press* (St. Paul).

As American cartoonists saw the visit.

The Pilgrims club gave Twain a luncheon at the Savoy on June 25, hailing him as "a true consolidator of nations. His delightful humor is of the kind which dissipates and destroys national prejudices. He has made the world better by his presence, and we rejoice to see him here."

Mark Twain joins other candidates assembling to receive honorary degrees at Oxford's Sheldonian Theatre on June 26, 1907. The brilliant list included Kipling, Rodin, and Saint-Saëns.

When the Oxford pageant took place the day after the degrees were conferred, the papers called it "Mark Twain's Pageant." This British cartoon shows General William Booth of the Salvation Army, Kipling, the Duke of Connaught, and Mark Twain marching— "Doctors All; or, More Innocents Abroad."

In England, Mark was asked why he always carried a cheap cotton umbrella. He replied, "Because that's the only kind of umbrella that an Englishman won't steal!"

Oxford gave out honors every year, but Mark Twain was the first foreigner in 50 years to be given a luncheon by the staff of *Punch*. In *Harper's* the coming event was announced by this cartoon.

AT OXFORD

When Mark Twain, dressed in his robe of scarlet and gray, was summoned to receive his academic honors, "a veritable cyclone" of applause broke out. "Most amiable and charming sir," Chancellor Curzon addressed him in Latin, "you shake the sides of the whole world with your merriment."

ENGLAND'S HOMAGE TO MARK TWAIN: NOTABLES AT PILGRIMS' LUNCHEON

MR. PUNCH IS TO ENTERTAIN MARK TWAIN. —News Item.

Punch saluted Mark Twain with this front-page cartoon, and as a surprise gave him the original at the luncheon.

Playing cards with his daughter Clara.

In his library at Stormfield.

AT HOME IN STORMFIELD

Mark Twain's last two years were spent at his new home in Redding, Connecticut. He had become tired of city life and its urgent pressures and decided a country home not too far from New York would be a welcome relief. In 1906 he bought over two hundred acres atop a hill, and with the $30,000 paid him for serial rights to part of his autobiography engaged John Mead Howells, the son of his old friend, to design a house. His only requirements were that the architect include a large billiard room, decorated in red, a living room big enough to hold his mechanical orchestrelle (Beethoven's Fifth was his favorite), and plenty of guest rooms. "I don't want to see it," he said of the house, "until the cat is purring on the hearth."

On June 18, 1908, he was met at the station by all Redding and escorted in flower-decked carriages to the hilltop where he entered the first home of his own in seventeen years. A dinner party, fireworks, and a boisterous round of billiards topped off his first day at home.

Mark Twain's last home, at Redding, Connecticut. He named it "Stormfield" because part of it was built with funds from his book, *Captain Stormfield's Visit to Heaven.*

282

Three months after Twain moved into Stormfield two burglars stole the family silver but were caught the next day after a pistol duel with police. Mark then tacked this notice on his front door.

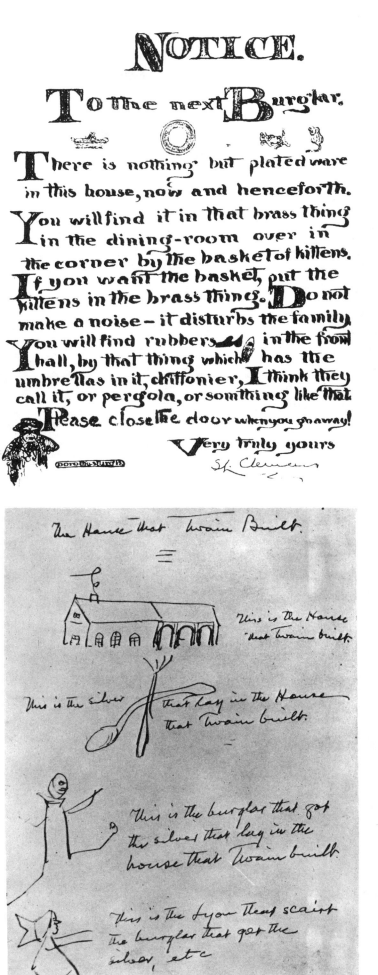

NOTICE.

To the next Burglar.

There is nothing but plated ware in this house, now and henceforth. You will find it in that brass thing in the dining-room over in the corner by the basket of kittens. If you want the basket, put the kittens in the brass thing. Do not make a noise — it disturbs the family. You will find rubbers in the front hall, by that thing which has the umbrellas in it, chiffonier, I think they call it, or pergola, or something like that. Please close the door when you go away!

Very truly yours

SL. Clemens

Mark joined other friends of the late Thomas Bailey Aldrich in dedicating the Aldrich Memorial Museum at Portsmouth, New Hampshire, in June, 1908. Outside, he posed with J. T. Trowbridge, the venerable writer.

The House that Twain Built.

This is the House that Twain built.

This is the silver that lay in the House that Twain built.

This is the burglar that got the silver that lay in the house that Twain built.

This is the Lyon that scairt the burglar that got the silver, etc

Another piece of Twainfoolery about the great silver robbery.

The sketch Leo Mielziner drew for the New York *Herald* on a visit to Redding in October, 1908. When the drawing was finished the artist showed it to Twain, who remarked, "Young man, that's the best likeness I have ever seen of myself. This reminds me of the time, 30 years ago, when Abbott Thayer came up to Hartford to do a sketch of me. I had a very bad cold that day; so I had to sit with a *bottle* of whiskey; and while Abbott drew, I drank. By and by he let me look at the sketch, and do you know, he had given me a *banana* for a nose. So I said, 'Abbott, I might be considered a *still-life*—but I am not a *fruit-piece!*' So Abbott consented to make the changes and he drew and I drank until I could hardly see the other side of the room. But I could still see that banana. And I'm so glad, young man, that *you* didn't give me a banana."

Clara Clemens.

Clara Clemens and Ossip Gabrilowitsch had met in Vienna in 1898 as pupils of the great piano teacher, Leschetizky. On October 6, 1909, they were married at Stormfield by Joe Twichell. The wedding group shows (*from left*) Twain in his Oxford robe, his nephew Jervis Langdon, Jean Clemens, Gabrilowitsch, Clara, and Twichell.

Taken in December, 1909, upon his return from Bermuda.

Ossip Gabrilowitsch.

In late December, 1909, Mark Twain returned from a month in Bermuda, to spend the holidays with Jean at Stormfield. A few days later, on Christmas Eve, Jean was found dead in her bathtub. After 14 years of epilepsy, her heart had failed during a convulsion. As Jean was taken to Elmira for burial, her father penned a tribute to her—his last piece of writing.

A WEDDING AND A FUNERAL

Jean Clemens.

Twichell and Twain, photographed by Jean Clemens in February, 1905. Twichell, whom Mark valued more than any other friend, officiated at Mark's and Clara's weddings, and buried Susy, Livy, and Jean. The two old friends spent many week ends in New York during Mark's last years. Twichell died in 1918.

A closer study of 74-year-old Mark Twain, made on the same occasion as the bowler hat pose on the opposite page.

MARK TWAIN GOES TO BERMUDA, BUT DENIES HE IS ILL

Doesn't Know How Impression Got Abroad That He Was Incapacitated, He Says.

HAS SOME TROUBLE LEFT IN HIS SIDE AND CHEST

Is Going Away for Month to Clear It Up—Shows Depression Due to Daughter's Death.

Mr. Samuel L. Clemons (Mark Twain) started alone to-day on the steamer Bermudian, for a month's visit to Bermuda. He still showed the depression consequent upon the sudden death of his daughter, Miss Jean Clemens, at the Clemens home at Redding, Conn., just before Christmas.

"I do not know exactly why the 'boys' got the impression that I was seriously ill or incapacitated before Christmas," said the humorist. "I have still some of my old trouble in my left side and chest and am going away for a month to clear it up. When I was here just before Christmas I certainly did not expect what happened a little later."

This was the only reference Mr. Clemens made to his daughter's death, but it could easily be seen that it had borne heavily upon him.

Alfred Payne Bigelow was at the pier to see Mr. Clemens off and wish him a pleasant journey. "Thank you," said the humorist when his friend extended his hand and said. "A pleasant journey."

In Bermuda, Mark played miniature golf with Woodrow Wilson and went swimming, picnicking, and boating. His angina troubled him now and then.

THE LAST YEAR

Ten days after Jean's death, Mark went back to Bermuda to spend the winter. On the night before he sailed he talked for the last time with Howells. A few days later Howells wrote him: "I shall feel it honor enough if they put on my tombstone 'He was born in the same century and general section of Middle Western country with Dr. Samuel L. Clemens, Oxon., and had his degree three years before him through a mistake of the University.'"

From Bermuda, Mark wrote Paine: "Good time, good home, tranquil contentment all day and every day." Here he is out riding with a young friend.

286

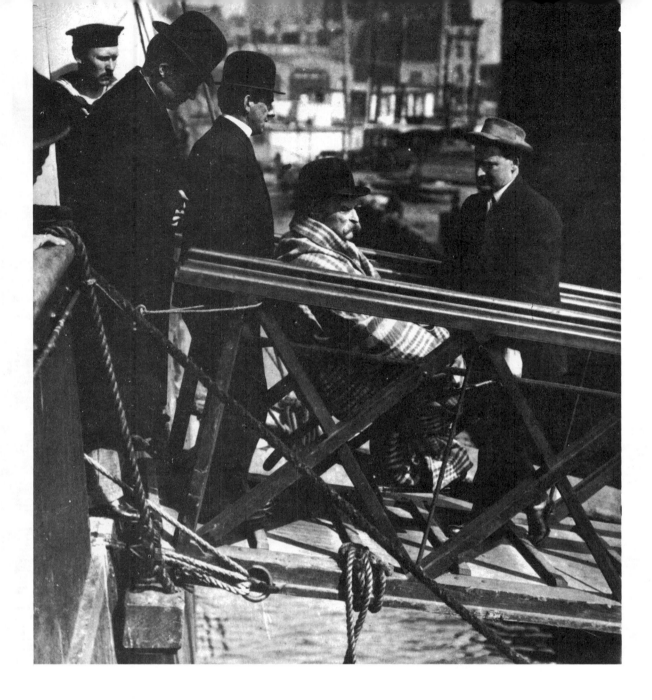

Late in March, 1910, Mark Twain's condition grew critical. After one especially bad attack he said, "Well, I had a picturesque night. Every pain I had was on exhibition . . . I am losing enough sleep to supply a worn-out army." Dying, he was taken back home; this picture of him being carried off the boat at New York on April 14, is the last taken of him.

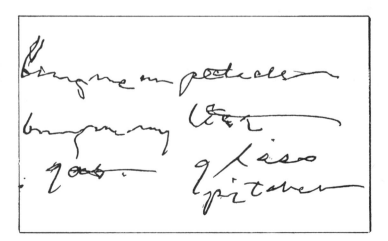

On his last day, when he could not speak intelligibly, Mark tried to write what he had to say. This—his last writing—was a request for his spectacles and a glass pitcher.

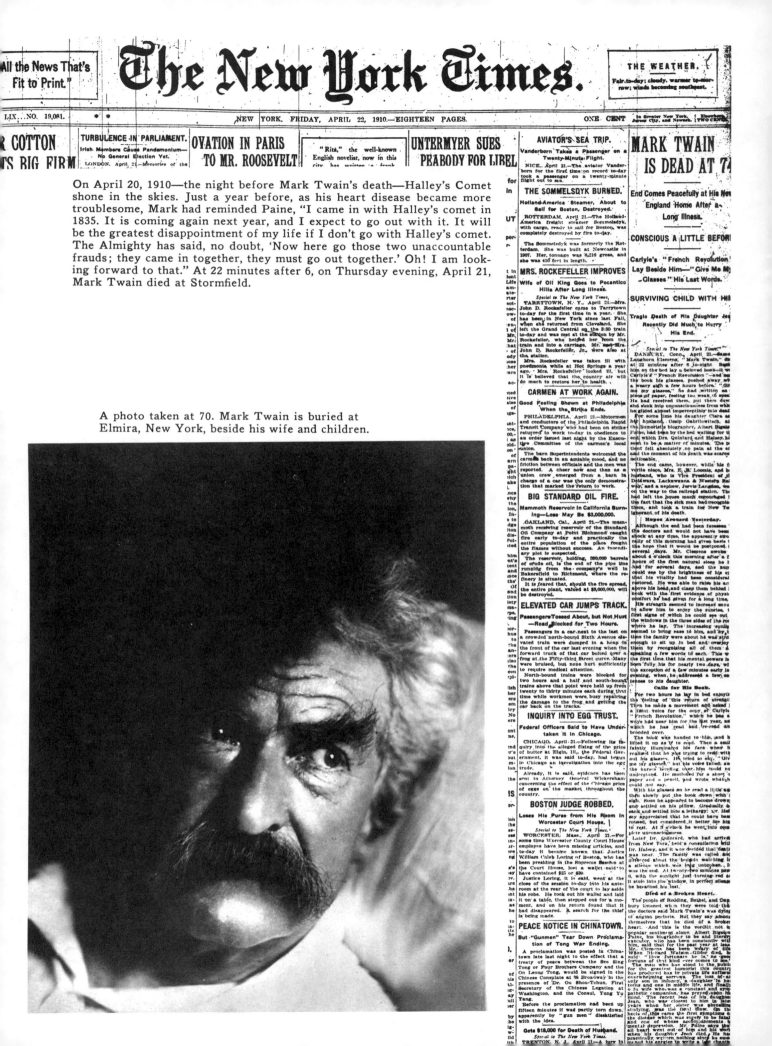

The New York Times.

THE WEATHER.
Fair to-day; cloudy, warmer to-morrow; winds becoming southeast.

NEW YORK, FRIDAY, APRIL 22, 1910.—EIGHTEEN PAGES.

...LIX...NO. 19,081.

ONE CENT
In Greater New York ... Jersey City, and Newark. } TWO CENTS

R COTTON
'S BIG FIRM

TURBULENCE IN PARLIAMENT.
Irish Members Cause Pandemonium—No General Election Yet.
LONDON, April 21.—Memories of the

OVATION IN PARIS TO MR. ROOSEVELT

"Rita," the well-known English novelist, now in this city, has written a frank

UNTERMYER SUES PEABODY FOR LIBEL

AVIATOR'S SEA TRIP.
Vanderborn Takes a Passenger on a Twenty-Minute Flight.
NICE, April 21.—The aviator Vanderborn for the first time on record to-day took a passenger on a twenty-minute flight out to sea.

MARK TWAIN IS DEAD AT 74

End Comes Peacefully at His New England Home After a Long Illness.

CONSCIOUS A LITTLE BEFORE

Carlyle's "French Revolution" Lay Beside Him—"Give Me My Glasses," His Last Words.

SURVIVING CHILD WITH HIM

Tragic Death of His Daughter Jean Recently Did Much to Hurry His End.

On April 20, 1910—the night before Mark Twain's death—Halley's Comet shone in the skies. Just a year before, as his heart disease became more troublesome, Mark had reminded Paine, "I came in with Halley's comet in 1835. It is coming again next year, and I expect to go out with it. It will be the greatest disappointment of my life if I don't go with Halley's comet. The Almighty has said, no doubt, 'Now here go those two unaccountable frauds; they came in together, they must go out together.' Oh! I am looking forward to that." At 22 minutes after 6, on Thursday evening, April 21, Mark Twain died at Stormfield.

A photo taken at 70. Mark Twain is buried at Elmira, New York, beside his wife and children.

THE SOMMELSDYK BURNED.
Holland-America Steamer, About to Sail for Boston, Destroyed.
ROTTERDAM, April 21.—The Holland-America freight steamer Sommelsdyk, with cargo, ready to sail for Boston, was completely destroyed by fire to-day.

MRS. ROCKEFELLER IMPROVES
Wife of Oil King Goes to Pocantico Hills After Long Illness.

CARMEN AT WORK AGAIN.
Good Feeling Shown at Philadelphia When the Strike Ends.

BIG STANDARD OIL FIRE.
Mammoth Reservoir in California Burning—Loss May Be $3,000,000.

ELEVATED CAR JUMPS TRACK.
Passengers Tossed About, but Not Hurt—Road Blocked for Two Hours.

INQUIRY INTO EGG TRUST.
Federal Officers Said to Have Undertaken it in Chicago.

BOSTON JUDGE ROBBED.
Loses His Purse from His Room in Worcester Court House.

PEACE NOTICE IN CHINATOWN.
But "Gunmen" Tear Down Proclamation of Tong War Ending.

Mark, dressed in his favorite white, was taken to the Brick Church in New York, where a huge crowd came to see him for the last time. Joe Twichell prayed brokenly, and then Howells came up to say good-by. "I looked a moment at the face I knew so well; and it was patient with the patience I had so often seen in it; something of a puzzle, a great silent dignity, an assent to what must be from the depths of a nature whose tragical seriousness broke in the laughter which the unwise took for the whole of him." I knew them all, Howells said—sages, poets, peers, critics, humorists—"but Clemens was sole, incomparable, the Lincoln of our literature."

A Reading List

For the reader who wants a full shelf of Twain to dip into at leisure there are the 1923 Definitive Edition and the 1929 Stormfield Edition.

To these can be added the large number of previously unpublished writings which have appeared posthumously; others will probably be added from time to time. Of interest to the general reader are *Mark Twain's Speeches* and *Mark Twain's Notebook*. There are several volumes of his personal correspondence: *Mark Twain's Letters, The Love Letters of Mark Twain, Mark Twain's Letters to Will Bowen, The Letters of Mark Twain to Mrs. Fairbanks.*

There are also some ten volumes of his newspaper pieces, usually written in the form of letters.

For the reader who wants handy and cheap volumes of some of the best of Twain there are *The Portable Mark Twain, The Complete Stories of Mark Twain,* and paperback editions of *Tom Sawyer, Huckleberry Finn,* and *Life on the Mississippi.*

Three versions of Twain's autobiographical writings have been issued: *Mark Twain's Autobiography* (1924), edited by Albert Bigelow Paine; *Mark Twain in Eruption* (1940), edited by Bernard De Voto; and *The Autobiography of Mark Twain* (1959), edited by Charles Neider.

Among the Twain biographies are several the general reader will enjoy. The first and still the most detailed is Albert Bigelow Paine's *Mark Twain: A Biography* (1912). A much briefer account is Jerry Allen's *The Adventures of Mark Twain.* From one of Twain's closest friends, William Dean Howells, came *My Mark Twain: Reminiscences and Criticisms.* Clara Clemens wrote *My Father, Mark Twain.* The family's housekeeper told her story through Mary Lawton's *A Lifetime With Mark Twain: The Memories of Katie Leary.*

There are many books focusing on one or another aspect of Twain's life. Again, for the general reader, Samuel C. Webster's *Mark Twain, Business Man* and Dixon Wecter's *Sam Clemens of Hannibal* are probably among the more interesting.

A few examples of what the critics have said about Mark Twain: Gladys Bellamy's *Mark Twain as a Literary Artist;* Van Wyck Brooks' *The Ordeal of Mark Twain* and the opposing view presented by Bernard De Voto in *Mark Twain's America;* DeLancy Ferguson's *Mark Twain: Man and Legend;* Philip S. Foner's *Mark Twain: Social Critic;* Arthur L. Scott's *Mark Twain: Selected Criticism;* Edward Wagenknecht's *Mark Twain: The Man and His Work.*

Finally, three useful references are *The Mark Twain Handbook,* by E. Hudson Long; *The Art, Humor and Humanity of Mark Twain,* edited by Minnie N. Brashear and Robert M. Rodney, and *Mark Twain at Your Fingertips,* edited by Caroline T. Harnsberger.

Nothing more delightful could be recommended to anybody—scholar or skimmer—than the actor Hal Holbrook's *Mark Twain Tonight!* You can enjoy it in both the book version and the long-playing record of his memorable impersonation of the great man on the platform.

A Visiting List

Mark Twain lived and worked in a great many American towns. The two where he spent most of his time are Hannibal, Missouri, and Hartford, Connecticut. Each place is worth visiting to see the Twain memorials.

In Hannibal, the Mark Twain Municipal Board displays the little house the Clemens family lived in. Right next door is the Twain Museum. Its walls are awash with pictures and its cabinets are bursting with memorabilia. Across the street is the Becky Thatcher house and, around any corner, the streets and hills Mark knew. To the east, the Mississippi.

In Hartford, at 351 Farmington Avenue, the big Twain house, after going through several hands, is now in the care of the Mark Twain Library and Memorial Commission. Many of the rooms have been restored to the way they were in those two happy decades when he lived there.

In Elmira, New York, where the Twain family spent so many summers at Quarry Farm, you can visit the cemetery where Mark, Livy, Susy and Jean lie. The library of Elmira's Strathmont Museum exhibits an illustrated history of Twain's life, with special emphasis on his summer residence. On the campus of Elmira College is the study in which he did some of his best work.

The Mark Twain Birthplace Shrine is in Mark Twain State Park, Florida, Missouri. It encloses the frame cabin in which the writer was born, as well as a library and museum which display material collected by the Mark Twain Research Foundation. The village of Florida is forty-three miles southwest of Hannibal, on Route 107.

The library Mark Twain founded in 1908 in the last place he lived, Redding, Connecticut, is operated by the Mark Twain Library Association. It is on Route 53. He gave many volumes from his personal library to help get it started, and these can be seen.

Picture Sources

Pictures, unless otherwise credited, are from the personal collection of the author. Key to picture position: t-top; c-center; b-bottom; l-left; r-right. Combinations: tl-top left, etc.

The following are abbreviations used for picture sources:

BA   Bettmann Archive
BB   Brown Brothers
BHS   Buffalo Historical Society
Cal SL California State Library
CHS   Chicago Historical Society
CS   Culver Service
CSL   Connecticut State Library
HTM   Hartford's Twain Memorial
LOC   Library of Congress
MTE   Mark Twain Estate
MTMH Mark Twain Museum, Hannibal
NHS   Nevada Historical Society
NYPL New York Public Library
SCW   Samuel C. Webster
U&U   Underwood & Underwood
YM   Yale University, Morse Collection

MISSOURI BOYHOOD

page

1 tl-BB; tr-BB
2 Henry Lewis, *Das Illustrirte Mississippithal*
4 MTE
5 MTMH
6 t-MTMH; b-*Life on the Mississippi*
7 tr-MTMH; bl-*Life on the Mississippi*

8 t-BB; b-MTMH
9 tl-MTE; tr-MTE; b-MTMH
11 MTE
12 l-*Tom Sawyer*
13 l-MTMH; r-MTMH
14 l-MTMH; r-MTMH
15 MTMH
16 t-MTMH; br-MTE; bl-Missouri Historical Society
17 NYPL
18 b-MTMH; t-NYPL
19 MTE
22 SCW
23 t-NHS; b-Harper & Brothers

TRAMP PRINTER

24 t-BB
25 t-NYPL; b-NYPL
27 tr-LOC; cl-LOC; b-LOC
28 NYPL
29 LOC
30 t-NYPL; b-NYPL
31 t-Muscatine Public Library
32 b-SCW

MISSISSIPPI PILOT

33 t-NYPL; bl-*Life on the Mississippi*; br-SCW
34 BB
35 MTMH
36 Captain Frederick Way
37 t-Captain Frederick Way; b-Cincinnati Public Library

Index